PRINCIPLES OF ECONOMICS: MICROECONOMICS

HARCOURT BRACE COLLEGE OUTLINE SERIES

PRINCIPLES OF ECONOMICS: MICROECONOMICS

E. David Emery

Department of Economics
St. Olaf College

Harcourt Brace College Publishers

Fort Worth   Philadelphia   San Diego
New York   Orlando   Austin   San Antonio
Toronto   Montreal   London   Sydney   Tokyo

Requests for permission to make copies of any part of the work should be mailed to: Permissions Department, Harcourt Brace & Company, 6277 Sea Harbor Drive, Orlando, Florida 32887-6777.

Printed in the United States of America

LIBRARY OF CONGRESS CATALOGING IN PUBLICATION DATA

Emery, E. David.
   Principles of economics, microeconomics

   (Harcourt Brace Jovanovich college outline series) (Books for professionals)
   Includes index.
   1. Microeconomics. I. Title. II. Series.
III. Series: Books for professionals.
HB172.E44   1984   338.5   84-12775

ISBN 0-15-600053-9

9 0 1 2 3 4 5 6 7 145 20 19 18 17 16 15 14 13

PREFACE

The study of economics is divided into two main parts, microeconomics and macroeconomics. Although *microeconomics* — or *micro*, for short — comes from the Greek word for "small," it is concerned less with the *small* elements in an economy than it is with the *individual* elements, whether they are small, like the average household, or large, like AT&T or General Motors. It is the study of how the choices of individual decision-making units and the functioning of individual markets determine how society's scarce resources are allocated and how income is distributed among its members.

Similarly, although *macroeconomics* — or *macro*, for short — comes from the Greek word for "large," it is concerned less with the *large* elements in an economy than it is with the collective or *aggregate* elements, regardless of their size. It is the study of how money and aggregate expenditure or investment behavior determine the levels of output, employment, and prices in an entire economy.

The subject of this book is microeconomics, and its purpose is twofold: first, to acquaint you with the basic subject matter of economics and with the tools of the discipline, and, second, to present you with a complete course in the principles of microeconomics in the clear, concise format of an outline. Like its companion, **PRINCIPLES OF ECONOMICS: MACROECONOMICS**, this outline is comprehensive enough to be used by itself for independent study, but you will find that many of its features make it an ideal supplement to an introductory college course or textbook on economics.

One of these features is the inclusion of sample **midterm** and **final examinations** in this outline. Like most college tests, these sample examinations are designed to measure not only your retention of information but also your understanding of and your ability to apply the knowledge that you have acquired. They are also designed to give you ample exposure to — as well as practice answering — the various types of questions that you are likely to encounter on a typical college exam.

Several other features, all of them practical study aids, appear at the end of each chapter:

RAISE YOUR GRADES This feature consists of a checkmarked list of open-ended, thought-provoking questions. By inviting you to compare concepts, interpret information, and examine the whys and wherefores of chapter material, these questions help you to assimilate ideas and prepare for class discussions, quizzes, and tests.

SUMMARY This feature provides a brief restatement of the main ideas in each chapter, including definitions of key terms. Because it is presented in the efficient form of a numbered list, you can use it to refresh your memory quickly before an exam.

RAPID REVIEW Like the summary, this feature is designed to provide you with a quick review of the principles presented in the body of each chapter. Consisting primarily of true–false, multiple-choice, and fill-in-the-blank questions, it allows you to test your memory and reinforce your learning at the same time. Should you have trouble answering any of these questions, you can locate and review the relevant sections of the outline by following the cross references provided.

SOLVED PROBLEMS Each chapter of this outline concludes with a series of problems that require more than just a simple one-word answer. Some ask you to apply abstract theories to concrete situations; others ask you to analyze and predict the outcome of a set of hypothetical circumstances; still others ask you to prepare graphs, interpret diagrams, analyze data, and perform elementary calculations. To make the most of these problems, try writing your own solutions first. Then compare your answers with those in the book.

Finally, of course, there is the outline format itself, which serves both as a clear guide to important ideas and as a convenient structure upon which to organize your knowledge. That format and the many other practical features of this outline, including the glossary at the back and the numerous examples in every chapter, combine to make it a valuable supplement to your college course work and textbook on the principles of microeconomics.

NORTHFIELD, MINNESOTA   E. DAVID EMERY

CONTENTS

1 THE ECONOMIC PROBLEM

THIS CHAPTER IS ABOUT

☑ **Scarcity**
☑ **Resources and Production**
☑ **Production Possibilities Boundary**
☑ **Choices and Opportunity Costs**
☑ **Resource Use: Four Fundamental Choices**

1-1. Scarcity

Our desire for material items such as food, clothing, cars, housing, and highways appears to be almost unlimited both individually and collectively. Yet the means to satisfy those wants—the goods and services we are able to produce—are limited. This is the problem of **scarcity**: our material wants exceed our ability to satisfy them from limited resources. The choices that individuals and societies make in response to scarcity are the subject matter of economics.

   Scarcity is a relative term in economics. The coal reserves in the United States may be as high as 1,700 billion tons, yet coal is a "scarce" resource: there isn't enough coal for all people to have as much as they desire at no cost.

EXAMPLE 1-1: Leonardo da Vinci's *Mona Lisa* is considered scarce by economists, yet the original artwork *Trains*, crayon on computer paper by 3-year-old Carl Emery, is not. Although there is only one original of each work, one is considered scarce and the other not because scarcity is relative. Not everyone who wants the original *Mona Lisa* can have it, but everyone who wants the original *Trains* (i.e., Carl's father) can.

A. Economics is the study of how scarce resources are used.

Every introductory economics textbook defines the term *economics* in its own unique way, but all of the definitions have elements in common. A typical definition reads something like this:

Economics is the study of how individuals and societies choose to use their scarce resources in order to best satisfy their material wants.

   There are three key words in this definition: *societies*, *choose*, and *best*. Economics is not just a study of wealth and the means to obtain it. Economists are concerned with the broader problem of how societies use their scarce resources. Scarcity implies the necessity of making choices. Therefore, choices on how to use scarce resources are an important concern of economics. Finally, the adjective *best* suggests that economists are concerned with the optimal or efficient use of resources, and indeed they are.

B. There are four methods to challenge scarcity.

There are four methods commonly used by societies to challenge or alleviate scarcity:

1. full employment of available resources
2. development of resources and technology
3. efficient organization of the production and distribution of goods
4. redistribution of goods or income among members of society

Although these methods may seem to be no more than common sense, none of them is used consistently by any society. How consistently, for example, do you think resources are "fully employed" in the United States? How consistently do you think production is efficiently organized in the USSR? Some of the methods, too, are controversial. For example, do you think every person in the United States favors more growth or a redistribution of income to the poor? Clearly different societies place different emphases on the methods they use to challenge scarcity.

1-2. Resources and Production

Individuals and societies satisfy their material wants with goods. Goods are produced from resources with the aid of technology. Resources include land, capital, and human resources. Economists give special meanings to all of these terms:

- **good:** any item or service that satisfies a material want
- **resource:** any item used to produce a good
- **land:** any naturally occurring resource used in production (any natural resource)
- **human resource:** any human skill used in production, including labor and entrepreneurial ability
- **capital:** any man-made item used in production
- **technology:** society's knowledge of production

EXAMPLE 1-2: A recording by your favorite musical group, be it Kiss or the Cleveland Orchestra, is a "good" to you (although it may be a pain to others in society). An acre of farm land and a tree used to produce lumber are both classified as "land" by an economist. The chief executive officer of IBM Corporation is a "human resource" and may provide labor as well as entrepreneurial or managerial ability. A building, a machine, and a road all fall into the economic category of "capital."

A. Resources are versatile and heterogeneous.

Resources are versatile and heterogeneous. The same set of resources can be used to produce a vast assortment of goods, but some resources, or some units of a resource, are more productive in one use than they are in another. Resources tend to be applied preferentially to more, rather than to less, productive uses.

B. Entrepreneurs are the organizers of production.

Entrepreneurs are individuals who organize production and bear the associated risks. Entrepreneurs perform three functions:

1. They decide what goods to produce in a market economy.
2. They take the initiative in assembling the resources necessary for production.
3. They reap the profits or losses resulting from their decisions.

Entrepreneurs play a critical role in a market economy. As the organizers of production, they must anticipate consumer wants and respond to changing tastes. They must also respond to changes in technology and in the availability of resources.

1-3. Production Possibilities Boundary

A **production possibility boundary (PPB)** is a schedule or curve illustrating the various combinations of goods that a society is capable of producing at any given time if technology and resources are fixed and all resources are fully and efficiently employed.

A hypothetical PPB for an economy producing only two goods, guns and butter, is shown in Figure 1-1.

A. A PPB has four important properties.

1. *A PPB is a boundary.* It shows the limit to what a society can produce with the technology and resources at its disposal. A society may wish to have more of all its goods, as shown by point *E* in Figure 1-1. However, it can't achieve point *E* with the technology and resources currently available to it. This limit is the essence of scarcity.

2. *A PPB illustrates maximum production points when all resources are fully and efficiently employed.* A society can operate inside its boundary, that is, below its potential, if it does not employ all of its resources fully and efficiently. If a society is operating below its potential, it is at a point such as *D* in Figure 1-1.

3. *A PPB has a negative or downward slope.* A negative slope indicates that more of one good can be produced only if less of another good is produced. Thus, movement along a PPB implies a trade-off between goods. For example, if society moves from point *A* to point *B* in Figure 1-1, it sacrifices 200 units of butter to acquire 50 additional guns.

4. *A PPB shifts when there is a change either in technology or in the availability of resources.* An increase in the availability of a resource used to produce both guns and butter would shift the PPB outward, as shown in Figure 1-2. An improvement in the technology of gun production, but not in the technology of butter production, would shift the PPB outward only on the gun axis, as shown in Figure 1-3.

B. Today's choices may affect the future position of a PPB.

A society's choices today may affect the position of its PPB in the future. A society may consciously seek to shift its PPB outward by developing resources, improving technology, or both. It may deliberately promote faster growth in its PPB by forgoing consumer goods today and choosing capital goods and research instead.

1-4. Choices and Opportunity Costs

Because it marks the limit of a society's production possibilities, a PPB illustrates two fundamental economic principles: the necessity of choice and the opportunity cost of choosing.

A. Society must make choices.

A PPB demonstrates that a society's resources and technology—and therefore its production possibilities—are limited. Since it cannot produce unlimited quantities of all goods, a society must make choices, both individually and collectively. Choice is inherent in scarcity.

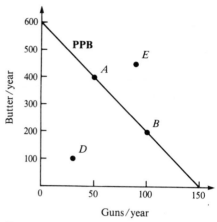

Figure 1-1
A production possibilities boundary (PPB) shows various combinations of two goods that a society is capable of producing.

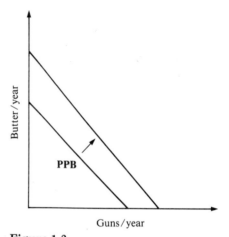

Figure 1-2
An increase in the resources used to produce both guns and butter shifts the PPB outward on both axes.

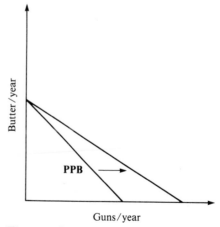

Figure 1-3
An improvement in the technology of gun production shifts the PPB outward only on the gun axis.

B. Opportunity costs are the values of forgone alternatives.

Choices involve sacrifices or costs. The negative slope of a PPB indicates that if a society chooses to produce more of one good, it must sacrifice or forgo some of another good. Since the other good, the forgone alternative, has a value, economists refer to this sacrifice as the opportunity cost of a good.

Opportunity cost is the amount of a good or goods that must be sacrificed or forgone to obtain a unit of another good.

EXAMPLE 1-3: If society chooses to move from point A to point B in Figure 1-1, it can produce 50 additional guns, but it must sacrifice 200 units of butter. The opportunity cost of each additional gun is thus four units of butter. The converse is also true. If society chooses to move from point B to point A, it can produce 200 additional units of butter, but it must sacrifice 50 guns. The opportunity cost of four units of butter is thus one gun.

Opportunity cost is a very important and useful economic concept. It enables economists to estimate costs and to weigh choices in a variety of situations.

EXAMPLE 1-4: The concept of opportunity cost can be used to evaluate two commonly accepted opinions about U.S. involvement in World War II: (1) that the cost of the war was very high, and (2) that the cost of the war, at least the part financed through the sale of government bonds, has been—and continues to be—borne by subsequent generations.

First, consider the cost of the war. To visualize the cost, imagine Figure 1-1 as the PPB of the United States at the time. The transition from a peacetime to a wartime economy involved moving from one point on the PPB to another. The opportunity cost of the war was the value of the consumer goods, the investment goods, and the leisure that had to be forgone to finance the war. Had all our resources been fully and efficiently employed before we entered the war, we might have started, say, at point A in 1940. Then we would have had to move, say, to point B in 1941. In that case the opportunity cost of the war would have been very high—higher than it actually was. However, in 1940 we were still recovering from the Great Depression of the 1930s, and our economy was operating *below* its potential, at a point such as D in Figure 1-1. Since we started at a point *inside* the boundary of our production possibilities, the opportunity cost of the war was *less* than it would have been if our economy had been fully employed in 1940.

Next, consider the burden of the cost of World War II. Has it been shifted to subsequent generations? No, the cost of the war was borne by those who sacrificed consumer goods, investment goods, and leisure to finance it. It was borne by people at the time who did without new cars, gasoline, sugar, meat; who worked extra hours; who sacrificed their careers to enter military service. Subsequent generations have inherited a larger national debt because of the deficit financing used during World War II, but we have also inherited the bonds that the government issued when it incurred the debt. When we pay off the debt (the bonds), we repay ourselves.

C. A bowed PPB indicates increasing opportunity costs.

A PPB usually curves or bows away from the origin of a set of axes, as shown in Figure 1-4. The bowed PPB in Figure 1-4 indicates that the number of units of butter that must be sacrificed to obtain an additional gun increases as society moves from point A to point B to point C, and that the number of guns that must be sacrificed to obtain an additional unit of butter increases as society moves from point C to point B to point A. In other words, the opportunity cost of acquiring an

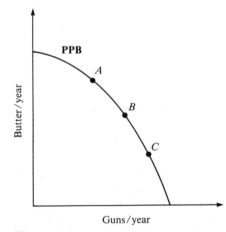

Figure 1-4
A bowed PPB indicates increasing opportunity costs.

additional gun increases with movement along the PPB toward the gun axis, and the opportunity cost of an additional unit of butter increases with movement along the PPB toward the butter axis. This principle is often referred to as the **law of increasing opportunity costs.**

D. The heterogeneity of resources contributes to increasing opportunity costs.

The fact that some resources are more productive in one use than they are in another is largely responsible for increasing opportunity costs. (The phenomenon of diminishing returns, which you will encounter in Chapter 9, also contributes to increasing opportunity costs.)

EXAMPLE 1-5: Some resources, such as farm land in Wisconsin, are better suited to the production of butter than they are to the production of guns. If these resources were withdrawn from the production of butter and applied instead to the production of guns, the output of butter would decline sharply, but the output of guns would not rise proportionately. Thus the opportunity cost of the few additional guns would be very high.

1-5. Resource Use: Four Fundamental Choices

Because of the basic economic problem of scarcity, every society faces four fundamental choices concerning the use of its resources:

1. how much of each good to produce
2. how to produce each good (i.e., what resources and technology to employ)
3. how to divide or apportion the goods it produces among its members
4. how fast to grow (i.e., how rapidly to shift its PPB outward)

These choices are inherent in the economic problem and are therefore universal. Every society, no matter how primitive or how technologically advanced, must make them.

RAISE YOUR GRADES

Can you explain...?

☑ why scarcity is relative in economics
☑ why different societies use different methods to challenge scarcity
☑ how an economist's definition of *capital* differs from a layperson's
☑ why entrepreneurs play a critical role in a market economy
☑ what a production possibilities boundary (PPB) indicates
☑ why a PPB has a negative slope
☑ what causes a PPB to shift
☑ what causes a society to move inside its PPB
☑ why economics has been called "the science of choice"
☑ how the opportunity cost of a good is calculated
☑ how the law of increasing opportunity costs affects the shape of a PPB
☑ why the heterogeneity of resources contributes to increasing costs
☑ how a society can promote growth in its PPB
☑ why all societies face four fundamental choices about resource use

SUMMARY

1. The basic economic problem is scarcity: our material wants exceed our ability to satisfy them from limited resources. *Economic scarcity* means that the desire for an item is greater than the free availability of the item in nature.

2. *Economics* is the study of how individuals and societies choose to use their scarce resources in order to best satisfy their material wants.

3. The four methods commonly used to challenge scarcity are (1) the full employment of available resources, (2) the development of resources and technology, (3) the efficient organization of the production and distribution of goods, and (4) the redistribution of goods or income among the members of a society.

4. *Goods* are items or services that satisfy material wants. They are produced from resources with the aid of technology.

5. *Resources* are items used to produce goods. Economists often classify resources as land, capital, and human resources.

6. *Land* is any naturally occurring resource (any natural resource) used in production.

7. A *human resource* is any human skill used in production, including labor and entrepreneurial ability.

8. *Capital* is any man-made item used in production.

9. *Technology* is society's knowledge of the production process.

10. Resources are versatile and heterogeneous: they may be used for many different purposes, but some resources are more productive in one use than they are in another.

11. *Entrepreneurs* are individuals who decide which goods to produce, who take the initiative in assembling the necessary resources, and who reap the profits or losses resulting from their decisions.

12. A *production possibilities boundary (PPB)* is a schedule or curve illustrating the various combinations of goods that a society is capable of producing at any given time if technology and resources are fixed and all resources are fully and efficiently employed.

13. A PPB has four important properties: (1) it is a boundary; (2) it can be reached only if all resources are fully and efficiently employed; (3) it has a negative slope; and (4) it shifts when there is a change in technology or in the availability of resources.

14. A society that forgoes consumption today, choosing capital goods and technology instead, will accelerate the growth of its PPB.

15. A PPB illustrates the necessity of making choices: once a society has reached the boundary of its production possibilities, it can increase production of one good only by decreasing production of another good.

16. *Opportunity cost* is the amount of a good or goods that must be sacrificed to obtain a unit of another good.

17. A PPB usually bows away from the origin of a set of axes because of increasing opportunity costs.

18. The law of increasing opportunity costs states that, if a society is operating at the boundary of its production possibilities, the opportunity cost of a good will increase with each additional unit of the good that is produced.

19. Costs increase because of the heterogeneity of resources and the phenomenon of diminishing returns.

20. Every society must make four fundamental choices about the use of its resources: (1) how much to produce, (2) how to produce it, (3) how to apportion it, and (4) how fast to grow.

RAPID REVIEW

1. The basic subject matter of economics is (**a**) money, (**b**) capital resources, (**c**) scarcity, (**d**) inflation. [See Section 1-1.]

2. Unpolluted air is a scarce resource because (**a**) people breathe too much, (**b**) the quantity freely available is less than the quantity people want, (**c**) government regulations limit its production, (**d**) very little is available, especially in cities like Los Angeles. [See Section 1-1.]

3. _____ is the study of how individuals and societies choose to use their scarce resources to satisfy their material wants. [See Section 1-1.]

4. A method *not* commonly used to alleviate scarcity is the (**a**) redistribution of income, (**b**) full employment of resources, (**c**) improvement of technology, (**d**) reduction of material wants. [See Section 1-1.]

5. Economists define *technology* as (**a**) society's knowledge of production, (**b**) applied science, (**c**) knowledge of science and mathematics, (**d**) none of these. [See Section 1-2.]

6. All of the following are capital resources *except* (**a**) a warehouse, (**b**) a tractor, (**c**) 100 shares of stock in IBM, (**d**) a delivery truck. [See Section 1-2.]

7. _____ are individuals who organize production and bear the associated risks. [See Section 1-2.]

8. A _____ is a schedule or curve illustrating the combinations of goods that a society is capable of producing at any time if it employs all of its given resources and technology fully and efficiently. [See Section 1-3.]

9. Which of the following is *not* a property of a PPB? (**a**) It has a positive slope. (**b**) It shifts when technology changes. (**c**) It can be achieved only with the full employment of resources. (**d**) It is a boundary. [See Section 1-3.]

10. A PPB will shift if (**a**) some resources are unemployed, (**b**) there is a change in a society's preference for goods, (**c**) there is a change in technology, (**d**) any of these conditions prevails. [See Section 1-3.]

11. *Opportunity cost* is (**a**) the amount of risk involved in an entrepreneurial venture, (**b**) the amount of a good or goods that must be sacrificed to obtain a unit of another good, (**c**) the amount of money it costs to produce a good, (**d**) none of these. [See Section 1-4.]

12. If you attend the movies tonight, you will pay $5 for a ticket and lose 3 hours of valuable study time. The opportunity cost of the movie is (**a**) $5, (**b**) 3 hours of study time, (**c**) both (**a**) and (**b**), (**d**) none of these. [See Section 1-4.]

13. A PPB that bows away from the origin of a set of axes indicates that the opportunity cost of the good on the *x*-axis (**a**) increases with movement toward the *x*-axis, (**b**) increases with movement toward the *y*-axis, (**c**) decreases as production of the good increases, (**d**) increases as production of the good on the *y*-axis increases. [See Section 1-4.]

14. The fundamental choices that a society must make about the use of its resources include (**a**) how much to produce, (**b**) how to produce, (**c**) how to distribute, (**d**) all of these. [See Section 1-5.]

Answers

1. (c)   2. (b)   3. *Economics*   4. (d)   5. (a)   6. (c)   7. *Entrepreneurs*
8. *PPB* (*production possibilities boundary*)   9. (a)   10. (c)   11. (b)   12. (c)   13. (a)
14. (d)

SOLVED PROBLEMS

PROBLEM 1-1   How can economists say that automobiles are scarce when millions are produced each year?

Answer: Automobiles are "scarce" in an economic sense because the number available *at no cost* is less than the number that people desire. As long as there are too few automobiles to meet this no-cost criterion, economists will classify them as scarce. [See Section 1-1.]

PROBLEM 1-2   Consider the following statement: "We would not have an economic problem if everyone simply decided that material goods were frivolous and quit wanting them." Is this statement true or false? Explain the rationale for your answer.

Answer: True. *If* everyone could make such a decision for *all* material goods, including food and shelter, scarcity would not be a problem. People would have no desires for material goods, and so no material resources would be required to satisfy them. Scarcity is a problem only because our desires for material goods exceed the limited resources available to satisfy them. [See Section 1-1.]

PROBLEM 1-3   Which of the four methods commonly used to challenge or alleviate scarcity is likely to be the most controversial in the United States? Explain.

Answer: The redistribution of goods or income is likely to be the most controversial for two reasons. First, whereas everybody might gain from the other three methods— efficiency, growth, and the full employment of resources—somebody must lose if income or goods are redistributed. Second, as a society, the United States traditionally has valued the rights and interests of the individual, both economic and political, over the rights and interests of the group. As a result, it tends to promote individual initiative and to resist any collective action, such as the redistribution of goods and income, that violates the economic interests of some individuals. [See Section 1-1.]

PROBLEM 1-4   Explain how it is possible to increase the output (production) of a good without increasing the input (resources) used to produce the good.

Answer: Output is a function of technology as well as the use of resources. An improvement in technology—society's knowledge of production—can increase output without also increasing input. [See Section 1-2.]

PROBLEM 1-5   What evidence can you cite to prove that garbage is not considered a "good" by most people?

Answer: Since people are willing to pay to have it removed, they obviously have more garbage than they want, even at no cost. To them, garbage *removal*, not garbage, is a good. Most people do not consider garbage a good because it does not satisfy a material want. [See Section 1-2.]

PROBLEM 1-6   Laypeople often refer to their holdings of stocks, bonds, and savings accounts as "capital." Explain why stocks, bonds, and saving accounts are not classified as capital by an economist.

Answer: Economists define *capital* as any man-made thing—such as a tool, a piece of machinery, a building—that is used directly in the production of a good. Stocks, bonds, and other financial assets are not *direct* inputs into the production of any good. [See Section 1-2.]

PROBLEM 1-7   Draw a PPB that exhibits increasing opportunity costs for a society producing two goods, tanks and tacos. On the same diagram, show the effect that a significant loss of resources would have on that society's PPB.

Answer: A PPB that exhibits increasing opportunity costs bows away from the origin of a set of axes, as shown in Figure 1-5. If the society producing the tanks and tacos were to lose a significant portion of its resources, its production possibilities would be reduced and its PPB would shift inward. [See Section 1-3.]

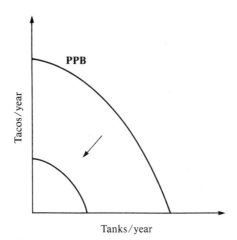

Figure 1-5

PROBLEM 1-8   Draw a PPB that exhibits constant (nonincreasing) opportunity costs for a society producing two goods, tanks and tacos. What would happen to that society's PPB if a significant portion of its labor force became unemployed?

Answer: A PPB that exhibits constant opportunity costs is a straight line, as shown in Figure 1-6. If the unemployment rate rose significantly, the PPB of the society producing the tanks and tacos would not shift because the same resources, though not fully employed, would still be available. Instead, the society would move inside its PPB, to a point such as *A* in Figure 1-6. [See Section 1-3.]

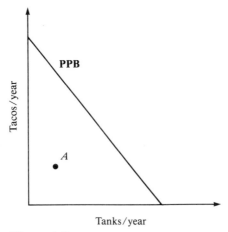

Figure 1-6

PROBLEM 1-9   How would you calculate the opportunity cost of your college education if you lived at home and went to school full time for four years?

Answer: The opportunity cost of your college education would be equal to the value of the alternatives you would have to forgo to attend school full time for four years. These alternatives would fall into two categories: **(1)** the value of the income you could earn if you worked full time instead, and **(2)** the value of the things you could buy if you did not spend your money on tuition and books. Your calculations might look something like this [see Section 1-4]:

Forgone alternative	Value
Income: 4 years @ $8,000/yr.	$32,000
Consumption: 4 years' tuition and books	10,000
Total	42,000

PROBLEM 1-10 Consider a simple island economy with one person, Robinson Crusoe, and two goods, fish and coconuts. Which of the four fundamental choices about the use of resources are relevant to this simple economy?

Answer: The first two choices, how much of each good to produce and how to produce it, are both clearly relevant to Robinson Crusoe's simple island economy. The third choice, how to distribute the goods produced, is less relevant because there is only one person on the island. However, even Robinson Crusoe must decide how to apportion his consumption of fish and coconuts between present and future time periods. If forgoing consumption today will promote growth in his economy, the fourth choice is also relevant. [See Section 1-5.]

2 ECONOMICS AS A DISCIPLINE

THIS CHAPTER IS ABOUT

☑ **Economics as a Social Science**
☑ **Microeconomics and Macroeconomics**
☑ **Theories in Economics**
☑ **Economic Theory Versus Economic Policy**
☑ **Barriers to Clear Thinking in Economics**

2-1. Economics as a Social Science

Economics is a social science. Like other social sciences, it uses systematic methods of observation, analysis, and reasoning to study society, its institutions, and the interrelationships of its members. On the basis of its studies, it makes generalizations and formulates theories to describe, to explain, and to make predictions about the economic variables that affect the lives of everyone. Chief among these variables is the economic behavior of human beings—the manner in which people respond, individually and collectively, to the basic economic problem of scarcity.

A. Economics begins with the proposition that human behavior is predictable.

The study of economics, like the study of psychology or the study of any other social science, necessarily begins with the proposition that human behavior is predictable. It does not, of course, assume that the behavior of any particular individual is always predictable. Neither does it assume that the behavior of human beings is as predictable, say, as the behavior of a falling object. However, it does assume, on the basis of observation and experience, that there are central or common tendencies in the behavior of large groups of people—that is, in the behavior of "typical" individuals. These central or common tendencies make prediction possible.

B. Economics assumes that people behave purposefully, rationally, and efficiently.

The study of economics is based on several axioms or principles concerning the economic behavior of "typical" human beings. Among the most important of these are the following three propositions:

1. People behave *purposefully*. Their actions are directed toward goals or objectives.
2. People behave *rationally*. Their actions are consistent with the pursuit of their goals.
3. People behave *efficiently*. They seek the best means to achieve their goals, given the constraints they face.

2-2. Microeconomics and Macroeconomics

For both pedagogical and epistemological reasons, the study of economics is divided into two main parts, microeconomics and macroeconomics.

- **Microeconomics** is the study of how the choices of individual decision-making units, such as households and producers, and the functioning of individual markets determine the allocation of society's scarce resources and the distribution of income.
- **Macroeconomics** is the study of how money and aggregate expenditure or investment behavior determine the levels of output, employment, and prices in an entire economy.

2-3. Theories in Economics

Economics centers around a core of economic theories.

A **theory** is a set of consistent and related statements that provides a logical explanation of observed phenomena and a basis for predicting future events.

Economists use theories to explain relationships between economic variables and to predict economic events.

EXAMPLE 2-1: Some textbooks may not refer to them as such; others may call them *models*. But competitive markets (supply and demand), perfect competition, monopoly, and Keynesian macroeconomics are all examples of economic theories.

A. Theories provide a framework for logical analysis.

Theories are sets of general principles. They are constructed to provide a logical framework for organizing and analyzing information about particular economic facts and events. Theories consist of three types of statements:

1. assumptions or premises
2. definitions
3. conclusions or implications

EXAMPLE 2-2: The theory of perfect competition has a long history in economics. Like other theories, it consists of sets of assumptions, definitions, and implications. Although you will study all of these in detail later on, here is an example of each type of statement:

- *Assumption:* There are many buyers and sellers in each market.
- *Definition:* *Many* means a number sufficiently large that no buyer or seller can perceive the effects of his or her individual actions on the market.
- *Implication:* The market price of a good will equal the marginal cost of producing the good in a perfectly competitive market.

B. Theories are abstractions.

Theories are, by their very nature, abstractions. They are literally "drawn away" or dissociated from specific instances. As a result, the assumptions of some theories may appear to be simplistic or unrealistic, but this appearance does not invalidate the theories. They are constructed to provide a framework for analysis, not to describe actual conditions in all their detail and complexity.

EXAMPLE 2-3: Many economic theories include the assumption that business firms seek to maximize their economic profits. Actual firms often claim that their goals are less selfish, that they seek, for example, to create jobs and stable communities. This apparent discrepancy between the abstract and the concrete does not invalidate the use of profit-based theories by economists. In the first place, regardless of their professed aims, firms may actually operate in a manner that parallels the behavior of profit-maximizing firms. In the second place, firms whose behavior does *not* parallel the behavior of profit-maximizing firms are less likely to survive in a competitive market economy than those whose behavior does. Thus, established firms tend to be profit seeking whether they acknowledge it or not.

C. Theories are accepted if their predictions are accurate.

Although theories are abstractions, they are accepted or rejected on their application to concrete facts and events. In fact, the term *theory* is reserved for those sets of statements that have withstood and continue to withstand the test of reality. Only those theories that consistently yield relatively accurate predictions about the real world attain acceptance, stature, and a place in textbooks.

2-4. Economic Theory Versus Economic Policy

Perhaps because it has such a profound and immediate effect on the lives of everyone, economics—literally, "the study of household management"—receives more public attention and seems to provoke more controversy than other academic disciplines. Entire newspapers, such as *The Wall Street Journal*, are devoted to business and economics. So are regular sections of most metropolitan daily newspapers and such national weekly magazines as *Time* and *Newsweek*.

The considerable attention focused on economics promotes interest in the subject, but it also creates confusion. By obscuring the distinction between economic theory and economic policy, the publicity tends to exaggerate the level of disagreement among professional economists and thus to encourage the notion that economics is less a body of serious knowledge than a collection of highly controversial opinions.

Of course this notion is misguided. Economists do disagree, often publicly and often vociferously, about economic *policy*; but about economic *theory* they are in substantial agreement. The distinction between theory and policy is an important one. In fact, economists have their own special terminology for it: positive versus normative economics.

- **Positive economics** is the study of what is (economic theory).
- **Normative economics** is the study of what should be (economic policy).

A. Economists substantially agree about economic theory.

There is substantial agreement among professional economists about the positive or theoretical aspects of economics. The reason for their agreement is that economics is a body of well-established general principles that provide plausible explanations for economic facts and events—that is, for the way things are. These principles or theories are not mere opinions. They are sets of statements that consistently yield accurate predictions about observable phenomena.

To say that there is substantial agreement among economists about economic theory is not of course to say that there is universal agreement among them, any more than there is—or could be—universal agreement among chemists, sociologists, or meteorologists. Although they agree about *most* economic theories, economists disagree about others—particularly, as you might expect, about relatively new theories and about theories that pertain to the forces at work in an economy as a whole. There are different schools of thought, for example, about the role of money in an economy. These disagreements should not undermine your confidence in economics as an academic discipline. Debate is universal—and necessary—at the frontiers of knowledge in any field.

B. Economists frequently disagree about economic policy.

Just as professional economists substantially agree about the body of knowledge called economics, so they usually disagree about how that knowledge should be applied in the solution of economic problems. The reason for widespread disagreement on economic policy or normative economics is that, like other people, economists have different backgrounds, different values, and different goals in life. These backgrounds, values, and goals are very influential in the shaping of economic policy, much more so than they are in the shaping of economic theory.

EXAMPLE 2-4: The theory of perfect competition is probably the most widely accepted, the most widely taught, and the most frequently applied theory in economics. Certainly it is a cornerstone of positive economics in Western societies. Yet economists disagree about the normative implications of the theory.

Take, for example, a specific application of the theory: the issue of the deregulation of natural gas prices in the United States. According to the theory of perfect competition, the price of a product will go up if an effective price ceiling is lifted and the price is allowed to respond to market forces. About this, the theoretical aspect of the issue, economists agree. They also agree that higher natural gas prices will encourage the efficient use of a limited resource by forcing people to reduce their consumption of natural gas.

But do all economists support deregulation? No. Some argue that although deregulation will increase efficiency, the benefits of that efficiency will be inequitable. Gas producers will reap high profits, but poor people will have to live in cold houses. Their argument is an argument about normative, not positive, economics. It is an argument about what should be, not about what is.

2-5. Barriers to Clear Thinking in Economics

Although admittedly less exact than physics or chemistry, economics is nevertheless a *science*. As such, its methods of gathering facts, drawing conclusions, and formulating hypotheses and generalizations are governed by the same rigorous standards as the methods of the natural sciences—even though its subject matter does not lend itself to the rigid controls of laboratory experimentation. In fact, precisely because it does not, students of economics must be constantly aware of the barriers to clear thinking in scientific analysis. Following are four of the more common ones.

A. Terminology may be misused or misunderstood.

Every discipline has its own specialized language or jargon to facilitate communication among its practitioners. Economics is no exception. The first barrier to clear thinking in economics, then, is an imperfect mastery of its vocabulary. This caution applies not only to new, obviously unfamiliar terms like *monopsony*, *marginal utility*, and *returns to scale*, but also to familiar words like *land*, *scarcity*, and *capital* to which economists assign peculiar meanings. The latter, particularly, can cause confusion among the uninitiated, just as popular preconceptions and misconceptions about economics itself can. To avoid that confusion, you must learn and use the vocabulary of economics with the same care and precision as you would learn and use the vocabulary of a subject, such as microbiology, with which you have no previous experience.

B. Association may be mistaken for causation.

Economists try to determine the causes of economic events because a knowledge of cause–effect relationships sometimes—though certainly not always—implies the ability to predict, and possibly to influence, those events. Establishing causal relationships in economics, however, is no simple matter. In the first place, the interrelationships of economic variables are often very complex. In the second place, manipulation of those variables for experimental purposes is usually impossible. In the third place, it is not always easy to distinguish causes from mere associations. Does one economic event cause another or does it merely precede it?

Our minds have been trained to perceive associated events as related, and occasionally we mistakenly infer causation from association. The rooster crows and the sun rises. That the crowing does not cause the sun to rise is obvious; that two closely associated economic events may actually be independent of one another, however, is often much more difficult to perceive. The mistake of inferring that a preceding event caused a subsequent one is called the *post hoc, ergo propter hoc* fallacy: "after this, therefore because of this." To avoid this barrier to clear thinking in economics, you must remember that neither chronological sequence nor association necessarily implies causation.

C. The *ceteris paribus* condition may be violated.

You will encounter the Latin phrase *ceteris paribus* frequently in economics textbooks. Literally, **ceteris paribus** means "other things being equal."

EXAMPLE 2-5: An economist might use the phrase *ceteris paribus* in a statement such as the following: "An increase in demand will increase market price, *ceteris paribus*." Translated, this statement means, "An increase in the demand for a good will result in an increase in its price if all of the other factors that influence the market price of the good are held constant."

Economists use the *ceteris paribus* condition in much the same way that natural scientists use the controlled environment of the laboratory: to examine the relationship between two economic variables in isolation.

Of course economists can't isolate and control economic variables in the same way that natural scientists can isolate and control physical variables in laboratory experiments. In fact, nature rarely cooperates by holding all other economic factors constant. As a result, economists have had to develop elaborate statistical techniques to overcome the methodological problem of testing hypotheses qualified by the *ceteris paribus* condition.

Although it is an artificial convenience rather than a reflection of the way things are, the *ceteris paribus* condition is very useful in economic analysis. You must, however, understand exactly which economic variables are comprehended by the phrase in any given situation. Otherwise you can violate the condition in your analysis by allowing to vary factors that should be held constant.

D. Unwarranted inferences may be drawn from the part to the whole.

Valid statements about individual experience may be invalid if they are applied to groups.

EXAMPLE 2-6: If one individual brings a large cooler of soft drinks to the beach on a hot day, he or she can make a handsome profit selling the drinks. However, if everyone brings a large cooler of soft drinks to the beach on the same hot day, no one can make a profit.

Drawing unwarranted inferences from the part to the whole is called the **fallacy of composition**. To avoid this barrier to clear thinking in economics, you must remember that statements that are true for an individual may not be true for a group.

RAISE YOUR GRADES

Can you explain...?

☑ why economics is classified as a social science
☑ why economists start with three main axioms concerning human behavior
☑ how theories are used in economics
☑ how theories become accepted
☑ why simplistic assumptions do not invalidate theories
☑ how the three types of statements in a theory interrelate
☑ how positive economics differs from normative economics
☑ why economists disagree about economic policy
☑ why terminology may be a barrier to clear thinking in economics
☑ what *post hoc, ergo propter hoc* means and why it is a fallacy
☑ why the *ceteris paribus* condition is useful in economic analysis
☑ why a valid statement about individual experience may be invalid if applied to a group

SUMMARY

1. Economics is a social science. It uses systematic methods to study the ways in which a society responds, individually and collectively, to the basic economic problem of scarcity.
2. Economics begins with the proposition that human behavior (i.e., the behavior of "typical" individuals) is predictable.
3. The study of economics is based on three main axioms or principles concerning human behavior: that it is purposeful, rational, and efficient.
4. Economics is divided into two parts. *Microeconomics* is the study of the individual decision-making units in an economy. *Macroeconomics* is the study of how money and aggregate expenditure or investment behavior determine the levels of output, employment, and prices in an economy as a whole.
5. The discipline of economics centers around a core of economic theories. *Theories* are sets of consistent and related statements that provide logical explanations of observed phenomena.
6. Theories provide a logical framework for organizing information about particular economic facts and events.
7. Economists use theories to explain relationships between economic variables and to predict economic events.
8. Theories consist of three types of statements: assumptions or premises, definitions, and logical conclusions or implications.
9. Theories are abstractions. Hence their assumptions, though valid, may seem simplistic. Simplistic assumptions do not invalidate theories.

10. Theories are accepted only if they consistently yield relatively accurate predictions about observable phenomena.
11. *Positive economics* is the study of what is (economic theory). *Normative economics* is the study of what should be (economic policy).
12. Economists are in substantial agreement about positive economics. They agree about most economic theories.
13. Economists disagree about some economic theories, especially those dealing with the forces at work in an economy as a whole. Disagreement is universal at the frontiers of any discipline.
14. Economists disagree about the best policies to use in solving particular economic problems (normative economics) because they have different backgrounds, experiences, values, and goals.
15. Economists use their own special jargon; they also attach uncommon meanings to common terms. Hence terminology can be a barrier to clear thinking in economics.
16. Mistaking chronological sequence or association for causation is called the *post hoc, ergo propter hoc* fallacy. The Latin phrase means "after this, therefore because of this."
17. *Ceteris paribus* is an artificial condition adopted by economists to examine, in isolation, the relationship between two economic variables. *Ceteris paribus* means "if all other relevant factors are held constant."
18. The *ceteris paribus* condition can present a barrier to clear thinking in economic analysis if factors that are assumed to be held constant are allowed to vary.
19. The testing of economic hypotheses qualified by the *ceteris paribus* condition is complicated by the fact that nature seldom cooperates by holding other things constant.
20. Valid statements about individual experience are not necessarily true of groups. Drawing unwarranted inferences from the part to the whole is called the *fallacy of composition*.

RAPID REVIEW

1. Economics is a branch of the _____ sciences. [See Section 2-1.]
2. The study of economics necessarily begins with the assumption that human behavior is _____. [See Section 2-1.]
3. Economics assumes that people behave in all of the following ways *except* (**a**) efficiently, (**b**) generously, (**c**) purposefully, (**d**) rationally. [See Section 2-1.]
4. The behavior of a particular individual is more predictable than the behavior of a typical individual within a group. True or false? [See Section 2-1.]
5. _____ is the study of how individual households and producers interacting in particular markets determine the allocation of society's scarce resources and the distribution of income. [See Section 2-2.]
6. Economists use _____ to explain relationships between economic variables and to predict economic phenomena. [See Section 2-3.]
7. Keynesian macroeconomics is an example of an economic theory or _____. [See Section 2-3.]
8. Theories may include all of the following types of statements *except* (**a**) implications, (**b**) definitions, (**c**) premises, (**d**) opinions. [See Section 2-3.]
9. Theories are rejected by economists (**a**) if they are dissociated from specific instances, (**b**) if their assumptions seem naive or unrealistic, (**c**) if they fail to provide complete descriptions of actual conditions, (**d**) for none of these reasons. [See Section 2-3.]

10. A theory would probably be accepted by economists if it consistently yielded more accurate predictions about economic phenomena than a competing theory. True or false? [See Section 2-3.]

11. The word *economics* literally means "the study of _____ management." [See Section 2-4.]

12. _____ *economics* is the study of what is; _____ *economics* is the study of what should be. [See Section 2-4.]

13. Economists substantially agree about economic _____; they often disagree about economic _____. [See Section 2-4.]

14. Economists disagree about positive economics because they have different backgrounds, values, and goals. True or false? [See Section 2-4.]

15. If you concluded mistakenly that the inflation of 1979 was caused by an increase in government spending in 1933, you would be guilty of the (a) *ceteris paribus* fallacy, (b) fallacy of composition, (c) *post hoc, ergo propter hoc* fallacy, (d) normative fallacy. [See Section 2-5.]

16. The Latin phrase *ceteris paribus* means (a) "where is the bus?" (b) "other things being equal," (c) "after this, therefore because of this," (d) if all other factors change at the same rate." [See Section 2-5.]

17. Drawing unwarranted inferences from the individual to the group is called the *fallacy of* _____. [See Section 2-5.]

18. Economists adopt the *ceteris paribus* condition because it gives them greater control over economic variables. True or false? [See Section 2-5.]

19. All of the following are actual or potential barriers to clear thinking in positive economics *except* (a) objectivity, (b) jargon, (c) fallacious reasoning, (d) violations of the *ceteris paribus* condition. [See Section 2-5.]

Answers

1. social   2. predictable   3. (b)   4. false   5. *Microeconomics*   6. theories
7. model   8. (d)   9. (d)   10. true   11. household   12. *Positive, normative*
13. theory, policy   14. false   15. (c)   16. (b)   17. *composition*   18. false   19. (a)

SOLVED PROBLEMS

PROBLEM 2-1 Economists start with the proposition that human behavior is purposeful, rational, and efficient. Are your current activities in pursuit of a career consistent with these propositions?

Answer: You must answer this question for yourself. If you are a college student majoring in business, engineering, computer science, premedicine, or some other applied field, you will probably conclude that your activities are consistent with the propositions. If you are majoring in the humanities or liberal arts, your current activities may appear to be directed more toward an education than toward a career. [See Section 2-1.]

PROBLEM 2-2 Economic theories often include the assumption that individuals seek to maximize their satisfaction or utility. Yet you may know of people whose behavior as consumers appears random or irrational. Does your observation render the economic models useless?

Answer: No. There need not be an exact correspondence between the assumptions of a theory and the realities to which those assumptions refer. Theories by their very nature are abstractions. As long as there is a tendency for consumers to behave as if they are seeking to maximize their satisfaction, the theories may accurately predict the behavior of groups of people and society in general. [See Sections 2-1 and 2-3.]

PROBLEM 2-3   Is gravity a theory or a fact?

Answer: It is a fact that mass is attracted to other units of mass, but explanations for this attraction are only theories. In fact, several theories have been advanced to explain this attraction. Like other theories, theories of gravity are constantly being revised and extended as more is learned. [See Section 2-3.]

PROBLEM 2-4   What events might lead a scientist to reject a theory?

Answer: Theories are accepted only if they yield predictions that are relatively more accurate than competing theories. If a theory were proposed that consistently yielded more accurate predictions about empirical phenomena than a previous theory, the previous theory would likely be rejected. [See Section 2-3.]

PROBLEM 2-5   Write four short statements on deficit spending by the federal government. Classify the statements as normative or positive.

Answer: Statements such as "Deficit spending causes inflation" or "Deficit spending will increase the level of national income" are positive or theoretical statements. Such statements can be tested against the facts, and the underlying theories can be either accepted or rejected.

   Statements such as "Deficit spending is immoral" or "The United States should not engage in deficit spending" are normative or policy statements. Such statements express a policy or position and cannot be scientifically tested. [See Section 2-4.]

PROBLEM 2-6   Comment on the following statement: "Economists publicly disagree on the best policy to cure inflation. Obviously, economics is simply a matter of opinion. I don't need to study economics to have opinions. I already know what I believe."

Answer: It is important to differentiate between economic theory and economic policy, between positive and normative economics. Economists do disagree publicly on economic policies (normative economics). However, they are in significant agreement on economic theories (positive economics). Your studies will focus primarily on economic theory, which is not just a matter of opinion. Your instructor is not likely to want your opinions on exams; rather he or she will want you to apply relevant economic theories. Don't substitute opinions for theories. [See Section 2-4.]

PROBLEM 2-7   Analyze the fallacy in the following statement: "I dump my garbage and sewage into the lake, and it has not caused any problems. Therefore, we do not need any pollution regulations for this lake."

Answer: The statement is an example of the fallacy of composition. If all of the people in the area dumped their garbage and sewage into the lake, it could cause pollution problems. [See Section 2-5.]

PROBLEM 2-8   Analyze the fallacy in the following statement: "Whenever we elect a Republican president, the economy goes into a recession or depression. Whenever we elect a Democratic president, we go to war."

Answer: This is an example of the *post hoc, ergo propter hoc* fallacy. Even if the statement had some basis in historical fact, there still would be no proof that the election of a particular party to the White House actually *caused* the events. [See Section 2-5.]

3 GRAPHING SKILLS

THIS CHAPTER IS ABOUT

☑ **The Use of Diagrams and Graphs in Economics**
☑ **Self-Test on Graphing**
☑ **Two-Dimensional Graphs and Diagrams**
☑ **Constructing a Graph**
☑ **Plotting Points on a Graph**
☑ **Connecting the Points on a Graph**
☑ **"Reading" the Lines on a Graph or Diagram**
☑ **Calculating the Slope of a Line**
☑ **Answers to Self-Test on Graphing**

3-1. The Use of Diagrams and Graphs in Economics

Economists make extensive use of diagrams and graphs to analyze relationships between economic variables. In this book, the words *diagram* and *graph* are both used to refer to a drawing that shows the relationships between two or more variables with respect to a set of axes. However, the two terms are distinguished in the following manner:

- A **diagram** is a drawing that shows general relationships between economic variables. On a diagram, the shape and direction of the lines are important, but the precise locations of particular points are not. In fact, there may be no numbers at all on the axes, as shown in Figure 3-1.

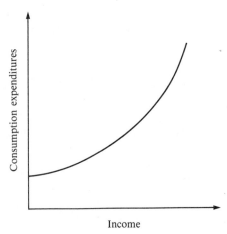

Figure 3-1
The shape and direction of the line(s) on a diagram show the general relationship between economic variables.

• A **graph** is a drawing that shows precise relationships between economic variables. On a graph, the exact location of a specific point, such as the intersection of two lines, is important, and so the numbers on the axes are critical. Economists use graphs to determine, for example, the equilibrium price and quantity in a market, as shown in Figure 3-2.

An ability to interpret and prepare diagrams and graphs is essential for the study of economics. Before you proceed any further in this book, then, measure your graphing ability by taking the self-test in Section 3-2. If you answer all of the questions correctly, proceed directly to Chapter 4. If you miss one or more answers, or if you have trouble answering any of the questions, study the rest of this chapter carefully before you move on. When you take the self-test, be honest. It is better to spend a little time now than to be confused each time you encounter a diagram or graph.

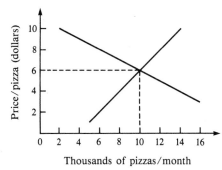

Figure 3-2
Economists use graphs to determine the precise location of specific points, such as the equilibrium price and quantity in a market.

3-2. Self-Test on Graphing

1. Plot the following points on the graph in Figure 3-3: (3, 5) and (8, 15).
2. Draw a line connecting the two points in Figure 3-3. Calculate the slope of the line.

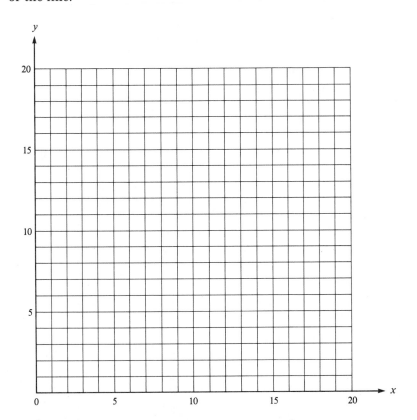

Figure 3-3

3. Consider the demand curve, line *DD*, in Figure 3-4. Describe the relationship between the price of pizza and the quantity demanded each month. What happens to the quantity demanded as the price of pizza increases? If the price of pizza increases by $2, how much does the quantity demanded change?
4. Suppose that pizza producers decide to provide more pizzas at each price than the supply curve, line *SS*, in Figure 3-4 indicates. Sketch a new supply curve in Figure 3-4 to show the change in supply. Label the new curve *S'S'*.

Turn to Section 3-9 to find the correct answers to this self-test. You should not skip the rest of this chapter unless you answered all of the questions correctly.

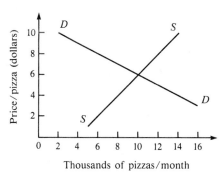

Figure 3-4

3-3. Two-Dimensional Graphs and Diagrams

Most diagrams and graphs, like the ones in this book, are two-dimensional. They show the relationship between two—and only two—variables.

EXAMPLE 3-1: The production possibilities boundaries (PPBs) that you encountered in Chapter 1 are two-dimensional diagrams. They illustrate how production of one good, such as butter, declines as production of another good, such as guns, rises. Other two-dimensional graphs and diagrams show the relationships between such economic variables as input and output, income and expenditures, price and quantity supplied or demanded.

3-4. Constructing a Graph

Two elements are necessary for the construction of a graph: numerical information about the relationship between two variables and a framework for displaying that information.

A. Two number lines provide the framework for a graph.

A **number line** is a line divided into sequentially numbered segments of equal length. A pair of crossed number lines, one horizontal and one vertical, as shown in Figure 3-5, provide the framework for displaying numerical information on a two-dimensional graph. The horizontal number line is used to locate the values of one variable; the vertical number line is used to locate the values of the second variable. These crossed number lines are called **coordinate axes**. By convention, the point of intersection of the two lines is the zero point on each axis. This point of intersection, designated as (0, 0), is called the **origin** of the axes.

As you can see in Figure 3-5, the numbers on the horizontal axis, called the **x-axis**, increase in value from left to right; they are negative on the left side of the vertical axis and positive on the right side of it. The numbers on the vertical axis, called the **y-axis**, increase in value from bottom to top; they are negative below the x-axis and positive above it. Since most numerical information in economics is positive, nearly all of the graphs (and diagrams) in this book show only the area above the x-axis and to the right of the y-axis. This area is called the *positive quadrant.*

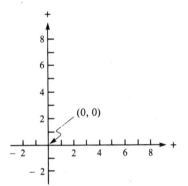

Figure 3-5
A pair of crossed number lines, called *coordinate axes*, provide the framework for a graph.

B. An equation or a schedule provides the numerical information for a graph.

Numerical information about the relationship between two variables may originate from an equation or a schedule. An equation or a schedule defines the relationship between two variables by specifying exactly how the set of values for one variable corresponds to the set of values for the other variable. These corresponding values are often presented in the form of paired numbers called **coordinates**, which correspond to points on a graph.

EXAMPLE 3-2: The following equation and schedule both yield the same numerical information about the relationship between two variables, price and quantity demanded. They both show how the quantity demanded each day varies as the price per unit changes: if the price per unit is $10, the quantity demanded each day is 0; if the price per unit is $8, the quantity demanded each day is 2; if the price per unit is $6, the quantity demanded each day is 4; and so on. If these corresponding values of price and quantity demanded are going to be displayed on a graph, they are often written, as they are here, as a set of paired coordinates. Each pair corresponds to a point on a graph.

Equation		
Price = 10 − quantity demanded		

Schedule		
Quantity/day	Price/unit	Paired Coordinates
0	$10	(0, 10)
2	8	(2, 8)
4	6	(4, 6)
6	4	(6, 4)
8	2	(8, 2)
10	0	(10, 0)

3-5. Plotting Points on a Graph

The corresponding values of two variables are called *coordinates* because they specify the location of the values in relation to the *coordinate* axes that provide the framework for a graph. By convention, the first coordinate is called the **x-coordinate** because it locates the value of one variable, called the **x-variable**, in relation to the *x*-axis. The second coordinate is called the **y-coordinate** because it locates the value of the second variable, called the **y-variable**, in relation to the *y*-axis. Together, the two coordinates specify a single point that can be displayed or *plotted* on a graph.

EXAMPLE 3-3: In the pair of coordinates (2, 8), 2 is the *x*-coordinate and 8 is the *y*-coordinate. The pair represents a point that is two units to the right of the origin on the *x*-axis and eight units above the origin on the *y*-axis, as shown in Figure 3-6. The point is a picture of a specific relationship between the variable on the *x*-axis and the variable on the *y*-axis. It "says" that when the value of the *x*-variable (e.g., quantity demanded) is 2, the value of the *y*-variable (e.g., price) is 8.

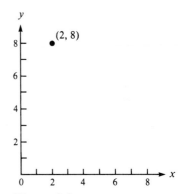

Figure 3-6
The first number in a pair of coordinates is located along the x-axis. The second number is located along the y-axis.

3-6. Connecting the Points on a Graph

After the points specified by a set of paired coordinates have been plotted on a graph, they are usually connected. A line presents a clearer, more immediate image of the relationship between two variables than several isolated points do. If the points fall in a straight line, a straight line is drawn through them. If they do not, as smooth a curve as possible is drawn to connect them. (The assumption, of course, is that the relationship between the two variables represented on the graph is consistent along the line—that is, not only *at* the plotted points, for which precise values are known, but also *between* the plotted points, for which precise values are not known. This assumption is useful, but it is not always strictly valid.)

In this chapter the word *line* is used to refer to any set of continuous points on a graph, whether it is straight or curved. Mathematically speaking, however, the correct term for a set of continuous points on a graph is *curve* (even if the "curve" happens to be a straight line). Since economists use *curve* in the mathematical sense, you will encounter many demand and supply "curves" that are actually straight lines. These curves are called *linear* curves.

3-7. "Reading" the Lines on a Graph or Diagram

A line on a graph or diagram makes the relationship between two variables more readily apparent than an equation, a schedule, or a set of paired coordinates. In fact, two properties of a line that are immediately obvious—its direction and its "shape"—provide instant information about the relationship between two variables.

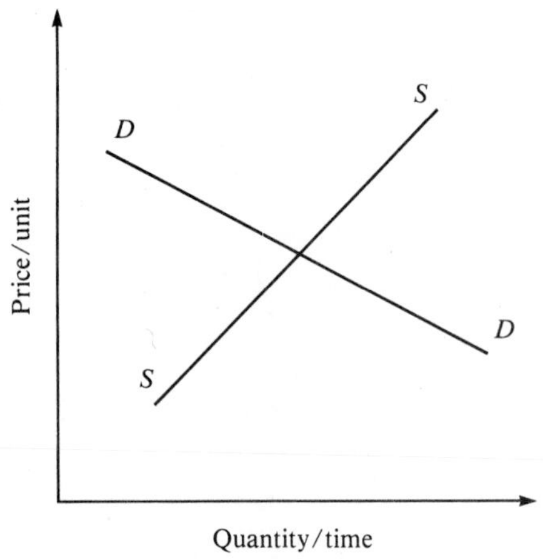

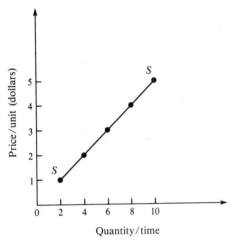

Figure 3-7
A positive slope (*SS*) indicates a direct relationship and a negative slope (*DD*) indicates an inverse relationship between two variables.

A. The direction of a line indicates whether the relationship between two variables is direct or inverse.

1. A line that moves in an upward (northeasterly) direction indicates a direct relationship between two variables. There is a **direct relationship** between two variables if they increase or decrease together.

EXAMPLE 3-4: Supply line *SS* in Figure 3-7 moves in an upward direction. It shows that price and quantity, the two variables represented on the diagram, are directly related: as price increases, quantity supplied increases; as price decreases, quantity supplied decreases.

2. A line that moves in a downward (southeasterly) direction indicates an inverse relationship between two variables. There is an **inverse relationship** between two variables if one increases as the other decreases.

EXAMPLE 3-5: Demand line *DD* in Figure 3-7 moves in a downward direction. It shows that price and quantity demanded are inversely related: as price increases, quantity demanded decreases; as price decreases, quantity demanded increases.

B. The "shape" of a line indicates whether or not the rate of change between two variables is constant.

1. A straight line indicates a constant rate of change between two variables.

EXAMPLE 3-6: Supply line *SS* in Figure 3-8 is straight, indicating a constant rate of change between price and quantity supplied. For every \$1 increase in price, quantity supplied increases by two units.

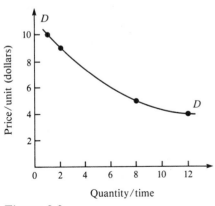

Figure 3-8
A straight line indicates a constant rate of change between two variables.

2. A curved line indicates an increasing or decreasing (inconstant) rate of change between two variables.

EXAMPLE 3-7: Demand line *DD* in Figure 3-9 is curved, indicating that the rate of change between quantity demanded and price is not constant. As price declines, quantity demanded increases at an increasing rate. As price declines from \$10 to \$9, quantity demanded increases by one unit; as price declines from \$5 to \$4, quantity demanded increases by four units.

3-8. Calculating the Slope of a Line

To determine the precise mathematical effect of a change in one variable on a second variable, economists calculate the slope of a line. The slope of a line is the measure of the relative rates of change between two variables. The slope of a line may be positive, negative, zero, or undefined; it may be constant or changing.

A. The slope of a line is the ratio of the rise to the run.

The **slope** of a line is the ratio of the rise of the line to the run of the line. The rise of a line is the vertical change or the change in the *y*-variable between two points on the line. The run of a line is the horizontal change or the change in the *x*-variable between the same two points on the line.

$$\text{slope} = \frac{\text{rise}}{\text{run}} = \frac{\text{change in } y\text{-variable}}{\text{change in } x\text{-variable}}$$

Figure 3-9
A curved line indicates an inconstant rate of change between two variables.

B. A positive slope indicates a direct relationship between two variables; a negative slope indicates an inverse relationship between two variables.

EXAMPLE 3-8: The slope of the line in Figure 3-10 is 1/2 (or 0.5). A slope of 1/2 indicates that there is a one-unit change in variable y for every two-unit change in variable x. Because 1/2 is positive, it also indicates that variable y and variable x are directly related: they increase or decrease together.

EXAMPLE 3-9: The slope of the line in Figure 3-11 is -5 (or $-5/1$). The slope is negative because variable x and variable y are inversely related. A slope of -5 implies a five-unit *decrease* in variable y for every one-unit *increase* in variable x (or, conversely, a five-unit *increase* in variable y for every one-unit *decrease* in variable x).

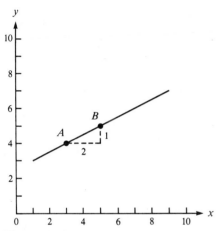

Figure 3-10
A slope of 1/2 indicates a one-unit increase in the *y*-variable for every two-unit increase in the *x*-variable.

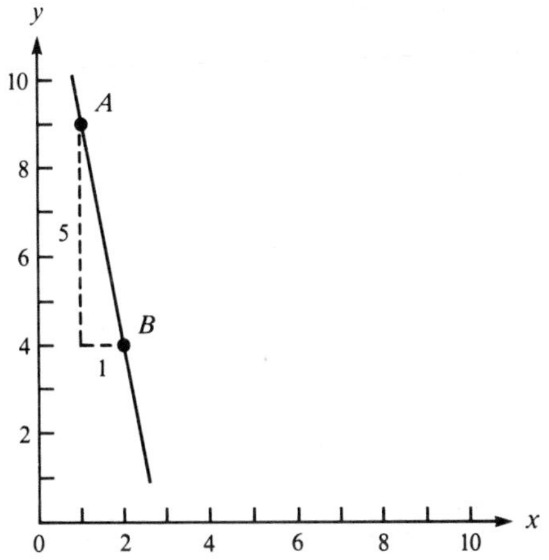

Figure 3-11
A slope of -5 indicates a five-unit decrease in the *y*-variable for every one-unit increase in the *x*-variable.

C. To calculate the slope of a line, use the slope formula.

To calculate the slope of a line, find the coordinates of two points on the line, (x_1, y_1) and (x_2, y_2). Substitute the values of those coordinates into the following formula:

$$\text{slope} = \frac{y_2 - y_1}{x_2 - x_1}$$

EXAMPLE 3-10: To calculate the slope of the line in Figure 3-11, pick any two points, such as A and B, on the line. Let A be the first point, (x_1, y_1), and B be the second point, (x_2, y_2). The coordinates of point A are (1, 9); the coordinates of point B are (2, 4). Substitute these values into the slope formula:

$$\text{slope} = \frac{y_2 - y_1}{x_2 - x_1} = \frac{4 - 9}{2 - 1} = \frac{-5}{1} = -5$$

Notice that reversing the order of the two points (letting B be the first point and A the second) does not change the arithmetic sign of the slope:

$$\frac{9 - 4}{1 - 2} = \frac{5}{-1} = -5$$

D. The slope of a straight line is constant; the slope of a curved line varies.

As you learned in Section 3-7, a straight line indicates a constant rate of change between two variables. Thus the slope of a straight line is the same between any two points on the line.

By contrast, the slope of a curved line varies between the points on the line, indicating a varying (increasing or decreasing) rate of change between two variables. Since the slope of a curved line varies, it must be calculated at each point or over each interval on the curve. To calculate the slope of a curved line at any point, find the slope of the straight line tangent to the curve at that point. (A straight line is tangent to a curve if it meets the curve at a single point. Only one line is tangent to a curve at a single point.) Alternatively, to approximate the slope of a curved line between two points, use the slope formula given in part C of this section.

E. The slope of a horizontal line is zero; the slope of a vertical line is undefined.

The slope of a horizontal line, any line parallel to the x-axis on a graph, is zero. A slope of zero indicates that there is no change in the variable on the y-axis with respect to the variable on the x-axis. If the rise of a line is zero, its slope must also be zero because the ratio of zero to any number (i.e., zero divided by any number) is always zero.

The slope of a vertical line, any line parallel to the y-axis on a graph, is undefined. A vertical line indicates that there is no change in the variable on the x-axis with respect to the variable on the y-axis. If the run of a line is zero, its slope must be undefined because the ratio of any number to zero (i.e., division by zero) is undefined. To say that the slope of a line is undefined is to say that its slope approaches infinity.

3-9. Answers to Self-Test on Graphing

1. Points (3, 5) and (8, 15) are plotted on the graph in Figure 3-12, which also shows the line connecting the two points.

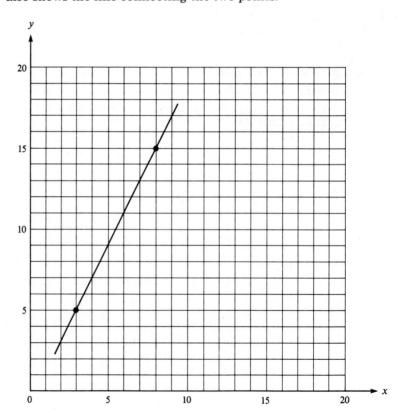

Figure 3-12

2. To calculate the slope of a line, find the ratio of the rise to the run.

$$\frac{y_2 - y_1}{x_2 - x_1} = \frac{15 - 5}{8 - 3} = \frac{10}{5} = 2$$

3. The negative (downward) slope of the demand curve, line *DD*, in Figure 3-4 (and shown again in Figure 3-13) indicates that the price of pizza and the quantity demanded are inversely related. The quantity demanded increases as price decreases and decreases as price increases. If the price of pizza increases by $2, the quantity demanded decreases by 4,000 units.

4. If pizza producers decide to provide more pizzas at each price than the supply curve, line *SS*, in Figure 3-4 indicates, the supply curve will shift to the right, as shown by *S'S'* in Figure 3-13.

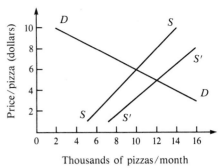

Figure 3-13
An increase in quantity supplied at each price causes a supply curve to shift right (*SS* to *S'S'*).

RAISE YOUR GRADES
Can you explain . . . ?

☑ why economists use diagrams and graphs
☑ why number lines are used to provide the framework for a graph
☑ where the information on a graph comes from
☑ why the paired values of two variables are called *coordinates*
☑ how points are plotted on a graph
☑ why a straight line can be called a curve
☑ how the slope of a line is calculated
☑ what a line with a positive or upward slope indicates
☑ what a line with a negative or downward slope indicates
☑ how the slope of a straight line differs from the slope of a curved line
☑ why the slope of a horizontal line is zero and the slope of a vertical line is undefined

SUMMARY

1. Economists use diagrams and graphs to show relationships between economic variables and to interpret numerical information.
2. A *diagram* is a drawing that shows general relationships between economic variables.
3. A *graph* is a drawing that shows precise relationships between economic variables.
4. Most diagrams and graphs are two-dimensional. They show the relationship between two, and only two, variables.
5. Two elements are necessary for the construction of a graph: numerical information about the relationship between two variables and a framework for displaying that information.
6. A pair of crossed number lines, called *coordinate axes*, provide the framework for a graph. These axes intersect at a point, (0, 0), called the *origin*.
7. The horizontal axis on a graph is called the *x-axis*; its values increase from left to right. The vertical axis on a graph is called the *y-axis*; its values increase from bottom to top.

8. An equation or a schedule defines the relationship between two variables and provides the numerical information for a graph.

9. The corresponding values of two variables are often presented in the form of paired numbers, called *coordinates*. Each pair of coordinates specifies a single point that can be plotted on a graph.

10. The first number in a pair of coordinates is called the *x-coordinate* because it locates the value of one variable along the *x*-axis. The second number is called the *y-coordinate* because it locates the value of the second variable along the *y*-axis.

11. After points have been plotted on a graph, they are usually connected to form a line. A line provides a clear, immediate image of the relationship between two variables.

12. A line that moves in an upward (northeasterly) direction indicates a direct relationship between two variables. If two variables are directly related, they increase or decrease together.

13. A line that moves in a downward (southeasterly) direction indicates an inverse relationship between two variables. If two variables are inversely related, one increases while the other decreases.

14. A straight line indicates a constant rate of change between two variables. A curved line indicates an increasing or decreasing (inconstant) rate of change between two variables.

15. Slope is the measure of the relative rates of change between two variables. The *slope* of a line is the ratio of the rise to the run.

16. The slope of a line can be found by substituting the coordinates of two points on the line into the slope formula:

$$\text{slope} = \frac{y_2 - y_1}{x_2 - x_1}$$

17. A positive slope indicates a direct relationship between two variables. A negative slope indicates an inverse relationship between two variables.

18. The slope of a straight line is constant. The slope of a curved line varies.

19. To find the slope of a curved line at any point, find the slope of the straight line tangent to the curve at that point. To approximate the slope of a curved line between two points, use the slope formula.

20. The slope of a horizontal line is zero. The slope of a vertical line is undefined.

RAPID REVIEW

1. A two-dimensional diagram or graph shows the relationship between two _____ with respect to a set of _____. [See Section 3-1.]

2. On a _____, the precise location of specific points is important; on a _____, the shape and the slope of a line provide all necessary information. [See Section 3-1.]

3. The crossed number lines that provide the framework for a graph are called _____ *axes*. [See Section 3-4.]

4. The vertical axis on a graph is called the _____; the horizontal axis on a graph is called the _____. [See Section 3-4.]

5. The point of intersection between the *x*- and *y*-axes on a graph is called the _____. [See Section 3-4.]

6. The numbers on the *x*-axis increase from (**a**) left to right, (**b**) top to bottom, (**c**) right to left, (**d**) bottom to top. [See Section 3-4.]

7. The numerical information that is plotted on a graph may be derived from (**a**) an equation, (**b**) a schedule, (**c**) a set of paired coordinates, (**d**) any of these sources. [See Section 3-4.]

8. If you were plotting the pair of coordinates (5, 3), you would locate the number 3 along the _____-axis. [See Section 3-5.]

9. If two variables increase or decrease together, they are _____ related. [See Section 3-7.]

10. A line with a downward or negative slope indicates that the relationship between two variables is _____. [See Section 3-7.]

11. A straight line indicates that the rate of change between two variables is _____. [See Section 3-7.]

12. The slope of a line is the _____ of the rise to the run. [See Section 3-8.]

13. A _____ slope indicates an inverse relationship between two variables. [See Section 3-8.]

14. A positive slope indicates that the relationship between two variables is (**a**) constant, (**b**) direct, (**c**) changing, (**d**) inverse. [See Section 3-8.]

15. The slope of a line between the points (5, 8) and (10, 18) is (**a**) 1, (**b**) 1/2, (**c**) 2, (**d**) −1/2. [See Section 3-8.]

Questions 16, 17, and 18 are based on Figure 3-14.

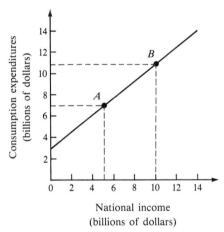

Figure 3-14

16. The slope of the line in Figure 3-14 indicates that the relationship between the two variables is _____: as national income increases, consumption expenditures _____. [See Sections 3-7 and 3-8.]

17. The rate of change between national income and consumption expenditures in Figure 3-14 is (**a**) increasing, (**b**) decreasing, (**c**) constant, (**d**) negative. [See Sections 3-7 and 3-8.]

18. The slope of the line between points *A* and *B* in Figure 3-14 is (**a**) 5/4, (**b**) 1.0, (**c**) −4/5, (**d**) 0.8. [See Section 3-8.]

19. To calculate the slope of a curved line at any point, you would find the slope of the straight line _____ to the curve at that point. [See Section 3-8.]

20. The slope of a horizontal line is _____. [See Section 3-8.]

Answers

1. variables, axes   2. *graph, diagram*   3. *coordinate*   4. *y-axis, x-axis*   5. *origin*
6. (**a**)   7. (**d**)   8. *y*   9. directly   10. inverse   11. constant   12. ratio   13. negative
14. (**b**)   15. (**c**)   16. direct, increase   17. (**c**)   18. (**d**)   19. tangent   20. zero

SOLVED PROBLEMS

PROBLEM 3-1 Find four pairs of coordinates, such as (3, 8), that satisfy the equation $y = 5 + x$.

Answer: Substitute any value for x in the equation and solve for y. [See Section 3-4.]

x	y	Paired coordinates
1	6	(1, 6)
2	7	(2, 7)
3	8	(3, 8)
5	10	(5,10)
10	15	(10,15)

PROBLEM 3-2 Figure 3-15 shows the relationship between the rate of interest and investment expenditures. Calculate the change in investment expenditures as the interest rate rises from 4 percent to 6 percent. Compare the change in investment for the 4–6 percent range with the change in investment for the 10–12 percent range. Is the relationship between rate of interest and investment expenditures direct or inverse?

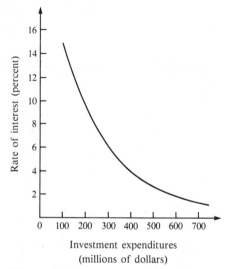

Figure 3-15

Answer: As the interest rate rises from 4 percent to 6 percent, investment expenditures decline by $100 million. As the interest rate rises from 10 percent to 12 percent, investment expenditures decline by only $50 million. Thus, the change in investment expenditures is greater in the 4–6 percent range than it is in the 10–12 percent range. The negative slope of the line in Figure 3-15 (notice that it moves in a downward or southeasterly direction) indicates that the relationship between the rate of interest and investment expenditures is inverse: one increases as the other decreases. [See Sections 3-7 and 3-8.]

PROBLEM 3-3 The following schedule shows the quantity of dollars demanded per month in exchange for yen at various rates or prices. Construct a set of axes, and graph this demand schedule. Following the conventions of economics, plot price on the y-axis and quantity on the x-axis. Then calculate the slope of the line. Are price and quantity directly or inversely related?

Quantity (dollars/month)	Price (yen/dollar)
100,000	700
150,000	600
200,000	500
250,000	400
300,000	300

Answer: Figure 3-16 is the graph of the demand schedule. The slope of the line is found by substituting the coordinates of any two points on the line into the slope formula:

$$\text{slope} = \frac{y_2 - y_1}{x_2 - x_1}$$

$$= \frac{600 - 700}{150,000 - 100,000}$$

$$= \frac{-100}{50,000}$$

$$= -0.002$$

A negative slope indicates an inverse relationship between the two variables: as price decreases, quantity demanded increases. [See Sections 3-4, 3-5, and 3-8.]

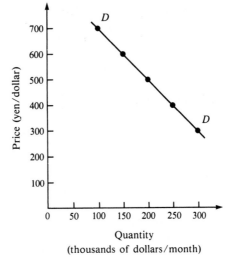

Figure 3-16

PROBLEM 3-4 The supply of wheat is based on the following hypothetical equation:

$$\text{Quantity supplied } (Q_S) = 10 + (5 \times \text{price of wheat})$$

Assume that quantity is measured in thousands of bushels per month and price in dollars per bushel. Use the equation to find quantity supplied at prices of $1, $2, $4, and $10 a bushel. Then plot your results on a graph to show the supply curve for wheat. Plot price on the *y*-axis and quantity on the *x*-axis.

Answer: Substitute each price into the equation and solve for quantity supplied.

$$Q_S = 10 + (5 \times 1)$$
$$= 15 \text{ thousand bushels/month}$$
$$Q_S = 10 + (5 \times 2)$$
$$= 20 \text{ thousand bushels/month}$$
$$Q_S = 10 + (5 \times 4)$$
$$= 30 \text{ thousand bushels/month}$$
$$Q_S = 10 + (5 \times 10)$$
$$= 60 \text{ thousand bushels/month}$$

Express your results as four pairs of coordinates (i.e., four quantity–price combinations): (15, $1), (20, $2), (30, $4), and (60, $10). Then plot the points on a graph. Figure 3-17 shows the supply curve (*SS*) for wheat. It is the graph of the hypothetical equation given in the problem. [See Sections 3-4 and 3-5.]

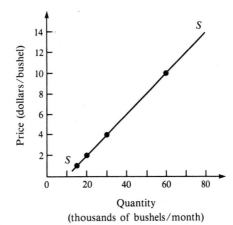

Figure 3-17

PROBLEM 3-5 Calculate the slope of the supply curve in Figure 3-17. Are price and quantity supplied directly or inversely related?

Answer: Since the supply curve in Figure 3-17 is a straight line, its slope is constant. Therefore, you can measure it between any two points on the line and the result will always be the same. Take (20, $2) and (30, $4), arbitrarily, and substitute them into the formula for determining slope:

$$\text{slope} = \frac{y_2 - y_1}{x_2 - x_1} = \frac{4 - 2}{30 - 20} = \frac{2}{10} = 0.2$$

Since the slope is positive, price and quantity supplied are directly related. [See Section 3-8.]

PROBLEM 3-6   A hypothetical aggregate production (AP) curve can be graphed from the following equation:

$$\text{Aggregate production (AP)} = \text{national income}$$

Calculate four sets of paired coordinates that satisfy the equation. Then, with national income on the x-axis, plot the points and construct the hypothetical AP curve. Estimate the slope of the curve just by looking at it.

Answer: This equation is so simple that it may seem difficult. Pick any four values for national income, such as (in millions of dollars) 100, 200, 300, and 400. Substitute those values into the equation for aggregate production. Since aggregate production equals national income, the values of the paired coordinates are always equal: (100, 100), (200, 200), (300, 300), (400, 400). Thus, no matter what values you arbitrarily assign to national income, the graph of the equation is a straight line extending from the origin at a 45-degree angle to the axes, as shown in Figure 3-18. Since the x- and y-coordinates are always equal, the slope of the aggregate production curve is 1. [See Sections 3-4, 3-5, and 3-8.]

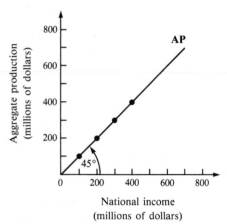

Figure 3-18

PROBLEM 3-7   The following aggregate supply schedule relates various price levels to alternative levels of national income (in millions of dollars).

Aggregate Supply Schedule

National income	Price level
$ 0	100
100	100
300	100
500	100

Express the related levels of national income and price levels in the form of paired coordinates. Then, with national income on the x-axis, plot the points and construct the aggregate supply (AS) curve. Calculate the slope of the AS curve.

Answer: If national income is plotted along the x-axis, the figures in the national income column are the x-coordinates and the figures in the price level column are the y-coordinates. Thus the paired coordinates for the aggregate supply (AS) curve are (0, 100), (100, 100), (300, 100), and (500, 100). When these points are plotted on a graph, they form a horizontal line, as shown in Figure 3-19. A horizontal line has a slope equal to zero. [See Sections 3-4, 3-5, and 3-8.]

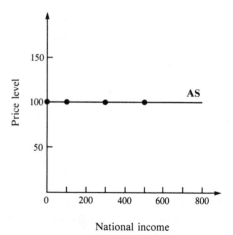

Figure 3-19

4 THE CIRCULAR FLOW MODEL OF AN ECONOMY

4-1. Specialization and the Division of Labor

Long ago people learned that they could challenge scarcity more effectively through cooperation than they could through self-sufficiency. They discovered that they could produce more goods and services and thus satisfy more of their material wants through specialization and the division of labor.

- **Specialization** is the concentration of effort in a particular activity of production.
- The **division of labor** is the distribution of the activities of production among the members of a society.

EXAMPLE 4-1: Specialization, and the division of labor that it necessarily implies, is so predominant in our society that we seldom think about it. All of us consume a variety of goods and services, yet we perform only a limited number of the tasks of production in our specialized jobs as clerks, lawyers, engineers, stockbrokers, assembly line workers, housekeepers, and so on.

A. Specialization increases productivity.

Specialization increases the level and the efficiency of production for four main reasons:

1. It saves time lost by nonspecialized workers in transferring from one task to another.
2. It allows the unique talents of individual workers to be more fully utilized.
3. It permits the establishment of efficient routines and the training of workers to perform those routines.
4. It facilitates the design of capital goods (e.g., machinery) to enhance human effort.

B. Specialization creates three problems.

Although specialization enhances productivity, it also generates problems.

1. Specialization entails *interdependence*. Since no one in a specialized society performs more than one or a few productive tasks, everyone is dependent on others to provide the many goods and services he or she needs or wants.

2. Specialization requires *coordination*. In a specialized society, production and consumption are two separate, isolated activities. Thus, society must provide a system of coordination to ensure that decisions made about production coincide with decisions made about consumption.

3. Specialization necessitates *exchange*. Since specialized workers do not produce for their own consumption, society must provide them with a convenient, efficient means of exchanging what they do produce for what they need and want.

EXAMPLE 4-2: The problems of interdependence, coordination, and exchange are illustrated by the infamous case of the man working in a factory that produces camshafts (highly machined metal rods used in internal-combustion engines). First, because his productive activities are highly specialized, the camshaft worker is totally dependent on those people in his society who specialize in the production of food, clothing, shelter, and the many other goods and services that he requires. Second, because the camshafts he produces are useless by themselves, their production must be coordinated with the production of particular engines, which in turn must be coordinated with the production of particular automobile bodies, which in turn must be coordinated with the needs and wants of consumers. Finally, because he has no use for the many camshafts that he produces, the worker must be able to exchange them for the goods and services he needs. (Otherwise, all he gets is the shaft.)

4-2. The Circular Flow Model

The **circular flow model** is a picture of how economic activity is organized in a specialized society faced with the problems of interdependence, coordination, and exchange. Like any other economic model, the circular flow model is an abstraction. As such, it is a very simplified picture. Nevertheless, it suggests some of the problems that can arise in coordinating activity in a complex economy.

A. The circular flow model is divided into two sectors.

There are two basic types of economic activity: production and consumption. Since decisions about these two types of activity are made separately in a specialized society, the circular flow model in Figure 4-1 is divided into two distinct sectors, producers and households. The function of the producers, of course, is to produce products (goods and services) for the consumption of the households. The households, then, are the consumers, but they also perform another—very important—function in the economy.

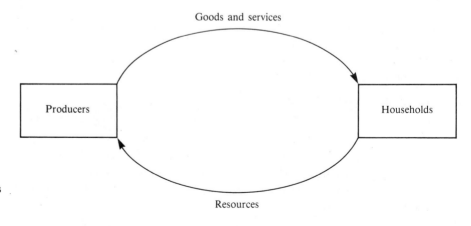

Figure 4-1
The circular flow model shows the isolation of the producing and consuming sectors in a specialized society as well as the flows of resources and products between them.

To produce goods and services, producers need resources—natural, human, and capital resources. The circular flow model in Figure 4-1 assumes that all of these resources are owned by households, either directly or indirectly. Thus the model shows a *circular* flow of economic activity. It shows resources flowing from the households to the producers, and it shows products (goods and services) flowing from the producers to the households. These flows of resources and products are referred to as **real flows**.

B. Money facilitates exchange between the two sectors.

If the exchange of resources and products in an economy were direct, Figure 4-1 would be an accurate (though incomplete and highly simplified) picture of the basic organization of economic activity in a specialized society. However, the direct exchange of resources and products, a practice called **barter**, is very inefficient because it requires a coincidence of wants. For example, the hungry worker in the camshaft factory would have to find a farmer in need of a camshaft before he could complete an exchange.

A convenient means of exchanging resources and products is absolutely essential in a specialized society. Without one, people cannot satisfy their many and changing wants. To enable them to do so (and thus to promote specialization and higher productivity), societies invented money.

Money is anything generally accepted as (**a**) a medium of exchange, (**b**) a store of value, and (**c**) a unit of account.

Because it is an indirect method of exchange and does not require a coincidence of wants, money allows people to buy and sell their resources and products more freely. It also permits them to sell in one period and to defer buying until a later period.

C. Money flows complement real flows.

Figure 4-2 shows how money fits into the circular flow of economic activity in a specialized society. The upper portion of the figure shows how money flows from households to producers in exchange for goods and services. This flow of money is called **business receipts**. The

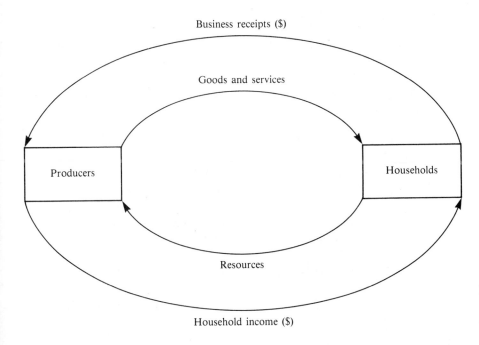

Figure 4-2
Real flows are clockwise. Money flows are counterclockwise.

lower portion of the figure shows how money flows from producers to households in exchange for resources. This flow of money is called **household income**.

Real flows are so called because, unlike money, resources and products (goods and services) have inherent value: people can wear them or eat them or make something with them. The outer circle of the figure represents money flows. As their name suggests, **money flows** represent the circular movement of money in exchange for resources and products in a specialized society. Real flows and money flows are complementary: that is, resources and products flow in a clockwise direction; household income and business receipts flow in a counter-clockwise direction.

D. The circular flow model illustrates the need for coordination.

Though simple, the circular flow model illustrates the vital need for coordination between the isolated producing and consuming sectors in a specialized society. Coordination implies both communication and motivation. On the one hand, producers must be informed about and must be motivated to produce the goods and services that households want. On the other hand, households must be informed about and must be motivated to supply the resources that producers need. Coordination is provided by economic systems.

4-3. Economic Systems

Various sets of institutions have evolved for coordinating economic activity and for making the four fundamental choices about resource use discussed in Chapter 1 (see Section 1-5). These sets of institutions are referred to as economic systems.

An **economic system** is a set of institutions for making basic economic choices and for coordinating economic activity in a society.

Economic systems are classified on the basis of two criteria: the ownership of resources and the allocation of resources.

A. Resources may be owned privately or collectively.

There are two major types of resource ownership: capitalism and socialism.

- **Capitalism** is the private ownership of the nonhuman resources of production.
- **Socialism** is the collective ownership of the nonhuman resources of production.

(Note that economists define *capitalism* and *socialism* only in terms of resource ownership.)

EXAMPLE 4-3: The economic system of the United States is characterized primarily by the private ownership of resources. Although highways, parks, water and sewerage facilities, public schools, and the like are collectively owned through various levels of government, most factories and businesses in the United States are owned by individuals. By contrast, the economic system of the USSR relies primarily upon the collective ownership of resources.

B. Resources may be allocated by tradition, by markets, or by planning.

Resources, and the goods that they are used to produce, are commonly allocated in one of three ways: by tradition, by markets, or by planning.

1. In a **traditional economy**, goods and resources are allocated according to historical patterns. The pace of change in the modern world has made reliance upon historical patterns increasingly impractical. Hence today, even in the more traditionally run, less developed nations, the allocation of resources is commonly determined by markets or planning.
2. In a **market economy**, goods and resources are allocated according to the decisions of individual producers and consumers.
3. In a **planned economy**, goods and resources are allocated according to the central directions of a government agency. Those directions may be advisory, or they may be mandatory. **Indicative planning** serves only as a guide for decision makers. **Command planning** has the force of law.

The major difference between a market economy and a planned economy is that, whereas a planned economy relies upon the *centralized* decisions of a government agency, a market economy depends on the *decentralized* decisions of all its participants.

EXAMPLE 4-4: The Soviet Union exemplifies the planning system. There, goods and resources are allocated primarily according to the centralized decisions of a government planning agency. The United States exemplifies the market system. Although the government does engage in indicative planning through such agencies as the Department of Commerce, goods and resources in this country are allocated primarily according to the decisions of individual producers and consumers in the marketplace.

C. Most nations have mixed economic systems.

Most nations have mixed economic systems. Socialist economies often allow some resources to be privately owned. Market economies often engage in some form of planning.

Economist John Kenneth Galbraith argues that economic systems are determined more by technology than they are by ideology. According to him, to the extent that modern industrial nations employ similar technology, their economic systems tend to converge.

4-4. Mixed Capitalist Market Systems

The economic system of the United States is a mixed system. It is primarily capitalist and market directed, but some resources are collectively owned and allocated through planning by various units of government. This particular mixture has two important implications for the circular flow model of economic activity in the United States:

1. The flows of resources and products are directed and coordinated primarily through a system of markets, as shown in Figure 4-3 on the following page, rather than through a central planning agency.
2. The flows are much affected by the actions of government.

A. Markets consist of customers and vendors.

A **market** consists of customers (buyers or demanders) and vendors (sellers or suppliers) interacting to determine the price of an item and the quantity produced and exchanged. In the markets for resources, producers are the customers and households are the vendors, as shown in Figure 4-3. In the markets for goods and services, the relationship is reversed: households are the customers and producers are the vendors.

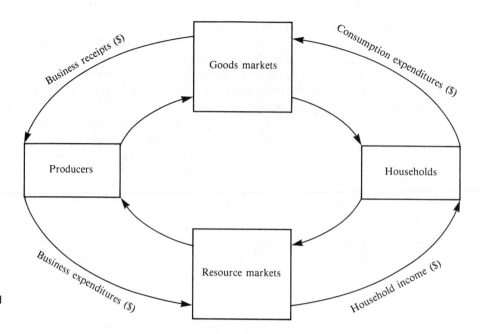

Figure 4-3
In the mixed capitalist market economy of the United States, the flows of resources and products are coordinated primarily through markets.

The interaction between customers and vendors in a market may be geographically localized, as it is at the New York securities market on Wall Street or at the Chicago commodities market. However, the interaction usually is much more diffused. In fact, each time you buy or sell something, you are participating in a market. You are helping to determine both the price of the item and the quantity produced and exchanged.

B. There are many markets in an economy.

There is at least one market (and one price) for each distinct good or resource in a market-directed economy. An economy with two goods and three resources, for example, utilizes at least five markets and generates at least five prices.

C. Prices serve as signals in a market economy.

Prices serve as signals to both buyers and sellers in a market economy. Buyers respond to price changes by increasing or decreasing their purchases of goods. Sellers respond to price changes by varying the quantities of goods that they offer for sale and by changing the mixture of resources that they use to produce goods.

A market economy cannot function efficiently unless it is generating correct signals or prices. For this reason, a market economy is often referred to as a *price system.*

D. Markets provide a framework for making the four fundamental choices.

Markets provide a framework for making the four fundamental choices about resource use.

1. The first choice, how much to produce, is made through the interaction of individual buyers and sellers in the market for each good.

2. The second choice, how to produce, is made by the individual producers of each good. They make choices that will minimize the costs of production.

3. The third choice, how to apportion (for whom to produce), is made by individual households according to their income. The income of a household is dependent upon the value of the resources that it can and does provide to producers. The greater the value of its resources, the higher its income.

4. The fourth choice, how fast to grow, is made by individual households and producers when they choose between consumer and investment goods. Forgoing consumer goods for capital goods leads to a faster rate of growth in the economy (and to higher productivity).

E. Governments affect real flows and money flows in industrialized economies.

The governments of all industrialized nations, even those with capitalist market systems that are theoretically self-regulating, influence the flows of resources and money in their economies. Government involvement takes four forms:

1. *Consumption and production*: Governments purchase a substantial share of the goods and services produced in the economies of industrialized nations. Their productions include defense, roads, parks, and the services of public employees.
2. *Planning*: Governments are involved in planning for their nations' economies. In some European nations, governments are so involved in economic planning that the distinction between market economies and planned economies has become blurred.
3. *Ownership*: In the United States, the government owns a significant portion of the nation's resources. These resources consist primarily of the natural resources held "in trust" by the Department of the Interior and the resources devoted to the production of such public services as defense, transportation, and mail delivery. In some European countries, governments are directly involved in the ownership or joint ownership of factories and businesses.
4. *Welfare*: Governments often assume responsibility for ensuring minimum standards of nutrition, health care, and education. The programs that fulfill these responsibilities are funded through taxes. Because they transfer income or benefits from one group of people to another, economists often refer to welfare programs as *transfer programs*.

RAISE YOUR GRADES

Can you explain ... ?

☑ why specialization increases productivity
☑ why specialization creates problems
☑ why the circular flow model is divided into two sectors
☑ what money is and why it was invented
☑ how economic systems are classified
☑ how capitalism differs from socialism
☑ how a market economy differs from a planned economy
☑ why prices are important in the market system
☑ how the four fundamental choices are made in a market economy
☑ how governments are involved in the economies of industrialized nations

SUMMARY

1. *Specialization* is the concentration of effort in a particular activity of production. The *division of labor* is the distribution of the activities of production among the members of a society.

2. Specialization increases production because it (1) saves time, (2) allows a fuller utilization of talent, (3) permits the establishment of efficient routines, and (4) facilitates the design of capital goods to enhance human effort.

3. Specialization creates three problems: interdependence, coordination, and exchange.

4. The circular flow model is a picture of how economic activity is organized in a specialized society.

5. The circular flow model is divided into two sectors because decisions about production and consumption are made separately in a specialized society.

6. The circular flow model shows the flows of resources from households to producers and the flows of goods and services from producers to households. These flows are called *real flows*.

7. Specialization necessitates exchange. Exchange can (and sometimes does) take place directly through a practice called *barter*. However, barter is inefficient because it requires a coincidence of wants.

8. Money was invented to facilitate exchange in specialized societies. *Money* is anything generally accepted as (a) a medium of exchange, (b) a store of value, and (c) a unit of account.

9. *Money flows* represent the movement of money in exchange for resources and products in the circular flow model of an economy. The money that flows from producers to households in exchange for resources is called *household income*; the money that flows from households to producers in exchange for goods and services is called *business receipts*.

10. In the circular flow model, money flows complement real flows: household income and business receipts flow in a counterclockwise direction; resources and goods and services flow in a clockwise direction.

11. The circular flow model illustrates the need for coordination between the producing and consuming sectors of an economy. Coordination, which implies both communication and motivation, is provided by economic systems.

12. An *economic system* is a set of institutions for making basic economic choices and for coordinating economic activity in a society.

13. Economic systems are classified on the basis of two criteria: the ownership of resources and the allocation of resources.

14. Resources may be owned privately or collectively. *Capitalism* is the private ownership of the nonhuman resources of production; *socialism* is the collective ownership of the nonhuman resources of production.

15. Resources may be allocated in three ways: (1) by tradition, according to historical patterns; (2) by markets, according to the decisions of individual producers and consumers; and (3) by planning, according to the central directions of a government agency.

16. Most nations have mixed economic systems.

17. In the mixed capitalist market system of the United States, most resources are privately owned and are allocated primarily through markets. However, the system is extensively influenced by government actions.

18. A *market* consists of customers and vendors interacting to determine the price of an item and the quantity produced and exchanged. There are many markets in an economy, at least one for each good or resource.
19. Prices serve as signals in a market economy, which is often referred to as a *price system*. A market functions efficiently only if it generates correct signals or prices.
20. The market system provides a framework for making the four fundamental choices about resource use.
21. Governments play a significant role in the economies of industrialized nations. They influence the production and consumption of goods through direct purchases and direct production. They also plan economic activity, own resources, and assume responsibility for ensuring minimum levels of nutrition, health care, and education.

RAPID REVIEW

1. _____ is the concentration of effort in a particular activity of production. [See Section 4-1.]
2. Which of the following is *not* a reason that specialization increases productivity? (a) It allows a fuller utilization of individual talent. (b) It saves time. (c) It necessitates exchange. (d) It permits the establishment of efficient routines. [See Section 4-1.]
3. In the circular flow model, _____ are assumed to own all of the resources of production. [See Section 4-2.]
4. In the circular flow model of a market economy, producers are (a) the source of household income, (b) customers in the markets for resources, (c) suppliers in the markets for goods and resources, (d) all of these. [See Sections 4-2 and 4-4.]
5. The flows of resources and goods and services in the circular flow model are called _____ *flows*. [See Section 4-2.]
6. The use of money is a more convenient and efficient practice than barter because it allows exchange in spite of a noncoincidence of wants. True or false? [See Section 4-2.]
7. Which of the following is *not* a necessary characteristic of money? (a) It has inherent value. (b) It acts as a unit of account. (c) It is generally accepted as a medium of exchange for goods and services. (d) It retains value over time. [See Section 4-2.]
8. In the circular flow model, the money flowing from households to producers in exchange for goods and services is called _____ _____. [See Section 4-2.]
9. Economic systems are sets of institutions that provide _____ between the producing and consuming sectors in a specialized society. [See Section 4-3.]
10. _____ is the private ownership of nonhuman productive resources; _____ is the collective ownership of nonhuman productive resources. [See Section 4-3.]
11. Because of the pace of change in the modern world, resource allocation is rarely determined by _____. [See Section 4-3.]
12. In a _____ economy, resources are allocated according to the decentralized decisions of all the participants. [See Section 4-3.]
13. In a _____ economy, resources are allocated according to the central directions of a government agency. [See Section 4-3.]
14. A _____ consists of customers and vendors interacting to determine the price of an item and the quantity produced and exchanged. [See Section 4-4.]
15. The minimum number of markets in an economy with three goods and five resources is _____. [See Section 4-4.]

16. In a market economy, _____ serve as signals to buyers and sellers. [See Section 4-4.]

17. A market system is often referred to as a _____ *system.* [See Section 4-4.]

18. In the market system, households are _____ in the markets for resources and _____ in the markets for goods and services. [See Section 4-4.]

19. Government involvement in the U.S. economy includes all of the following *except* (a) the financing of health care programs, (b) the production of highways, (c) the ownership of most factories, (d) the consumption of defense goods. [See Section 4-4.]

20. Welfare programs are often referred to as _____ *programs.* [See Section 4-4.]

Answers

1. *Specialization*   2. (c)   3. households   4. (d)   5. *real*   6. true   7. (a)
8. *business receipts*   9. coordination   10. *Capitalism, socialism*   11. tradition
12. market   13. planned   14. market   15. eight   16. prices   17. *price*
18. vendors (sellers or suppliers), customers (buyers or demanders)   19. (c)   20. *transfer*

SOLVED PROBLEMS

PROBLEM 4-1   Explain how specialization would improve productivity even for a "simple" task such as cleaning an office.

Answer: Specialization would improve productivity even for a "simple" task such as office cleaning in a variety of ways. First, it would allow for the establishment of efficient routines and the training of individuals in specific cleaning techniques. Second, it would justify the design and production of sophisticated equipment that would be used on a regular, not just an occasional, basis to enhance human effort. Finally, it would save time that would otherwise be lost if office workers had to transfer between their regular work and cleaning. [See Section 4-1.]

PROBLEM 4-2   Is it possible that the problems associated with specialization and the division of labor might lead a society to reduce its level of specialization?

Answer: Yes, the problems of interdependence, coordination, and exchange can present obstacles that might prompt a society to reduce its level of specialization. Take, for example, a society that is constantly thrown into chaos by striking specialists—sanitation workers, transportation workers, police and fire personnel, production workers of all types. The people in such a society might decide to deal with some of the problems associated with high-level specialization by electing to become more self-sufficient. [See Section 4-1.]

PROBLEM 4-3   Reproduce the circular flow model. Label all the parts, including the real flows and the money flows. Draw arrows to indicate the directions of the flows.

Answer: Your drawing should look like the circular flow model in Figure 4-2. [See Section 4-2.]

PROBLEM 4-4   Why are producers and households shown on separate sides of the circular flow model?

Answer: Producers and households are separate and distinct decision-making units in a specialized economy. Producers make decisions about production. They decide how to produce goods, what quantities to make available at varying prices, and what mix of inputs to use (i.e., what quantities of resources to purchase at varying prices). Households make decisions about consumption. They decide what quantities of goods to purchase at varying prices. Since they are also assumed to own all resources, c all claims to resources, households also decide what quantities of resources to provide at varying prices. [See Section 4-2.]

PROBLEM 4-5 Suppose that an economy experienced hyperinflation to such an extent that people would no longer accept money as payment. (Money would no longer serve as a medium of exchange.) How would the degree of specialization and division of labor in the economy most likely be affected?

Answer: If money ceased to function as a medium of exchange, people very likely would revert to barter and would try to exchange their goods and services directly. Since bartering is a less efficient and less convenient method of exchange than the use of money, the level of specialization in the economy would decline. Individuals would be forced to become more self-sufficient, and productivity would decline. [See Section 4-2.]

PROBLEM 4-6 Consider three items: fresh strawberries, wheat, and paper. Which of these items would make the best money—that is, which item is best suited for use as a medium of exchange, a store of value, and a unit of account? Explain your answer.

Answer: Strawberries are too perishable to act as a store of value, but either wheat or paper is suitable for use as money. To say which is better is difficult. Paper, of course, is more commonly used, but wheat has the advantage of being intrinsically valuable as food. People have to be fairly sophisticated (or gullible) to accept paper in exchange for such valuable things as houses and cows. [See Section 4-2.]

PROBLEM 4-7 Explain the differences between a capitalist market economic system and a socialist planned economic system.

Answer: Economic systems differ in the way that resources are owned and allocated. In a capitalist market system, nonhuman resources are owned privately and are allocated through a system of markets. In a socialist planned system, nonhuman resources are owned collectively and are allocated through a centralized planning process. [See Section 4-3.]

PROBLEM 4-8 Why do most nations have mixed capitalist–socialist, market–planned economic systems instead of relying solely on private ownership and market allocations or on collective ownership and planned allocations?

Answer: Each form of resource ownership and allocation generates its own peculiar set of problems. Mixed systems are an attempt to gain the benefits, and at the same time to avoid the problems, inherent in each. [See Section 4-3.]

PROBLEM 4-9 Some people argue that socialism is not compatible with the market system, that is, that a socialist state cannot use the market system to coordinate a complex economy. Discuss possible points of incompatibility between socialism and the market system.

Answer: Coordination of a complex economy requires motivation as well as communication between the producing and consuming sectors. Some people argue that a socialist system lacks the motivation necessary to ensure proper responses from either producers or consumers. They argue, for example, that producers may not respond to shortages by increasing production if they can't profit materially from their actions. At the same time, households may not seek the education or training required to meet the resource needs of producers if, in doing so, they experience no significant material gains.

A key issue is the criterion, or the criteria, used by the socialist system to divide income among members of the society. If distribution reflects the contributions of each individual to production, motivation may not be a problem. [See Sections 4-2 and 4-3.]

PROBLEM 4-10   If the price of gasoline were to increase in a market economy, what response, if any, would you expect from the producers and consumers of gasoline? Why?

Answer: Prices serve as signals to producers and consumers in the market system, and both groups would be expected to respond to a price change. The producers of gasoline would probably increase their output as the price rose so that they could increase their profits. The consumers of gasoline, on the other hand, would probably reduce their consumption as much as possible in order to offset the increase in price. [See Section 4-4.]

PROBLEM 4-11   Explain how the four fundamental economic choices are made in a capitalist market economy.

Answer: The decision about how much of each good to produce is made through the interaction of buyers and sellers in the market for that good. The decision about how to produce is made by individual producers, who seek to minimize the costs of production. The decision about how to apportion is made in the market for resources, where customers (households) and vendors (producers) interact to determine the value of the productive resources provided by each household. That value in turn determines the income of each household, which in turn determines the share that each household will have in the goods and services produced. The fourth choice, how fast to grow, is made by individual consumers and producers when they forgo (or don't forgo) current consumption to invest in new plants and equipment. [See Section 4-4.]

PROBLEM 4-12   Explain why economists refer to welfare programs, such as food stamps and Medicaid, as *transfer programs*.

Answer: Welfare programs are often referred to as *transfer programs* because they do not involve exchange. Instead, as the name suggests, they *transfer* income or benefits from one group of people to another. The first group receives nothing and the second group gives nothing in exchange for the income or benefits. Obvious welfare programs are those sponsored by the government and funded usually through taxes. Private individuals and firms, however, also make transfer payments when they donate gifts to colleges and other nonprofit organizations. [See Section 4-4.]

5 DEMAND AND SUPPLY: The Mechanics of a Market

THIS CHAPTER IS ABOUT

- ☑ **Demand and Supply**
- ☑ **Consumer Behavior: Demand**
- ☑ **Individual Demand and Market Demand**
- ☑ **Properties of Demand Curves**
- ☑ *Demand* **Versus** *Quantity Demanded*
- ☑ **Producer Behavior: Supply**
- ☑ **Individual Supply and Market Supply**
- ☑ **Properties of Supply Curves**
- ☑ *Supply* **Versus** *Quantity Supplied*
- ☑ **Equilibrium of Demand and Supply**
- ☑ **Adjustments in Market Equilibrium**

5-1. Demand and Supply

In a market economy, as you learned in Chapter 4, there is no central authority to make decisions about production and consumption. Instead, all of the participants in the economy are free to make their own decisions and to pursue their own self-interests. Consumers are free to make buying decisions that will maximize their satisfaction; producers are free to make selling decisions that will maximize their profits; and the individual decisions of both are coordinated through a complex system of markets.

To understand how such a potentially chaotic system can work in the absence of a guiding force, you must understand the mechanics of demand and supply. Economists use these two basic concepts to explain how a market functions: how buyers behave (demand), how sellers behave (supply), and how the two interact to determine both the market price of a good and the quantity produced and exchanged.

[*Note*: Like most discussions of demand and supply, this one focuses on the markets for goods and services, where households are demanders and producers are suppliers. However, the two concepts apply equally to the markets for resources, where producers are demanders and households are suppliers.]

5-2. Consumer Behavior: Demand

Economists use the concept of demand to describe, to analyze, and to make predictions about the behavior of buyers in a market.

Demand is a schedule or curve that relates the various quantities of an item that a buyer is willing and able to purchase at any given time to alternative prices, *ceteris paribus*.

Two parts of this definition merit further development: the word *relates* and the phrase *ceteris paribus*.

A. *Demand* **expresses a** *relationship* **between quantity demanded and price.**

Demand does not refer to quantity alone. It refers to a *relationship* between quantity and price. Experience shows that the quantity of an item that consumers seek to purchase is dependent on the price of the item. Hence demand is expressed not as a single value nor as a single set of values. Rather, it is expressed as a schedule or curve that relates the set of values for one variable, quantity, to the set of values for another variable, price.

B. The concept of demand assumes that variables other than price are held constant.

Many factors besides the price of a good determine how much of it (if any) a consumer will seek to purchase at any given time. Prominent among these factors are the consumer's income and tastes, the prices of other goods, and the consumer's expectations about the future.

EXAMPLE 5-1: The number of pizzas that you will seek to purchase this month depends on a number of things: the price of pizza; your appetite for it; your income; the prices of related goods, such as tacos and torpedo sandwiches; the prices of other goods that you need and want, such as textbooks and theater tickets; your expectations about the future, especially about whether your income is likely to increase or decrease and whether the price of pizza is likely to go up or down. Taking all of these (and other relevant) variables into consideration, you will choose to buy pizza in the quantity that will give you the greatest satisfaction or utility.

Technically, then, demand is not a simple relationship between quantity and price. Rather, quantity demanded (Q_D) is an outcome or function of many variables, only one of which is price:

$$Q_D = f(\text{price, income, tastes, prices of other goods, expectations}, \ldots)$$

Economists do not ignore these other variables. However, when they define *demand*, they do hold them constant. In doing so, they can present a clearer picture of the consistent and predictable effect that price has on quantity demanded. This effect is essential to an understanding of how the market system works.

5-3. Individual Demand and Market Demand

The demand schedule or curve for a market is an aggregation of the demand schedules or curves for all of the individual buyers in the market. To obtain a market demand schedule or curve, economists simply add the quantities that individual buyers seek to purchase at each price.

The quantity–price relationship in a market is affected by the same *ceteris paribus* variables that affect an individual demand curve. It is also affected by the number of buyers in the market. The greater the number of buyers, the larger the quantity sought at each price, *ceteris paribus*.

EXAMPLE 5-2: The following schedule is a hypothetical market demand schedule for pizza. It reflects the pizza-buying intentions of all the demanders in the market. The market demand curve that corresponds to the schedule is shown in Figure 5-1. (Notice that the plotting of the demand curve on the graph follows a rigid convention in economics: price is located along the *y*-axis and quantity is located along the *x*-axis. *Remember this convention.*)

Demand Schedule	
Price/pizza	Pizzas/month
$9	4,000
8	6,000
7	8,000
6	10,000
5	12,000
4	14,000

Demand Curve

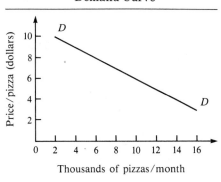

Figure 5-1
A demand curve shows the various quantities of an item that buyers seek to purchase at alternative prices, *ceteris paribus*.

5-4. Properties of Demand Curves

Demand curves, which are simply graphic representations of demand schedules, have three main properties. These properties are common to *all* demand curves.

A. Demand curves have negative slopes.

The slope of a demand curve is negative. (Notice the negative or downward slope of the demand curve in Figure 5-1.) As you learned in Chapter 3, a negative slope indicates an inverse relationship between two variables, in this case, price and quantity demanded: as price increases, quantity demanded decreases; as price decreases, quantity demanded increases. This inverse relationship is so regular that it is often referred to as the **law of demand**. There are two explanations for this relationship: the substitution effect and the income effect.

1. The **substitution effect** means that as the price of an item increases, consumers seek to purchase other (substitute) items that provide approximately the same amount of satisfaction.
2. The **income effect** means that as the price of an item increases, consumers are unable to purchase as many units of the item with the same dollar income. Economists refer to this loss of purchasing power as a reduction in **real income**.

EXAMPLE 5-3: You may be very fond of pizza, but if the price of a pizza increases, say, from $4 to $8 and your dollar or money income remains the same, you will experience a sharp decline in your pizza-purchasing power. You will be able to buy only half as many pizzas as before, and so the price increase, in effect, will make you poorer. This decline in your real income (the income effect) will prompt you to reduce your consumption of pizzas. It will also prompt you to increase your consumption of other, more economical, foods, such as hamburgers or meatball heroes (the substitution effect).

B. Demand curves shift when *ceteris paribus* variables change.

Since a demand curve is drawn in only two dimensions, it can reflect the effects of only one variable, price, on a second variable, quantity demanded. Other variables that affect quantity demanded, such as buyer income and the prices of other goods, must be assumed to remain constant. Of course these other variables, the *ceteris paribus* variables, can change just as easily as price. How is a change in a *ceteris paribus* variable reflected on a two-dimensional graph? By a shift in the position of the demand curve.

A demand curve can shift to the right or to the left. The direction of the shift depends on the relationship between the quantity demanded

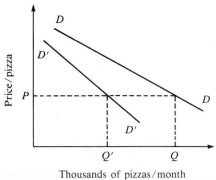

Figure 5-2
A demand curve shifts, reflecting a change in demand, when one or more of the *ceteris paribus* variables change.

and the *ceteris paribus* variable. A shift to the *right* (e.g., as a result of an increase in the number of buyers in a market) reflects an *increase* in the quantity demanded at each price. A shift to the *left* (e.g., as a result of a decrease in the number of buyers in a market) reflects a *decrease* in the quantity demanded at each price.

EXAMPLE 5-4: The number of buyers in the market for pizza is a *ceteris paribus* variable that affects the quantity demanded at each price. Consider a college town in which the number of pizza buyers declines during the summer months. Figure 5-2 shows the effect that summer vacation (and hence a decrease in the number of buyers) has on the demand curve for pizza in the town. Line *DD* is the hypothetical demand curve during the month of May. Line *D'D'* is the demand curve during the month of June, when classes are no longer in session. The leftward shift of the demand curve depicts graphically the decrease in the number of pizzas demanded at each price as a result of a decrease in the number of buyers in the market. At price *P*, for example, quantity demanded declines from *Q* to *Q'*.

C. Demand curves are "snapshots" at one instant in time.

A demand curve portrays a price–quantity relationship at a particular time only. It does not (and cannot) show the history of a price–quantity relationship over a period of time. The reason for this is simple: over a period of time, *ceteris paribus* variables (e.g., taste, income) change. Any change in a *ceteris paribus* variable causes a demand curve to shift. After a shift, a demand curve shows a *different* set of price–quantity combinations than it did initially.

5-5. *Demand* Versus *Quantity Demanded*

The terminology that economists use when they discuss demand relationships is confusing. *Demand* and *quantity demanded*, though they sound alike, do not have the same meaning. *Demand* refers to an entire curve or schedule; therefore *change in demand* refers to a shift in a demand curve or, in a demand schedule, to a change in the quantity demanded *at each price level* as a result of a change in a *ceteris paribus* variable.

EXAMPLE 5-5: The shift in the demand curve in Figure 5-2, from *DD* to *D'D'*, illustrates the meaning of *change in demand*. Specifically, it illustrates a *decrease* in demand because the quantity demanded *at each price* on line *D'D'* is lower than the quantity demanded *at each price* on line *DD*. A shift in the opposite direction (i.e., to the right) would illustrate an *increase* in demand.

Change in quantity demanded refers to movement along a specific demand curve as a result of a change in price. As price changes, buyers change the quantity that they seek to purchase.

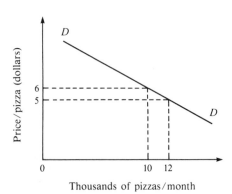

Figure 5-3
Change in quantity demanded refers to movement from one point to another on a given demand curve as a result of a change in price.

EXAMPLE 5-6: Figure 5-3 illustrates the meaning of *change in quantity demanded*. It shows how the quantity of pizza that buyers seek to purchase each month varies as the price of pizza varies. At a price of $6, the quantity demanded is 10,000 pizzas a month. At a price of $5, the quantity demanded is 12,000 pizzas a month. Thus, if the price of pizzas declines from $6 to $5, buyers will seek to purchase 2,000 additional pizzas each month.

5-6. Producer Behavior: Supply

Economists use the concept of supply to describe, to analyze, and to make predictions about the behavior of vendors in a market.

Supply is a curve or schedule that relates the various quantities of an item that vendors are seeking to sell at any given time to alternative prices, *ceteris paribus*.

Notice how similar this definition is to the definition of *demand*. Only a few key words have been changed. A word and a phrase that haven't changed and once again require further comment are *relates* and *ceteris paribus*.

A. *Supply* **expresses a *relationship* between quantity supplied and price.**

Like *demand*, *supply* refers not to quantity alone, but to a *relationship* between quantity and price. Just as buyers seek to purchase different quantities at different prices, so vendors seek to sell different quantities at different prices.

B. **The concept of supply assumes that variables other than price are held constant.**

Many factors besides the price of a good determine how much of it a producer will seek to sell at any given time. Prominent among these factors are the prices of the resources used in production, the prices of other goods, the technology available, and the producer's expectations about the future. Mathematically put, quantity supplied (Q_s) is an outcome or function of all these variables:

$$Q_s = g(\text{price, prices of inputs, prices of other goods, technology, expectations,} \ldots)$$

Given these, and other, variables, a producer can be expected to supply a good or service in the quantity that will maximize profits (or minimize losses). (This is one of the basic assumptions of the theory or model of competitive markets. So, too, is the assumption that consumers will seek to purchase goods and services in quantities that will maximize their satisfaction or utility.)

5-7. Individual Supply and Market Supply

The difference between an individual supply curve and a market supply curve is the same as the difference between an individual demand curve and a market demand curve. A market supply curve is an aggregation of individual supply curves. It shows the selling intentions of all the vendors in a market. The greater the number of vendors, the larger the quantity supplied at each price, *ceteris paribus*.

EXAMPLE 5-7: The following schedule is a hypothetical market supply schedule for pizza. It reflects the pizza-selling intentions of all the suppliers in the market. The market supply curve that corresponds to the schedule is shown in Figure 5-4. It is a graph of the price–quantity relationships presented in the supply schedule.

Supply Schedule

Price/pizza	Pizzas/month
$9	13,000
8	12,000
7	11,000
6	10,000
5	9,000
4	8,000

Supply Curve

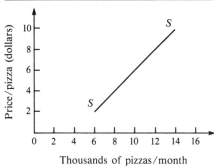

Figure 5-4
A supply curve shows the various quantities of an item that vendors seek to sell at alternative prices, *ceteris paribus*.

5-8. Properties of Supply Curves

Supply curves, like demand curves, have three main properties.

A. Supply curves have positive slopes.

The slope of a supply curve is always positive. (Notice the positive or upward slope of the supply curve in Figure 5-4.) A positive or upward slope indicates that price and quantity supplied are directly related: as price increases, quantity supplied also increases; as price decreases, quantity supplied also decreases.

The reason that price and quantity supplied are directly related is this: a producer who is already supplying at a level that maximizes profits (this, remember, is a basic assumption) will be inspired to expand production only if the increased output will yield higher profits. Therefore higher prices are required to call forth higher levels of production, *ceteris paribus*.

EXAMPLE 5-8: Picture yourself as the owner of a pizza parlor near a college campus. You have calculated that at the current price of $5 a pizza, you can maximize your profits by providing 9,000 pizzas a month, which is the number that you are currently producing. Suppose, now, that a student approaches you with a proposal to deliver pizzas to the dormitories on campus. You will take the orders and prepare the pizzas. She will deliver the pizzas in her van and pay you $5 per pizza. Should you accept her proposal and expand production?

Assume that, to increase output, you would have to install an additional oven and hire another worker or two. Assume, also, that the current workload has you worn to a frazzle. If both of these assumptions are true and you are maximizing profits at your current level of production, you should not accept the proposal unless the student agrees to increase the price that she is willing to pay you for each pizza. Otherwise your profits will decrease, not increase, and you will probably get an ulcer in the bargain.

B. Supply curves shift when *ceteris paribus* variables change.

Like a demand curve, a supply curve is drawn with the assumption that all variables except price and quantity remain constant. Thus, along a supply curve, only price and quantity vary. If another variable changes, the effect is the same as it is on a demand curve: the entire curve shifts, either to the right or to the left. The direction of the shift depends on the relationship between the *ceteris paribus* variable and quantity supplied. A shift to the right (e.g., as a result of an improvement in technology) reflects an increase in the quantity supplied at each price. A shift to the left (e.g., as a result of an increase in the prices of inputs) reflects a decrease in the quantity supplied at each price.

EXAMPLE 5-9: Figure 5-5 illustrates the effect that a change in a *ceteris paribus* variable has on a supply curve. In this case, the *ceteris paribus* variable is the price of cheese. As the figure shows, when the price of cheese increases, the pizza market supply curve shifts left, from *SS* to *S'S'*. The leftward shift indicates a decrease in the number of pizzas supplied at each possible price. At price *P*, for example, quantity supplied declines from *Q* to *Q'*.

C. Supply curves are "snapshots" at one instant in time.

A supply curve, like a demand curve, portrays a price–quantity relationship at one particular time only. It does not show changes in the relationship over time.

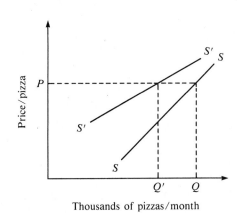

Figure 5-5
A supply curve shifts, reflecting a change in supply, when one or more of the *ceteris paribus* variables change.

5-9. *Supply* Versus *Quantity Supplied*

Like *demand* and *quantity demanded*, *supply* and *quantity supplied* have different meanings. *Supply*, remember, refers to an entire curve or schedule. Thus, *change in supply* refers to a shift in a supply curve or to a change in the whole set of price–quantity combinations in a supply schedule as a result of a change in a *ceteris paribus* variable.

EXAMPLE 5-10: The shift in the supply curve in Figure 5-5, from *SS* to *S′S′*, illustrates the meaning of *change in supply*. Specifically, it shows a *decrease* in supply.

Quantity supplied, on the other hand, refers only to one point on a supply curve or to one price–quantity combination on a supply schedule. *Change in quantity supplied*, then, refers to movement from one point to another on the same supply curve or from one price–quantity combination to another on the same supply schedule as a result of a change in price.

EXAMPLE 5-11: Figure 5-6 illustrates the meaning of *change in quantity supplied*. As price increases from $5 to $6, quantity supplied increases from 9,000 to 10,000 pizzas per month.

5-10. Equilibrium of Demand and Supply

Demand and supply curves are models—simplified pictures—of how buyers and sellers behave in a market. To show how they interact to determine price and quantity produced and exchanged, economists plot both curves on the same graph. The point at which the two curves intersect is called the point of equilibrium in the market.

Economists use the term **equilibrium** to describe a state in which all internal forces or variables are balanced and there is no tendency to change.

At the point of equilibrium in a market, the intentions of buyers correspond exactly to the intentions of sellers: that is, the quantity that buyers seek to purchase (the quantity demanded) is exactly equal to the quantity that suppliers seek to sell (the quantity supplied). As you would expect, this quantity is called the **equilibrium quantity**, and the corresponding price is called the **equilibrium price**.

EXAMPLE 5-12: In Figure 5-7, the market for pizzas is in equilibrium at a price of $6 and a quantity of 10,000 per month. At that price, the quantity of pizza supplied equals the quantity of pizza demanded.

The market would not be in equilibrium at a price of $4 because buyers would seek to purchase 14,000 pizzas while suppliers would seek to sell only 8,000 pizzas. The shortage of 6,000 pizzas would prompt buyers to compete for the pizzas available, bidding the price up.

Similarly, the market would not be in equilibrium at a price of $8 because, at that price, buyers would seek to purchase only 6,000 pizzas while sellers would seek to sell 12,000 pizzas. The surplus would induce sellers to bid the price down so that they could sell their excess pizzas.

5-11. Adjustments in Market Equilibrium

If the relationship between price and quantity were unaffected by other variables, the equilibrium point in a market would be a fixed point. As it is, however, demand and supply curves are constantly shifting to the right or to the left in response to changes in *ceteris paribus* variables. When they

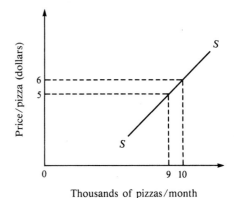

Figure 5-6
Change in quantity supplied refers to movement from one point to another on a given supply curve as a result of a change in price.

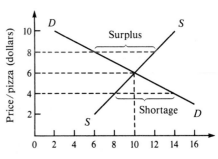

Figure 5-7
A market is in equilibrium when quantity demanded equals quantity supplied.

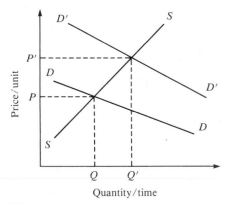

Figure 5-8
When demand increases (when a demand curve shifts right), price and quantity exchanged both increase.

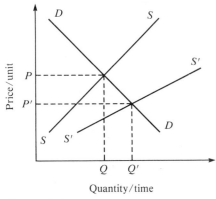

Figure 5-9
When supply increases (when a supply curve shifts right), price decreases and quantity exchanged increases.

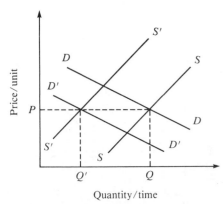

Figure 5-10
When demand and supply both shift in the same direction, quantity shifts with them. The effect on price is indeterminate.

do, equilibrium price and quantity shift, too, establishing a new point of balance between the opposing forces in a market. This flexibility in the market system allows prices and quantities to adjust naturally to changes in demand or supply conditions.

A. Changes in *either* demand or supply have predictable effects on *both* price and quantity.

1. When *demand decreases* (i.e., when a demand curve shifts left) and supply remains constant, equilibrium *price and quantity* both *decrease.*

2. When *demand increases* (i.e., when a demand curve shifts right) and supply remains constant, equilibrium *price and quantity* both *increase.*

EXAMPLE 5-13: Figure 5-8 illustrates the effect of an increase in demand when supply remains constant. The position of the supply curve, SS, doesn't change, but the demand curve shifts right, from DD to $D'D'$. As it does so, the equilibrium price increases from P to P' and the equilibrium quantity increases from Q to Q'. Thus, as more people compete for a good, its relative scarcity increases, and so does its price.

3. When *supply decreases* (i.e., when a supply curve shifts left) and demand remains constant, equilibrium *price increases* and equilibrium *quantity decreases.*

4. When *supply increases* (i.e., when a supply curve shifts right) and demand remains constant, equilibrium *price decreases* and equilibrium *quantity increases.*

EXAMPLE 5-14: Figure 5-9 illustrates the effect of an increase in supply when demand remains constant. The position of the demand curve, DD, doesn't change, but the supply curve shifts right, from SS to $S'S'$. As supply increases, the equilibrium quantity in the market also increases, from Q to Q', but the equilibrium price decreases, from P to P'. An increase in supply reduces the relative scarcity of a good, and the price of the good adjusts downward accordingly.

B. Changes in *both* demand and supply have predictable effects on *either* price or quantity.

Two general statements can be made about simultaneous changes in demand and supply.

1. When demand and supply both increase or decrease, the effect on equilibrium quantity is always known, but the effect on equilibrium price depends on the relative magnitudes of the changes.

    *   When *demand and supply* both *increase* (shift right), equilibrium *quantity* always *increases.*
    *   When *demand and supply* both *decrease* (shift left), equilibrium *quantity* always *decreases.*

EXAMPLE 5-15: Figure 5-10 illustrates the effect of a simultaneous decrease in both demand and supply. As the supply curve shifts left, from SS to $S'S'$, and the demand curve shifts in the same direction, from DD to $D'D'$, the equilibrium quantity in the market also declines, from Q to Q'. In this particular example, the equilibrium price remains constant, but if the relative magnitudes of the changes in demand and supply are different, price can either increase or decrease.

2. When demand or supply increases and the other decreases, the effect on equilibrium price is always known, but the effect on equilibrium quantity depends on the relative magnitudes of the changes.

- When *demand increases* (shifts right) and *supply decreases* (shifts left), equilibrium *price* always *increases.*
- When *demand decreases* (shifts left) and *supply increases* (shifts right), equilibrium *price* always *decreases.*

EXAMPLE 5-16: Figure 5-11 illustrates the effect of an increase in demand coupled with a simultaneous decrease in supply. As demand increases from DD to $D'D'$ and supply decreases from SS to $S'S'$, the equilibrium price of the hypothetical good must increase, from P to P', because its relative scarcity increases. In this particular example, the equilibrium quantity of the good decreases, from Q to Q', but if demand and supply increase and decrease in different proportions, quantity can either increase or remain the same.

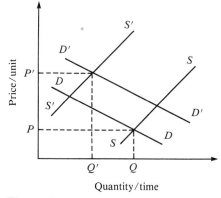

Figure 5-11
When demand and supply shift in opposite directions, the effect on price is determinate, but the effect on quantity is not.

RAISE YOUR GRADES

Can you explain...?

☑ how expectations affect consumer behavior
☑ how a market demand schedule differs from an individual demand schedule
☑ why the "law of demand" is valid
☑ how the substitution effect differs from the income effect
☑ how and why demand curves shift
☑ how *demand* differs from *quantity demanded*
☑ why the prices of other goods affect producer behavior
☑ why price and quantity supplied are positively related
☑ what a rightward shift in a supply curve means
☑ why demand and supply curves do not show historical relationships between price and quantity
☑ how *change in supply* and *change in quantity supplied* differ in meaning
☑ why the intersection of a market supply and a market demand curve is the point of equilibrium in the market
☑ what happens to price and quantity when demand and supply both increase
☑ why price decreases when a demand curve shifts left and a supply curve shifts right

SUMMARY

1. In a market economy, the free choices of individual buyers and sellers are coordinated through a system of markets.
2. The market system rests on two basic assumptions about consumer and producer behavior: **(1)** consumers make buying decisions that maximize their satisfaction or utility; **(2)** producers make selling decisions that maximize their profits (or minimize their losses).
3. Economists use the concepts of demand and supply to explain how the market system works: how buyers behave, how sellers behave, and

how the two interact to determine price and quantity produced and exchanged.

4. The concepts of demand and supply apply to resource markets as well as to product markets.

5. *Demand* is a schedule or curve that relates the various quantities of an item that a buyer is willing and able to purchase at any given time to various prices, *ceteris paribus*.

6. The quantity of an item that a consumer seeks to buy is an outcome or function of many variables: price, income, tastes, prices of other goods, expectations about the future, and so on. Consumers buy in quantities that maximize satisfaction.

7. A market demand schedule or curve is an aggregation of the individual demand schedules or curves of all the buyers in the market. The greater the number of buyers in the market, the larger the quantity demanded at each price, *ceteris paribus*.

8. Demand curves have three main properties: (1) they have negative slopes; (2) they shift when *ceteris paribus* variables change; (3) they depict price–quantity relationships at one time only.

9. The law of demand states that price and quantity demanded are inversely related: as price increases, quantity demanded decreases; as price decreases, quantity demanded increases. There are two explanations for the law of demand: the substitution effect and the income effect.

10. The *substitution effect* means that as the price of an item increases, consumers seek to purchase other (substitute) items. The *income effect* means that as the price of an item increases, consumers experience a loss in real income or purchasing power: they are unable to buy as many units of the item with the same dollar income.

11. *Change in demand* refers to a shift in a demand curve as a result of a change in a *ceteris paribus* variable. *Change in quantity demanded* refers to movement along a specific demand curve as a result of a change in price.

12. *Supply* is a curve or schedule that relates the various quantities of an item that vendors are seeking to sell at any given time to various prices, *ceteris paribus*.

13. The quantity of an item that a producer seeks to sell is an outcome or function of many variables: price, prices of inputs, prices of other goods, technology, expectations about the future, and so on. Producers produce in quantities that maximize profits (or minimize losses).

14. A market supply schedule or curve shows the selling intentions of all the individual vendors in the market. The greater the number of vendors in the market, the larger the quantity supplied at each price, *ceteris paribus*.

15. Supply curves have three main properties: (1) they have positive slopes; (2) they shift when *ceteris paribus* variables change; (3) they depict price–quantity relationships at one time only.

16. Price and quantity supplied are directly related: they increase and decrease together. Higher prices are required to bring forth greater effort and larger quantities from producers.

17. *Change in supply* refers to a shift in a supply curve as a result of a change in a *ceteris paribus* variable. *Change in quantity supplied* refers to movement along a specific supply curve as a result of a change in price.

18. Economists use the term *equilibrium* to describe a state in which all internal forces or variables are balanced and there is no tendency to change.

19. Equilibrium in a market is the point at which the demand and supply curves for the market intersect. At that point, quantity supplied equals quantity demanded.
20. The equilibrium price and quantity in a market fluctuate. They adjust to changes in demand and supply conditions.
21. When demand decreases (increases) and supply remains constant, equilibrium price and quantity also decrease (increase).
22. When supply decreases (increases) and demand remains constant, equilibrium quantity also decreases (increases), but equilibrium price increases (decreases).
23. When demand and supply both increase (decrease), equilibrium quantity also increases (decreases). Equilibrium price increases, decreases, or remains the same depending on the relative magnitudes of the changes in demand and supply.
24. When demand increases (decreases) and supply decreases (increases), equilibrium price increases (decreases). Equilibrium quantity increases, decreases, or remains the same depending on the relative magnitudes of the changes in demand and supply.

RAPID REVIEW

1. In a competitive market system, consumers are assumed to buy in quantities that maximize their _____, and producers are assumed to produce in quantities that maximize their _____. [See Section 5-1.]
2. _____ is a curve or schedule that relates the various quantities of an item that a buyer is willing and able to purchase to various prices, *ceteris paribus*. [See Section 5-2.]
3. Along a demand curve, only _____ and _____ vary. [See Section 5-2.]
4. When demand curves are plotted on a graph, _____ is always located along the *x*-axis and _____ is always located along the *y*-axis. [See Section 5-3.]
5. Which of the following is *not* true of a market demand curve? (**a**) It portrays a price–quantity relationship at a particular time only. (**b**) It has a positive slope. (**c**) It shifts if the income of buyers changes. (**d**) It is affected by the same *ceteris paribus* variables that affect an individual demand curve. [See Sections 5-3 and 5-4.]
6. The law of demand states that price and quantity demanded are _____ related. [See Section 5-4.]
7. A consumer whose salary does not increase as rapidly as prices increase suffers a loss in _____ income. [See Section 5-4.]
8. The _____ effect implies that consumers will seek to purchase more of a good if its price declines relative to the prices of similar goods. [See Section 5-4.]
9. Demand curves show the historical relationship between the price of a good and the quantity demanded. True or false? [See Section 5-4.]
10. By definition, demand can't increase when (**a**) income increases, (**b**) income decreases, (**c**) price increases, (**d**) tastes change. [See Section 5-5.]
11. *Supply* is a curve or schedule that relates the various quantities that vendors are seeking to sell at alternative _____, *ceteris paribus*. [See Section 5-6.]
12. A _____ supply curve shows the selling intentions of all the individual producers in a market. [See Section 5-7.]
13. An increase in the number of producers in a market will cause the supply curve for that market to shift _____, *ceteris paribus*. [See Sections 5-7 and 5-8.]
14. The relationship between price and quantity supplied is _____. [See Section 5-8.]

15. *Change in quantity supplied* refers to movement along a supply curve as a result of a change in price. True or false? [See Section 5-9.]

16. If the price of cream declines, the supply of ice cream will (**a**) decrease or shift left, (**b**) decrease or shift right, (**c**) increase or shift right, (**d**) increase or shift left. [See Section 5-9.]

17. If the price of ice cream declines, the supply of ice cream will decline. True or false? [See Section 5-9.]

18. The point at which the demand and supply curves in a market intersect is called the point of _____ in the market. [See Section 5-10.]

19. Increases in supply lead to _____ prices and _____ quantities exchanged, *ceteris paribus*. [See Section 5-11.]

20. If demand increases while supply decreases, you can be sure that _____ will increase. [See Section 5-11.]

Answers

1. satisfaction or utility, profits   2. *Demand*   3. price, quantity   4. quantity, price   5. (**b**)
6. inversely   7. real   8. substitution   9. false   10. (**c**)   11. prices   12. market
13. right   14. direct (or positive)   15. true   16. (**c**)   17. false   18. *equilibrium*
19. lower, higher   20. price

SOLVED PROBLEMS

PROBLEM 5-1   Graph the points and construct a demand curve from the following demand schedule for steak. Label the axes.

Demand for Steak

Price/pound	Pounds/month
$10	0
8	2,000
6	4,000
4	6,000
2	8,000

Answer: The points are plotted in Figure 5-12. In accordance with economic convention, quantity (pounds per month) is plotted on the *x*-axis and price (dollars per pound) is plotted on the *y*-axis. [See Section 5-3.]

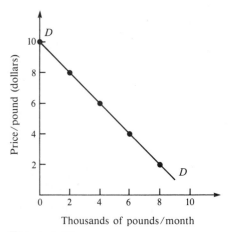

Figure 5-12

PROBLEM 5-2   Show that the demand for steak in Problem 5-1 obeys the law of demand.

Answer: The law of demand states that price and quantity demanded are inversely related: as one increases, the other decreases. The demand schedule for steak shows in tabular form that quantity demanded increases as the price of steak decreases. The demand curve shows the same inverse relationship in graphic form: it has a negative or downward slope. [See Section 5-4.]

PROBLEM 5-3 What would happen to the demand curve for steak in Problem 5-1 if many people lost their jobs. What would happen to the demand curve if many people expected to lose their jobs? Sketch the changes on the graph in Figure 5-12.

Answer: Unemployment would reduce consumer income, a *ceteris paribus* variable. When a *ceteris paribus* variable changes, it causes a demand curve to shift. In this case the demand curve would shift left, from DD to $D'D'$ in Figure 5-13, because the demand for steak would decrease: that is, consumers would seek to purchase smaller quantities of steak at every price. The expectation of unemployment most probably would have the same effect. [See Section 5-4.]

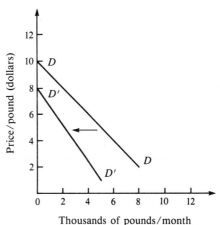

Figure 5-13

PROBLEM 5-4 Given the following data on the price and sales of diamonds, can you conclude that diamonds are an exception to the law of demand?

Year	Price/carat	Number of carats sold
1950	$ 200	45,000
1960	400	65,000
1970	650	100,000
1980	1,100	185,000

Answer: No. A demand schedule is valid for a particular time only because it is prepared under the assumption that all variables other than price and quantity remain constant. Over a period of 30 years, the other variables undergo many changes, and each time they change, the result is a new set of price–quantity combinations and a shift in the demand curve for diamonds, as shown in Figure 5-14. Two factors that might account for an increase in the demand for diamonds between 1950 and 1980 are consumer income, which has increased, and the number of buyers in the diamond market, which may also have increased as a result of an increase in the population. [See Section 5-4.]

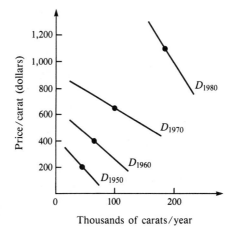

Figure 5-14

PROBLEM 5-5 Explain the difference between *change in demand* and *change in quantity demanded.*

Answer: Change in demand refers to a shift in the position of a demand curve as a result of a change in a *ceteris paribus* variable. *Change in quantity demanded* refers to movement along a given demand curve as a result of a change in price. [See Section 5-5.]

PROBLEM 5-6   Construct a supply curve for steak from the following supply schedule. Label the axes. [*Suggestion*: Plot your supply curve on the same graph that you prepared for Problem 5-1.]

Supply of Steak	
Price/pound	Pounds/month
$10	10,000
8	8,000
6	6,000
4	4,000
2	2,000

Answer: Your supply curve should look like the supply curve in Figure 5-15, with price plotted on the *y*-axis and quantity plotted on the *x*-axis. [See Section 5-6.]

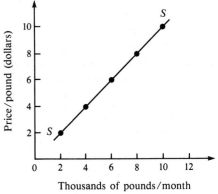

Figure 5-15

PROBLEM 5-7   Explain why a supply curve has a positive slope.

Answer: A supply curve shows the quantities that producers are willing to provide at various prices, *ceteris paribus*. It has a positive slope, indicating a direct relationship between price and quantity supplied, because, in the market system, higher prices (and the prospect of greater profits) provide the incentive that producers need to expand their efforts and produce in larger quantities. [See Section 5-8.]

PROBLEM 5-8   What would happen to the supply curve for steak in Figure 5-15 if the price of corn, an input in the production of choice steak, decreased?

Answer: Figure 5-16 illustrates the effect that a decrease in the price of corn, a *ceteris paribus* variable, would have on the supply curve for steak. A decrease in the price of an input would result in a decrease in the cost— and thus an increase in the profitability—of producing choice steak. Hence producers would be motivated to supply more steak at each price level, and the market supply curve would shift right, from *SS* to *S'S'*. [See Section 5-8.]

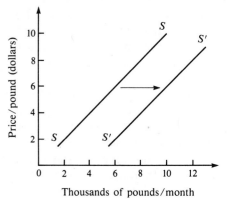

Figure 5-16

PROBLEM 5-9   Using the demand and supply schedules in Problems 5-1 and 5-6, find the equilibrium price and quantity in the market for steak.

Answer: Ordinarily, to find market equilibrium from schedules rather than curves, you look for the price–quantity combination in the demand schedule that matches a price–quantity combination in the supply schedule. That combination represents the point of equilibrium in the market, that is, the price at which quantity supplied and quantity demanded are equal.

In this case, however, the equilibrium price and quantity for steak are not given explicitly in the schedules, and so you must infer them by finding the midpoint between the two price–quantity combinations that are nearest to being equal. Here, that point is obviously $5 and 5,000 pounds.

Of course you can also solve the problem graphically. Just find the coordinates of the point at which the demand and supply curves that you constructed intersect, as shown in Figure 5-17. The *x*-coordinate is the equilibrium quantity and the *y*-coordinate is the equilibrium price. [See Section 5-10.]

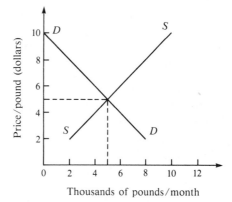

Figure 5-17

PROBLEM 5-10 Explain why an increase in the number of producers in a market causes the market supply curve to shift right.

Answer: If all other things are equal, an increase in the number of producers in a market results in an increase in the quantity supplied *at each price*. An increase in the quantity supplied *at each price* (i.e., an increase in supply) causes a market supply curve to shift right, as shown in Figure 5-18. [See Section 5-9.]

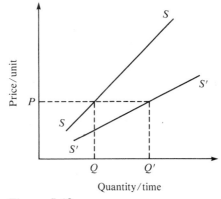

Figure 5-18

PROBLEM 5-11 Assume that the corn market is in equilibrium. Then the United States agrees to sell a million tons of corn to the USSR. Analyze the effect of the agreement on the price and quantity exchanged in the U.S. corn market. Draw an appropriate diagram.

Answer: If the Soviets seek to purchase a substantial amount of U.S. corn, the result will be an increase in the number of buyers and hence in the demand for corn in the U.S. market. This increase will cause the demand curve for corn to shift right, as shown in Figure 5-19. When a demand curve shifts right and supply remains constant, equilibrium price and quantity both increase. Thus, as the demand curve shifts right from *DD* to *D'D'*, the equilibrium price will increase from *P* to *P'* and the equilibrium quantity will increase from *Q* to *Q'*. [See Sections 5-3 and 5-11.]

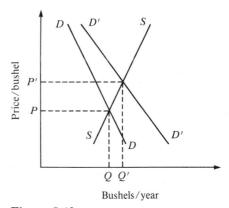

Figure 5-19

PROBLEM 5-12 Assume that the widget market is in equilibrium. Then Japanese producers begin exporting widgets to the United States. Analyze the effect of the imports on the price of widgets, the quantity exchanged, and the quantity produced by U.S. firms. Draw an appropriate diagram.

Answer: If Japanese widget producers begin exporting their products to the United States, the number of suppliers in the U.S. widget market will increase and so will the supply of widgets. An increase in supply will result in a decrease in price and an increase in quantity exchanged, as shown in Figure 5-20. As the supply of widgets increases from SS to $S'S'$, the price will drop from P to P' and the quantity exchanged will increase from Q to Q'. At a price of P', U.S. producers will find it profitable to produce only at a level of Q'', which is on their supply curve. As a result, they will be forced to cut back their production from Q to Q''. The gap between Q'' and Q' will be filled by the Japanese imports. [See Sections 5-7 and 5-11.]

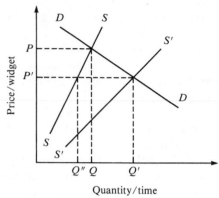

Figure 5-20

6 SUPPLY AND DEMAND ANALYSIS

THIS CHAPTER IS ABOUT

- ☑ **Economic Analysis**
- ☑ **Demand Shifts: Substitutes and Complements**
- ☑ **Demand Shifts: Superior and Inferior Goods**
- ☑ **Price Ceilings**
- ☑ **Price Floors**
- ☑ **Excise Taxes**

6-1. Economic Analysis

Supply and demand analysis is deceptive. It appears simple and logical when you read about it or when you watch someone else do it, but when you are called upon to do it yourself, you may be confused about where to start and how to proceed. Which curve shifts? Which way does it shift? The purpose of this chapter is to demonstrate a few extensions, modifications, and applications of supply and demand analysis.

6-2. Demand Shifts: Substitutes and Complements

As you learned in Chapter 5, one of the *ceteris paribus* variables that can cause a change in the demand for a good is the price of another good. Whether a change in the price of one good will cause demand for another good to increase, decrease, or remain the same depends on the relationship between the two goods. The demand for hamburger, for example, is affected in different ways by a change in the price of steak, in the price of hamburger buns, and in the price of books.

A. An increase in the price of a substitute for a good increases demand for the good.

Substitute goods are goods that can be used in place of one another, such as pens and pencils, paint and wallpaper, hamburger and steak. If two goods are substitutes and the price of one increases, demand for the other will increase.

EXAMPLE 6-1: An increase in the price of steak will result in an increase in the demand for hamburger. Consumers will substitute the relatively cheaper hamburger for steak, and they will seek to purchase larger quantities of hamburger at every price. This process of substitution will cause the demand curve for hamburger to shift right, as shown in Figure 6-1. As it does so, both the quantity exchanged and the price of hamburger will increase, from Q to Q' and P to P', respectively.

B. An increase in the price of a complement to a good decreases demand for the good.

Complementary goods are goods that are used in conjunction with one another, such as pens and paper, paint and paintbrushes, ham-

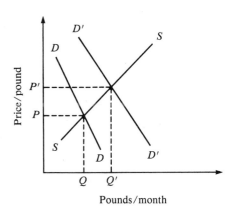

Figure 6-1
When the price of steak rises, the demand curve for hamburger, a substitute, shifts right (*DD* to *D'D'*).

61

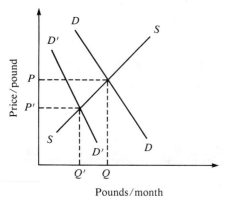

Figure 6-2
When the price of hamburger buns rises, the demand curve for hamburger, a complement, shifts left (*DD* to *D'D'*).

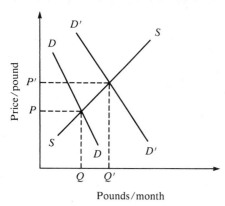

Figure 6-3
An increase in income causes the demand curve for a superior good, such as steak, to shift right (*DD* to *D'D'*).

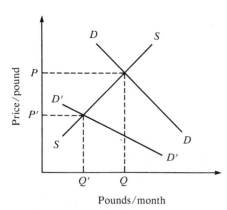

Figure 6-4
As income increases, demand for an income-inferior good, such as hamburger, decreases (*DD* to *D'D'*).

burger and buns. If two goods are complements and the price of one increases, demand for the other will decrease.

EXAMPLE 6-2: An increase in the price of hamburger buns will result in a decrease in the demand for hamburger. Since consumers will have to pay more for the combination of hamburger and bun, they will reduce their consumption of both goods. This reduction in consumption will cause the demand curve for hamburger to shift left, as shown in Figure 6-2. As consumers seek to purchase smaller quantities of hamburger at every price, the quantity exchanged will decline, from *Q* to *Q'*, and the price will also decline, from *P* to *P'*.

C. A change in the price of an independent good has no effect.

Independent goods are goods that are unrelated in usual consumption patterns, such as hamburgers and books, gasoline and earrings, pens and pajamas. If two goods are independent, a change in the price of one will have no direct effect on demand for the other.

6-3. Demand Shifts: Superior and Inferior Goods

Another *ceteris paribus* variable that can cause the demand for a good to change is consumer income. Again, whether the demand for a good will increase, decrease, or remain the same as income changes depends on the relationship between the good and income. A good may be income superior, income inferior, or income independent.

A. An increase in income increases demand for a superior good.

An **income-superior good** is a good whose consumption increases as income increases. Steak, private education, and designer clothes are examples of income-superior goods.

EXAMPLE 6-3: An increase in income will cause the demand curve for a superior good such as steak to shift right, as shown in Figure 6-3. As consumers seek to purchase more steak at each price, both the quantity exchanged and the price will increase, from *Q* to *Q'* and *P* to *P'*, respectively.

B. An increase in income decreases demand for an inferior good.

An **income-inferior good** is a good whose consumption decreases as income increases. Hamburger and used cars and used clothing are examples of income-inferior goods.

EXAMPLE 6-4: An increase in income will cause the demand curve for an inferior good such as hamburger to shift left, as shown in Figure 6-4. As consumers seek to purchase less hamburger at each price, both the quantity exchanged and the price will decrease, from *Q* to *Q'* and *P* to *P'*, respectively.

C. A change in income does not affect independent goods.

An **income-independent good** is a good whose consumption does not vary with income. Salt and toothbrushes are examples of income-independent goods. A change in consumer income will not shift the demand curve for an income-independent good.

6-4. Price Ceilings

A **price ceiling** sets a maximum price that can be charged in the market for a good. If a price ceiling is imposed on a good, the price of the good cannot exceed the ceiling, regardless of market forces. Price ceilings, then, represent a departure from purely competitive market conditions. They are designed, of course, to control market price, but they have other effects as well.

A. An effective ceiling reduces price.

An *effective* price ceiling is one that is set *below* the equilibrium level in a market. An effective ceiling forces price down and prevents it from rising again to equilibrium, but it also results in a decline in quantity supplied.

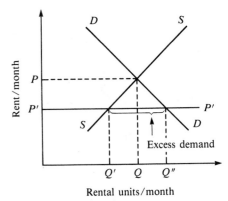

Figure 6-5
An effective price ceiling ($P'P'$) holds the market price of a good below equilibrium and creates excess demand.

EXAMPLE 6-5: Rent control is a program of limiting the rent (use price) of apartments by imposing a price ceiling. Assume that the rental market is initially in equilibrium at price P and quantity Q, as shown in Figure 6-5. Then a ceiling price of P' is imposed on the rental market. The ceiling will effectively reduce the market price for rental units from P to P', but at the new price of P', landlords will find it profitable to make available only Q' units. As a result, the number of rental units will eventually decline from Q to Q'.

B. An effective price ceiling results in excess demand.

The purpose of a price ceiling is to reduce price. If price decreases, quantity supplied also decreases, but quantity demanded increases. Therefore a price ceiling must result in excess demand.

EXAMPLE 6-6: The imposition of ceiling price P' on rental housing in Figure 6-5 will have two simultaneous effects: quantity supplied will decrease from Q to Q' and quantity demanded will increase from Q to Q''. The difference between Q'', the quantity that people will seek to rent, and Q', the quantity that landlords will be willing to make available, represents the excess demand that the price ceiling will create.

Although rent control is designed to make housing more affordable, especially for lower income groups, it can, and often does, have detrimental effects. Not only does it encourage landlords to demand extra payments in various forms, such as bribes, but also it allows them to discriminate, at no cost, against some of the very groups that it is designed to help, such as minorities and people with children.

6-5. Price Floors

A **price floor** sets a minimum or floor on the price that can be charged in the market for a good. If a price floor is imposed on a good, the price of the good cannot fall below the floor or support price, regardless of market forces. Like price ceilings, price floors represent a departure from purely competitive market conditions.

EXAMPLE 6-7: The agricultural assistance programs of the federal government have often taken the form of price floors for crops. The federal government establishes price floors by agreeing to purchase, at a support price, all of the corn, wheat, or other crop that producers are offering to sell.

A. An effective floor raises price.

An *effective* price floor is one that is set *above* the equilibrium price in a market. An effective floor forces price up, but it also results in a decline in quantity demanded by private buyers.

EXAMPLE 6-8: Assume that the market for corn is initially in equilibrium at price P and quantity Q, as shown in Figure 6-6 on the following page. If the federal government establishes a floor at price P', the market

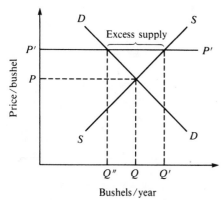

Figure 6-6
An effective price floor (*P'P'*) holds the market price of a good above equilibrium and creates excess supply.

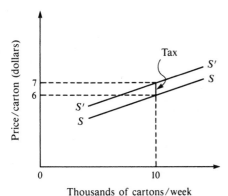

Figure 6-7
An excise tax collected from suppliers causes a vertical shift equal to the tax in the supply curve for a good such as cigarettes.

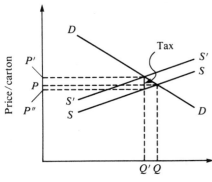

Figure 6-8
Under normal conditions, an excise tax collected from suppliers increases price (*P* to *P'*) and reduces quantity exchanged (*Q* to *Q'*).

price will increase from *P* to that price. As it does so, the total quantity sold to private buyers and the government combined will also increase, from *Q* to *Q'*, but private purchases will actually decline, from *Q* to *Q''*. As market demand curve *DD* shows, at support price *P'*, private buyers are willing and able to purchase only *Q''* bushels of corn per year.

B. An effective price floor results in excess supply.

Just as an effective price ceiling results in excess demand so an effective price floor results in excess supply.

EXAMPLE 6-9: At support price *P'* in Figure 6-6, producers will seek to sell *Q'* bushels of corn, but private buyers will seek to purchase only *Q''* bushels. The difference between quantity supplied and quantity demanded, *Q'* minus *Q''*, represents the excess supply that the price floor will create. Under normal market conditions, an excess supply will drive the price of a product down. To prevent this from happening, and thus to ensure that the market price will not fall below the support price, the federal government must do one of two things. Either it must buy and store all of the surplus corn, or it must seek to shift the market supply curve to the left by limiting the number of acres of corn that may be planted. Both approaches have been tried in the past.

6-6. Excise Taxes

An **excise tax** is a tax levied on a particular good. The taxes imposed by the federal government on gasoline, tires, liquor, and cigarettes are examples of excise taxes. An excise tax collected from the consumers of a good produces slightly different results than an excise tax collected from producers (see Problem 6-8 at the end of this chapter), but only under very unusual demand and supply conditions is the burden of an excise tax borne exclusively by either buyers or sellers.

A. An excise tax collected from producers shifts a supply curve to the left.

If an excise tax is collected from the producers of a good, it will shift the supply curve for the good to the left. Measured vertically, the shift in the supply curve will be exactly equal to the amount of the tax.

EXAMPLE 6-10: Assume that the market for cigarettes is initially in equilibrium at a price of $6 a carton and a quantity of 10,000 cartons a week, as shown in Figure 6-7. Then the federal government levies an excise tax of $1 per carton on cigarettes, which it will collect from producers. The excise tax will cause the supply curve for cigarettes to shift left, from *SS* (before the tax) to *S'S'* (after the tax). Since producers who were willing to provide 10,000 cartons at a price of $6 before the tax presumably will be willing to provide the same number of cartons at a price of $7 after the tax, the vertical distance between supply curve *SS* and supply curve *S'S'* will be exactly $1, the amount of the tax.

B. Under normal conditions, an excise tax collected from producers increases price and reduces quantity exchanged.

Except in extreme cases, an excise tax collected from producers will result in an increase in price and a decrease in quantity exchanged.

EXAMPLE 6-11: Figure 6-8 shows the effect that an excise tax collected from vendors will have on equilibrium price and quantity in the market for cigarettes. As the supply curve shifts left, from *SS* to *S'S'*, the equilibrium price in the market will increase from P to P', *including tax*. At the higher price of P', *including tax*, buyers will seek to purchase fewer cartons of cigarettes, and quantity demanded will decline from Q to Q'.

Notice, now, that the price increase $(P' - P)$ is less than the amount of the tax, which is represented by the vertical distance between the two supply curves $(P' - P'')$. This indicates that cigarette producers will actually realize a smaller price (P'') for their products than they did before the excise tax was imposed (P). It also indicates that, although the tax will be collected from producers, the burden will fall on consumers and producers alike. Producers will have to absorb the difference between P'' and P, and consumers will have to pay the difference between P and P'.

As the example suggests, the share of the burden of an excise tax (what economists call the *incidence* of a tax) depends more on demand and supply conditions than it does on the party from whom the tax is collected.

C. If demand is perfectly inelastic, buyers bear the full burden of an excise tax.

Demand is **perfectly inelastic** if quantity demanded does not vary with price, that is, if buyers seek to purchase the same quantity of a good no matter what its price is. Perfectly inelastic demand is represented on a graph by a vertical demand curve. If an excise tax is imposed on a product for which demand is perfectly inelastic, buyers bear the full burden of the tax.

EXAMPLE 6-12: Figure 6-9 illustrates the effect of an excise tax on a product for which demand is perfectly inelastic. Notice that the demand curve, D, is vertical. Assuming that the tax is collected from producers, the supply curve will shift left, from SS to $S'S'$. The shift in the supply curve will cause the equilibrium price in the market to increase, from P to P', the amount of the tax, but instead of decreasing, quantity demanded will remain constant. Since consumers will seek to purchase the same quantity of the good in spite of the price increase, they will bear the full burden of the excise tax.

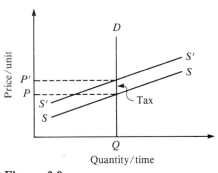

Figure 6-9
When demand is perfectly inelastic, a demand curve is vertical and buyers bear the full burden of an excise tax.

D. If demand is perfectly elastic, sellers bear the full burden of an excise tax.

Demand is **perfectly elastic** if buyers reduce their purchases of a good to zero if its price rises even slightly. Perfectly elastic demand is represented on a graph by a horizontal demand curve. If an excise tax is imposed on a product for which demand is perfectly elastic, sellers bear the full burden of the tax.

EXAMPLE 6-13: Figure 6-10 illustrates the effect of an excise tax on a product for which demand is perfectly elastic. Notice that the demand curve, D, is horizontal. Again, assuming that the tax is collected from producers, the supply curve will shift left. Since buyers will reduce their purchases to zero if the price of the product rises above P, price must remain constant. Therefore, as quantity exchanged declines from Q to Q', sellers will absorb the full impact of the excise tax.

E. If demand is normal, buyers and sellers share the burden of an excise tax.

Perfect inelasticity and perfect elasticity represent the two extremes between which most normal demand curves fall. If an excise tax is imposed on a product for which the demand curve is neither vertical

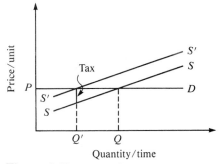

Figure 6-10
When demand is perfectly elastic, a demand curve is horizontal and sellers bear the full burden of an excise tax.

nor horizontal but somewhere in between, buyers and sellers share the burden of the tax. Their shares are determined by the position of the curve in relation to the two extremes. The more nearly vertical the demand curve, the greater the burden on buyers. The more nearly horizontal the demand curve, the greater the burden on sellers.

RAISE YOUR GRADES
Can you explain ... ?

☑ why demand for a good increases when the price of a substitute good increases
☑ why the demand curve for a good shifts left when the price of a complementary good increases
☑ why demand for superior goods is directly related to income
☑ why demand for inferior goods decreases as income increases
☑ how price ceilings and price floors interfere with the mechanism of supply and demand
☑ why effective price ceilings create excess demand
☑ why some economists argue that rent control programs are ineffective
☑ why effective price floors create excess supply
☑ how price ceilings and price floors may foster discrimination
☑ how an excise tax collected from producers affects the supply curve in a market
☑ why producers and consumers usually share an excise tax
☑ how producer and consumer shares of an excise tax are determined

SUMMARY

1. A change in the price of a substitute or a complement causes the demand curve for a related good to shift.
2. *Substitute goods* are goods that can be used in place of one another. If two goods are substitutes, an increase in the price of one will result in an increase in demand for the other.
3. *Complementary goods* are goods that are used in conjunction with one another. If two goods are complements, an increase in the price of one will result in a decrease in demand for the other.
4. *Independent goods* are goods that are unrelated in usual consumption patterns. Hence a change in the price of one will not affect demand for the other.
5. A change in consumer income causes the demand curves for income-superior and income-inferior goods to shift.
6. An *income-superior good* is a good whose consumption increases as income increases.
7. An *income-inferior good* is a good whose consumption decreases as income increases.
8. An *income-independent good* is a good whose consumption does not vary with income.
9. A *price ceiling* sets a maximum price that can be charged in the market for a good. An effective price ceiling reduces price and results in excess demand.

10. A *price floor* sets a minimum price that can be charged in the market for a good. An effective price floor increases price and results in excess supply.

11. An *excise tax* is a tax levied on a particular good. An excise tax collected from the producers of a good shifts the supply curve for the good to the left. Measured vertically, the shift equals the amount of the tax.

12. Except in extreme cases, an excise tax collected from producers increases price and reduces quantity exchanged.

13. The burden of an excise tax does not necessarily fall solely on the party from whom it is collected. In fact, it is usually shared by producers and consumers in proportions that are determined by demand and supply conditions.

14. Demand is *perfectly inelastic* if quantity demanded does not vary with price. If demand is perfectly inelastic, a demand curve is vertical and buyers bear the full burden of an excise tax.

15. Demand is *perfectly elastic* if buyers reduce their purchases of a good to zero if its price rises even slightly. If demand is perfectly inelastic, a demand curve is horizontal and sellers bear the full burden of an excise tax.

16. Most demand curves are neither vertical nor horizontal. However, the more nearly vertical a demand curve, the greater the burden of an excise tax on buyers. The more nearly horizontal a demand curve, the greater the burden of an excise tax on sellers.

RAPID REVIEW

1. A decrease in the price of a good will cause the demand for a substitute good to _____. [See Section 6-2.]

2. Tennis balls and tennis rackets are considered _____ goods because they are used in conjunction with one another. [See Section 6-2.]

3. An increase in the price of a good complementary to good X will _____ the price of good X and _____ the quantity of good X exchanged. [See Section 6-2.]

4. Goods that are not related in normal consumption patterns are called _____ goods. [See Section 6-2.]

5. Of the following goods, the one most likely to be classified as income inferior is (a) lobster, (b) potatoes, (c) magazines, (d) vacations in the Bahamas. [See Section 6-3.]

6. If your income decreases, your demand for a superior good will _____ . [See Section 6-3.]

7. Assume that good X is income inferior. If national income declines, (a) the price of X should decrease, (b) the quantity of X exchanged should decline, (c) the market demand curve for X should shift left, (d) the price of X should increase. [See Section 6-3.]

8. An effective price ceiling _____ price and results in excess _____ . [See Section 6-4.]

9. A ceiling imposed above the equilibrium price in a market will (a) result in excess demand, (b) result in excess supply, (c) increase price, (d) produce no change in the equilibrium price and quantity in the market. [See Section 6-4.]

10. If the government imposes an effective price floor in the wheat market, the price of wheat will _____ . [See Section 6-5.]

11. An *excise tax* is (a) a tax on income, (b) a tax on profits, (c) a tax on a specific item, (d) a sales tax. [See Section 6-6.]

12. An excise tax collected from the producers of a good (**a**) shifts the demand curve for the good to the right, (**b**) shifts the supply curve for the good to the right, (**c**) shifts the supply curve for the good to the left, (**d**) shifts the demand curve for the good to the left. [See Section 6-6.]

13. If the demand curve for a good is completely insensitive to price, an excise tax collected from the producers of the good will be (**a**) borne completely by the producers, (**b**) borne completely by consumers, (**c**) shared equally by producers and consumers, (**d**) shared, but borne mostly by buyers. [See Section 6-6.]

14. Demand is said to be perfectly _____ if buyers reduce their purchases to zero if price rises even slightly. [See Section 6-6.]

15. The more nearly horizontal a demand curve, the greater the burden of an excise tax on _____ . [See Section 6-6.]

Answers

1. decrease   2. complementary   3. decrease, decrease   4. independent   5. (**b**)
6. decrease   7. (**d**)   8. reduces, demand   9. (**d**)   10. increase   11. (**c**)   12. (**c**)
13. (**b**)   14. elastic   15. sellers (producers)

SOLVED PROBLEMS

PROBLEM 6-1   Assume that the state government imposes an excise tax on margarine. Analyze the impact of the tax on the price of butter and the quantity of butter sold each month. Draw an appropriate diagram.

Answer: If the state government imposes an excise tax on margarine, the price of margarine will increase. Since butter and margarine are substitute goods, an increase in the price of margarine will increase the demand for butter. This increase in demand will be reflected by a rightward shift in the demand curve for butter, as shown in Figure 6-11. As the demand curve for butter shifts right (*DD* to *D'D'*), the price of butter will increase (*P* to *P'*), and so will the quantity sold (*Q* to *Q'*). [See Sections 6-2 and 6-6.]

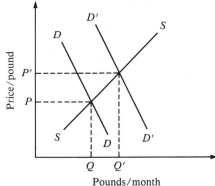

Figure 6-11

PROBLEM 6-2   Analyze the impact of a margarine tax on the equilibrium price and quantity in the market for bread.

Answer: Since margarine and bread are complementary goods, an increase in the price of margarine (theoretically, at least) will result in a decrease in the demand for bread. As the demand curve for bread shifts left, from *DD* to *D'D'* in Figure 6-12, the equilibrium price and quantity in the market will both decline, from *P* to *P'* and *Q* to *Q'*, respectively. (As you can see, taxing margarine is a real bread-and-butter issue.) [See Section 6-2.]

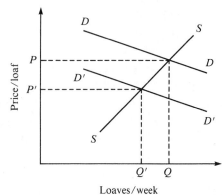

Figure 6-12

PROBLEM 6-3 Analyze the effect of a recession (a drop in national income and production) on the number of people luxuriating at Rosy's Resort and the number of people roughing it at It's the Pitts' Campground. Draw an appropriate diagram.

Answer: The question suggests that Rosy's Resort is an income-superior good and that It's the Pitts' Campground is an income-inferior good. If that is the case, a decline in national income will reduce the demand for accommodations at Rosy's and increase the demand for campsites at the Pitts'. In other words, the number of vacation days spent at Rosy's Resort will decrease and the number of vacation days spent at It's the Pitts' Campground will increase, as shown in Figure 6-13. [See Section 6-3.]

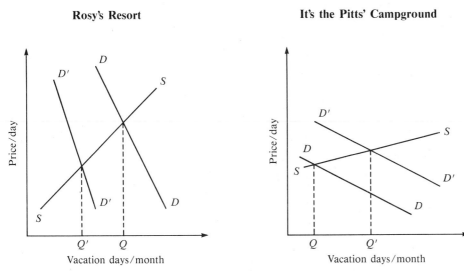

Figure 6-13

PROBLEM 6-4 You learned in Chapter 5 that a change in consumer income, a *ceteris paribus* variable, causes the demand curve for a good to shift. What type of good is an exception to this rule?

Answer: An income-independent good is an exception to this rule. By definition, the demand curve for an income-independent good, such as salt, does not shift with changes in consumer income. [See Section 6-3.]

PROBLEM 6-5 Assume that the local government imposes an effective price ceiling on new textbooks. Analyze the effects of the ceiling on price and quantity sold in the market for new textbooks. Do the same for the used textbook market, assuming that the ceiling price does not apply to used books. Draw appropriate diagrams.

Answer: An effective price ceiling on new texts will reduce both price and quantity exchanged in the new textbook market, as shown in Figure 6-14. Price will drop from *P*, the

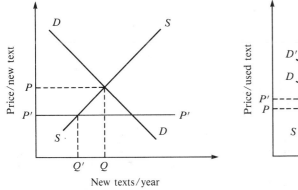

Figure 6-14

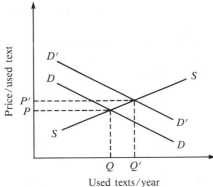

Figure 6-15

market equilibrium price, to P', the ceiling price, and quantity sold will decline from Q, the market equilibrium quantity, to Q', the quantity that suppliers will be willing to make available at the ceiling price.

The price ceiling will have the opposite effect on the market for used texts. Some or all of the excess demand in the new book market will spill over into the used book market and cause the demand curve for used books to shift right, as shown in Figure 6-15 on the preceding page. As the demand for used books increases from DD to $D'D'$, price will increase from P to P' and quantity exchanged will increase from Q to Q'. [See Section 6-4.]

PROBLEM 6-6 The minimum wage law in the United States specifies a price floor for the hourly wages of most workers. Assume that the price floor is effective (i.e., above the equilibrium rate) for workers who are not highly skilled. Analyze the impact of the law on the wages and employment of those workers, particularly minority workers. Draw an appropriate diagram.

Answer: Figure 6-16 illustrates the effect that the minimum wage law has on price (wage rate) and quantity exchanged (employment or hours worked) in the market for unskilled labor. As price is forced up from P, the market equilibrium price, to P', the floor price or minimum wage, quantity demanded decreases from H to H'. In other words, wages increase and employment decreases. At the same time, quantity supplied (employment sought) increases (from H to H''), and the result is a surplus of labor that makes discrimination against minorities essentially cost free for employers. [See Section 6-5.]

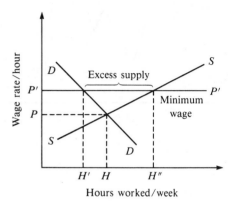

Figure 6-16

PROBLEM 6-7 Assume that the government increases the excise tax on whisky by $2 per gallon and collects the tax from distillers. Analyze the effect of the tax increase on the price and the quantity of whisky sold. Who will bear the tax increase? Draw an appropriate diagram.

Answer: A tax increase collected from distillers will shift the supply curve for whisky to the left. The vertical distance between the initial supply curve and the new supply curve will equal the amount of the tax, $2 per gallon. Assuming that the demand curve for whisky is neither vertical nor horizontal, the shift in the supply curve will cause the price of whisky to increase, but by less than the amount of the tax, and it will cause the quantity sold to decrease. Under these circumstances, the tax increase will be shared by buyers and sellers, as shown in Figure 6-17. Sellers will collect price P' for each gallon, but after they pay the tax

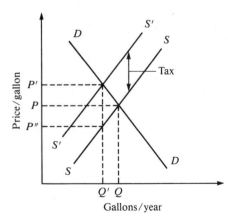

Figure 6-17

increase, they will realize only P'' dollars per gallon. Thus they must absorb the difference between P'' and P, and buyers must pay the difference between P and P'. [See Section 6-6.]

PROBLEM 6-8 Assume that the government increases the excise tax on cigarettes by $1 per carton and collects the tax from *consumers*. Analyze the effect of the tax increase on the price and quantity of cigarettes sold. Who will bear the burden of the tax increase? Draw an appropriate diagram.

Answer: To answer this question, you must extrapolate from the discussion of excise taxes in Section 6-6, which is limited to excise taxes that are collected from producers. As you should be able to deduce, an excise tax collected from buyers, rather than sellers, will cause the demand, rather than the supply, curve for a good to shift left. Thus, if the $1 increase in the excise tax on cigarettes is collected from consumers, the demand curve for cigarettes will shift left, as shown in Figure 6-18. The vertical distance between the new demand curve, $D'D'$, and the initial demand curve, DD, will be $1, the amount of the tax increase. Consumers will pay more per carton as a result of the increase (P'' instead of P), but the price

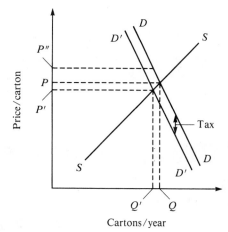

Figure 6-18

excluding tax and the quantity sold will both decline, from P to P' and Q to Q', respectively. Even though the tax increase will be collected from consumers, it will be shared by producers, who will receive a lower price per carton after the increase is levied. In other words, of the distance P' to P'', which represents the $1 tax increase in Figure 6-18, producers will bear the portion between P' and P and consumers will bear the portion between P and P''. Since demand for cigarettes is relatively inelastic (insensitive to price), the demand curve in Figure 6-18 is more nearly vertical than horizontal, and consumers are shown to bear a larger share of the tax increase. [See Section 6-6.]

7 PRICE ELASTICITY OF DEMAND

THIS CHAPTER IS ABOUT

- ☑ **Price Sensitivity**
- ☑ **Price Elasticity of Demand**
- ☑ **Measuring Price Elasticity of Demand with the Arc Formula**
- ☑ **Price Elasticity of Demand and Slope**
- ☑ **Price Elasticity of Demand and Total Revenue**
- ☑ **Determinants of Price Elasticity of Demand**
- ☑ **Other Elasticities**

7-1. Price Sensitivity

Price sensitivity of demand is a measure of the degree to which consumers respond to price changes by increasing or decreasing the quantities that they purchase. Price sensitivity of demand is a critical factor in the pricing decisions of firms, the taxing decisions of legislators, and the forecasting decisions of product managers. Firms need to know how far they can raise the prices of their products before consumers will drastically reduce their purchases. Legislators need to know whether an excise tax under consideration will reduce consumption by 50 percent or only 5 percent. Product managers need to know what adjustments to make in production levels if the prices of their products are raised or lowered. As usual, economists have their own special term for the sensitivity of quantity demanded to price. They call it *price elasticity of demand*.

7-2. Price Elasticity of Demand

Price elasticity of demand is a unit-free measure of the relative sensitivity of quantity demanded to changes in price. More technically:

Price elasticity of demand (E) is the percentage change in quantity demanded for a 1 percent change in price.

A *high* price elasticity indicates that quantity demanded varies significantly as price changes. A *low* price elasticity indicates the opposite, that quantity demanded varies little as price changes.

EXAMPLE 7-1: The price elasticity of demand for plain white bread and tickets on Northwest Orient Airlines is high. If the prices of these two goods were increased by, say, 50 percent, quantity demanded would decline significantly. Consumers would either look for substitutes or decide to do without. By contrast, the price elasticity of demand for such goods as insulin and salt is low. A 50 percent increase in the price of either would produce only a small decline in quantity demanded.

A. Price elasticity of demand is a positive ratio.

Price elasticity of demand is a positive ratio of a percentage change in quantity demanded to a percentage change in price. It is found by means of the following formula, in which the symbol Δ (delta) is used to represent the word *change*:

$$\text{Price elasticity of demand } (E) = \left| \frac{\% \, \Delta \text{ in quantity demanded}}{\% \, \Delta \text{ in price}} \right|$$

If you know the percentage change in quantity demanded that will result from a given percentage change in price, you can calculate the price elasticity of demand for a good very simply by substituting the known values into the elasticity formula.

EXAMPLE 7-2: If a 10 percent increase in the price of widgets produces a 30 percent decrease in quantity demanded, the price elasticity of demand for widgets is 3:

$$E = \left| \frac{-30\%}{10\%} \right| = 3$$

If you don't know the percentage changes in quantity demanded and price, you can find them by dividing the change in quantity by the initial quantity and the change in price by the initial price. Thus, if (Q_1, P_1) and (Q_2, P_2) are two quantity–price combinations, the elasticity formula can be restated as follows:

$$E = \left| \frac{(Q_2 - Q_1)/Q_1}{(P_2 - P_1)/P_1} \right|$$

EXAMPLE 7-3: Assume that at an initial price of $100, consumers seek to purchase 10,000 units of a hypothetical good, and at an increased price of $110, they seek to purchase only 8,000 units. To calculate the price elasticity of demand for the good, substitute the values you are given into the restated formula.

$$E = \left| \frac{(8{,}000 - 10{,}000)/10{,}000}{(\$110 - \$100)/\$100} \right|$$

$$= \left| \frac{-2{,}000/10{,}000}{\$10/\$100} \right|$$

$$= \left| \frac{-20\%}{10\%} \right|$$

$$= 2$$

(As you will learn in Section 7-3, economists use another method to calculate percentage changes *between* two quantity–price combinations.)

B. Price elasticity of demand is a unit-free measure.

Notice that, when elasticity is calculated, changes in quantity and price are expressed as percentages. If they were expressed in units of measure, such as pounds or barrels for quantity and dollars or marks for price, elasticity would not be a standard measure. Instead, it would vary, depending on the units used. It would also have to be written as a ratio—of bushels to lira, for example.

Expressing changes in price and quantity as percentages makes elasticity a unit-free measure that can be written as a simple number, such as 3 in Example 7-2. That number, which is called the *elasticity coefficient*, is the quotient of the percentage change in quantity divided by the percentage change in price. An elasticity coefficient of 3 means that a 1 percent change in price results in a 3 percent change in quantity demanded.

C. Price elasticity of demand is positive by convention.

According to the law of demand, price and quantity demanded are inversely related. This inverse relationship implies that changes in price and quantity, whether they are measured in percentages or units, always have opposite arithmetic signs: if one is positive, the other is negative. Technically, then, price elasticity of demand coefficients should always be negative. However, since negative coefficients would place economists in the awkward position of having to say that a price elasticity of -4 was *greater* than one of -2, they have arbitrarily agreed to express price elasticity of demand in positive terms. That's why the vertical bars symbolizing positive or absolute value are placed on either side of the ratio in the elasticity formula.

D. The elasticity formula can be manipulated to find percentage changes.

Like other formulas, the formula for calculating the price elasticity of demand for a good can be manipulated. In other words, it can be used to find percentage changes in price and quantity just as easily as it can be used to find elasticity. Of course the values of two of the three variables must be known. But if they are, the value of the third variable, whichever one it is, can be determined by means of the formula.

EXAMPLE 7-4: The product manager for Widgets International is trying to calculate the change in production that should accompany an increase in the price of widgets. She knows that the price elasticity of demand for widgets is 0.5. She also knows that the price of widgets will be increased by 20 percent. To determine the decline in quantity demanded that will accompany the price increase, then, all she needs to do is to plug those values into the elasticity formula, add the necessary minus sign (price elasticity of demand is positive by convention but negative in reality), and cross multiply:

$$-0.5 = \frac{x\%}{20\%}$$

$$x\% = -0.5 \times .20$$

$$x\% = -0.10 \text{ or } -10\%$$

Thus, when the price of widgets is increased by 20 percent, she should plan to reduce production by 10 percent to compensate for the decline in quantity demanded.

E. Demand is classified as elastic, unitary elastic, or inelastic.

Depending on whether price elasticity is greater than, equal to, or less than one, demand is classified as elastic, unitary elastic, or inelastic, respectively. These classifications and their interpretations are shown in the following table.

Elasticity	Classification	Interpretation
$E > 1$	elastic	$\% \Delta Q > \% \Delta P$
$E = 1$	unitary elastic	$\% \Delta Q = \% \Delta P$
$E < 1$	inelastic	$\% \Delta Q < \% \Delta P$

EXAMPLE 7-5: In Example 7-4 the price elasticity coefficient of widgets is given as 0.5. Since 0.5 is less than 1, the demand for widgets is said to be inelastic. This means that consumers are relatively unresponsive to changes in the price of widgets. If the price of widgets is increased,

consumers will seek to purchase them in smaller quantities, but the percentage decrease in their consumption will be less than the percentage increase in price. In fact, it will be only half the percentage increase in price. (An elasticity coefficient of 0.5 means that a 1 percent increase in price will bring about a decrease in quantity demanded equal to 1/2 of 1 percent.)

F. Demand may be perfectly inelastic or perfectly elastic.

As you learned in Chapter 6, at its two extremes, demand is perfectly inelastic and perfectly elastic. The graph of perfectly inelastic demand is a vertical line, as shown in Figure 7-1. A vertical demand curve has an elasticity of zero, which means that consumers are completely unresponsive to changes in price. In Figure 7-1, for example, even though price increases from $4 to $5, quantity demanded remains constant.

By contrast, the graph of perfectly elastic demand is a horizontal line, as shown in Figure 7-2. A horizontal demand curve has an elasticity that approaches infinity, which means that consumers are extremely sensitive to changes in price. If price increases even slightly, they will reduce their consumption to zero. If price decreases even slightly, they will increase their consumption substantially.

7-3. Measuring Price Elasticity of Demand with the Arc Formula

One problem arises in the determination of price elasticity, and that is the calculation of the percentage changes in price and quantity when no "initial" price or quantity is specified. An example serves to illustrate the problem.

EXAMPLE 7-6: Take the two quantity–price combinations given in Example 7-3: (10,000, $100) and (8,000, $110). In that example, elasticity is calculated on the basis of the first quantity–price combination because it is designated as the "initial" combination. But what if you were simply asked to calculate the elasticity between the two points and you used the second combination instead? The absolute differences in price and quantity would still be the same, but since they would have to be divided by different values, they would yield different percentages and a different elasticity coefficient.

$$E = \left| \frac{(10,000 - 8,000)/8,000}{(\$100 - \$110)/\$110} \right|$$

$$= \left| \frac{2,000/8,000}{-\$10/\$110} \right|$$

$$= \left| \frac{25\%}{-9\%} \right|$$

$$= 2.78$$

In other words, if the percentage changes are calculated on the basis of the first quantity–price combination, as they are in Example 7-3, the elasticity coefficient of the hypothetical good is 2. If they are calculated on the basis of the second quantity–price combination, as they are here, the elasticity coefficient is 2.78.

To avoid the problem, economists use a less ambiguous method of determining percentage changes. Instead of basing their calculations on

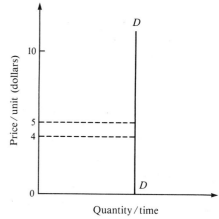

Figure 7-1
A vertical demand curve is perfectly inelastic: $E = 0$.

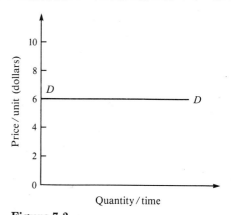

Figure 7-2
A horizontal demand curve is perfectly elastic: E approaches infinity.

one or the other of two quantity–price combinations, they use them both: that is, they use the *average* of the two. Thus, to find the percentage change in price, they divide the change or the difference by the average of the two prices; to find the percentage change in quantity, they divide the change or the difference by the average of the two quantities.

$$E = \left| \frac{\dfrac{\Delta \text{ in quantity}}{\text{average quantity}}}{\dfrac{\Delta \text{ in price}}{\text{average price}}} \right|$$

This formula for calculating price elasticity *between* two quantity–price combinations is called the **midpoint** or **arc formula**. Again, if (Q_1, P_1) and (Q_2, P_2) are two points on a demand curve or two quantity–price combinations in a demand schedule, the arc formula can be restated as follows:

$$E = \left| \frac{\dfrac{Q_2 - Q_1}{(Q_2 + Q_1)/2}}{\dfrac{P_2 - P_1}{(P_2 + P_1)/2}} \right|$$

The arc formula looks more complicated than it really is. Once you understand how it is derived, you can memorize it in its simplified form:

$$E = \left| \frac{Q_2 - Q_1}{P_2 - P_1} \times \frac{P_2 + P_1}{Q_2 + Q_1} \right|$$

EXAMPLE 7-7: You can calculate the average elasticity between any two quantity–price combinations in a demand schedule or any two points on a demand curve with the arc formula. Take, for example, the following demand schedule and the corresponding demand curve, Figure 7-3:

Demand Schedule

Point	Quantity/time	Price/unit
A	10	$9
B	20	8
C	40	6
D	60	4
E	70	3
F	80	2

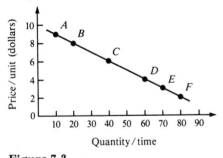

Figure 7-3
The arc formula measures elasticity midway between two points, such as *C* and *D*, on a demand curve.

As the following calculations show, the average elasticity between points *A* and *B* is 5.67:

$$E = \left| \frac{20 - 10}{8 - 9} \times \frac{8 + 9}{20 + 10} \right| = \frac{10}{1} \times \frac{17}{30} = \frac{17}{3} = 5.67$$

The average elasticity between points *C* and *D* is 1.0:

$$E = \left| \frac{60 - 40}{4 - 6} \times \frac{4 + 6}{60 + 40} \right| = \frac{20}{2} \times \frac{10}{100} = \frac{200}{200} = 1.0$$

The average elasticity between points *E* and *F* is 0.33:

$$E = \left| \frac{80 - 70}{2 - 3} \times \frac{3 + 2}{80 + 70} \right| = \frac{10}{1} \times \frac{5}{150} = \frac{1}{3} = 0.33$$

7-4. Price Elasticity of Demand and Slope

A. Price elasticity of demand is inversely related to the slope of a demand curve.

In Chapter 3 you learned that a horizontal line has a slope of zero and a vertical line has a slope that approaches infinity. In Section 7-2 of this chapter you learned that a horizontal line has an elasticity approaching infinity and a vertical line has an elasticity of zero. From these two bits of information you can conclude that price elasticity of demand is inversely related to the slope of a demand curve. Other things being equal, the steeper the slope of a demand curve, the lower the price elasticity of demand; the flatter the slope of a demand curve, the higher the price elasticity of demand.

EXAMPLE 7-8: Figure 7-4 shows two demand curves. Demand curve *DD* has a relatively steep slope but a relatively low elasticity. Demand curve *D'D'* has a relatively flat slope but a relatively high elasticity. Although the labels are not technically correct, economists routinely refer to relatively steep demand curves like *DD* as "inelastic" and to relatively flat demand curves like *D'D'* as "elastic."

You can see the mathematical reason that price elasticity is inversely related to the slope of a demand curve if you compare the arc elasticity formula with the formula for calculating slope (see Chapter 3):

$$E = \left| \frac{Q_2 - Q_1}{P_2 - P_1} \times \frac{P_2 + P_1}{Q_2 + Q_1} \right| \qquad \text{slope} = \frac{P_2 - P_1}{Q_2 - Q_1}$$

Notice that the first term of the arc elasticity formula is an exact inversion of the slope formula. Therefore, as slope increases, price elasticity of demand decreases, and as slope decreases, price elasticity of demand increases, *ceteris paribus*.

B. Price elasticity varies along a linear demand curve.

Price elasticity is inversely related to slope, but whereas slope remains constant along a straight or linear demand curve, price elasticity doesn't.

EXAMPLE 7-9: Figure 7-5 shows how price elasticity varies along the linear demand curve in Figure 7-3. Although slope is a constant −0.1 all along the curve, price elasticity declines from the upper left-hand to the lower right-hand portion of the curve. Between points *A* and *B*, it is elastic (5.67, as you know from the calculations in Example 7-7). Between points *C* and *D*, it is unitary elastic (1.0). And between points *E* and *F*, it is inelastic (0.33).

The reason that price elasticity varies even when slope doesn't is this: slope is measured in absolute terms; price elasticity is measured in relative terms. Price elasticity, remember, is a *percentage* change in quantity relative to a *percentage* change in price. Thus, a given change in price (or quantity) will register as a relatively large percentage if price (or quantity) is small, but it will register as a relatively small percentage if price (or quantity) is large.

EXAMPLE 7-10: If the price of a good were raised from $1 to $2, the $1 change would represent an increase of 100 percent ($1 is 100 percent of $1). If the price of the good were raised from $10 to $11, the same $1 change would represent an increase of only 10 percent ($1 is 10 percent of $10).

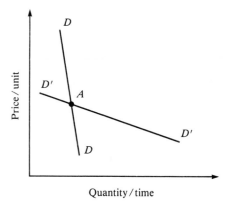

Figure 7-4
Demand curve *DD* has a steeper slope and therefore a lower elasticity at point *A* than demand curve *D'D'*.

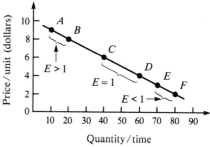

Figure 7-5
Price elasticity of demand varies along a linear demand curve. It is high when price is high and low when price is low.

Again, if you look at the simplified arc formula, you can see the mathematical reason that price elasticity varies along a linear demand curve even though slope doesn't. Since the first factor in the arc formula is the inverse of the slope, it remains constant no matter where elasticity is measured on a linear demand curve. However, the second factor, which is the ratio of the sum of two prices to the sum of two quantities obviously varies, depending on the prices and quantities involved. If the sum of the two prices (the numerator) is relatively high and the sum of the two quantities (the denominator) is relatively low, the value of the second factor is relatively high and so is elasticity. This occurs at the upper left-hand end of a demand curve.

If, on the other hand, the sum of the two prices (the numerator) is relatively low and the sum of the two quantities (the denominator) is relatively high, the value of the second term is relatively low and so is elasticity. This occurs at the lower right-hand end of a demand curve. Thus, although slope doesn't vary along a linear demand curve, price elasticity does.

EXAMPLE 7-11: Look again at Example 7-7, where price elasticity is calculated between three different pairs of points on the same linear demand curve (Figures 7-3 and 7-5). Although price and quantity are different at each point, the first factor in all three calculations has the same absolute value (10/1) because it is the positive inverse of the slope of the curve, which is constant (-0.1 or $-1/10$). The value of the second factor, however, varies considerably. Between points A and B, it has a value of 17/3, but between points E and F, which are exactly the same distance apart, it has a value of only 1/3. As you can see, between points A and B, price is relatively high and quantity is relatively low, and between points E and F, quantity is relatively high and price is relatively low. These relative differences account for the variation in price elasticity along a linear demand curve.

7-5. Price Elasticity of Demand and Total Revenue

Price elasticity of demand determines the change in total revenue (or, from the point of view of consumers, total expenditures) that results from a change in price. **Total revenue** is the product of price and quantity exchanged:

$$\text{Total revenue} = \text{price} \times \text{quantity exchanged}$$

Since price and quantity exchanged are inversely related, increases in price do not always bring about increases in total revenue. Increases in price bring about increases in total revenue only if demand is inelastic. If demand is elastic, increases in price bring about decreases in total revenue.

EXAMPLE 7-12: The following demand schedule and Figure 7-6 show the effect that changes in price have on total revenue.

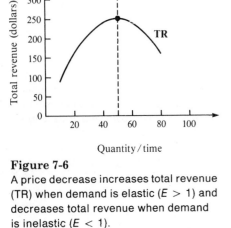

Figure 7-6
A price decrease increases total revenue (TR) when demand is elastic ($E > 1$) and decreases total revenue when demand is inelastic ($E < 1$).

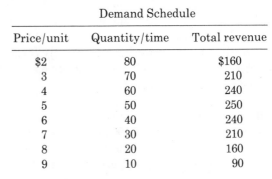

Demand Schedule		
Price/unit	Quantity/time	Total revenue
$2	80	$160
3	70	210
4	60	240
5	50	250
6	40	240
7	30	210
8	20	160
9	10	90

As you can see, increases in price bring about increases in total revenue only in the top half of the schedule, where price is relatively low and quantity is relatively high. In that area, as Figure 7-6 shows, demand is inelastic. In the bottom half of the schedule, where price is relatively high and quantity is relatively low, increases in price bring about decreases in total revenue. In that area, as Figure 7-6 shows, demand is elastic.

Figure 7-6 is an excellent picture of the interrelationship of price, elasticity, and total revenue, one that you should commit to memory. On the left side of the dashed line, the negative slope of the demand curve in the upper portion and the positive slope of the total revenue curve in the lower portion show that, when demand is elastic ($E > 1$), price and total revenue are inversely related. In other words, when demand is elastic, increases in price are too small, proportionately, to compensate for the decreases in quantity that they provoke. Therefore, when demand is elastic, decreases in price result in increases in total revenue and increases in price result in decreases in total revenue.

On the right side of the dashed line, where demand is inelastic ($E < 1$), the demand curve and the total revenue curve both have negative slopes, which indicates that price and total revenue are directly related when demand is inelastic. A direct relationship between price and total revenue means that, when demand is inelastic, increases in price more than compensate for the decreases in quantity that they produce. Therefore, when demand is inelastic, decreases in price result in decreases in total revenue and increases in price result in increases in total revenue.

In the middle of the figure, where demand is unitary elastic ($E = 1$), total revenue is unaffected by changes in price because those changes are exactly offset by changes in quantity.

The interrelationship of price, elasticity, and total revenue is summarized in the following table:

Elasticity	Price change	Revenue change
elastic	increase	decrease
	decrease	increase
unitary elastic	increase	no change
	decrease	no change
inelastic	increase	increase
	decrease	decrease

If you look again at the elasticity formula in Section 7-2, you can see the mathematical reason for the interrelationship of price, elasticity, and total revenue that is summarized graphically in Figure 7-6 and verbally in the preceding table. When demand is elastic ($E > 1$), total revenue is inversely related to price because percentage decreases in quantity exceed percentage increases in price. For example, when elasticity is 2, a 10 percent increase in price produces a 20 percent decrease in quantity exchanged, thus causing total revenue to fall.

On the other hand, when demand is inelastic ($E < 1$), total revenue is directly related to price because percentage increases in price exceed percentage decreases in quantity. For example, when elasticity is 0.3, a 10 percent increase in price reduces quantity exchanged by only 3 percent, so total revenue rises.

Of course, when elasticity is unitary ($E = 1$), the percentage increase in price is exactly equal to the percentage decrease in quantity exchanged, so total revenue doesn't change.

7-6. Determinants of Price Elasticity of Demand

Price elasticity of demand is affected by the same variables that affect demand. These variables and their effects on elasticity can be summarized as follows:

1. The better the substitutes for a good, the more elastic the demand.
2. The larger the portion of income spent on a good, the more elastic the demand.
3. The longer the time period, the more elastic the demand. Given time, people find or develop substitute goods.
4. The more luxurious a good, the more elastic the demand. Luxuries, such as vacations in Europe, tend to have a higher price elasticity than necessities, such as prescription drugs.

7-7. Other Elasticities

The concept of elasticity is applicable to other variables besides price and quantity demanded. In fact, since elasticity is simply a ratio of percentage changes, it can be applied to any two economic variables that change in conjunction with one another. Price and quantity supplied are two of the more common ones. So are income and quantity demanded.

A. **Price elasticity of supply measures producer sensitivity to price changes.**

Price elasticity of supply is the percentage change in quantity supplied for a 1 percent change in price.

$$\text{Price elasticity of supply } (E_S) = \frac{\% \, \Delta \text{ in quantity supplied}}{\% \, \Delta \text{ in price}}$$

Price elasticity of supply is calculated in the same way that price elasticity of demand is calculated, that is, by means of the arc formula. Since price and quantity supplied are directly related, price elasticity of supply coefficients are always positive.

B. **Income elasticity of demand measures consumer sensitivity to income changes.**

Income elasticity of demand is the percentage change in quantity demanded for a 1 percent change in income.

$$\text{Income elasticity of demand } (E_I) = \frac{\% \, \Delta \text{ in quantity demanded}}{\% \, \Delta \text{ in price}}$$

Income elasticity of demand is positive, zero, or negative, depending on whether a good is income superior, income independent, or income inferior. If consumers purchase more of a good, such as steak, as their income rises, the income elasticity of demand for the good is positive. If consumers purchase the same amount of a good, such as salt, as their income rises, the income elasticity of demand for the good is zero. Finally, if consumers purchase less of a good, such as macaroni, as their income rises, the income elasticity of demand for the good is negative.

RAISE YOUR GRADES

Can you explain...?

☑ why price elasticity of demand is positive
☑ why a vertical demand curve has an elasticity of zero
☑ why elasticity approaches infinity for a horizontal demand curve

☑ why elasticity is inversely related to the slope of a demand curve
☑ why elasticity varies along a linear demand curve
☑ how total revenue is related to price elasticity of demand
☑ how price elasticity of supply differs from price elasticity of demand
☑ what the arithmetic sign of an income elasticity coefficient signifies

SUMMARY

1. Price elasticity of demand is a measure of the relative sensitivity of quantity demanded to changes in price. More technically, *price elasticity of demand* is the percentage change in quantity demanded for a 1 percent change in price.

2. Price elasticity of demand (E) is a ratio that is found by means of the following formula:

$$E = \left| \frac{\% \, \Delta \text{ in quantity demanded}}{\% \, \Delta \text{ in price}} \right|$$

3. Price elasticity of demand is a unit-free measure that is conventionally expressed in terms of its positive or absolute value.

4. Demand is elastic if $E > 1$. Demand is unitary elastic if $E = 1$. Demand is inelastic if $E < 1$.

5. If demand is elastic, consumers are very sensitive to price changes. If demand is inelastic, consumers are insensitive to price changes.

6. Vertical demand curves represent perfect inelasticity ($E = 0$); horizontal demand curves, perfect elasticity (E approaches infinity).

7. The arc elasticity formula measures the average elasticity between two points on a demand curve or schedule. It divides the difference between the two quantities by the average of the two quantities and the difference between the two prices by the average of the two prices.

8. Expressed in its simplest form, the formula for measuring the average elasticity between points (Q_1, P_1) and (Q_2, P_2) on a demand curve is

$$E = \left| \frac{Q_2 - Q_1}{P_2 - P_1} \times \frac{P_2 + P_1}{Q_2 + Q_1} \right|$$

9. Price elasticity of demand is inversely related to the slope of a demand curve. Other things being equal, the steeper the slope of a demand curve, the lower the elasticity of demand; the flatter the slope of a demand curve, the higher the elasticity of demand.

10. Price elasticity varies along a linear demand curve. Elasticity is high when price is high and quantity is low. Elasticity is low when price is low and quantity is high.

11. Total revenue, which is equal to price times quantity exchanged, is inversely related to price when demand is elastic and directly related to price when demand is inelastic. When demand is unitary elastic, total revenue is unaffected by price changes.

12. Price elasticity of demand is affected by the same variables that affect demand. Other things being equal, the elasticity of demand for a good tends to be greater (1) the better the substitutes for the good, (2) the larger the portion of income spent on the good, (3) the longer the time period, (4) the more luxurious the good.

13. The concept of elasticity is applicable to any two economic variables that change in conjunction with one another.

14. *Price elasticity of supply* is the percentage change in quantity supplied for a 1 percent change in price. A price elasticity of supply coefficient is always positive.

15. *Income elasticity of demand* is the percentage change in quantity demanded for a 1 percent change in income. Income elasticity of demand is positive if a good is income superior, zero if a good is income independent, and negative if a good is income inferior.

RAPID REVIEW

1. Price elasticity of demand measures the percentage change in quantity demanded for a 1 percent change in _____. [See Section 7-2.]

2. If a 10 percent decrease in the price of a good results in a 30 percent increase in quantity demanded, the price elasticity of demand for the good equals _____. [See Section 7-2.]

3. If the price elasticity of demand for a good is 1.5, a 10 percent increase in the price of the good will result in a _____ percent _____ in quantity demanded. [See Section 7-2.]

4. Since price and quantity demanded are inversely related, the arithmetic sign of a price elasticity coefficient is _____ only by convention. [See Section 7-2.]

5. If $E < 1$, demand is said to be _____. [See Section 7-2.]

6. If demand is unitary elastic, a _____ percent _____ in price will result in a 2 percent increase in quantity demanded. [See Section 7-2.]

7. A vertical demand curve has a price elasticity equal to _____. [See Section 7-2.]

8. A horizontal demand curve indicates that consumers are extremely sensitive to changes in price. True or false? [See Section 7-2.]

9. The _____ elasticity formula measures the average elasticity between two points on a demand curve. [See Section 7-3.]

10. Price elasticity of demand is _____ related to the slope of a demand curve. [See Section 7-4.]

11. Other things being equal, the flatter the slope of a demand curve, the _____ the price elasticity of demand. [See Section 7-4.]

12. On a linear demand curve, the _____ the price, the lower the elasticity. [See Section 7-4.]

13. A price decrease will increase total revenue only if demand is _____. [See Section 7-5.]

14. If $E = 1$, a price increase will increase total revenue. True or false? [See Section 7-5.]

15. The slope of a total revenue curve is directly related to the slope of a demand curve when demand is _____. [See Section 7-5.]

16. If no good substitutes for a good are available, demand tends to be _____. [See Section 7-6.]

17. Other things being equal, the longer the time period, the more price elastic the demand. True or false? [See Section 7-6.]

18. If a 5 percent increase in price results in a 10 percent increase in quantity supplied, price elasticity of supply equals _____. [See Section 7-7.]

19. The income elasticity of demand for an income-inferior good has a _____ arithmetic sign. [See Section 7-7.]

Answers

1. price   2. 3   3. 15, decrease   4. positive   5. inelastic   6. 2, decrease   7. zero
8. true   9. arc   10. inversely   11. higher   12. lower   13. elastic   14. false
15. inelastic   16. inelastic   17. true   18. 2   19. negative

SOLVED PROBLEMS

PROBLEM 7-1   Define *price elasticity of demand*. Explain why it is positive.

Answer: *Price elasticity of demand* is the percentage change in quantity demanded for a 1 percent change in price:

$$E = \left| \frac{\% \, \Delta Q}{\% \, \Delta P} \right|$$

Since price and quantity demanded are inversely related, price elasticity coefficients should be negative. However, economists conventionally express them in terms of their positive or absolute value because it is more convenient (and more logical, mathematically) to say that a price elasticity of 4 is greater than a price elasticity of 2 than it is to say that a price elasticity of -4 is greater than a price elasticity of -2. [See Section 7-2.]

PROBLEM 7-2   Explain why price elasticity of demand is a single unit-free number, such as 2, rather than a ratio of two numbers with different unit values, such as 20 quarts to $10.

Answer: Price elasticity of demand is a single unit-free number, such as 2, because it is a ratio of *percentage* changes. When the percentage changes are calculated, the units in which quantity and price are measured cancel out.

   For example, when you use the arc formula in Section 7-3 to determine the percentage change in quantity from, say, 4 pounds to 2 pounds, you divide the change in quantity (2 pounds) by the average quantity (3 pounds), and the pounds cancel out:

$$\frac{2 \text{ pounds}}{3 \text{ pounds}} = 0.67 \text{ or } 67\%$$

Likewise, when you determine the percentage change in price from, say, 10¢ to 20¢, you divide the change in price (10¢) by the average price (15¢), and the cents cancel out:

$$\frac{10¢}{15¢} = 0.67 \text{ or } 67\%$$

Thus, when you express the percentage change in quantity and the percentage change in price as a ratio, as you do when you calculate price elasticity of demand, the result is a single unit-free number:

$$\frac{67\%}{67\%} = 1$$

Elasticity is expressed as a ratio of percentage changes because percentages are comparable even when units of measure differ. [See Section 7-2.]

PROBLEM 7-3   Find the price elasticity of demand for a good if a 15 percent decrease in the price of the good results in a 45 percent increase in quantity demanded. Is demand for the good elastic or inelastic?

Answer: If a 15 percent decrease in price results in a 45 percent increase in quantity demanded, the price elasticity coefficient for the good is 3:

$$E = \left| \frac{\% \, \Delta \text{ in quantity}}{\% \, \Delta \text{ in price}} \right| = \left| \frac{45\%}{-15\%} \right| = 3$$

Since $E > 1$, demand for the good is obviously elastic. [See Section 7-2.]

PROBLEM 7-4 The product manager for Gizmos Unlimited is planning a 20 percent increase in the price of gizmos. If the price elasticity of demand for gizmos is 0.75, by how much should he increase or decrease production?

Answer: Since an increase in price will bring about a decrease in quantity demanded, the product manager should decrease production. To determine how much, substitute the values given in the problem into the elasticity formula, add the necessary minus sign to the arbitrarily positive elasticity coefficient, and solve for the percentage change in quantity demanded.

$$E = \left| \frac{\% \, \Delta Q}{\% \, \Delta P} \right|$$

$$-0.75 = \frac{\% \, \Delta Q}{20\%}$$

$$\% \, \Delta Q = 0.20 \times -0.75$$

$$= -15\%$$

The product manager for Gizmos Unlimited should plan a 15 percent decrease in production to compensate for the decrease in quantity demanded that will result from the 20 percent increase in price. [See Section 7-2.]

PROBLEM 7-5 The makers of brand X raised the price of their product from $3 to $5 a unit. As a result, sales declined from 2,000 units a month to 1,000. Calculate the average price elasticity of demand for brand X between the two quantity–price combinations. Is demand for brand X elastic or inelastic between them?

Answer: Use the arc formula to calculate the elasticity between the two quantity–price combinations:

$$E = \left| \frac{Q_2 - Q_1}{P_2 - P_1} \times \frac{P_2 + P_1}{Q_2 + Q_1} \right|$$

$$= \left| \frac{1,000 - 2,000}{\$5 - \$3} \times \frac{\$5 + \$3}{1,000 + 2,000} \right|$$

$$= \frac{1,000}{\$2} \times \frac{\$8}{3,000}$$

$$= \frac{8}{6} = 1.33$$

Since $E > 1$, demand for brand X is elastic between the two quantity–price combinations. [See Section 7-3.]

PROBLEM 7-6 The slope of a linear demand curve is -4. Calculate the price elasticity of demand over the arc on the curve where the average quantity equals 200 and the average price equals $8. Is demand elastic or inelastic?

Answer: Remember that the first term of the arc elasticity formula is an exact inversion of the slope formula. Therefore, all you need to do is to substitute the inverse of the slope into the formula along with the average price and quantity that you are given:

$$E = \left| \frac{1}{\text{slope}} \times \frac{\text{average price}}{\text{average quantity}} \right|$$

$$= \left| \frac{1}{-4} \times \frac{8}{200} \right|$$

$$= 0.01$$

Since $E < 1$, demand is inelastic. [See Sections 7-3 and 7-4.]

PROBLEM 7-7 Consider the three pairs of points on the demand curve in Figure 7-7, *A* and *B*, *C* and *D*, and *E* and *F*. Between which two points is elasticity highest? Between which two points is it lowest? Explain the rationale for your answer.

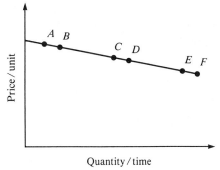

Figure 7-7

Answer: On a linear demand curve like the one in Figure 7-7, elasticity varies directly with price: it increases as price increases and decreases as price decreases. Therefore, elasticity is highest between points *A* and *B* and lowest between points *E* and *F*. The arc formula suggests the reason. Since the first term of the formula is the exact inverse of the slope formula, it remains constant whenever slope remains constant—that is, whenever a demand curve, like the one in Figure 7-7, is linear. However, the second term of the formula, which is the ratio of the sum of two prices to the sum of two quantities, does not. In fact, it is different between every pair of points on a linear demand curve. Therefore, since price and quantity demanded are inversely related, the higher the prices, the higher the ratio and the higher the elasticity; the lower the prices, the lower the ratio and the lower the elasticity. [See Section 7-4.]

PROBLEM 7-8 Calculate total revenue for points *A* through *D* in the following demand schedule. Then classify the price elasticity between points *A* and *B*, *B* and *C*, and *C* and *D* as inelastic, unitary elastic, or elastic. Explain your classifications.

Demand Schedule

Point	Price/unit	Quantity/time
A	$10	200
B	7	300
C	5	400
D	3	500

Answer: Total revenue is the product of price and quantity sold. The following table shows the total revenue for each of the four price–quantity combinations given in the demand schedule.

Point	Total revenue
A	$2,000
B	2,100
C	2,000
D	1,500

Notice that, although price *decreases* between points *A* and *B*, *B* and *C*, and *C* and *D*, total revenue *decreases* only between points *B* and *C* and *C* and *D*. Between points *A* and *B* it increases. Since a price *decrease* brings about an *increase* in total revenue only when demand is elastic, demand must be elastic between points *A* and *B*. Between points *B* and *C* and *C* and *D*, where a price *decrease* brings about a *decrease* in total revenue, demand must be inelastic.

Remember that elasticity is a ratio of a percentage change in quantity to a percentage change in price. When that ratio is greater than one ($E > 1$), the percentage change in quantity is greater than the percentage change in price. So, when demand is elastic, an increase (decrease) in price is always more than offset by the decrease (increase) in quantity that it produces, and total revenue decreases (increases). Conversely, when that ratio is less than one ($E < 1$), the percentage change in quantity is less than the percentage change in price. So, when demand is inelastic, an increase (decrease) in price always more than offsets the decrease (increase) in quantity that it produces, and total revenue increases (decreases). [See Section 7-5.]

PROBLEM 7-9   Fly-by-Night Airways is suffering from low revenues and inadequate profits. The manager reports the following facts about the company for the preceding month:

Average fare	$100
Number of riders	2,000
Price elasticity of demand	1.5

The president of the company is proposing a fare increase to $110. Should she go ahead with the increase? Explain your answer.

Answer: No. Since $E = 1.5$, the 10 percent increase that the president is proposing (from $100 to $110) will cause a 15 percent decrease in the number of passengers (from 2,000 to 1,700) and a drop in total revenue (from $200,000 to $187,000 a month). If there are empty seats on Fly-by-Night flights, the president should *decrease* the fare. Only by decreasing price can she bring about an increase in total revenue when demand is elastic ($E > 1$). [See Section 7-5.]

PROBLEM 7-10   As the price of good X increases from $6 to $8, quantity supplied increases from 20,000 to 22,000 units per month. Using the arc formula, calculate the price elasticity of supply for good X.

Answer: Price elasticity of supply is calculated in the same way that price elasticity of demand is calculated, except that, since price and quantity supplied are directly related, there is no need for the vertical bars that signify absolute value. Price elasticity of supply is always positive [see Section 7-7].

$$E_S = \frac{Q_2 - Q_1}{P_2 - P_1} \times \frac{P_2 + P_1}{Q_2 + Q_1}$$

$$= \frac{22,000 - 20,000}{\$8 - \$6} \times \frac{\$8 + \$6}{22,000 + 20,000}$$

$$= \frac{2,000}{\$2} \times \frac{\$14}{42,000} = 0.33$$

PROBLEM 7-11   If the income elasticity of demand for a good is -2.5, find the change in quantity demanded that will result from a 10 percent decline in income. Classify the good as income superior, income independent, or income inferior. Explain your answer.

Answer: An income elasticity coefficient of -2.5 tells you two things. First, the negative sign tells you that income and quantity demanded are inversely related. Therefore, the good is income inferior and a decrease in income will result in an increase in quantity demanded. Second, the 2.5 tells you that a 1 percent change in income will result in a 2.5 percent change in quantity demanded. Therefore, a 10 percent decrease in income will result in a 25 percent increase in quantity demanded.

You can also find the change in quantity demanded by substituting the values given into the formula for determining income elasticity of demand [see Section 7-7]:

$$E_I = \frac{\% \Delta Q}{\% \Delta I}$$

$$-2.5 = \frac{\% \Delta Q}{-10\%}$$

$$\% \Delta Q = -10\% \times -2.5$$

$$= +25\%$$

8 CONSUMER CHOICE AND DEMAND

THIS CHAPTER IS ABOUT

☑ **Consumer Behavior**
☑ **The Marginal Utility Approach**
☑ **The Indifference Curve Approach**
☑ **Indifference Curve Analysis**

8-1. Consumer Behavior

Much of economics is concerned with consumer behavior, the behavior of people as they seek to acquire goods and services that will satisfy their needs and wants. In analyzing consumer behavior, economists begin with a few basic assumptions:

1. Consumers' wants and needs fall into certain broad categories: food, shelter, transportation, health, and so on. Consumers can satisfy their wants or needs in any broad category with a variety of different goods and services.
2. Consumers are constrained in their search for satisfaction by the limits of their income. Typical consumers can't afford to satisfy all of their whims and wants.
3. Consumers behave purposefully, rationally, and efficiently (as you recall from Chapter 2). Given the constraints of a limited income, they purchase goods and services in quantities and combinations that will afford them the greatest satisfaction or utility possible.

Economists analyze consumer behavior in two alternative ways. One way is called the *marginal utility approach*. The other way is called the *indifference curve approach*. Although the methods of the two approaches are different, they both seek to explain why changes in prices and income have predictable effects on consumer behavior.

8-2. The Marginal Utility Approach

The marginal utility approach to analyzing consumer behavior is based on the premise that the amount of utility or satisfaction that a consumer derives from a good is quantifiable. A bagel, for instance, might provide you with, say, 30 units of utility; ten bagels might provide you with, say, 120 units of utility. These units of utility are called *utils* for short.

Total utility is the cumulative satisfaction that a consumer derives from the consumption of successive units of a good.

If you were to graph the cumulative satisfaction that you derive from consuming various quantities of bagels a week, your total utility curve might look something like the typical one in Figure 8-1.

A. The marginal utility of a good diminishes.

The total utility curve in Figure 8-1 has a decreasing slope. The decreasing slope indicates that the more bagels you consume, the less

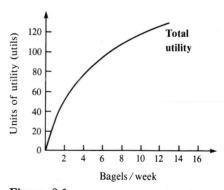

Figure 8-1
Total utility increases at a decreasing rate as additional units of a good are consumed.

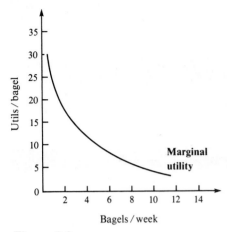

Figure 8-2
Marginal utility diminishes as additional units of a good are consumed.

satisfaction you derive from each *additional* bagel. Economists refer to the satisfaction that a consumer derives from each *additional* unit of a good as *marginal utility*.

Marginal utility is the change in total utility for a one-unit change in quantity consumed.

As a general rule, the satisfaction that a consumer derives from each additional unit of a good decreases with consumption. This rule is known as the **law of diminishing marginal utility**.

Figure 8-2 shows the marginal utility curve that corresponds to the total utility curve in Figure 8-1. Since each successive bagel provides fewer units of utility than the one before it, the curve has a negative or downward slope.

EXAMPLE 8-1: If you've ever eaten a dozen candy bars in a single sitting, you are familiar with the law of diminishing marginal utility. If you were very hungry for sweets at the time, you no doubt derived a good deal of satisfaction from the first one that you ate, and probably even the second one, and (depending on your size and your appetite) maybe even the third, fourth, and fifth. At some point, however, your craving for sweets was satisfied, and though you might still have derived a modicum of pleasure from eating one or two additional candy bars, they did not contribute as much to your total satisfaction as the first one did. In fact, they might actually have made you sick, in which case, if you continued eating, the marginal utility that you derived from the additional candy bars was negative and your total utility began to decline.

B. Maximum satisfaction is attained when the ratio of marginal utility to price is the same for all goods.

The measurement of utility—for various products as well as for various quantities of the same product—is a highly personal, highly subjective matter. Since we all spend our limited incomes on many different goods and services, it can also be very complicated. However, the rule for maximizing utility is both objective and fairly simple. As consumers we maximize our utility when the last dollar that we spend on each product that we purchase provides us with the same increase in satisfaction. In other words, we maximize our utility when the ratio of marginal utility to price is the same for each product in our commodity bundle.

If we let MU stand for marginal utility, *P* for price, and A, B, and Z for all of the goods and services in our respective commodity bundles, we can restate the rule for maximizing utility in the following formula:

$$\frac{MU_A}{P_A} = \frac{MU_B}{P_B} = \cdots = \frac{MU_Z}{P_Z}$$

EXAMPLE 8-2: Assume for the sake of simplicity that you earn an income of $10 and you spend it all on two goods, hamburgers and French fries. The price of one hamburger is $2 and the price of one order of French fries is $1. The units of utility that you derive from consuming successive units of each good are shown in the following marginal utility schedules:

Hamburgers		French Fries	
Quantity	MU	Quantity	MU
1	50	1	35
2	45	2	30
3	40	3	25
4	35	4	20
5	30	5	15
6	25	6	10

If you apply the rule for maximizing utility, you will spend your $10 on three hamburgers ($6) and four orders of French fries ($4) because the ratio of marginal utility to price for the third hamburger is the same as the ratio of marginal utility to price for the fourth order of French fries:

$$\frac{MU_H}{P_H} = \frac{40}{\$2} = \frac{20}{\$1} \qquad \frac{MU_F}{P_F} = \frac{20}{\$1}$$

As you can see, if you buy three hamburgers and four orders of French fries, the last dollar that you spend on hamburgers will provide you with the same increase in satisfaction, 20 units of utility, as the last dollar that you spend on French fries.

How can you be sure that the combination of three hamburgers and four orders of French fries will provide you with more satisfaction than any other combination of the two goods? Simply compare it with other combinations. For example, with your $10 you can buy one less hamburger and two more orders of French fries. If you do, you will gain an additional 25 utils from the fifth and sixth orders of French fries, but you will lose 40 utils by giving up the third hamburger—a net loss of 15 utils. Similarly, with your $10 you can buy one more hamburger and two fewer orders of French fries. If you do so, you will gain an additional 35 utils from the fourth hamburger, but you will lose 45 utils by giving up the third and fourth orders of French fries—a net loss of 10 utils. The same is true of other affordable combinations. They all provide less satisfaction than you can obtain with your limited budget if the ratio of marginal utility to price is the same for both of the goods in your commodity basket.

C. The marginal utility approach explains the law of demand.

As you recall from Chapter 5, the law of demand states that price and quantity demanded are inversely related. The rule for maximizing satisfaction in the marginal utility approach to consumer choice explains that inverse relationship. According to the rule, maximum satisfaction is attained when the ratio of marginal utility to price is the same for all of the goods in a consumer's commodity bundle. If the price of one of the goods is raised, the ratio of marginal utility to price for that good will obviously be lower than it is for the other goods in the bundle, and the balance required for maximum utility will be upset. To restore it, the consumer will have to offset the price increase by increasing the marginal utility of the good proportionately, and the only way to do that, given the law of diminishing marginal utility, is by *decreasing* quantity consumed.

EXAMPLE 8-3: Assume that the price of hamburgers in Example 8-2 is increased from $2 to $3 and that everything else remains constant. Now, you can still afford to buy three hamburgers, and, if you do buy them, they will still yield the same amount of total utility (50 + 45 + 40 = 135 utils). However, since you will have to pay $9 for them instead of $6, you will obviously derive less satisfaction *per dollar* spent on hamburgers than you did before the price increase. Moreover, since you still have only $10 to spend, if you choose to continue buying three hamburgers, you will have to give up three orders of French fries, which means, in effect, that you will have to sacrifice 75 utils (the aggregate marginal utility of the second, third, and fourth orders of French fries, which you can still purchase for $3) to gain a mere 40 utils (the marginal utility of the third hamburger). Needless to say, if you are a rational consumer, you will not be willing to make such a sacrifice.

Instead, you will seek to maximize your utility under the new conditions by buying fewer hamburgers and more French fries. If you do so, you will increase the ratio of marginal utility to price for hamburgers, you will decrease the ratio of marginal utility to price for French fries, and you will thus establish a new point of balance between the two. That new point will be two hamburgers and five orders of French fries.

$$\frac{MU_H}{P_H} = \frac{45}{\$3} = \frac{15}{\$1} \qquad \frac{MU_F}{P_F} = \frac{15}{\$1}$$

Since the two ratios are equal at that point, you can be sure that you are maximizing your utility. No other affordable combination of hamburgers and French fries will provide you with as much satisfaction. You can also be sure that you are confirming the validity of the law of demand: other things being equal, if price increases, quantity demanded decreases.

D. Value is related to marginal rather than total utility.

Early economists were puzzled by a paradox of value: why are diamonds, which are not essential to life, more expensive than water, which is? The concept of marginal utility—or, more precisely, the distinction between marginal utility and total utility—helps to resolve this paradox.

The value that a consumer places on a good, which is reflected in the price that he or she is willing to pay for the good, is related to the marginal, rather than the total, utility that the consumer derives from the good. As you may be able to infer from the law of diminishing marginal utility, as consumers we tend to place a low value on additional units of a good that we consume in very large quantities. This is true of a plentiful good such as water. Thus, although the total utility that we derive from water is immense, the marginal utility that we derive from an additional unit of water—and hence the price that we are willing to pay for it—is low. Conversely, we tend to place a high value on additional units of a good that we consume in very small quantities. This is true of a relatively scarce good such as diamonds. Thus, although the total utility that we derive from diamonds is low, the marginal utility that we derive from an additional diamond—and hence the price that we are willing to pay for it—is high.

8-3. The Indifference Curve Approach

Unlike the marginal utility approach to consumer behavior, the indifference curve approach does not assume that consumers can quantify their levels of satisfaction. It assumes only that they can rank various combinations of goods in order of their preference. For example, given the choice between combination A and combination B, a consumer need only be able to state a preference for A or B, if one affords more satisfaction than the other, or express an indifference to the choice, if both combinations afford the same amount of utility.

The indifference curve approach involves indifference curves and budget lines.

A. An indifference curve connects points of equal satisfaction.

An **indifference curve** is a set of points representing various combinations of two goods that yield the same level of satisfaction to a consumer—combinations, in other words, about which a consumer is *indifferent*.

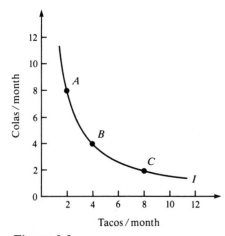

Figure 8-3
Combinations of goods along an indifference curve (*I*) provide equal satisfaction or utility.

EXAMPLE 8-4: Figure 8-3 shows a hypothetical indifference curve (*I*) for Jane Smith. Each point on the curve represents a different combination or bundle of two goods, tacos and colas. For instance, point *A* represents two tacos and eight colas; point *B*, four tacos and four colas; point *C*, eight tacos and two colas. The curve is called an indifference curve for an obvious reason: Jane Smith doesn't care which combination of tacos and colas she chooses because, from her point of view, they are all equally satisfactory. All of them will provide her with the same level of utility.

B. Indifference curves have four properties.

1. *Indifference curves have negative slopes.* Economists assume that goods provide utility. An indifference curve shows combinations of two goods, each of which provides utility. The utility level remains constant along an indifference curve. Therefore an indifference curve must have a negative slope. A negative slope implies that, if a consumer receives more units of one good, he or she can maintain a constant utility level only by sacrificing some of the other good.

2. *Indifference curves bow inward toward the origin of a graph.* Economists assume that, given two goods and a constant level of utility, the amount of one good that a consumer will exchange for an additional unit of the second good diminishes with each successive exchange. Therefore indifference curves bow inward toward the origin of a graph. The inward bow of an indifference curve reflects what economists refer to as the diminishing *marginal rate of substitution* of the good represented on the *x*-axis (good X) for the good represented on the *y*-axis (good Y).

   The **marginal rate of substitution (MRS)** of good X for good Y is the number of units of good Y that can be replaced by one additional unit of good X.

   When the rate at which good X can be substituted for good Y diminishes, a curve bows inward: the absolute value of its slope decreases. The MRS of good X for good Y is equal to the absolute value of the slope of an indifference curve.

EXAMPLE 8-5: The hypothetical indifference curve for Jane Smith in Figure 8-3 bows inward toward the origin of the graph, indicating a diminishing marginal rate of substitution of tacos for colas for Jane Smith. Between points *A* and *B*, Jane Smith is willing to give up as many as two colas to obtain an additional taco. (The absolute value of the average slope between points *A* and *B* is 2.) Between points *B* and *C*, however, she is willing to give up no more than half a cola to obtain an additional taco. (The absolute value of the average slope between points *B* and *C* is 1/2.)

3. *Indifference curves that lie to the northeast represent higher levels of satisfaction.* Economists assume that consumers always prefer more of a good to less. On an indifference diagram, commodity bundles that contain more of both goods are represented by points that lie to the northeast. Therefore indifference curves that lie to the northeast represent higher levels of satisfaction.

EXAMPLE 8-6: Figure 8-4 shows two hypothetical indifference curves for Jane Smith, I_1 and I_2. Indifference curve I_2 lies to the northeast of indifference curve I_1 and thus represents more colas and tacos and a higher level of satisfaction for Jane Smith. At point *D*, for example, Jane Smith has eight colas and eight tacos as compared with the four colas and four tacos that she has at point *B* on indifference curve I_1.

Jane Smith ranks all of the combinations of colas and tacos on indifference curve I_1 as equally satisfactory. Likewise, she ranks all of the combinations of colas and tacos on indifference curve I_2 as equally

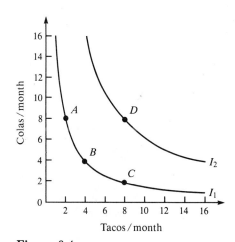

Figure 8-4
Indifference curve I_2 lies to the northeast of I_1 and thus represents a higher level of satisfaction.

satisfactory. However, because all of the combinations on indifference curve I_2 provide her with a higher level of satisfaction, she naturally prefers any one of them to any combination on indifference curve I_1. If point D is within her budget, then, Jane Smith will prefer it to point A, B, C, or any other point on indifference curve I_1.

4. *Indifference curves do not intersect.* Economists assume that consumers are rational. Intersecting indifference curves would imply irrationality in the ranking of commodity bundles. Therefore indifference curves do not intersect.

C. A budget line shows affordable combinations.

Indifference curves reveal a consumer's preferences for various combinations of two goods, but they don't show which combinations the consumer can actually afford. A budget line does that.

A **budget line** is a set of points representing various combinations of two goods that a consumer can purchase, at given prices, with a given expenditure.

A budget line is drawn from the *y*-axis on a graph to the *x*-axis. The *y*-intercept, the point at which the budget line begins on the *y*-axis, represents the number of units of good Y (whatever it happens to be) that a consumer can purchase, at a given price, if he or she spends his or her entire budget on good Y and does not buy any units of good X. Similarly, the *x*-intercept, the point at which the budget line ends on the *x*-axis, represents the number of units of good X that a consumer can purchase, at a given price, if he or she spends his or her entire budget on good X and does not buy any units of good Y.

As long as the prices of the two goods are constant, a budget line is linear (straight), and all of the points on the line that lie on or between the *y*-intercept and the *x*-intercept represent various affordable combinations of the two goods that will exhaust the consumer's budget. The consumer can also purchase combinations that lie inside (to the left of) the budget line for a smaller expenditure, but those outside (to the right) are not affordable.

EXAMPLE 8-7: Let's assume that Jane Smith has a budget of $10 to spend on colas and tacos each month. Colas are selling for 50¢ apiece; tacos, for $1 apiece. We can locate the two extremes of her budget line, the *y*- and *x*-intercepts, if we assume that she spends all of her money on colas, on the one hand, and all of her money on tacos, on the other hand. If she spends all of her money on colas, she can purchase 20 colas ($10 ÷ $0.50 = 20), so the *y*-intercept of her budget line is 20, as shown in Figure 8-5. If she spends all of her money on tacos, she can purchase 10 tacos ($10 ÷ $1 = 10), so the *x*-intercept of her budget line is 10. Now, assuming that the prices of colas and tacos are constant, we can complete Jane Smith's budget line for colas and tacos simply by connecting the two points.

The budget line (*BB*) in Figure 8-5 doesn't tell us which combinations of tacos and colas Jane Smith prefers—which ones, in other words, provide her with the highest level of satisfaction or utility. It tells us only which ones she can afford. Given the prices of tacos and colas and a limited budget of $10, Jane can afford the combinations that lie on her budget line because they all cost exactly $10. She can also afford the combinations that lie inside her budget line because they all cost less than $10. But she can't afford the combinations that lie to the right of her budget line because they all cost more than $10.

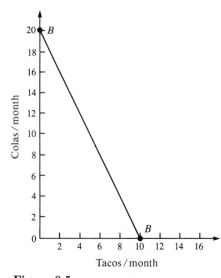

Figure 8-5

A budget line (*BB*) shows combinations of two goods, at given prices, that a consumer can purchase with a given expenditure.

D. A budget line has four important properties.

1. *A budget line has a negative slope.* A negative slope implies that, if a consumer purchases more units of one good, he or she must purchase fewer units of the other good in order to maintain a constant level of expenditure.

2. *A budget line has a slope equal to the negative ratio of the price of good X to the price of good Y.*

$$\text{slope} = -\frac{P_X}{P_Y}$$

EXAMPLE 8-8: The slope of Jane Smith's hypothetical budget line in Figure 8-5 is the negative ratio of the price of tacos, $1, to the price of colas, $0.50: $-(\$1/\$0.50) = -2$. A slope of -2 means that Jane Smith must give up two colas in order to obtain one additional taco.

3. *A budget line shifts when a consumer's income changes.* A change in a consumer's income results in a parallel shift in the consumer's budget line. An increase in income shifts the consumer's budget line right, indicating that he or she can afford to buy more of both goods. A decrease in income shifts the consumer's budget line left, indicating that he or she can't afford to buy as much of either good.

EXAMPLE 8-9: If Jane Smith's income increased, her budget line for colas and tacos would shift right, as shown in Figure 8-6. Because she would be able to purchase proportionately more colas or tacos or some combination of the two, her new budget line, $B'B'$, would be parallel to her old budget line, BB.

4. *A budget line rotates when the price of a good changes.* If the price of good X changes and the price of good Y doesn't, the budget line remains fixed on the y-intercept and rotates along the x-axis, indicating that more or fewer units of good X can be purchased with the same amount of money. If the price of good Y changes and the price of good X doesn't, the budget line remains fixed on the x-intercept and rotates along the y-axis, indicating that more or fewer units of good Y can be purchased with the same amount of money.

EXAMPLE 8-10: Budget line BB in Figure 8-7 is Jane Smith's original $10 budget line for colas and tacos. Let's assume, now, that the price of tacos increases from $1 to $2. If Jane's income and the price of colas (50¢) remain constant, she will still be able to buy 20 colas with her $10, so the y-intercept of her budget line will stay where it is. However, she will now be able to afford only half as many tacos, so her x-intercept will decline from 10 to 5. Since the budget line will remain anchored at 20 colas on the y-axis, the decline in the x-intercept will cause the budget line to rotate from BB to BB' in Figure 8-7. As the new budget line shows, the only commodity bundle that will *not* be affected by the increase in the price of tacos is the bundle that contains only colas. All of the other bundles include some tacos and will therefore be smaller than they were before the price increase.

E. Maximum satisfaction is attained when the budget line is tangent to an indifference curve.

A consumer attains maximum satisfaction by choosing the affordable combination of two goods that provides the highest level of satisfaction possible. That combination is represented graphically by the

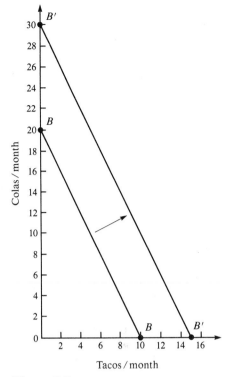

Figure 8-6
An increase in a consumer's income causes a parallel shift to the right in the consumer's budget line (BB to $B'B'$).

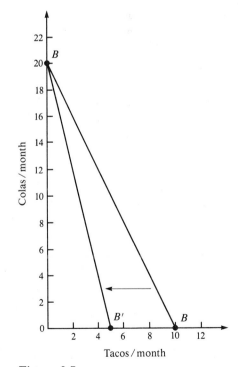

Figure 8-7
An increase in the price of tacos rotates the budget line clockwise through a point on the cola axis (BB to BB').

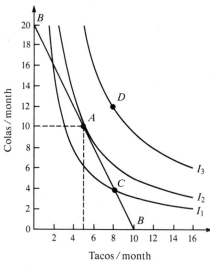

Figure 8-8
Maximum consumer satisfaction is represented by *A*, the point of tangency between the budget line (*BB*) and the highest attainable indifference curve (I_2).

point where the consumer's highest attainable indifference curve is tangent to his or her budget line.

EXAMPLE 8-11: Figure 8-8 shows Jane Smith's budget line (*BB*) for colas and tacos and three of her indifference curves for the two goods, I_1, I_2, and I_3. If Jane Smith follows the rule for maximizing her satisfaction, she will select commodity bundle *A*. Point *A* is on her budget line, which means that it is affordable, and it is also on her highest attainable indifference curve, which means that it will provide her with more satisfaction than any other affordable combination.

Point *D* on indifference curve I_3 represents a higher level of satisfaction, but it is unaffordable. Point *C* is on her budget line and is therefore affordable, but it is also on a lower indifference curve, I_1, and so it represents a lower level of satisfaction. (Notice that I_1 *intersects* the budget line; it is not *tangent* to it, as I_2 is.) With her particular tastes and preferences, Jane Smith can get more satisfaction for the same expenditure simply by choosing point *A* over point *C*.

F. At the point of maximum satisfaction, the slopes of the budget line and the indifference curve are equal.

As you recall from Chapter 3, the slope of a curve at any point is equal to the slope of the straight line tangent to the curve at that point. Thus, the slope of a consumer's highest attainable indifference curve is equal to the slope of the consumer's budget line at the point of tangency between the two curves. Now, the slope of the consumer's indifference curve is equal to the negative value of the marginal rate of substitution (MRS) of good X for good Y. The slope of the consumer's budget line is equal to the negative ratio of the price of good X to the price of good Y. Therefore, at the point at which the consumer attains maximum satisfaction, the MRS of good X for good Y is equal to the ratio of the price of good X to the price of good Y:

$$\text{MRS} = \frac{P_X}{P_Y}$$

At point *A* in Figure 8-8, the MRS of tacos for colas is equal to the ratio of the price of tacos ($1) to the price of colas ($0.50), which is equal to 2.

8-4. Indifference Curve Analysis

In Chapters 5 and 6 you learned about the predictable effects that changes in income and price have on consumer behavior. Indifference curve analysis can be used to substantiate and to illustrate those effects.

A. An increase in income increases demand for an income-superior good.

Figure 8-9 uses indifference curve analysis to illustrate the effect that an increase in consumer income has on the consumer's demand curve for an income-superior good. As you recall from Chapter 6, an income-superior good, by definition, is a good whose consumption increases as income increases.

As the upper portion of the figure shows, an increase in consumer income causes a parallel shift to the right in the consumer's budget line (from *BB* to *B'B'*). When the budget line shifts, the point of maximum satisfaction for the consumer also shifts because the new budget line is tangent to a higher indifference curve. In this case, the point shifts from *A* to *E*, where the consumer—Jane Smith, again—maximizes her satisfaction by consuming more colas and more tacos, which for her are both income-superior goods. Point *A*, as you can see, represents

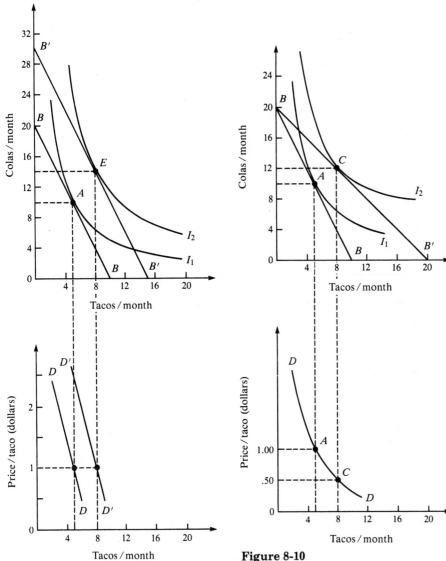

Figure 8-9

An increase in income causes the consumer's budget line (upper portion) and the consumer's demand curve for an income-superior good (lower portion) to shift right, *ceteris paribus.*

Figure 8-10

A decrease in the price of tacos rotates the budget line outward on the *x*-axis (upper portion), resulting in an increase in quantity consumed. The demand curve for tacos (lower portion) has a negative slope.

only five tacos and ten colas; point *E* represents eight tacos and fourteen colas.

The lower portion of Figure 8-9 illustrates the effect that the increase in Jane Smith's income has on her demand curve for tacos. (The effect on her demand curve for colas is similar.) Since she will seek to purchase eight tacos instead of five for the same price, $1, her demand curve for tacos will shift right, from *DD* to *D'D'*, indicating that she is both willing and able to purchase a larger number of tacos at each price at which they might be offered.

B. A decrease in the price of a good increases the quantity demanded of the good.

Figure 8-10 uses indifference curve analysis to illustrate the effect that a decrease in the price of a good has on the quantity demanded of the good when consumer income and the prices of other goods are held constant. As the upper portion of the figure shows, a reduction in the price of tacos from $1 to 50¢ causes Jane Smith's budget line to rotate outward on the x-axis (from BB to BB'). As a result of the rotation, her budget line becomes tangent to a higher indifference curve, I_2, and her optimal commodity bundle shifts from point A to point C. Point A represents a bundle that contains only five tacos. Point C represents a bundle that contains eight tacos. Thus, as the price of tacos goes down, Jane Smith maximizes her satisfaction by increasing the quantity of tacos that she consumes.

The lower portion of the figure illustrates the effect that a reduction in the price of tacos has on the quantity of tacos that Jane Smith demands. It shows, in other words, how Jane Smith's demand curve for tacos is derived. At a price of $1, Jane Smith is willing and able to purchase five tacos. At a price of 50¢, she is willing and able to purchase eight tacos. Thus, as you can see, her demand curve for tacos has a downward or negative slope, which is consistent with the inverse relationship between price and quantity demanded predicated in the law of demand.

RAISE YOUR GRADES
Can you explain...?

☑ why consumers seldom satisfy all of their material wants
☑ why the marginal utility of a good diminishes as more units of the good are consumed
☑ how a consumer attains maximum satisfaction in the marginal utility approach
☑ how the law of demand can be derived from the marginal utility approach
☑ how the paradox of value is resolved
☑ why indifference curves have negative slopes
☑ why indifference curves bow inward toward the origin of a graph
☑ why budget lines are usually straight lines
☑ why a change in consumer income causes a budget line to shift
☑ how a consumer's optimal commodity bundle is identified in the indifference curve approach
☑ how a demand curve can be derived through indifference curve analysis

SUMMARY

1. In analyzing consumer behavior, economists assume (1) that consumers can satisfy their general wants and needs with a variety of goods and services; (2) that consumers are constrained in their search for satisfaction by the limits of their incomes; (3) that consumers aim to satisfy as many of their wants and needs as their limited incomes allow.
2. Economists analyze consumer behavior in two alternative ways: the marginal utility approach and the indifference curve approach.
3. The marginal utility approach is based on the premise that the satisfaction or utility that a consumer derives from a good is quantifiable.

4. *Total utility* is the cumulative satisfaction that a consumer derives from the consumption of successive units of a good.

5. *Marginal utility* is the satisfaction that a consumer derives from the consumption of each *additional* unit of a good. More technically, *marginal utility* is the change in total utility for a one-unit change in quantity consumed.

6. As a general rule, the satisfaction that a consumer derives from each additional unit of a good diminishes with consumption. This rule is known as the *law of diminishing marginal utility*.

7. In the marginal utility approach, a consumer attains maximum satisfaction when the ratio of marginal utility to price (the marginal utility per dollar) is the same for all goods consumed.

8. Other things being equal, an increase in the price of a good reduces its marginal utility per dollar, and a decrease in the consumption of a good increases its marginal utility per dollar. Therefore, when the price of a good goes up, a utility-maximizing consumer buys less of the good. This behavior explains the law of demand.

9. The distinction between total and marginal utility resolves the diamond–water paradox of value. Value is related to marginal utility, not total utility. Water provides more total utility than diamonds, but it is so plentiful that its marginal utility is low.

10. The indifference curve approach is based on the premise that consumers can rank various combinations of goods in order of their preference.

11. An *indifference curve* is a set of points representing various combinations of two goods that yield the same level of satisfaction to a consumer.

12. Indifference curves have four properties: (**1**) they have negative slopes; (**2**) they bow inward toward the origin of a graph; (**3**) they represent increasing levels of satisfaction to the northeast; (**4**) they do not intersect.

13. The *marginal rate of substitution* (*MRS*) of good X for good Y is the number of units of good Y that a consumer maintaining a constant level of satisfaction will give up in order to obtain an additional unit of good X. The MRS of good X for good Y diminishes along an indifference curve.

14. The MRS of good X for good Y is equal to the absolute value of the slope of an indifference curve.

15. A *budget line* is a set of points representing various combinations of two goods, at given prices, that a consumer can purchase with a given expenditure.

16. Budget lines have four properties: (**1**) they have negative slopes; (**2**) they have slopes equal to the negative ratio of the price of good X to the price of good Y; (**3**) they shift in a parallel manner when consumer income changes; (**4**) they rotate when the price of good X or the price of good Y changes.

17. In the indifference curve approach, maximum consumer satisfaction is represented graphically by the point of tangency between the consumer's budget line and the consumer's highest attainable indifference curve.

18. In the indifference curve approach, at the point of maximum consumer satisfaction the MRS of good X for good Y is equal to the ratio of the price of good X to the price of good Y: $MRS = P_X/P_Y$.

19. An increase in income shifts a consumer's budget line to the right and makes it tangent to a higher indifference curve. If the new point of tangency represents an increase in the consumption of a good, the good is income superior and the consumer's demand curve for the good

shifts right. If it represents a decrease in the consumption of a good, the good is income inferior and the consumer's demand curve for the good shifts left.

20. A decrease in the price of good X rotates a consumer's budget line outward on the *x*-axis and makes it tangent to a higher indifference curve. The new point of tangency nearly always represents an increase in the consumption of good X, which explains the law of demand.

21. A consumer's demand curve for a good can be derived through indifference curve analysis by varying the price of the good and holding income and the prices of other goods constant. As the price of the good is varied, the consumer's budget line rotates and becomes tangent to various indifference curves. The points of tangency represent quantity demanded at the various prices.

RAPID REVIEW

1. Consumers can satisfy their wants and needs in a broad category such as food with a _____ of different goods and services. [See Section 8-1.]

2. Consumers purchase goods and services in quantities and combinations that yield the maximum _____ attainable with their limited incomes. [See Section 8-1.]

3. Two common approaches to the study of consumer behavior are the _____ _____ approach and the _____ _____ approach. [See Section 8-1.]

4. _____ *utility* is the change in total utility for a one-unit change in quantity consumed. [See Section 8-2.]

5. As a general rule, total utility diminishes as additional units of a good are consumed. True or false? [See Section 8-2.]

6. If the third doughnut that you consume provides you with 8 units of utility, the fourth one will provide you with (**a**) 8 utils, (**b**) more than 8 utils, (**c**) less than 8 utils, (**d**) twice as many utils. [See Section 8-2.]

7. In the marginal utility approach, a consumer attains maximum satisfaction when the ratios of marginal utility to price are _____ for all goods purchased. [See Section 8-2.]

8. If the price of doughnuts declines, a consumer will buy (**a**) fewer doughnuts so that their marginal utility will increase, (**b**) fewer doughnuts so that their marginal utility will decrease, (**c**) more doughnuts so that their marginal utility will increase, (**d**) more doughnuts so that their marginal utility will decrease. [See Section 8-2.]

9. The price of a pound of gold is higher than the price of a pound of corn because gold provides more total utility than corn. True or false? [See Section 8-2.]

10. The indifference curve approach requires that consumers be able to rank various _____ of goods in order of preference. [See Section 8-3.]

11. An *indifference curve* is a locus of points representing various combinations of two goods that yield various levels of satisfaction to a consumer. True or false? [See Section 8-3.]

12. Indifference curves (**a**) have positive slopes, (**b**) bow outward from the origin of a graph, (**c**) do not intersect, (**d**) all of these. [See Section 8-3.]

13. The _____ _____ of substitution of good X for good Y is the number of units of good Y that a consumer will give up in exchange for an additional unit of good X and still maintain a constant level of satisfaction. [See Section 8-3.]

14. A _____ line shows all of the combinations of two goods that a consumer can purchase, at given prices, with a given expenditure. [See Section 8-3.]

15. If a combination of goods costs less than a consumer's available budget, it is represented graphically by a point that lies (**a**) on the consumer's highest possible indifference curve, (**b**) on the consumer's budget line, (**c**) to the right of the consumer's budget line, (**d**) to the left of the consumer's budget line. [See Section 8-3.]

16. The slope of a budget line is equal in absolute value to the ratio of the _____ of good X and good Y. [See Section 8-3.]

17. An increase in the price of good Y causes a consumer's budget line to (**a**) rotate outward on the *y*-axis, (**b**) shift right in a parallel manner, (**c**) rotate outward on the *x*-axis, (**d**) rotate inward on the *y*-axis. [See Section 8-3.]

18. In the indifference curve approach, optimal satisfaction is represented graphically by the point at which the consumer's budget line is _____ to the consumer's highest attainable indifference curve. [See Section 8-3.]

19. If the price of good X equals $4 and the price of good Y equals $1, then the MRS of good X for good Y equals _____ at the point where a consumer with a limited budget attains maximum satisfaction. [See Section 8-3.]

20. As a result of a decrease in income, a consumer's budget line shifts _____ and becomes tangent to a lower indifference curve. If the point of tangency represents an increase in the consumption of a good, the good is income _____ and the consumer's demand curve for the good shifts _____. [See Section 8-4.]

21. A consumer's _____ curve for a good can be derived through indifference curve analysis by varying the price of the good while holding income and the prices of other goods constant. [See Section 8-4.]

Answers
1. variety   **2.** satisfaction or utility   **3.** marginal utility, indifference curve   **4.** *Marginal*
5. false   **6.** (**c**)   **7.** equal or the same   **8.** (**d**)   **9.** false   **10.** combinations   **11.** false
12. (**c**)   **13.** marginal rate   **14.** budget   **15.** (**d**)   **16.** prices   **17.** (**d**)   **18.** tangent
19. 4/1 or 4   **20.** left, inferior, right   **21.** demand

SOLVED PROBLEMS

PROBLEM 8-1 As you recall from Chapter 2, economists assume that people, as economic entities, behave purposefully and efficiently. Explain the relevance of these two assumptions to theories of consumer behavior.

Answer: To say that people behave purposefully is to say that their actions are directed toward the achievement of some goal. That goal for people *as consumers* is utility—the satisfaction of material needs and wants. Thus economists base their theories of consumer behavior on the assumption that consumers purchase goods and services that provide the satisfaction that they seek for their material needs and wants.

To say that people behave efficiently is to say that they seek the best way to achieve their goals. The best way for people *as consumers* to satisfy their many needs and wants is to spend their limited incomes on goods and services that provide as much utility as possible. Thus economists base their analysis of consumer behavior on the assumption that consumers purchase goods and services in quantities and in combinations that satisfy as many of their material needs and wants as market prices and their own limited incomes will allow. [See Section 8-1.]

PROBLEM 8-2 (*Marginal utility approach*) Construct a graph of the total utility that you might derive from consuming slices of your favorite pizza. Assume that you must consume all of the slices within a one-hour period. Does your total utility curve display diminishing marginal utility? Explain your answer.

Answer: Figure 8-11 is a graph of a typical total utility curve. It shows the cumulative satisfaction that you might derive from consuming successive slices of your favorite pizza in a one-hour period. Your graph, of course, might look somewhat different. Since the measurement of utility or satisfaction is subjective, you may have higher or lower units of utility (utils) on your *y*-axis.

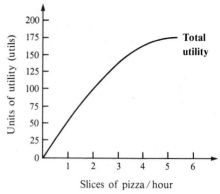

Figure 8-11

The total utility curve shown here does exhibit diminishing marginal utility: the slope of the curve decreases as the number of slices of pizza consumed increases. The decreasing slope indicates that each additional slice of pizza contributes less to your total utility than the preceding piece did. In other words, the marginal satisfaction that you derive from consuming the fifth or the sixth piece is less than the marginal satisfaction that you derive from consuming the first or the second one. Diminishing marginal utility is such a common phenomenon that economists refer to it as a law.

Linear total utility curves and total utility curves that turn up instead of down do not display diminishing marginal utility. These types of total utility curves are rare. [See Section 8-2.]

PROBLEM 8-3 (*Marginal utility approach*) Assume that you have $40 to spend on gold-plated necklaces and T-shirts. The price of a necklace is $10; the price of a T-shirt is $5. The units of utility that you derive from consuming successive units of each good are shown in the following marginal utility schedules.

Necklaces		T-Shirts	
Quantity	MU	Quantity	MU
1	100	1	40
2	90	2	35
3	70	3	30
4	40	4	25
5	10	5	20

How should you allocate your funds on the two goods so that you get a maximum amount of utility from your $40 expenditure?

Answer: You will maximize your satisfaction if you allocate your funds for each purchase to the product that yields the higher utility per dollar—that is, the product with the higher MU-to-price ratio. Since the marginal utility of an additional unit of each good diminishes with consumption, the MU-to-price ratio also diminishes with quantity consumed. These ratios are shown in the following table:

Necklaces			T-Shirts		
Quantity	MU	MU/*P*	Quantity	MU	MU/*P*
1	100	10	1	40	8
2	90	9	2	35	7
3	70	7	3	30	6
4	40	4	4	25	5
5	10	1	5	20	4

The first item that you purchase should be a necklace. Even though it is twice as expensive as a T-shirt, the first necklace has a higher MU-to-price ratio than the first T-shirt (10 versus 8) and thus will provide you with more utility per dollar. The second item likewise should be a necklace (9 versus 8), but the third item should be a T-shirt (8 versus 7). The fourth and fifth items should be a necklace and a T-shirt. Since the MU-to-price ratio is the same for the third necklace (7) and the second T-shirt (7), the order in which you purchase them is unimportant. Three necklaces ($30) and two T-shirts ($10) will exhaust your $40 budget. [See Section 8-2.]

PROBLEM 8-4 (*Marginal utility approach*) Consumer X purchases two items, steak and spinach. The marginal utility of steak is 40 and the price $5. The marginal utility of spinach is 10 and the price $1. Explain why Consumer X is not maximizing his utility. How should he adjust his purchases to increase his satisfaction?

Answer: Consumer X is not maximizing his utility because the MU-to-price ratios of the two goods that he is purchasing are not equal. For steak the ratio is 40/5 or 8; for spinach the ratio is 10/1 or 10. Since the ratio for spinach is higher, Consumer X can increase his total utility by increasing his consumption of spinach. [See Section 8-2.]

PROBLEM 8-5 (*Marginal utility approach*) Suppose that you have a budget of $90 for records and textbooks. The units of utility that you derive from consuming successive units of the two goods are shown in the following marginal utility schedules.

Records		Textbooks	
Quantity	MU	Quantity	MU
1	20	1	60
2	15	2	40
3	10	3	20
4	8	4	5

The price of records is $10; the price of textbooks is $20. Assuming that you spend your entire $90 budget, explain the order in which you should select the two items so that you maximize your utility with each purchase.

Answer: You should make your purchasing decisions in the same way that you made your purchasing decisions about gold-plated necklaces and T-shirts in Problem 8-3. Each time you make a purchase, you should allocate your funds to the item that has the higher MU-to-price ratio and thus will afford you more marginal utility per dollar.

In this case the first item that you select should be a textbook because the first textbook provides more marginal utility per dollar (60/20 = 3) than the first record (20/10 = 2). The second and third items should be a record and a textbook in either order. Both provide 2 utils per dollar (20/10 = 2; 40/20 = 2). The fourth item should be a record because the second record provides more utils per dollar (15/10 = 1.5) than the third textbook (20/20 = 1). The fifth and sixth items again should be a record and a textbook, and again you may select them in either order because they both provide 1 util per dollar (10/10 = 1; 20/20 = 1). Three textbooks at $20 each and three records at $10 each will exhaust your $90 budget. [See Section 8-2.]

PROBLEM 8-6 (*Marginal utility approach*) Assume that the price of textbooks in Problem 8-5 rises to $30 while the price of records, your budget, and your marginal utility schedules for the two items remain constant. What combination of records and textbooks will maximize your utility now? Do textbooks obey the law of demand? Explain your answer.

Answer: After the price increase, your optimal combination will be three records and two textbooks, which you will purchase in the following order: record (20/10) or textbook (60/30); record (20/10) or textbook (60/30); record (15/10); textbook (40/30); record (10/10). Although the MU-to-price ratios for the two items are not equal (the 40/30 ratio for the second textbook is greater than the 10/10 ratio for the third record), they are as close as you can get without purchasing fractions of the two items. If you could purchase fractions of each good, you could equalize their MU-to-price ratios.

Yes, textbooks do obey the law of demand. The increase in their price leads you to reduce the quantity that you consume. [See Section 8-2.]

PROBLEM 8-7 (*Marginal utility approach*) Assume that you are shipwrecked in the Pacific Ocean. You find yourself lying in the searing sun on a barren atoll with little or no drinking water. Explain why the diamond–water paradox of value is irrelevant to your situation.

Answer: The diamond–water paradox of value arises because water is usually so plentiful and we consume so much of it that we place a lower value on it than we do on diamonds. This usual situation is represented graphically by point *A* on the total utility curve for water in Figure 8-12. However, if you were shipwrecked on a barren atoll where drinking water was either unavailable or very scarce, you would place a much higher marginal value on it than you would ordinarily. In fact, you would no doubt place a much higher marginal value on a glass of water than you would on a diamond, which, under the circumstances, would be of little or no use to you in your struggle for survival. This unusual situation is represented graphically by point *B* in Figure 8-12. [See Section 8-2.]

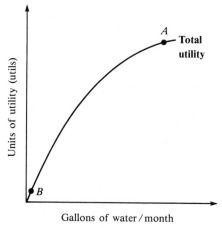

Figure 8-12

PROBLEM 8-8 (*Indifference curve approach*) Figure 8-13 shows three hypothetical indifference curves for Consumer Y. Points *A*, *B*, *C*, *D*, and *E* all represent various combinations of records and textbooks. Which combination represents the lowest level of satisfaction for Consumer Y? Which one represents the highest level? About which combinations is Consumer Y indifferent? Explain your answers.

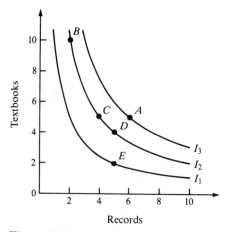

Figure 8-13

Answer: Point *E* lies on the lowest of the three indifference curves—the one closest to the origin of the graph—and thus represents the smallest bundle of records and textbooks, five and two, respectively. Point *A* lies on the highest of the three indifference curves—the one farthest to the northeast—and thus represents the largest bundle of records and textbooks, six and five, respectively. Since economists assume that goods provide utility and that more goods therefore provide more utility, point *A* represents the highest level of satisfaction for Consumer Y and point *E* the lowest.

Points *B*, *C*, and *D* all lie on the same indifference curve and thus represent the same level of satisfaction for Consumer Y. Since Consumer Y ranks bundles *B*, *C*, and *D* as equally satisfactory, she is indifferent about whether she receives two records and ten textbooks (*B*), four records and five textbooks (*C*), or five records and four textbooks (*D*). [See Section 8-3.]

PROBLEM 8-9 (*Indifference curve approach*) Consider the strange, atypical indifference curves in Figures 8-14 and 8-15. Interpret the relationship between good X and good Y in each figure. Give examples of goods that might be related in these ways.

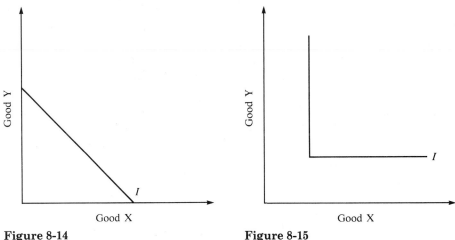

Figure 8-14   **Figure 8-15**

Answer: Good X and good Y in Figure 8-14 are perfect substitutes for one another. Two goods that might be perfect substitutes for one another are two brands of cola soft drinks. If a consumer doesn't prefer one brand to another, a bottle of brand X can be substituted for a bottle of brand Y without altering the consumer's level of satisfaction. Other goods that might be perfect substitutes for one another are bushels of wheat, corn, or another commodity; brands of milk; brands of cornflakes; brands of beer; and so on.

Good X and good Y in Figure 8-15 are used only in fixed proportions. Goods that are ordinarily used only in fixed proportions are right and left shoes, right and left gloves, and so on. So long as the extras could be stored or disposed of at no cost, a consumer would be indifferent to a choice between one right shoe and one left shoe, on the one hand (or foot), and one right shoe and, say, four left shoes, on the other. [See Section 8-3.]

PROBLEM 8-10 (*Indifference curve approach*) Consider indifference curve I_2 in Figure 8-13 once again. Demonstrate that the marginal rate of substitution (MRS) of records for textbooks diminishes along the curve.

Answer: As you recall from Section 8-3, the MRS of good X for good Y is the number of units of good Y that can be replaced by one additional unit of good X on the same indifference curve. In this case good X is records and good Y is textbooks. If you compare the number of textbooks that can be replaced by one record between points *B* and *C* with the number of textbooks that can be replaced by one record between points *C* and *D*, you will see that the MRS of records for textbooks diminishes along the indifference curve.

Between points *B* and *C*, five textbooks can be replaced by two records, so the MRS is 2.5 between points *B* and *C*. Between points *C* and *D*, one textbook can be replaced by one record, so the MRS is only 1 between points *C* and *D*. As you proceed along the curve, the MRS of records for textbooks, which is equal to the absolute value of the slope of the curve, continues to diminish. [See Section 8-3.]

PROBLEM 8-11 (*Indifference curve approach*) Figure 8-16 shows two intersecting indifference curves for a hypothetical consumer. Consider the points marked *A*, *B*, and *C*. Explain why intersecting indifference curves don't make sense for normal goods.

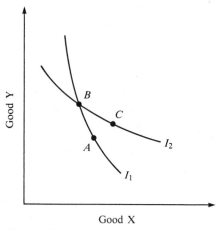

Figure 8-16

Answer: Points *A* and *B* lie on the same indifference curve (I_1); hence the consumer must be indifferent to the combinations of good X and good Y that these two points represent. Similarly, points *B* and *C* lie on the same indifference curve (I_2); hence the consumer must be indifferent to the combinations that they represent. If the consumer is indifferent to points *A* and *B* and to points *B* and *C*, then the consumer should also be indifferent to points *A* and *C*. However, point *C*, which lies to the northeast of point *A*, represents more records and more textbooks than point *A* does. Therefore the consumer cannot be indifferent to points *A* and *C* without contradicting one of the basic assumptions of consumer theory: that consumers always prefer a larger quantity of a good to a smaller quantity. Given that assumption, indifference curves cannot intersect. [See Section 8-3.]

PROBLEM 8-12 (*Indifference curve approach*) Construct your budget line for records and textbooks. Locate records along the *x*-axis and textbooks along the *y*-axis. The price of a record is $10; the price of a textbook is $20; your budget for the two goods is $90. Find the slope of your budget line.

Answer: One way to construct a budget line is to find the *x*- and *y*-intercepts of the line and then connect them. The *x*-intercept, in this case, is the number of units of good X (records) that you can purchase with your $90 if you don't purchase any units of good Y (textbooks). Thus the *x*-intercept of your budget line is 9 ($90 ÷ $10 = 9), as shown in Figure 8-17. The *y*-intercept is the number of units of good Y (textbooks) that you can purchase with your $90 if you don't buy any units of good X (records). Thus the *y*-intercept of your budget line is 4.5

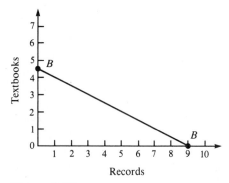

Figure 8-17

($90 ÷ $20 = 4.5), as also shown in Figure 8-17. The slope of your budget line is the ratio of the rise (the *y*-intercept) to the run (the *x*-intercept):

$$\text{slope} = \frac{-4.5}{9} = -0.5$$

This ratio is the same as the negative ratio of the price of good X (records) to the price of good Y (textbooks) [see Section 8-3]:

$$\text{slope} = -\frac{\$10}{\$20} = -0.5$$

PROBLEM 8-13 (*Indifference curve approach*) Figure 8-18 shows Consumer X's budget line, *BB*, and two of his indifference curves for tacos and colas, I_1 and I_2. Explain why Consumer X is not maximizing his satisfaction at point *A*.

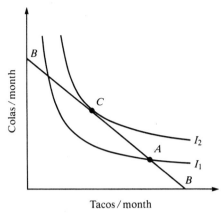

Figure 8-18

Answer: Points *A* and *C* both lie on Consumer X's budget line, which means that they both are affordable, they both cost the same amount of money, and they both exhaust his budget. Point *A*, however, lies on a lower indifference curve than point *C*. Therefore, Consumer X will attain a higher level of satisfaction if he reduces his purchases of tacos and increases his purchases of colas and thereby moves from point *A* to point *C*.

Point *C* fulfills the two requirements for utility maximization in the indifference curve approach: (1) it lies on the consumer's budget line, and (2) it lies on the highest of the consumer's attainable indifference curves. In other words, it is the point of tangency between the budget line and an indifference curve. [See Section 8-3.]

PROBLEM 8-14 (*Indifference curve approach*) Using indifference curve analysis, demonstrate graphically that a decrease in the price of a good will increase the quantity of the good demanded.

Answer: Begin by labeling a pair of axes "Good X" and "Good Y." Then sketch in a budget line with an indifference curve tangent to it. Label the budget line *BB* and the point of tangency *A*, as shown in Figure 8-19. A decrease in the price of good X will rotate the budget line outward on the *x*-axis, so sketch in a second budget line to represent the effect of the price decrease. It should extend from point *B* on the *y*-axis to point *B'* somewhere to the right of point *B* on the *x*-axis. Now draw in another indifference curve that is tangent to the new budget line, *BB'*. Label the new point of tangency *F*.

In all likelihood your diagram will look very much like the one shown here in Figure 8-19, with point *F* lying to the right of point *A*. Since point *F* represents a larger quantity (*Q'*) of good X than point *A* (*Q*), you have demonstrated graphically that a decrease in the price of good X will increase the consumption of good X, *ceteris paribus*. [See Section 8-4.]

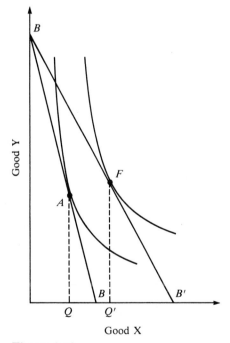

Figure 8-19

PROBLEM 8-15 (*Indifference curve approach*) Using the diagram that you just drew for Problem 8-14, find two quantity–price combinations on the demand curve for good X. Derive the demand curve for good X from your diagram. [*Note:* Your quantity–price combinations need not have numerical values. You may label them (*Q, P*) and (*Q', P'*).]

Answer: Points *A* and *F* in Figure 8-19 represent two quantity–price combinations in the demand schedule or on the demand curve for good X. Point *A* represents point (Q, P). Point *F* represents point (Q', P'). Although you may not have assigned numerical values to these points on your diagram, you know that quantity Q' is larger than quantity Q because it lies to the right of it on the *x*-axis. You also know that price P' is less than price P because the budget line rotates outward on the *x*-axis and becomes tangent to another indifference curve at point *F* as a result of a *decrease* in the price of good X.

To derive the demand curve for good X, then, simply construct another set of axes below your diagram for Problem 8-14. Label the *x*-axis "Quantity of good X per time period." (This label is not identical with the label on the *x*-axis in Figure 8-19, but it has exactly the same meaning, so you're measuring the same thing—quantity of good X—on the *x*-axis in both the upper and lower portions of your diagram.) Next, label the *y*-axis "Price per unit of good X," and make two tick marks on it, one for price P' and one *above* it for price P. (Price P, remember, is greater than price P'. How much greater doesn't matter.)

Now, to locate points (Q, P) and (Q', P') on the demand curve for good X, simply draw four lines. The first one should be parallel to the *y*-axis and should extend from point *A* in the upper portion of the diagram to the *x*-axis in the lower portion of the diagram, as shown in Figure 8-20. The second one should also be

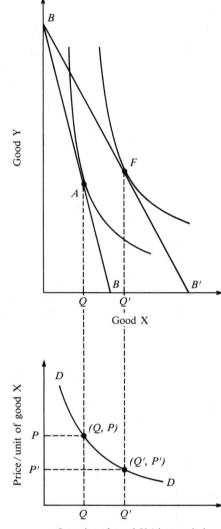

Figure 8-20

parallel to the *y*-axis and should extend from point *F* in the upper portion of the diagram to the *x*-axis in the lower portion. The third and fourth lines should be parallel to the *x*-axis and should extend from price *P* to the first line and from price P' to the second line, respectively.

The point at which the first and the third lines meet is point (Q, P), and the point at which the second and the fourth lines meet is point (Q', P'), as shown in Figure 8-20. To construct the demand curve for good X, simply connect these two points. Your demand curve, like the one in Figure 8-20, will have a negative slope. [See Section 8-4.]

9 PRODUCTION AND INPUT USE

9-1. Production

As you recall from Chapter 4, there are two separate sectors in the circular flow model of a market economy, the household sector and the producer sector. In the last two chapters you have been learning about the household sector—about consumer choices and demand. In this chapter you will begin learning about the producer sector—about producer choices and supply.

Later on you will be introduced to the economic theories or models of the various market structures that affect decisions about production: perfect competition, monopoly, monopolistic competition, and oligopoly. But first you must learn the rudiments of production, the basic concepts that apply to all market structures. These concepts are the focus of this chapter and the two that follow. Here you will learn about production functions, about fixed and variable inputs, about short-run and long-run production, and about economic efficiency in the selection of input combinations. In the next two chapters you will learn about production costs and about how producers maximize their profits.

9-2. Production Functions

As you recall from Chapter 1, goods are produced from three types of resources—land or natural resources, labor or human resources, and capital or man-made resources—with the aid of technology, society's knowledge of production. The relationship between output, technology, and these three types of resources can be expressed in terms of a production function.

A **production function** is an expression relating the maximum amount of a good that can be produced in a time period to various combinations of labor, capital, and natural resources and to technology.

$$\text{Output} = f(\text{labor, capital, natural resources})$$

Economists refer to the resources that are used to produce goods as *inputs* or *factors*. Technology, of course, is not itself an input or physical component of the production process. Rather it is the *means* by which various combinations of inputs are transformed into goods and services. Technology is *incorporated* in the factors of production—particularly the human and capital resources. Thus society's knowledge of production is present but invisible in the preceding production function.

A. Most goods are produced from both fixed and variable inputs.

- **Fixed inputs** are factors of production that do *not* vary in quantity with changes in output.
- **Variable inputs** are factors of production that *do* vary in quantity with changes in output.

EXAMPLE 9-1: A plant built to generate electricity is an example of a fixed input, and the fossil fuel used to generate the electricity is an example of a variable input. The amount of fuel used can be altered at any time to meet the load on the generating system and thus to increase or decrease output (kilowatt hours). The capacity and efficiency of the plant itself, however, can't be varied on a daily or even a yearly basis. The plant is a fixed input until it is either modified or abandoned.

B. Fixed inputs can be altered in the long run but not the short run.

The distinction between fixed and variable inputs gives rise to the distinction between two time periods in economic analysis: the short run and the long run.

- The **short run** is a time period within which at least one input is fixed.
- The **long run** is a time period within which *no* inputs are fixed—a time period, in other words, long enough for *all* inputs to be varied.

As the phrase *long enough* suggests, the short run and the long run are relative, not absolute, periods of time. The long run is relatively short for a young entrepreneur's summertime lemonade stand; the short run is relatively long for a nuclear power plant that takes years to build and depreciate.

Since all inputs (and therefore all costs) can be varied in the long run, producers obviously have more choices in the long run than they do in the short run. In the short run their decisions are necessarily influenced by the factors (and therefore the costs) of production that can't be altered.

9-3. Short-Run Production

Fixed inputs have two principal implications for short-run production:

1. Fixed inputs imply fixed costs. *Fixed costs* are costs that must be paid even if production is temporarily halted.
2. Fixed inputs limit the freedom of management to modify production. Because management has limited control over fixed inputs in the short run, the costs of production tend to be higher in the short run than they are in the long run.

EXAMPLE 9-2: As you learned in Example 9-1, a plant that generates electricity is a fixed input in the production of electricity. If for any reason the plant shuts down temporarily, it ceases to generate electricity, but it continues to generate costs—repair costs, maintenance costs, land-use costs, and so on. These costs are fixed costs—costs over which management has limited control in the short run.

Management similarly has limited control in the short run over the capacity or efficiency of an existing plant. The plant may be outdated technologically; it may be too small to meet current demands for electricity; it may be located in an area that prevents it from serving its present market as efficiently as possible. Nevertheless, management has no choice in the short run but to make do with what it has. Only in the long run can a new plant be constructed.

A. The law of diminishing returns applies to short-run production.

The **law of diminishing returns** states that, if one or more inputs are fixed, beyond some point the addition to output of each successive unit of a variable input declines. The law of diminishing returns implies that as more units of a variable input, such as labor, are added to a production process that includes at least one fixed input, beyond some point total output—or *total product*, as it is also called—increases at a decreasing rate. The effect of the law of diminishing returns on total output is illustrated in Figure 9-1. After the second unit of labor is added, diminishing returns set in, and the slope of the total product curve decreases.

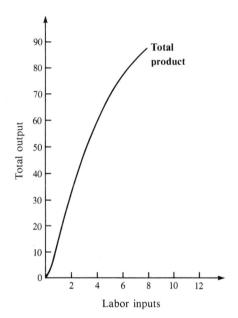

Figure 9-1
Because of the law of diminishing returns, total product increases at a decreasing rate beyond some point in the short run.

EXAMPLE 9-3: The law of diminishing returns was the basis for Thomas Malthus's gloomy predictions in the late 1700s about the fate of mankind. Malthus observed that the human population tends to increase rapidly under favorable conditions. He also observed that while labor (the human population) is a variable input in the production of food, tillable land is a fixed input. Therefore, he reasoned, beyond some point each additional unit of labor added to the production of food would yield less food than the unit before it, and the ratio of food to labor (the human population) would decline. This effect is shown in simplified form in the following table:

Land (fixed input)	1	1	1	1	1	1	1	1	1
Labor (variable input)	0	1	2	3	4	5	6	7	8
Total output (food)	0	16	34	48	60	70	78	84	88
Food/labor ratio	0	16	17	16	15	14	13	12	11

On the basis of his two observations, Malthus concluded that the growth of the population would outstrip the growth of the food supply. As a result, he predicted, mankind was doomed to spend its existence on the brink of starvation.

B. The law of diminishing returns implies diminishing marginal physical product.

Since the law of diminishing returns concerns the addition to output of each successive unit of a variable input, it can also be called the law of diminishing marginal product or the law of diminishing marginal physical product.

Marginal product or **marginal physical product (MPP)** is the change in total output (or total product) for a one-unit change in a variable input.

$$\text{MPP} = \frac{\text{change in output}}{\text{change in one input}}$$

The marginal physical product of labor in Example 9-3 is shown in the following table:

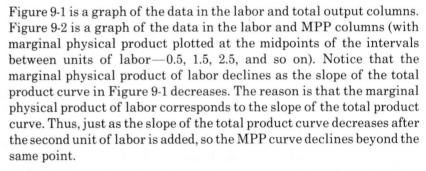

Labor	Total output	MPP
0	0	
		16
1	16	
		18
2	34	
		14
3	48	
		12
4	60	
		10
5	70	
		8
6	78	
		6
7	84	
		4
8	88	

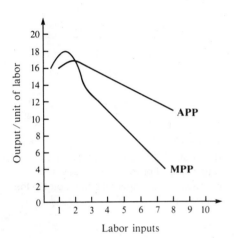

Figure 9-2
An MPP curve declines beyond the point of diminishing returns in the short run. Whenever MPP falls below APP, APP declines.

Figure 9-1 is a graph of the data in the labor and total output columns. Figure 9-2 is a graph of the data in the labor and MPP columns (with marginal physical product plotted at the midpoints of the intervals between units of labor—0.5, 1.5, 2.5, and so on). Notice that the marginal physical product of labor declines as the slope of the total product curve in Figure 9-1 decreases. The reason is that the marginal physical product of labor corresponds to the slope of the total product curve. Thus, just as the slope of the total product curve decreases after the second unit of labor is added, so the MPP curve declines beyond the same point.

C. **Average physical product declines whenever marginal physical product falls below average physical product.**

The ratio of food to labor in the table in Example 9-3 has a technical name: *average product* or *average physical product*.

Average product or **average physical product (APP)** is output per unit of a variable input.

$$\text{APP} = \frac{\text{output}}{\text{input}}$$

The graph of the average physical product of labor in Example 9-3 is shown in Figure 9-2 with the graph of the marginal physical product of labor. Notice the relationship between the APP curve and the MPP curve: beyond the second unit of labor, the MPP curve falls below the APP curve, and the APP curve begins to decline. Average physical product is always related to marginal physical product in the same way. Whenever marginal physical product exceeds average physical product, average physical product rises; whenever marginal physical product falls below average physical product, average physical product declines.

D. The law of diminishing returns implies rising costs and lower productivity in the short run.

The law of diminishing marginal physical product has two major implications for short-run costs and productivity.

1. The variable cost, and therefore the total cost, of producing additional units of output increases as output is expanded in the short run. In other words, when marginal physical product is declining, it takes more units of a variable input to produce each additional unit of output.
2. Productivity, which is the average product of labor, eventually declines in the short run if additional units of labor are added to fixed quantities of capital and natural resources.

9-4. Long-Run Production

Long-run production and long-run costs differ from their short-run counterparts.

1. Because there are no fixed inputs in the long run, the law of diminishing returns doesn't apply to long-run production.
2. The costs of production can be at their lowest possible level in the long run because everything—including plant size, location, number of plants, and technology—can be varied.
3. Larger plants *may* be able to produce a good with fewer input units per unit of output. In other words, doubling all inputs may more than double output; or, production may be doubled with less than twice the initial amount of resources.
4. If a larger plant is able to produce a unit of output with fewer input units, the result obviously is a lower cost per unit of output. Cost per unit of output may even decline as plant size and output simultaneously increase.

A belief that larger plants can produce goods at a lower cost per unit than smaller plants is almost an article of faith in the United States.

EXAMPLE 9-4: Generation of electricity is often cited as a production process in which increasing plant size results in more efficient production. This conviction has led to an increase in the size of electricity-generating plants over the years. In 1960, fewer than 7 percent of the fossil-fueled plants had over 500 megawatts of generating capacity; by 1981, over 40 percent had that much or more.

Larger, however, is not necessarily synonymous with *more efficient*. In the production of some goods and services, increases in plant size result in higher, not lower, per-unit costs.

9-5. Choice of Inputs

Most goods can be produced from a variety of different input combinations. The task of the production manager is to find the combination that will produce a good of a given quality at the lowest possible cost.

EXAMPLE 9-5: The following table lists various hypothetical input combinations, all of which will produce ten widgets. If the price of labor is $5 a unit and the price of capital services is $2 a unit, the widget production manager will minimize total costs by choosing combination C, eight units of labor and five units of capital.

Input combination	Units of labor	Units of capital	Number of widgets	Total cost
A	4	17	10	$54
B	6	11	10	52
C	8	5	10	50
D	10	2	10	54

A. Production costs are minimized when the ratios of MPP to price are the same for all inputs.

As you recall from the discussion of the marginal utility approach to consumer choice in Chapter 8, a consumer achieves maximum satisfaction or utility by ensuring that the ratios of marginal utility to price are the same for all of the goods in his or her commodity bundle. This rule for maximizing utility is very similar to the rule for minimizing production costs. To minimize the costs of production, a producer must ensure that the ratios of marginal physical product to price are the same for all inputs. If L, K, and N stand for labor, capital, and natural resources, respectively, and P stands for price, this rule for minimizing costs can be restated very simply in the following formula:

$$\frac{MPP_L}{P_L} = \frac{MPP_K}{P_K} = \frac{MPP_N}{P_N}$$

EXAMPLE 9-6: You can see the logic of the equal ratios rule if you examine a situation in which the ratios of marginal physical product to price are not equal for all inputs. Suppose that a widget producer selects inputs with unequal MPP-to-price ratios:

$$\frac{MPP_L}{P_L} = \frac{32}{4} = 8 \qquad \frac{MPP_K}{P_K} = \frac{4}{1} = 4$$

An MPP-to-price ratio of 8 means that an additional dollar spent on labor will yield eight additional widgets. Similarly, an MPP-to-price ratio of 4 means that an additional dollar spent on capital will yield only four additional widgets. Clearly the producer will be able to produce more widgets with the same expenditure if she adjusts her mix of inputs to include more labor and less capital, even though the price of labor is $4 a unit and the price of capital is only $1 a unit.

For instance, if she reduces capital inputs by four units, she will reduce output by 16 widgets, but she will then have $4 extra to spend on labor. With that $4 she can hire only one additional unit of labor, but that one additional unit of labor will increase output by 32 widgets. The net result of the adjustment, then, will be a gain of 16 widgets. As this example suggests, whenever the ratios of marginal physical product to price are *not* equal for all inputs, an adjustment in the use of inputs will increase output without also increasing total expenditure.

B. Relative input use reflects relative input prices.

The equal ratios rule for minimizing the costs of production logically implies that the relative use of inputs reflects the relative prices (as well as the relative marginal physical products) of the inputs. Thus an increase in the relative price of labor would lower the MPP-to-price ratio of labor and lead producers to substitute capital for labor, *ceteris paribus*. Similarly, an increase in the relative price of capital would lower the MPP-to-price ratio for capital and lead producers to substitute labor for capital, *ceteris paribus*.

EXAMPLE 9-7: If the price of labor in Example 9-6 were increased from $4 to $16, the MPP-to-price ratio of labor would decline from 8 to 2, meaning that an additional dollar spent on labor would now yield only two additional widgets instead of eight. After the price increase, the production manager would have to readjust her mix of inputs in order to minimize costs. Logically she would do so by subtracting units of labor and adding units of capital. As she did so, the MPP and thus the MPP-to-price ratio of labor would *increase* and the MPP and thus the MPP-to-price ratio of capital would *decrease*. She would continue adding capital and subtracting labor until the two ratios were again equal. Once the ratios were equal, no further adjustments that she could make would reduce production costs.

C. The least-cost input combination is economically efficient.

The input combination that produces a good at the least cost is economically efficient. It utilizes those inputs that have the lowest opportunity cost to society and thereby minimizes the required sacrifice of other goods.

RAISE YOUR GRADES

Can you explain . . . ?

☑ why economists differentiate between the short run and the long run in their analysis of production
☑ what the law of diminishing returns signifies
☑ how marginal physical product differs from average physical product
☑ why the law of diminishing returns doesn't apply to long-run production
☑ why cost per unit produced may decline in the long run
☑ how a production manager chooses inputs to minimize costs
☑ how an increase in the price of capital affects the capital intensity of production
☑ why the least-cost input combination is economically efficient

SUMMARY

1. A *production function* is an expression relating the maximum amount of a good that can be produced in a time period to technology and to various combinations of labor, capital, and natural resources.
2. *Fixed inputs* are factors of production that do *not* vary in quantity with changes in output. *Variable inputs* are factors of production that *do* vary in quantity with changes in output.
3. There are two time periods in economic analysis. The *short run* is a time period in which the quantity of at least one input is fixed. The *long run* is a time period in which the quantities of all inputs can be varied.
4. Fixed inputs have two principal implications for short-run production: (1) they imply fixed costs, and (2) they limit the freedom of management to modify production.
5. The law of diminishing returns applies to short-run production. The *law of diminishing returns* states that, if one or more inputs are fixed,

beyond some point the addition to output of each successive unit of a variable input declines.

6. The law of diminishing returns implies diminishing marginal product or marginal physical product.

7. *Marginal product* or *marginal physical product (MPP)* is the change in total output (or total product) for a one-unit change in a variable input.

8. *Average product* or *average physical product (APP)* is output per unit of a variable input.

9. Whenever marginal physical product exceeds average physical product, average physical product rises; whenever marginal physical product falls below average physical product, average physical product declines.

10. The law of diminishing returns implies that productivity (the average physical product of labor) will decline and the variable cost of producing a unit of output will increase as output is expanded beyond some point in the short run.

11. The law of diminishing returns does not apply to long-run production because the quantities of all inputs can be varied in the long run.

12. The costs of production can be at their lowest possible level in the long run.

13. Larger plants *may* be able to produce a good with fewer input units per unit of output: that is, doubling all inputs may more than double output.

14. If a larger plant is able to produce a unit of output with fewer input units, the result is a lower cost per unit of output.

15. The task of a production manager is to find the combination of inputs that will produce a good of a given quality at the lowest possible cost.

16. Production costs are minimized when the ratios of marginal physical product to price are the same for all inputs.

17. The equal ratios rule for minimizing the costs of production implies that the relative use of inputs reflects the relative prices of inputs. For example, an increase in the relative price of labor would lead producers to substitute other inputs for labor, *ceteris paribus*.

18. The least-cost input combination is economically efficient: it utilizes those inputs that have the lowest opportunity cost to society.

RAPID REVIEW

1. An expression relating the maximum quantity of a good that can be produced to various sets of inputs and technology is called a _____ _____. [See Section 9-2.]

2. An input that varies in quantity with output is called a _____ *input*. [See Section 9-2.]

3. The time period for a production process in which four out of five inputs are variable is the long run. True or false? [See Section 9-2.]

4. Management has less flexibility in the short run than in the long run; therefore, short-run costs per unit are usually higher than long-run costs per unit. True or false? [See Section 9-3.]

5. If other inputs are fixed, beyond some point the addition to output of each successive unit of a variable input _____. [See Section 9-3.]

6. _____ _____ _____ is the change in output for a one-unit change in a variable input. [See Section 9-3.]

7. Average physical product (APP) is calculated by dividing _____ by units of an _____. [See Section 9-3.]

8. Whenever marginal physical product falls below average physical product, average physical product _____. [See Section 9-3.]

9. The law of diminishing marginal physical product implies that the variable cost of producing each additional unit of output _____ beyond some point in the short run. [See Section 9-3.]

10. _____ is the average physical product of labor. It _____ in the short run if additional units of labor are added to fixed quantities of capital and natural resources. [See Section 9-3.]

11. The law of diminishing returns applies to the long run because the same inputs are present in the long run as in the short run. True or false? [See Section 9-4.]

12. "Larger plants produce goods with fewer input units per unit of output than smaller plants." This statement is (**a**) always false, (**b**) sometimes true, (**c**) true only of plants that generate electricity, (**d**) always true. [See Section 9-4.]

13. Production costs are minimized when the ratios of _____ physical product to _____ are equal for all inputs used. [See Section 9-5.]

14. A decrease in the relative price of capital inputs would lead producers to decrease the use of capital relative to labor, *ceteris paribus*. True or false? [See Section 9-5.]

15. A combination of inputs is economically efficient if it utilizes those inputs that have the lowest _____ cost to society. [See Section 9-5.]

Answers
1. *production function*   2. *variable*   3. false   4. true   5. diminishes or decreases
6. *Marginal physical product*   7. output, input   8. declines or decreases   9. increases or rises   10. *Productivity*, declines   11. false   12. (**b**)   13. marginal, price
14. false   15. opportunity

SOLVED PROBLEMS

PROBLEM 9-1   Interpret the following expression:

$$\text{Gizmos} = g(\text{energy, capital, labor})$$

Answer: The expression is called a *production function*. All it says, basically, is that what comes out of a production process (the output) is determined by what goes into the production process (the input). In this particular case, the expression says that the maximum number of gizmos that can be produced in any given time period is determined by the amounts and the combinations of energy, capital, and labor that are used to produce them. Technology, of course, is what makes the production of gizmos possible, even though it is not explicitly mentioned in the production function. Society's knowledge of production is incorporated in its human and capital resources. [See Section 9-2.]

PROBLEM 9-2   The following inputs are used in the production of automobiles: (**a**) workers paid by the hour, (**b**) rolled steel sheets for car bodies, (**c**) a building housing an assembly line, (**d**) a robot that paints cars, (**e**) a manager hired by the year. Classify these inputs as fixed or variable.

Answer: Although classification depends in part on interpretation, the inputs would ordinarily be classified as follows: (a) variable, (b) variable, (c) fixed, if owned or leased long term, (d) fixed, if owned or leased long term, (e) fixed, if on an annual contract. [See Section 9-2.]

PROBLEM 9-3 Explain why short-run costs per unit must always be greater than or equal to long-run costs per unit. [*Hint:* Consider the definitions of *short run* and *long run*.]

Answer: Short-run costs per unit must always be greater than or equal to long-run costs per unit because production managers have fewer options in the short run than they do in the long run. In the long run they can vary all inputs and thereby minimize production costs absolutely. In the short run, however, they may be stuck with plants of the wrong size, in the wrong location, or with obsolete technology. As a result, they cannot reduce costs to their lowest possible level. At best, short-run costs can only equal long-run costs. [See Sections 9-3 and 9-4.]

PROBLEM 9-4 The production of corn requires land, labor, seed, fertilizer, and machinery services (tractor hours). If land is a fixed input, which inputs are likely to be subject to the law of diminishing returns?

Answer: If land is a fixed input in the production of corn, all of the other inputs are likely to be subject to the law of diminishing returns. Beyond some point, each additional unit of labor, seed, fertilizer, or machinery services will contribute *less* to the total production of corn than the one before it. Another way of saying the same thing is this: if other inputs are held constant, beyond some point, doubling an input will less than double output. In fact, if some inputs, such as labor and machinery services, are increased to the extreme, they will actually result in a *decrease* in total product because too many farmhands and too many tractors will destroy the corn crop. [See Section 9-3.]

PROBLEM 9-5 Given the following production schedule for the Widget Works, calculate the average and marginal physical products of fuel. Does the law of diminishing marginal physical product apply to the use of fuel at the Widget Works?

Units of capital	Gallons of fuel	Widgets a day
50	10	1
50	22	2
50	36	3
50	52	4

Answer: The following table shows the average physical product (APP) and the marginal physical product (MPP) of fuel at the Widget Works:

Gallons of fuel	Widgets a day	APP	MPP
0	0	0	
			1/10
10	1	1/10	
			1/12
22	2	2/22	
			1/14
36	3	3/36	
			1/16
52	4	4/52	

As the decreasing values of the fractions in the MPP column show, the law of diminishing returns does apply to the use of fuel in the production of widgets. [See Section 9-3.]

PROBLEM 9-6 Graph the data in Problem 9-5. Plot the total product curve on one graph and the average physical product (APP) and marginal physical product (MPP) curves on a second one. Label the axes and the three curves. [*Hint:* Use Figures 9-1 and 9-2 as models.]

Answer: The total product curve is shown in Figure 9-3. The MPP and APP curves are shown in Figure 9-4. [See Section 9-3.]

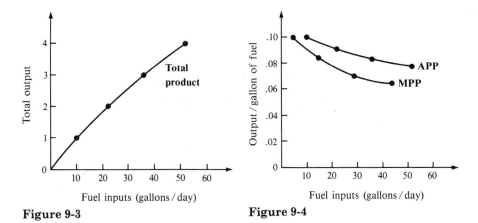

Figure 9-3   **Figure 9-4**

PROBLEM 9-7 The law of diminishing returns dictates that beyond some point variable cost per unit must increase as output increases in the short run. Must variable cost per unit increase as output increases beyond some point in the long run? What factor or factors influence long-run costs per unit of output?

Answer: Since the law of diminishing returns doesn't apply to long-run production, there is no "some point" beyond which variable (and therefore total) cost per unit must necessarily rise in the long run. Like short-run costs, long-run costs per unit are determined by the relationship between inputs and output. The only difference is that, since there are no fixed inputs in the long run, there are no fixed costs, either. Variable cost per unit *is* total cost per unit in the long run. [See Section 9-4.]

PROBLEM 9-8 In a particular generating plant the MPP-to-price ratio for fuel is 10/10 and the MPP-to-price ratio for capital is 8/4. If the returns on both inputs are diminishing, what adjustments should the manager of the plant make in order to minimize the costs of production?

Answer: Since the MPP-to-price ratio is higher for capital than it is for fuel, a dollar spent on capital will increase output more than a dollar spent on fuel. Therefore, the plant manager should decrease fuel inputs and increase capital inputs until the MPP-to-price ratios are equal. [See Section 9-5.]

PROBLEM 9-9 Explain why, beyond the point of diminishing returns, decreasing the use of a variable input, such as fuel in Problem 9-8, will increase its marginal product, *ceteris paribus.*

Answer: The law of diminishing returns states that, beyond some point, the marginal physical product of an input declines as additional units of the input are added to a production process. If the use of an input has gone beyond the point of diminishing returns, then, *decreasing* use will *increase* marginal physical product, *ceteris paribus.* [See Section 9-5.]

10 *ECONOMIC COSTS*

THIS CHAPTER IS ABOUT

☑ **Economic Costs**
☑ **Short-Run Production Costs**
☑ **Short-Run Cost Curves**
☑ **Long-Run Costs and Long-Run Cost Curves**

10-1. Economic Costs

Economists are concerned with the costs of *all* resources used in production, regardless of who owns them. This perspective influences their definitions of costs, profits, and optimal production levels.

You were introduced to the concept of opportunity cost in the discussion of production possibility boundaries in Chapter 1. That concept forms the basis for another cost concept, economic cost.

The **economic cost** of a good is the value of the alternatives that society must forgo in order to obtain it.

To determine the economic cost of a good, economists ask themselves what *society* must sacrifice in order to produce another unit of the good. That sacrifice—or the value of that sacrifice—is the economic cost of the good.

A. Economic costs include both private and external costs.

Since the economic cost of a good is a measure of what *society* must sacrifice in order to obtain the good, it includes external costs as well as private costs.

- **Private costs** are costs or sacrifices borne by individuals who are directly involved in the production or consumption of an item.
- **External costs** are costs or sacrifices borne by individuals who are *not* directly involved in the production or consumption of an item. External costs are also called *third-party costs*.

EXAMPLE 10-1: The Dew Point Chemical Company manufactures pesticides and other chemical products. It disposes of its chemical wastes by dumping them in a river. As a result of the dumping, the river can no longer be used for swimming, fishing, and other recreational purposes. Moreover, cities downstream must install elaborate purification systems to make the river water drinkable.

The costs of the labor, raw materials, energy, and so on that the company incurs in the production of its chemicals are private costs. The costs of combatting the pollution that the company is imposing on people downstream, as well as the costs of the lost recreation, are external or third-party costs.

B. Private costs may be explicit or implicit.

The economist's concern with counting all costs leads to consideration of two categories of private costs: explicit and implicit.

- **Explicit costs** are the market values of resources *purchased* by a producer.
- **Implicit costs** are the market values of self-owned, self-employed resources.

There are two important points to remember about implicit costs:

1. Self-owned, self-employed resources are valued at their opportunity costs, that is, what they could earn in their next-best uses.
2. Some implicit costs are routinely excluded from accounting calculations of costs or expenses.

EXAMPLE 10-2: Pierre resigned from his $40,000-a-year job as executive chef for a major restaurant chain, McQuick's. He took his life's savings of $50,000 and started an ethnic restaurant in St. Paul, Minnesota. At the close of the first year of business, his accountant gave him the following list of expenses and said, "You had $85,000 in expenses last year."

Expenses	
Food	$15,000
Hired labor	35,000
Utilities	10,000
Lease on building	8,000
Miscellaneous	17,000
Total	$85,000

Pierre, who had a knowledge of economics, looked at the list and said, "Yes, my expenses were $85,000, but my costs were much greater. I estimate my costs at $130,000."

Pierre's assessment of his costs differed from his accountant's assessment of his expenses because, whereas the accountant considered only Pierre's explicit costs of doing business, Pierre considered both his explicit costs and his implicit costs. In this case, Pierre's implicit costs included the cost of his own time and the cost of using his own savings to finance the venture. Pierre valued his time at $40,000 a year, the amount he could have been earning in his next-best use as a chef. He valued the use of his savings at $5,000 a year, the 10 percent annual interest it could have been earning for him in its next-best use. Adding his $45,000 in implicit costs to the accountant's $85,000 in explicit costs, Pierre determined that the total private costs of his first year in the restaurant business were $130,000.

C. Production costs are opportunity costs.

The cost of producing a good is the sum of the opportunity costs of the inputs used to produce it. Since input use varies between the short run and the long run, economists analyze production costs in each time period separately.

10-2. Short-Run Production Costs

As you already know from Chapter 9, the *short run* is defined as a time period in which at least one input is fixed. This definition implies that some or all of the other inputs in short-run production are variable. Fixed inputs generate fixed costs; variable inputs generate variable costs.

- **Fixed costs (FC)** are costs that do *not* vary with output and are incurred even if production falls to zero in the short run.
- **Variable costs (VC)** are costs that *do* vary with output.

EXAMPLE 10-3: The list of Pierre's expenses in Example 10-2 provides illustrations of both fixed and variable costs. If Pierre had a long-term lease on his building, the $8,000 that he paid for rent in the first year was a fixed cost. He would have had to pay the same amount whether he had shut down for the winter or not. The food and labor, on the other hand, were variable costs generated by variable inputs. He incurred them only when the restaurant was actually operating.

A. Total cost is the sum of fixed and variable costs.

The **total cost (TC)** of production is the sum of fixed and variable costs.

$$\text{Total cost (TC)} = \text{fixed costs} + \text{variable costs}$$

Since fixed and variable costs are also the products of addition—the sums of the costs associated with all fixed and all variable inputs, respectively—they are also classified as total costs. Thus, fixed costs are also called *total fixed costs* (*TFC*), and variable costs are also called *total variable costs* (*TVC*).

B. Average cost is total cost divided by total output.

The **average cost (AC)** or **average total cost (ATC)** of production is the total cost of production divided by the total quantity produced.

$$\text{Average cost (AC or ATC)} = \text{total cost} \div \text{total output}$$

Average cost is the *unit* or *per-unit* cost of production.

Average fixed and average variable costs are also calculated. As their names suggest, they are found by dividing total fixed costs and total variable costs, respectively, by total output:

$$\text{Average fixed cost (AFC)} = \text{total fixed costs} \div \text{total output}$$

$$\text{Average variable cost (AVC)} = \text{total variable costs} \div \text{total output}$$

As you may infer, average total cost is the sum of average fixed cost and average variable cost.

$$\text{ATC} = \text{AFC} + \text{AVC}$$

C. Marginal cost is the change in total cost for a one-unit change in output.

Marginal cost (MC) is the change in total cost for a one-unit change in output. Like average cost, marginal cost is a unit cost: it is the cost of producing one *additional* unit of a good. It can be found by dividing the change in total cost by the change in quantity produced from one output level to another:

$$\text{Marginal cost (MC)} = \text{change in total cost} \div \text{change in output}$$

Since total fixed cost doesn't change in the short run, marginal cost can also be found by dividing the change in total variable cost by the change in output.

EXAMPLE 10-4: The following table shows how the total output of food (Q) yielded by a single plot of land (fixed input) varies as different amounts of labor (variable input) are added to the production process:

Units of land (fixed input)	1	1	1	1	1
Units of labor (variable input)	1	2	4	9	16
Units of output (Q)	1	2	3	4	5

If the price of land services is $50 a unit and the price of labor is $10 a unit, the fixed, variable, total, average, and marginal costs of producing the food are as follows:

Fixed cost (FC)	$50	$50	$50	$ 50	$ 50
Variable cost (VC)	10	20	40	90	160
Total cost (TC = FC + VC)	60	70	90	140	210
Average cost (TC ÷ Q)	60	35	30	35	42
Marginal cost (ΔTC ÷ ΔQ)		$10	$20	$50	$70

10-3. Short-Run Cost Curves

Production costs are frequently presented graphically. When they are, they are known as *cost curves*.

A. Total costs are graphed with output and cost on the axes.

Fixed, variable, and total costs are graphed with output or quantity on the horizontal axis and cost on the vertical axis. Figure 10-1 shows the graphs of the fixed, variable, and total costs in Example 10-4. Note the following features of these cost curves:

1. The fixed cost (FC) curve is a horizontal line because fixed cost doesn't vary with output.
2. The slope of the variable cost (VC) curve increases (gets steeper) at an increasing rate because of the law of diminishing returns.
3. The total cost (TC) curve is a vertical summation of the fixed cost (FC) and the variable cost (VC) curves.

B. Average and marginal costs are graphed with output and cost per unit on the axes.

Average and marginal cost curves are graphed with output or quantity on the horizontal axis and cost per unit of output on the vertical axis. Figure 10-2 shows the graphs of the average total costs (ATC) and the marginal costs (MC) in Example 10-4. It also shows the average fixed costs (AFC = FC ÷ Q) and the average variable costs (AVC = VC ÷ Q) for the same data. Note the following features of these cost curves:

1. The average fixed cost (AFC) curve declines throughout its length because a fixed cost is divided by increasingly larger output levels.
2. The average variable cost (AVC) curve rises beyond some point because of the law of diminishing returns.
3. The average cost or average total cost (ATC) curve is a vertical summation of the average fixed cost (AFC) and the average variable cost (AVC) curves. Since the vertical distance between the AVC and the ATC curves represents the average fixed cost and since the average fixed cost declines, the AVC curve approaches the ATC curve as output increases.
4. The marginal cost (MC) curve rises beyond some point because of the law of diminishing returns. It always intersects the AVC and the ATC curves at their lowest points.

C. AVC and ATC curves typically are U-shaped.

Average variable cost (AVC) and average total cost (ATC) curves are usually U-shaped. An AVC curve typically is U-shaped because the average variable cost of producing a good generally decreases at first and then increases beyond some point as a result of the law of diminishing returns. An ATC curve typically is U-shaped because it is the vertical summation of an average fixed cost (AFC) curve, which

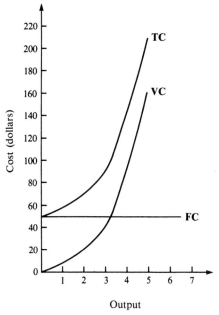

Figure 10-1
A total cost (TC) curve is a vertical summation of a fixed cost (FC) curve and a variable cost (VC) curve: TC = FC + VC.

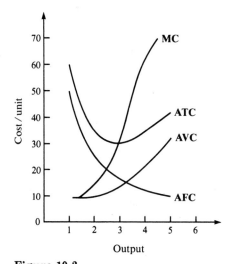

Figure 10-2
Average and marginal costs are graphed with output or quantity on the *x*-axis and cost per unit on the *y*-axis.

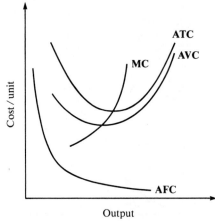

Figure 10-3
A model cost diagram shows the typical shapes of and the necessary geometrical relationships among AFC, AVC, ATC, and MC curves.

declines throughout its length, and an average variable cost (AVC) curve, which rises beyond some point.

Figure 10-3 is a model cost diagram that you would do well to memorize. It shows the typical shapes of and the necessary geometric relationships among AFC, AVC, ATC, and MC curves. You should be able to label the axes correctly and to duplicate the shapes and the relative positions of all four curves.

10-4. Long-Run Costs and Long-Run Cost Curves

Long-run costs and long-run cost curves differ from their short-run counterparts in four ways.

1. There are no fixed inputs in the long run, so fixed costs equal zero. Since all costs are variable in the long run, total cost is the same as variable cost (TC = VC).
2. The law of diminishing returns doesn't apply to long-run production and thus doesn't influence the shapes of long-run cost curves.
3. Plant size and rate of production vary continuously along a long-run cost curve because *all* inputs are variable. A long-run cost curve shows the lowest possible costs of production when all factors, including plant size, are adjusted.
4. Producers can't build a single plant whose average cost curve corresponds to a long-run average cost (LRAC) curve. Once a particular plant is built, it has its own short-run cost curves and the long-run cost curve does not apply to production costs in that plant. Long-run cost curves are often called *planning curves*.

A. An LRAC curve is an envelope.

A long-run average cost (LRAC) curve is an envelope, a curve tangent to a family or series of short-run average cost (SRAC) curves. Each point on an LRAC curve corresponds to a point on an SRAC curve for a particular plant size (fixed input) and rate of production. Figure 10-4 shows three such plant sizes and the points of tangency between their SRAC curves and the LRAC curve derived from them. Notice that, when long-run average costs are diminishing (on the left side of point *A* in Figure 10-4), the point of tangency between the LRAC curve and the SRAC curve is on the left side of the SRAC curve, where short-run costs are also diminishing. Conversely, when long-run average costs are increasing (on the right side of point *A* in Figure 10-4), the point of tangency between the LRAC curve and the SRAC curve is on the right side of the SRAC curve, where short-run costs are also increasing. Only at its minimum point (point *A* in Figure 10-4) is the LRAC curve tangent to an SRAC curve at the minimum point of the SRAC curve.

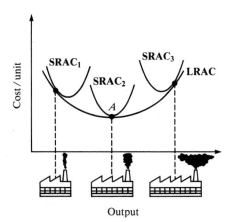

Figure 10-4
An LRAC curve is an envelope, a curve that encloses a series of SRAC curves. Both output and plant size vary along an LRAC curve.

B. An LRAC curve reflects economies, diseconomies, or constant economies of scale.

An LRAC curve reflects what economists refer to as *scale economies*.

- **Economies of scale** are reflected in a downward-sloping LRAC curve: long-run average cost decreases as plant size and rate of production increase.
- **Diseconomies of scale** are reflected in an upward-sloping LRAC curve: long-run average cost increases as plant size and rate of production increase.
- **Constant economies of scale** are reflected in a horizontal LRAC curve: long-run average cost remains constant as plant size and rate of production increase.

An LRAC curve may reflect more than one of these three conditions. For example, the U-shaped LRAC curve in Figure 10-4 reflects economies of scale up to point *A* and diseconomies of scale beyond point *A*. The LRAC curve in Figure 10-5 reflects all three conditions: economies, constant economies, and diseconomies of scale.

C. Scale economies may influence market structure.

The advantages or disadvantages of producing a product on a large scale may influence the structure of the market for the product, that is, the number and the size of the producers or sellers. When economies of scale are virtually unlimited, a market is usually characterized by one or at most a few large plants (and one or at most a few large producers). Conversely, when diseconomies of scale occur at very low levels of output, a market is usually characterized by many small plants (and often by many small producers).

EXAMPLE 10-5: Figure 10-6 shows the conditions for a natural monopoly. The negative or downward slope of the LRAC curve indicates that the advantages of large-scale production are so great that a single large plant (producer) can satisfy existing demand at a much lower cost than many small plants (producers). In fact demand, as curve *DD* shows, is insufficient to exhaust the economies of large-scale production. Public utilities, such as water, sewerage, electricity, and natural gas services, are presumed to show virtually unlimited economies of scale (decreasing LRAC curves).

In contrast, Figure 10-7 shows the conditions for perfect (or potentially perfect) competition. The steep upward slope of the LRAC curve indicates that diseconomies of scale set in at very low levels of output and thus make large-scale production more costly than small-scale production. Demand can be satisfied at a lower cost by many small plants (producers) than by one or a few large ones. The production of agricultural commodities such as wheat, barley, corn, and rice is presumed to show diseconomies of scale (increasing LRAC curves) beyond some point.

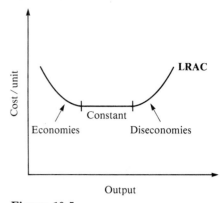

Figure 10-5
An LRAC curve may exhibit economies of scale, constant economies of scale, or diseconomies of scale.

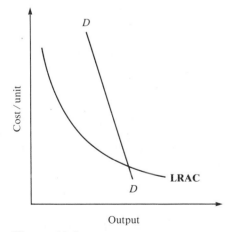

Figure 10-6
When economies of scale are significant relative to demand, conditions are right for a natural monopoly. Production costs will be minimized if the market is served by one large plant.

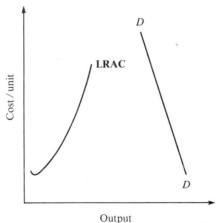

Figure 10-7
When diseconomies of scale are significant relative to demand, conditions are right for perfect competition. Production costs will be minimized if the market is served by many small plants.

RAISE YOUR GRADES

Can you explain ... ?

☑ how private costs differ from external costs
☑ how the values of implicit costs are established
☑ why accounting costs may differ from economic costs
☑ what the vertical distance between an ATC and an AVC curve represents
☑ how MC and AVC and MC and ATC curves are related geometrically
☑ why marginal costs must rise beyond some point in the short run
☑ what an envelope curve is
☑ why an LRAC curve is often called a *planning curve*
☑ how economies of scale differ from diseconomies of scale
☑ how scale economies may influence market structure

SUMMARY

1. The *economic cost* of a good is the value of the alternatives that society must forgo to produce it. Economic cost includes private costs and external costs.
2. *Private costs* are the values of the sacrifices borne by individuals directly involved in the production or consumption of an item.
3. *External* or *third-party costs* are the values of the sacrifices borne by individuals not directly involved in the production or consumption of an item.
4. Private costs may be explicit or implicit.
5. *Explicit costs* are the market values of resources purchased for use in production.
6. *Implicit costs* are the market values of self-owned, self-employed resources used in production. Self-owned, self-employed resources are valued at their opportunity costs—what they could earn in their next-best uses.
7. *Production cost* is the sum of the opportunity costs of all inputs.
8. *Fixed costs (FC)* are costs generated by fixed inputs. Fixed costs do *not* vary with output and are incurred even if output falls to zero in the short run.
9. *Variable costs (VC)* are costs generated by variable inputs. Variable costs *do* vary with output.
10. *Total cost (TC)* in the short run is the sum of fixed and variable costs.
11. *Average cost (AC)* or *average total cost (ATC)* is total cost divided by total output.
12. *Marginal cost (MC)* is the change in total cost for a one-unit change in output.
13. A total fixed cost (FC) curve is a horizontal line. An average fixed cost (AFC) curve declines throughout its length.
14. Short-run MC and average variable cost (AVC) curves rise beyond some point as a result of the law of diminishing returns.
15. A short-run TC curve is a vertical summation of an FC and a VC curve. A short-run ATC curve is a vertical summation of an AFC and an AVC curve.

16. AVC and ATC curves typically are U-shaped. MC curves intersect AVC and ATC curves at the minimum points of the AVC and ATC curves.

17. There are no fixed inputs in the long run, so fixed costs equal zero. In the long run total cost equals variable cost.

18. The law of diminishing returns doesn't apply to long-run production and thus doesn't influence the shape of long-run cost curves.

19. A long-run average cost (LRAC) curve shows the lowest possible costs of production when all factors, including plant size, are adjusted.

20. An LRAC curve is an envelope, a curve that is tangent to and encloses a series of short-run average cost (SRAC) curves. Both output and plant size vary along an LRAC curve.

21. Large-scale production may or may not be economical. *Economies of scale* occur when long-run average cost decreases as plant size and output increase. *Diseconomies of scale* occur when long-run average cost increases as plant size and output increase.

22. Scale economies may influence market structure—the number and the size of the producers or sellers in a market.

RAPID REVIEW

1. The economic cost of a good is the value to _____ of the alternatives that must be forgone to obtain it. [See Section 10-1.]

2. _____ costs are sacrifices borne by individuals who are *not* directly involved in the production or consumption of a good. [See Section 10-1.]

3. The cost of lumber purchased by a building contractor is (**a**) a fixed cost, (**b**) an implicit cost, (**c**) an external cost, (**d**) an explicit cost. [See Section 10-1.]

4. Of the two types of private costs, accountants routinely exclude some _____ costs in their calculations of expenses. [See Section 10-1.]

5. Self-owned, self-employed resources are valued at their _____ costs, what they could earn in their next-best uses. [See Section 10-1.]

6. A 5-year lease on a truck is an example of (**a**) a fixed cost, (**b**) a variable cost, (**c**) a total cost, (**d**) an implicit cost. [See Section 10-2.]

7. Gasoline for a delivery truck is an example of (**a**) a third-party cost, (**b**) a variable cost, (**c**) an implicit cost, (**d**) a fixed cost. [See Section 10-2.]

8. Total cost in the short run is the sum of _____ and _____ costs. [See Section 10-2.]

9. _____ and _____ costs are unit or per-unit costs. [See Section 10-2.]

10. If total cost equals $75 when output is five units, average total cost equals _____. [See Section 10-2.]

11. If total cost increases from $100 to $150 as output increases from 25 to 30 units, marginal cost equals _____. [See Section 10-2.]

12. The law of diminishing returns implies that beyond some output level average variable cost will (**a**) increase, (**b**) decrease, (**c**) remain constant, (**d**) exceed average total cost. [See Section 10-3.]

13. In the short run _____ and _____ curves typically are U-shaped. [See Section 10-3.]

14. In the long run all costs are _____. [See Section 10-4.]

15. In the long run all inputs can be varied, so long-run costs (**a**) are always less than short-run costs, (**b**) are always greater than or equal to short-run costs, (**c**) never equal short-run costs, (**d**) never exceed short-run costs. [See Section 10-4.]

16. A firm could build a plant whose average cost curve was congruent with its LRAC curve. True or false? [See Section 10-4.]

17. The law of diminishing returns determines the shape of long-run cost curves. True or false? [See Section 10-4.]

18. Each point on an LRAC curve corresponds to a different rate of production and a different plant size. True or false? [See Section 10-4.]

19. An LRAC curve with a positive slope reflects _____ of scale. [See Section 10-4.]

20. A market may be served by a single large plant when there are significant _____ of scale relative to industry demand. [See Section 10-4.]

Answers

1. society   **2.** *External* or *third-party*   **3. (d)**   **4.** implicit   **5.** opportunity   **6. (a)**
7. (b)   **8.** fixed, variable   **9.** Average, marginal   **10.** $15   **11.** $50 ÷ 5 = $10
12. (a)   **13.** AVC, ATC   **14.** variable   **15. (d)**   **16.** false   **17.** false   **18.** true
19. diseconomies   **20.** economies

SOLVED PROBLEMS

PROBLEM 10-1   Consider the following two statements:

Speaker A: "The cost of pollution control to my firm is enormous."
Speaker B: "The cost of pollution is enormous."

How does Speaker A's use of the word *cost* differ from Speaker B's?

Answer: Speaker A uses the word *cost* to refer to private costs, the costs that an individual firm must bear to control the pollution that it generates in the production of some good. Speaker B uses the word *cost* to refer to external or third-party costs, the costs associated with pollution that society must bear. [See Section 10-1.]

PROBLEM 10-2   Think of yourself as the producer of your own good health. List some typical explicit and implicit costs that you incur in the production of your health.

Answer: The explicit costs of producing your good health are the values of the resources that you purchase to produce it. Typical explicit costs for health production include the values of physician services, prescription drugs, vitamins, memberships in health clubs, and so on. The implicit costs of your good health are the values of the self-owned, self-employed resources that you use to produce it. Typical implicit costs for health production include the value of time spent exercising and consulting physicians. [See Section 10-1.]

PROBLEM 10-3   Assume that you have an appointment with a physician who is helping you to produce your good health. You take 3 hours off from work in order to spend 10 minutes with the physician. You pay the physician $40. You spend $5 in cab fare to get to and from the appointment. Your hourly wage is $6. From an economist's point of view, what is the cost of your visit with the physician?

Answer: An economist considers *all* costs, implicit costs as well as explicit costs. In this case, the explicit costs of your health production are the doctor's fee and the cab fare ($40 + $5 = $45). The implicit cost is the value of your time, the 3 hours of work at $6 an hour that you have to forgo to keep the appointment (3 × $6 = $18). Thus, from an economist's point of view, the total cost of your visit with the physician is $63, the sum of the implicit and explicit costs. [See Section 10-1.]

PROBLEM 10-4 The following short-run production schedule shows the units of labor and capital that are used to produce various quantities of a hypothetical good.

Inputs		
Labor	Capital	Output
0	100	0
5	100	1
12	100	2
21	100	3
32	100	4
45	100	5

Assume that the price of capital is $3 per unit and the price of labor is $5 per unit. Prepare a cost schedule that shows the fixed, variable, total, and marginal costs for each level of output.

Answer: The fixed cost is the cost associated with the fixed input, in this case capital. You find it by multiplying the number of units of capital (100) by the price of capital ($3 a unit). By definition, the fixed cost is the same for all levels of output.

The variable cost is the cost associated with the variable input, in this case labor. You find it by multiplying the number of units of labor used at each level of output by the price of labor ($5 a unit).

The total cost is the sum of the fixed and variable costs at each level of output. The marginal cost is the change in total cost divided by the change in quantity from one level of output to another. All of these costs are shown in the following cost schedule [see Section 10-2]:

	Costs			
Output	Fixed	Variable	Total	Marginal
0	$300	$ 0	$300	
				$25
1	300	25	325	
				35
2	300	60	360	
				45
3	300	105	405	
				55
4	300	160	460	
				65
5	300	225	525	

PROBLEM 10-5 Explain how total costs in Problem 10-4 can be $300 when output equals zero.

Answer: Short-run total costs, as you know, are the sum of fixed costs and variable costs. Although variable costs are zero when output is zero, fixed costs are positive in the short run even when production ceases. Fixed costs represent commitments to fixed inputs that must be paid regardless of short-run output. In Problem 10-4 that commitment is $300. [See Section 10-2.]

PROBLEM 10-6 Use the information in Problem 10-4 to prepare an average cost schedule. Calculate average fixed, average variable, and average total costs for each level of output.

Answer: You find the average costs for each level of output by dividing the fixed, variable, and total costs at each level by the output at each level. The average costs of producing various quantities of the hypothetical good in Problem 10-4 are shown in the following schedule [see Section 10-2]:

| | Average Costs | | |
Output	Fixed	Variable	Total
0	$ —	$ —	$ —
1	300	25	325
2	150	30	180
3	100	35	135
4	75	40	115
5	60	45	105

PROBLEM 10-7   Plot the average costs in Problem 10-6 and the marginal costs in Problem 10-4 on the same graph. Plot the marginal costs at the midpoints of the intervals between output levels (i.e., 0.5, 1.5, and so on). Label the axes and the four curves.

Answer: Figure 10-8 shows the graphs of the marginal and average costs in the cost schedules in Problems 10-4 and 10-6. [See Section10-3.]

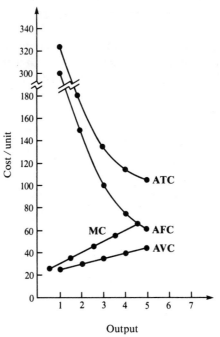

Figure 10-8

PROBLEM 10-8   As you recall from Chapter 9, the law of diminishing returns states that, beyond some point, larger and larger increments of a variable input are required to produce each additional unit of output. Explain why the marginal cost (MC) curve in Figure 10-8 is consistent with the law of diminishing returns.

Answer: The slope of the MC curve in Figure 10-8 is positive. An MC curve with a positive or upward slope indicates that the cost of producing each additional unit of a good is rising. There are only two causes of an increase in marginal cost in the short run: an increase in the *price* of a variable input and an increase in the *use* of a variable input. Since the price of the only variable input (labor) in Problem 10-4 is constant, we can conclude that the use of the variable input must be rising. In other words, we can conclude that more and more units of labor are being required to produce each additional unit of the good. This conclusion is consistent with the law of diminishing returns. [See Section 10-3.]

PROBLEM 10-9 Figure 10-9 shows three hypothetical cost curves, a marginal cost (MC) curve, an average variable cost (AVC) curve, and an average total cost (ATC) curve. It also shows a line parallel to the *y*-axis that intersects all three curves at output *Q*. Identify the segment of the line that represents each of the following unit costs at output *Q*: average total cost, average variable cost, average fixed cost, and marginal cost.

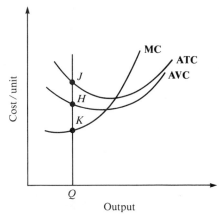

Figure 10-9

Answer: Average total cost is represented by the line segment *QJ*; average variable cost, by the line segment *QH*; and marginal cost, by the line segment *QK*. There is no average fixed cost (AFC) curve in the diagram, but you can find average fixed cost by subtracting average variable cost (*QH*) from average total cost (*QJ*). The difference is line segment *HJ*. [See Section 10-3.]

PROBLEM 10-10 Explain why an ATC curve is usually U-shaped.

Answer: An ATC curve is a vertical summation of an AFC curve and an AVC curve. An AFC curve declines throughout its length because it shows a fixed cost being divided by increasingly larger levels of output. An AVC curve, on the other hand, usually declines only up to a point; then it begins to rise at an ever-increasing rate as a result of the law of diminishing marginal physical product. (As progressively larger increases in a variable input are required to produce each additional unit-increase in total output, average variable cost must increase.) Vertical summation of a falling AFC curve and a rising AVC curve usually results in a U-shaped curve. [See Section 10-3.]

PROBLEM 10-11 Explain why average total cost, or average cost, in the long run never exceeds average total cost in the short run.

Answer: A long-run average cost (LRAC) curve, remember, is a *planning* curve. It does *not* show the average costs of production at any particular plant. It shows the *lowest possible* average costs of production when *all* factors, including the size, location, and technological sophistication of plants and equipment, are adjusted. By definition, then, long-run average (total) cost never exceeds short-run average total cost.

In the long run a firm can vary all of its costs because it can vary all of its inputs. Therefore it can reduce its average cost of production to the lowest possible level in the long run. In the short run a firm does not have the same control over its average total costs because it does not have the same control over all of its resources. By definition, at least one input (and therefore at least one cost) is fixed in the short run. If that fixed input is optimal in size, location, technology, and so on, the cost of employing it, and thus the average cost of production, may be no higher than it would be in the long run. But it can *never* be lower. [See Section 10-4.]

PROBLEM 10-12 Are diseconomies of scale attributable to the law of diminishing returns? If not, to what are they attributable? Explain your answer.

Answer: No. The law of diminishing returns applies only to the short run, when at least one input is fixed. Diseconomies of scale apply only to the long run, when all inputs, including plant size, are variable. In fact, diseconomies of scale—increasing average costs in the long run—are directly attributable to size, that is, to large-scale production. They may result from engineering or organizational problems (problems of communication and coordination on a very large scale). [See Section 10-4.]

PROBLEM 10-13 Sketch four LRAC curves, (a) one to reflect constant economies of scale, (b) a second to reflect economies of scale, (c) a third to reflect diseconomies of scale, and (d) a fourth to reflect all three of these conditions. Label the axes.

Answer: The four curves are shown in Figure 10-10. [See Section 10-4.]

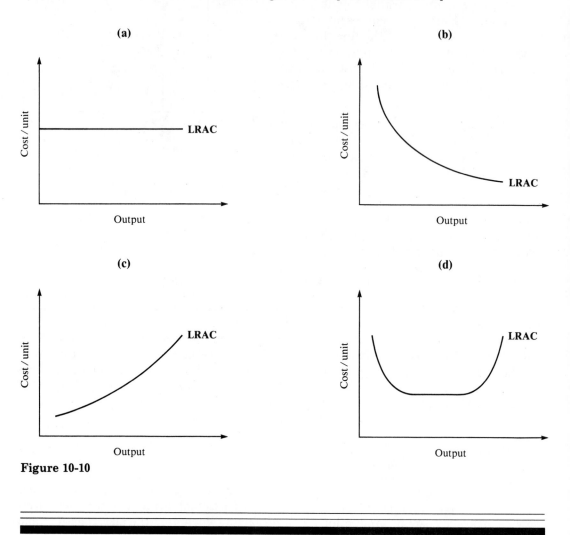

Figure 10-10

11 *PROFIT MAXIMIZATION BY FIRMS*

THIS CHAPTER IS ABOUT

☑ **Firms**
☑ **Economic Profits**
☑ **Output and Profits**
☑ **Shutdown Rules**
☑ **Three Rules for Profit Maximization**

11-1. Firms

Just as economists assume that consumers aim to maximize their satisfaction or utility, so they assume that most producers aim to maximize their profits. As the qualifier *most* suggests, not all producers aim to maximize their profits. Those that do belong to a specific class known as *firms*.

A **firm** is a profit-oriented decision-making unit with an internal organization for producing or trading a good.

There are two notable advantages to organizing production or trade internally. Internal organization allows for greater specialization, and it reduces the transaction costs associated with market interactions.

A. Firms reduce transaction costs.

Firms organize production internally in order to reduce the transaction costs associated with participation in markets. Market participants must search out information on prices, quantities, and quality; they must negotiate agreements; and, in some cases, they must formalize agreements through written contracts. These procedures are costly, and the costs associated with them are incurred at every stage in a production process that is conducted through market interactions with independent agents. Firms seek to reduce or to avoid these costs by purchasing or hiring resources and organizing and directing productive activities from within.

EXAMPLE 11-1: You could produce your own car from such basic components as the engine, chassis, tires, and so on. However, unless you were a specialist in reading blueprints, purchasing parts, and assembling automobiles, the process would be prohibitively costly for you or for any other individual. That's why firms like the Ford Motor Company exist. By organizing the production of automobiles internally, they can reduce transaction costs and produce cars much more efficiently than any individual can.

B. Firms perform the entrepreneurial functions in a market economy.

As you recall from Chapter 1, an *entrepreneur* is an individual who organizes production, bears the associated risks, and reaps the associated rewards. In a market economy, firms perform the functions of an entrepreneur. They decide:

1. how much to produce
2. how to produce
3. what prices to charge
4. how to differentiate their products from those of other producers

C. Firms are organized in three common ways.

There are three common forms of legal organization for firms.

1. A **sole proprietorship** is a firm that is owned and controlled by one individual who reaps the profits and bears the liability for the debts of the organization.
2. A **partnership** is a firm that is owned and controlled by two or more individuals who share the profits and the liability for the debts of the organization.
3. A **corporation** is a firm that is legally distinct from the individuals who own and may control it. Those individuals (shareholders or stockholders) reap the profits of the organization, but the corporation itself, which is a legal entity, is liable for its own debts.

11-2. Economic Profits

Profits are the carrot in a capitalist market system. They provide the motivation necessary to inspire a firm to undertake the risks of organizing the production of some good or service. But what do economists mean by the word *profit*? Do they simply mean the difference between what a firm takes in and what it pays out? Not quite.

Economic profit is the difference between total revenue and private costs.

As you recall from Chapter 7, total revenue (TR) is the product of price (P) and quantity sold (Q):

$$TR = P \times Q$$

As you recall from the last chapter, private costs (or *total costs*, as they are commonly referred to in this context) include both explicit costs (the costs of purchased resources) and implicit costs (the opportunity costs of self-owned, self-employed resources). Thus:

$$\text{Economic profit} = (P \times Q) - \text{explicit costs} - \text{implicit costs}$$

A. An economic profit of zero is acceptable to a firm.

Because economists deduct implicit costs as well as explicit costs from a firm's total revenue, their calculations of profit include a normal return on *all* inputs, including the time, energy, and other resources provided by an entrepreneur. For this reason, an economic profit of zero is acceptable to a firm, even in the long run. An economic profit of zero implies that the resources employed by the firm are earning as much in their present use as they could elsewhere in the economy. Firms seek, of course, to earn positive profits, but competition in a market economy tends to push profits down toward zero.

B. Economic profit differs from accounting net income.

Just as economic costs differ from accounting costs, so economic profit differs from what accountants refer to as *net income*. *Net income* is the difference between total revenue and accounting costs. Accounting costs, as you may recall from Chapter 10, exclude some implicit costs. One of the implicit costs that they exclude is a return on stockholders' equity. Thus, whereas an economic profit of zero might be perfectly satisfactory to the stockholders of a corporation, a net income of zero would be highly unsatisfactory. The former would bring them a normal return on their equity; the latter would bring them no returns.

EXAMPLE 11-2: Consider Pierre, the chef in Chapter 10 who left his $40,000-a-year job at McQuick's to open a restaurant of his own. In his first year of business Pierre incurred accounting costs of $85,000 and private costs of $130,000. If his total revenue that year was $110,000, Pierre's net income (total revenue minus accounting costs) was positive:

$$\text{Net income} = \$110,000 - \$85,000 = +\$25,000$$

However, his economic profit (total revenue minus private costs) was negative:

$$\text{Economic profit} = \$110,000 - \$130,000 = -\$20,000$$

The concept of a negative profit might seem self-contradictory to you, but it really isn't. What an economic profit of $-\$20,000$ means is that the resources Pierre used in his restaurant produced $20,000 less than they could have produced in their next-best use. In other words, if Pierre had kept his job as a chef at McQuick's, he would have had an additional $20,000 at the end of the year.

11-3. Output and Profits

In order to maximize profits, a firm must select its optimal level of production. It can do so by examining the relationship either between its total revenue and its total cost or between its marginal revenue and its marginal cost at various levels of output.

A. A firm's optimal output level is the level at which its total revenue minus its total cost is at a maximum.

Since *profit* is defined as the difference between revenue and production costs, a firm that maximizes that difference will maximize its profits.

EXAMPLE 11-3: The following schedule shows the total revenue (TR), total cost (TC), and total profit (TR − TC) data for various levels of output at Olie's Widget Works.

Total output	Total revenue	Total cost	Total profit
10	$ 50	$100	−$50
20	100	120	− 20
30	150	150	0
40	200	190	10
45	225	212	13
50	250	240	10
60	300	300	0
70	350	370	− 20

In order to maximize his profits, Olie should produce at an output level of 45 widgets. As the fourth column shows, at that level of production the positive difference between his total revenue and his total cost is greater than at any other level.

$$\text{Total profit} = \$225 - \$212 = \$13$$

B. At a firm's optimal production level, the positive vertical distance between its TR and TC curves is greatest.

When the total revenue and total cost data for a firm are plotted against output on a graph, the vertical distance between the two

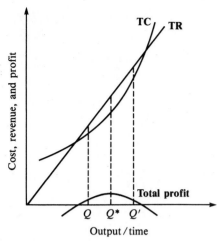

Figure 11-1
At a firm's profit-maximizing output level (Q*), the positive vertical distance between its TR and TC curves is greatest.

curves (whether positive or negative) represents the firm's total profit. The firm's profit-maximizing output level is the level at which the positive vertical distance between its TR and TC curves is greatest.

EXAMPLE 11-4: Figure 11-1 shows the TR and TC curves for a hypothetical firm. The vertical distance between the TR and TC curves represents the arithmetic difference between total revenue and total cost (TR − TC) at each level of output. That difference, the firm's total profit, is graphed as a separate curve at the bottom of the figure.

As you can see, in the area where the TR curve lies above the TC curve, indicating that total revenue is greater than total cost, profits are positive and the total profit curve lies above the *x*-axis. At the two points where the TR and TC curves intersect, indicating that total revenue and total cost are equal, total profits are zero and the total profit curve intersects the *x*-axis. Finally, in the two areas where the TR curve lies *below* the TC curve, indicating that total revenue is less than total cost, total profits are negative and the total profit curve falls below the *x*-axis.

Obviously this hypothetical firm will maximize its profits at output level Q*. At that level the positive vertical distance between its TR and TC curves is greatest.

C. At a firm's optimal level of production, the slopes of its TR and TC curves are equal.

At the output level at which a firm is maximizing its profits, the slopes of its TR and TC curves are equal. The slopes of two curves are equal where the two curves are neither converging nor diverging—that is, where straight lines tangent to the two curves are parallel.

At output level Q in Figure 11-1, the slopes of the TR and TC curves are not equal (tangents to the two curves are not parallel) because the two curves are diverging (the positive vertical distance between them is increasing). The firm can increase its profits by *increasing* its level of output.

At output level Q', the slopes of the TR and TC curves are not equal (tangents to the two curves are not parallel) because the two curves are converging (the positive vertical distance between them is decreasing). The firm can increase its profits by *decreasing* its level of output.

Only at output level Q* in Figure 11-1 are the slopes of the TR and TC curves equal (tangents to the two curves are parallel) because the curves are neither diverging nor converging. Thus, only at that output level is the firm maximizing its profits.

D. The slopes of a firm's TR and TC curves correspond to its marginal revenue and marginal cost, respectively.

The slope of a firm's total cost curve is the ratio of the change in its total cost to the change in its total output. As you may recall from the last chapter, the ratio of the change in total cost to the change in total output—which is to say, the change in total cost for a one-unit change in output or quantity sold—is known as *marginal cost (MC)*. Thus the slope of a firm's TC curve corresponds to its marginal cost.

Similarly, the slope of a firm's total revenue curve is the ratio of the change in its total revenue to the change in its total output. The ratio of the change in total revenue to the change in total output is known as *marginal revenue*.

Marginal revenue (MR) is the change in total revenue for a one-unit change in output or quantity sold.

Thus the slope of a firm's TR curve corresponds to its marginal revenue.

Now, since the slopes of a firm's TR and TC curves correspond to its marginal revenue and marginal cost, respectively, and since the slopes of a firm's TR and TC curves are equal at the output level at which the firm is maximizing its profits, then at the same level the firm's marginal revenue must equal its marginal cost.

E. At a firm's optimal level of production, its marginal revenue equals its marginal cost.

To maximize profits, a firm should produce that level of output at which its marginal revenue equals its marginal cost. The firm's marginal cost, of course, must also be rising at that level. If it were falling, the firm would be able to increase its profits by increasing its output. However, this condition is taken for granted and is often left unstated.

EXAMPLE 11-5: In the following table, the marginal revenue and marginal cost data for Olie's Widget Works have been added to the total revenue and total cost data from Example 11-3.

Marginal revenue	Total revenue	Total output	Total cost	Marginal cost
	$ 50	10	$100	
$5				$2
	100	20	120	
5				3
	150	30	150	
5				4
	200	40	190	
5				5
	250	50	240	
5				6
	300	60	300	
5				7
	350	70	370	

The marginal revenue figures were calculated by dividing the change in total revenue by the change in quantity produced from one output level to the next. For example:

$$(\$100 - \$50) \div (20 - 10) = \$50 \div 10 = \$5$$

In like manner, the marginal cost figures were calculated by dividing the change in total cost by the change in quantity produced from one output level to the next. For example:

$$(\$120 - \$100) \div (20 - 10) = \$20 \div 10 = \$2$$

The marginal revenue and marginal cost figures are shown in the intervals between output levels because, like elasticity in Chapter 7, they are calculated by means of a midpoint or arc formula.

As you can see in the table, Olie's marginal revenue equals his marginal cost in the interval between 40 and 50 widgets. Since his marginal cost is also rising in that interval, Olie's profit-maximizing output level is 45 units.

F. At a firm's optimal level of production, its MC curve intersects its MR curve from below.

Like its total cost and total revenue data, a firm's marginal cost (MC) and marginal revenue (MR) data can be plotted on a graph. Graphically, a firm's profit-maximizing output level is represented by the

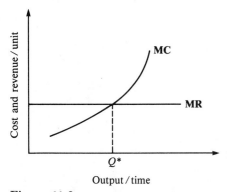

Figure 11-2
At a firm's profit-maximizing output level, its MC curve intersects its MR curve from below.

point at which its MC curve intersects its MR curve from below. At that point, its marginal revenue equals its marginal cost and its marginal cost is rising.

EXAMPLE 11-6: Figure 11-2 shows the MR and MC curves for a hypothetical firm. The firm's MC curve intersects its MR curve from below at output level Q^*. Q^*, therefore, is the firm's optimal level of production. At levels below Q^*, the revenue derived from producing an additional unit of output exceeds the cost of producing it. Hence profits can be increased by *increasing* output. At levels above Q^*, on the other hand, the cost of producing an additional unit of output exceeds the revenue derived from producing it. Hence profits can be increased by *decreasing* output.

11-4. Shutdown Rules

A firm can locate its most profitable positive level of output by the methods described in the preceding section. However, there are times when the most profitable course of action that a firm can take is to cease producing altogether. A firm should shut down whenever the losses from ceasing production are less than the losses from producing at any level of output. This is the essence of the two shutdown rules that follow.

A. In the short run, a firm should shut down if the price of its product is less than the average variable cost of producing it.

In the short run, whether or not a firm produces, it incurs the costs associated with its fixed inputs. Those costs, its total fixed costs, represent the *minimum* cost that the firm *must* bear in the short run. They also represent the *maximum* loss that the firm *need* sustain in the short run because it should shut down whenever its losses from producing are greater than its total fixed costs. When are a firm's losses from producing greater than its total fixed costs? When the price of its product is less than the average variable cost of producing it.

When the price (P) of a firm's product is less than the average variable cost (AVC) of producing it at any level of output (Q), the firm's total revenue ($P \times Q$) is less than its total variable costs (AVC $\times$ Q), so the firm loses not only all of its fixed costs but some of its variable costs, as well. Therefore the firm will lose less in the short run if it shuts down than if it produces. If it shuts down, it will limit its losses to its total fixed costs (TFC) because its total revenue (TR) and its total variable costs (TVC) will both be zero:

$$\begin{aligned} \text{Total profit} &= \text{TR} - (\text{TFC} + \text{TVC}) \\ &= 0 - (\text{TFC} - 0) \\ &= -\text{TFC} \end{aligned}$$

EXAMPLE 11-7: Figure 11-3 shows three prices for a hypothetical product that a firm is producing, P, P', and P''. At a price of P, the firm's optimal production level is Q. The firm should produce output Q because price P exceeds not only the average variable cost (AVC) but also the average total cost (ATC) of production. Therefore the firm's profits will be positive.

At a price of P', the firm's optimal production level is Q'. Since price P' is less than the average total cost (ATC) of production, the firm's profits will be negative. However, the firm should still produce output Q' because price P' is greater than the average variable cost (AVC) of production. In other words, price P' will cover some of the firm's fixed

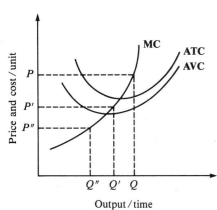

Figure 11-3
A firm should shut down in the short run if the price of its product is P''. P'' is less than the average variable cost (AVC) of producing output Q''.

costs as well as all of its variable costs. Therefore the firm will lose less in the short run if it produces than if it shuts down.

At a price of P'', the firm's marginal cost equals its marginal revenue at output Q''. Since price P'' is less than the average variable cost (AVC) of production, the firm will lose all of its fixed costs *plus* some of its variable costs if it produces in the short run, even at level Q''. Therefore the firm should shut down. If it shuts down, it will limit its losses to its fixed costs.

B. In the long run, a firm should shut down if the price of its product is less than the long-run average cost of producing it.

In the long run there are no fixed costs. All costs are variable and must be covered. In the long run, therefore, a firm should shut down if it does not expect the price of its product to cover the average total cost of production. Since a firm's total cost includes *all* of its private costs, implicit as well as explicit, if the price equals the average cost of production, all of the firm's costs will be covered. All of the resources the firm is employing will be earning as much as they could elsewhere in the economy. In other words, a firm should produce in the long run if it expects to earn an economic profit equal to or greater than zero. If it expects to earn an economic profit less than zero (a negative economic profit), it should shut down.

11-5. Three Rules for Profit Maximization

The methods of locating a firm's optimal production level in Section 11-3 and the shutdown rules in Section 11-4 can be condensed into three simple rules for profit maximization. *Memorize these rules.* You will use them over and over again in subsequent chapters.

Rule 1: If a firm produces, it should produce that level of output at which its marginal revenue equals its marginal cost (MR = MC).

Rule 2: In the short run, a firm should produce if the price of its product is greater than the average variable cost of production ($P >$ AVC).

Rule 3: In the long run, a firm should produce if its economic profit is equal to or greater than zero (i.e., if $P \geq$ AC).

RAISE YOUR GRADES

Can you explain...?

☑ why firms exist
☑ how corporations differ from partnerships and sole proprietorships
☑ why an economic profit of zero is acceptable
☑ how the economic profit of a firm differs from its accounting net income
☑ why a firm would produce quantity Q if tangents to its TR and TC curves were parallel at that level of output
☑ why a firm's marginal cost is equal to the slope of its TC curve
☑ why a firm's profits are maximized only if its MC curve intersects its MR curve *from below*
☑ why a firm should shut down in the short run if $P <$ AVC
☑ why a firm should shut down in the long run if its economic profit is negative

SUMMARY

1. A *firm* is a profit-oriented decision-making unit with an internal organization for producing or trading a good.
2. Firms are organized to allow greater specialization and to reduce the transaction costs associated with market interactions.
3. Firms bear the risks and reap the rewards of organizing production in a market economy. They decide how much and how to produce, what prices to charge, and how to differentiate their products from those of other producers.
4. There are three common forms of legal organization for firms: sole proprietorships, partnerships, and corporations.
5. A *sole proprietorship* is a firm that is owned and controlled by one individual who reaps the profits and bears the liability for the debts of the organization.
6. A *partnership* is a firm that is owned and controlled by two or more individuals who share the profits and the debt liability of the organization.
7. A *corporation* is a firm that is legally distinct from the individuals who own and may control it. Those individuals reap the profits of the organization, but they are not personally liable for its debts.
8. *Economic profit* is total revenue minus total private costs.
9. An economic profit of zero is acceptable, even in the long run, because it implies that the resources a firm is using are earning as much in their present use as they could elsewhere in the economy.
10. Economic profit differs from accounting net income. Calculations of accounting net income do not necessarily include *all* implicit costs; calculations of economic profit do.
11. A firm's optimal output level is the level at which its total revenue (TR) minus its total cost (TC) is at a maximum.
12. At a firm's profit-maximizing output level, the positive vertical distance between its TR and TC curves is greatest.
13. At a firm's profit-maximizing output level, the slopes of its TR and TC curves are equal—that is, tangents to the two curves are parallel.
14. The slopes of a firm's TR and TC curves correspond to its marginal revenue (MR) and its marginal cost (MC), respectively.
15. At a firm's profit-maximizing output level, its marginal revenue equals its marginal cost (MR = MC).
16. At a firm's profit-maximizing output level, its MC curve intersects its MR curve from below.
17. In the short run, a firm should shut down if the price (P) of its product is less than the average variable cost (AVC) of production (P < AVC). Shutting down in the short run limits a firm's losses to its fixed costs.
18. In the long run, a firm should shut down if the price (P) of its product is less than the average cost (AC) of production (P < AC)—that is, if its economic profit is negative.

RAPID REVIEW

1. In order to be classified as a firm, a producer must be _____ oriented. [See Section 11-1].
2. All of the following are classified as firms *except* (a) General Mills, (b) Sears Roebuck and Company, (c) Planned Parenthood, (d) American Telephone and Telegraph. [See Section 11-1.]
3. The internal organization of firms allows for greater _____ and a reduction in _____ costs. [See Section 11-1.]

4. Firms perform the _____ functions in a market economy. They bear the risks and reap the rewards of organizing _____ . [See Section 11-1.]

5. Firms may decide all of the following *except* (a) what prices they will charge, (b) how many competitors they will have, (c) how much they will produce, (d) how they will differentiate their products from those of their competitors. [See Section 11-1.]

6. A _____ consists of two or more individuals who share the ownership, control, profits, and debt liability of a firm. [See Section 11-1.]

7. Stockholders are personally liable for the debts of a corporation. True or false? [See Section 11-1.]

8. Economic profit equals _____ _____ minus _____ _____. [See Section 11-2.]

9. An economic profit of zero is acceptable, even in the long run, because it implies a normal return on all inputs. True or false? [See Section 11-2.]

10. A firm's accounting net income is always equivalent to its economic profit. True or false? [See Section 11-2.]

11. At a firm's profit-maximizing output level, the difference between its total revenue and its total cost is (a) greatest, (b) always equal to or greater than zero, (c) zero, (d) smallest. [See Section 11-3.]

12. A firm's total _____ is represented graphically by the vertical distance between its TR and TC curves. [See Section 11-3.]

13. A firm's optimal production level is represented graphically by the output at which tangents to its TR and TC curves are _____ . [See Section 11-3.]

14. *Marginal revenue* is the change in _____ _____ for a one-unit change in quantity sold. [See Section 11-3.]

15. If its marginal revenue is greater than its marginal cost, a firm can increase its profits by (a) maintaining the same level of output, (b) increasing output, (c) decreasing output, (d) shutting down in the short run. [See Section 11-3.]

16. A firm should produce in the short run if the price of its product is greater than the _____ _____ _____ of production. [See Section 11-4.]

17. In the short run, the maximum loss that a firm need sustain is its (a) total cost, (b) total fixed cost, (c) total variable cost, (d) average cost. [See Section 11-4.]

18. In the long run, the maximum loss a firm need sustain is (a) zero, (b) its total cost, (c) its variable cost, (d) its marginal cost. [See Section 11-4.]

19. In the long run, a firm should produce if (a) $P > AC$, (b) $P = AC$, (c) it expects to earn an economic profit of zero, (d) any of these conditions prevails. [See Section 11-4.]

20. If the price of a firm's product is $5 and the average total cost of production is $4, the firm should produce in the long run but not in the short run. True or false? [See Section 11-4.]

Answers

1. profit   2. (c)   3. specialization, transaction   4. entrepreneurial, production   5. (b)
6. partnership   7. false   8. total revenue, private (or total) costs   9. true   10. false
11. (a)   12. profit   13. parallel   14. total revenue   15. (b)   16. average variable cost
17. (b)   18. (a)   19. (d)   20. false

SOLVED PROBLEMS

PROBLEM 11-1   Explain why not all producers are classified as firms.

Answer: By definition, a *firm* is a profit-oriented producer. Therefore producers who are not profit oriented—government agencies, public libraries and museums, medical research groups like the American Cancer Society—are not classified as firms. [See Section 11-1.]

PROBLEM 11-2   Define *transaction costs* and explain how organizing production within a firm can reduce these costs.

Answer: Transaction costs are expenses incurred through market interactions or "arm's-length" exchanges between independent parties. They include acquiring information, negotiating agreements, and writing contracts. These costs are reduced when production is organized within a firm because management directly controls the resources of the firm. Once it hires a worker or acquires a capital input, it does not have to negotiate an agreement or draw up a contract for every task that it wants the worker or the capital input to perform. It can simply specify that the tasks be done. [See Section 11-1.]

PROBLEM 11-3   Explain why most people buy complex goods, such as stereo receivers, instead of producing them themselves.

Answer: The internal organization of a firm enables it to eliminate many of the numerous transaction costs that individuals would incur if they tried to produce such complex goods as stereo receivers on their own. The internal organization of a firm also enables it to hire and train specialists in every phase of a production process and to purchase state-of-the-art materials and equipment. As a result, a firm can usually produce a complex good of a higher quality than most individuals could achieve, and it can usually do so at a much lower cost. Since consumers maximize their satisfaction by acquiring goods of the highest quality at the lowest possible price, most people buy complex goods instead of producing them themselves. [See Section 11-1.]

PROBLEM 11-4   Explain the difference between a partnership and a corporation.

Answer: A primary difference between a partnership and a corporation is that the participants in a corporation, the stockholders, have no debt liability. Partners are personally liable for the debts of their partnership. Stockholders have no personal liability for the debts of a corporation. [See Section 11-1.]

PROBLEM 11-5   Assume that you are the owner and manager of the Widget Works. Your economic profit last year was zero. Now your brother-in-law is urging you to sell the business and get into something "more profitable." Explain why his argument makes no sense.

Answer: If your economic profit last year was zero, your total revenue for the year was just equal to your total costs, including your implicit costs, the costs associated with your own time and resources. You valued your time and resources at what they could have been earning in their next-best uses in society. Therefore, unless you undervalued your implicit costs, you and your resources were earning as much at the Widget Works as you and they could have been earning elsewhere in a competitive economy. There are no "more profitable" alternatives. [See Section 11-2.]

PROBLEM 11-6   Explain how an economic profit of zero could be the norm in a competitive market in the long run.

Answer: A positive economic profit implies that entrepreneurial inputs are earning more in their present use than they could be earning in any alternative use. If the entrepreneurs in a market were earning a positive economic profit, other entrepreneurs would enter the market, which would lead to an increase in market supply. If market demand remained constant, the increase in supply would drive price down until profits equaled zero.

Conversely, a negative profit implies that entrepreneurial inputs are earning less in their present use than they could be earning in an alternative use. If the entrepreneurs in a market were earning a negative economic profit, some of them would exit from the market, which would lead to a decrease in market supply. If market demand remained constant, the decrease in supply would drive price up until profits equaled zero. [See Section 11-2.]

PROBLEM 11-7   The following table shows the total output, total revenue, and total cost data for a hypothetical firm. Find the firm's optimal production level.

Total output	Total revenue	Total cost
0	$ 0	$ 50
5	25	55
10	50	65
15	75	80
20	100	100
25	125	125
30	150	155
35	175	190

Answer: A firm maximizes its profits at the output level at which its total revenue minus its total cost is at a maximum. The fourth column in the following table shows the difference between the hypothetical firm's total revenue and its total cost—that is, its total profit—at each level of output.

Total output	Total revenue	Total cost	Total profit
0	$ 0	$ 50	−$50
5	25	55	− 30
10	50	65	− 15
15	75	80	− 5
20	100	100	0
25	125	125	0
30	150	155	− 5
35	175	190	− 15

As you can see, the maximum profit that the firm can earn is zero at output levels of 20 or 25 units. If it can choose its output between 20 and 25 units, the firm's optimal production level is 22.5 units. [See Section 11-3.]

PROBLEM 11-8   Figure 11-4 shows the total cost (TC) and total revenue (TR) curves for the Gizmo Group. Find the Gizmo Group's profit-maximizing output level.

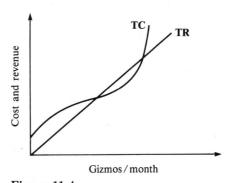

Figure 11-4

Answer: A firm's profit-maximizing output level is represented graphically by the point at which the positive vertical distance between its TR and TC curves is the greatest. To locate that point precisely, you must find the point at which the slopes of the firm's TR and TC curves are equal. Technically, that's the point at which a tangent to the TR curve is parallel to a tangent to the TC curve. As Figure 11-5 shows, that point for the Gizmo Group is output Q^*. [See Section 11-3.]

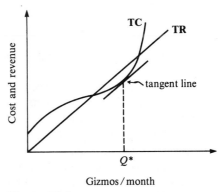

Figure 11-5

PROBLEM 11-9 Prepare marginal cost and marginal revenue schedules for the hypothetical firm in Problem 11-7.

Answer: To prepare the firm's marginal cost schedule, divide the change in its total cost by the change in its total output from one level to the next. To prepare the firm's marginal revenue schedule, divide the change in its total revenue by the change in its total output from one level to the next. Write the marginal cost and marginal revenue figures in the intervals between quantities, as shown in the following table [see Section 11-3]:

Marginal revenue	Total revenue	Total output	Total cost	Marginal cost
	$ 0	0	$ 50	
$5				$1
	25	5	55	
5				2
	50	10	65	
5				3
	75	15	80	
5				4
	100	20	100	
5				5
	125	25	125	
5				6
	150	30	155	
5				7
	175	35	190	

PROBLEM 11-10 Given the marginal cost and marginal revenue schedules for the hypothetical firm in Problem 11-9, find the firm's profit-maximizing output level.

Answer: A firm maximizes its profits at the output level at which its marginal revenue equals its marginal cost. For the hypothetical firm in the problem, then, the profit-maximizing output level is between 20 and 25 units. In that interval the firm's marginal revenue ($5) equals its marginal cost ($5). Therefore, if the firm produces, it should produce 20 to 25 (or 22.5) units of output. [See Section 11-3.]

PROBLEM 11-11 Figure 11-6 shows the short-run marginal revenue (MR), marginal cost (MC), average variable cost (AVC), and average total cost (ATC) curves for the Widget Works. If the firm produces in the short run, at what level of output will it maximize its profits? Will it produce in the short run if the price of a widget is $8?

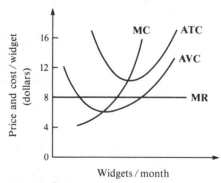

Figure 11-6

Answer: The profit-maximizing output level for the Widget Works is represented graphically by the point at which its MC curve intersects its MR curve from below. As Figure 11-7 shows, that level of output is quantity Q'.

Yes, at a price of $8 per widget, the firm will produce quantity Q' in the short run, even though it will be earning a negative profit. Since the price of a widget will be greater than the average variable cost of production, if the firm produces, it will recover all of its variable costs *plus* some of its fixed costs. If it shuts down, it won't have any variable costs, but it won't be able to recover any of its fixed costs, either. Therefore, it will be more profitable for it to produce than to shut down. [See Sections 11-3 and 11-4.]

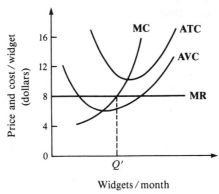

Figure 11-7

PROBLEM 11-12 The Widget Works reports the following cost and revenue data:

Output (*Q*):	100 widgets
Average fixed cost (AFC):	$20
Average variable cost (AVC):	$40
Marginal cost (MC):	$50
Marginal revenue (MR):	$50
Price (*P*):	$50

Calculate the profit the firm will earn if it produces and if it shuts down. Should it produce in the short run? How about the long run?

Answer: To calculate the profit the Widget Works will earn if it produces, first find its total cost (TC):

$$TC = Q(AFC) + Q(AVC)$$
$$= 100(\$20) + 100(\$40)$$
$$= \$6,000$$

Then find its total revenue (TR):

$$TR = Q \times P$$
$$= 100 \times \$50$$
$$= \$5,000$$

Then subtract its total cost from its total revenue: $5,000 − $6,000 = −$1,000.

To calculate the profit the Widget Works will earn if it shuts down, simply subtract the firm's total fixed cost from zero (its total revenue if it doesn't produce): $0 − $2,000 = −$2,000.

Since the Widget Works will earn a greater profit if it produces than if it shuts down, it should produce in the short run. However, it should *not* produce in the long run because its economic profit will be negative.

Another way to answer the question is this: Since the price of a widget ($50) is greater than the average variable cost of producing it ($40), the firm should produce in the short run. However, since the price of a widget ($50) is less than the average total cost of producing it ($60), the firm should *not* produce in the long run. [See Section 11-4.]

PROBLEM 11-13 Explain why a firm will shut down in the long run if the price of its product is less than the average cost of production.

Answer: If the price of its product is less than the long-run average cost of production, a firm's profit will be negative. A negative profit means that the inputs the firm is using have higher values in their next-best uses. Since all inputs—even capital inputs—are variable in the long run, the firm should reassign its inputs to uses with higher values, namely, to the production of other goods. [See Section 11-4.]

MIDTERM EXAMINATION

Chapters 1–11

DIRECTIONS: This examination consists of three types of questions worth a total of **100 points**. The questions in Part 1 are multiple choice. Select the single best answer to each one. The questions in Part 2 are numerical. Perform the calculations required, and fill in the blanks with the correct answers. The questions in Part 3 are analytical. Write a short-essay answer to each question, applying what you have learned about economic theory and drawing diagrams, as requested, to support your analysis. You should complete the entire examination in **90 minutes**. Answers follow the examination.

Part 1: Multiple Choice (60 points)

1. Economics is concerned with the allocation of
   (a) unlimited resources to satisfy limited material wants
   (b) scarce resources to satisfy unlimited material wants
   (c) power in a society
   (d) limited resources to satisfy very limited material wants

2. All of the following directly influence the potential level of output in an economy *except*
   (a) labor
   (b) natural resources
   (c) technology
   (d) shares of stock in major corporations

Questions 3, 4, and 5 are based on Figure ME-1, which shows the production possibilities boundary (PPB) of a hypothetical nation that produces only two goods, tractors and swimming pools.

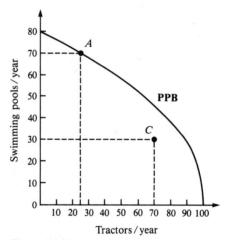

Figure ME-1

3. The nation's economy would be at a point inside its PPB, such as point *C*, if
   (a) its resources were less than fully employed
   (b) the economy were experiencing growth
   (c) the capital stock of the nation were to decrease
   (d) the capital stock of the nation were to increase

4. If the nation's economy were initially at point *A*, the cost of obtaining 10 additional swimming pools would
   (a) be 25 tractors
   (b) decrease as more swimming pools were built
   (c) be 10 tractors
   (d) be zero because fewer tractors would be produced

5. Which of the following would *not* cause a shift in the nation's PPB?
   (a) an improvement in the technology of producing tractors
   (b) a decrease in the unemployment rate
   (c) a reduction in the quantity of natural resources available
   (d) All of these would shift the nation's PPB.

6. Economics begins with the axiom that the behavior of typical human beings is
   (a) rational
   (b) purposeful
   (c) efficient
   (d) all of these

7. Using supply and demand analysis to predict the effect upon price of a change in demand is an example of
   (a) the fallacy of composition
   (b) the application of an economic theory
   (c) the *post hoc, ergo propter hoc* fallacy
   (d) a violation of the *ceteris paribus* condition

8. Positive economics is concerned with
   (a) economic policy (what should be)
   (b) positive, as opposed to deficit, financing
   (c) economic theory (what is)
   (d) the management of information by the government to achieve a more positive investment climate

9. The circular flow model depicts
   (a) a simple economy with only two people
   (b) a simple economy in which exchange occurs only through barter
   (c) a complex economy characterized by specialization, the division of labor, and the use of money
   (d) a complex economy characterized by the use of money but not by specialization or the division of labor

10. Specialization and the division of labor do all of the following *except*
    (a) increase interdependence
    (b) decrease the productive capabilities of an economy
    (c) necessitate exchange
    (d) increase the problems associated with the coordination of economic activity in a complex society

11. The economic system of the USSR (the Soviet Union) is best classified as
    (a) market socialist
    (b) market capitalist
    (c) planned socialist
    (d) planned capitalist

12. Which of the following is *not* a common economic role of government in a mixed capitalist market economy?
    (a) specifying production goals for all goods
    (b) owning some resources
    (c) guaranteeing minimum levels of nutrition, education, and health care services
    (d) producing some goods and services

13. Which of the following will *not* cause an increase in the demand for a good, *ceteris paribus*?
    (a) an increase in the income of consumers
    (b) a decrease in the price of a complementary good
    (c) a decrease in the price of the good
    (d) All of these will cause an increase in the demand for the good.

14. As the price of a good declines,
    (a) the income effect will result in a larger quantity of the good being demanded
    (b) the substitution effect will result in a smaller quantity of the good being demanded
    (c) the substitution and income effects will both result in a smaller quantity of the good being demanded
    (d) both (a) and (b) will occur

15. An increase in the price of an input used to produce a good will
    (a) shift the supply curve for the good to the right
    (b) shift the supply curve for the good to the left
    (c) increase the supply of the good
    (d) affect the quantity of the good supplied but not the supply of the good

16. Which of the following is *not* characteristic of a market supply curve?
    (a) It has a positive slope.
    (b) It shifts when one of the *ceteris paribus* variables changes.
    (c) It offers a historical perspective on the relationship between price and quantity supplied.
    (d) It is an aggregation of the supply curves of all the vendors in the market.

17. If demand increases while supply decreases,
    (a) price will decrease
    (b) both price and quantity exchanged will decrease
    (c) price will increase but quantity exchanged may either increase or decrease
    (d) both price and quantity exchanged will increase

18. An effective price floor imposed on a good will result in
    (a) a decrease in the price of the good
    (b) an increase in the price of the good but a decrease in the quantity of the good supplied
    (c) an increase in both the price of the good and the quantity of the good supplied
    (d) a decrease in both the price of the good and the quantity of the good exchanged

19. If other things remain constant, an increase in the price of tennis rackets most likely will lead to
    (a) an increase in the price of tennis balls
    (b) a decrease in the price of tennis balls
    (c) a decrease in the demand for tennis rackets
    (d) an increase in the demand for tennis balls

20. In the short run, an increase in the excise tax on whisky will
    (a) be absorbed entirely by the distillers
    (b) lead to an increase in the quantity of whisky exchanged
    (c) increase the price of whisky by an amount equal to the tax
    (d) increase the price of whisky by an amount less than the tax

21. If the quantity of gizmos sold declines by 20% when the price of gizmos increases by 5%, then the elasticity of demand for gizmos equals
    (a) 1/4   (b) −1/4   (c) 4   (d) none of these

22. If a demand curve is vertical,
    (a) it has a very high elasticity
    (b) it is perfectly elastic
    (c) it is unitary elastic
    (d) it has an elasticity of zero

23. In an effort to cut its operating deficits, the Metropolitan Transit Commission (MTC) has increased the price of a bus ride from 50¢ to 75¢. Obviously the MTC believes that the demand for bus rides is
  (a) elastic
  (b) unitary elastic
  (c) inelastic
  (d) unrelated to elasticity

24. An increase in the price of good X will lead, *ceteris paribus*, to
  (a) an increase in the marginal utility of good X
  (b) an increase in the amount of good X purchased by a typical consumer
  (c) a decrease in the amount of good X purchased by a typical consumer
  (d) both (a) and (c)

25. According to the marginal utility approach to consumer choice, the value of a good is determined by
  (a) the total utility derived from the good
  (b) the average utility derived from the good
  (c) the marginal utility derived from the last unit acquired
  (d) its contribution to the well-being of society

26. Which of the following statements is *not* true of indifference curves?
  (a) They are nonintersecting.
  (b) They are negatively sloped.
  (c) They increase in value to the northeast.
  (d) They bow away from the origin of a graph.

27. The marginal rate of substitution of good X for good Y
  (a) measures the quantity of good Y that can be replaced by an equal amount of good X
  (b) measures the quantity of good Y that can be replaced by one unit of good X
  (c) measures the slope of a consumer's budget line
  (d) increases over time

28. Which of the following is most likely to be a fixed input in the production of automobiles?
  (a) steel
  (b) labor
  (c) a manager
  (d) an assembly plant

29. It is repeatedly observed that, beyond a point, larger and larger inputs of fuel are needed to produce each additional unit of a good. This persistent observation is known in economics as
  (a) the law of diminishing marginal utility
  (b) the law of demand
  (c) the law of diminishing returns
  (d) the law of increasing costs

30. As output is expanded in the short run, eventually
  (a) productivity will rise
  (b) per-unit costs will decline
  (c) productivity will decline and per-unit costs will rise
  (d) productivity will rise and per-unit costs will decline

31. As output and plant size are expanded in the long run,
  (a) marginal physical product will always diminish
  (b) per-unit costs may reach their lowest possible levels
  (c) costs per unit will always decline
  (d) all of these will occur

32. The following table shows the prices of two inputs, labor and capital, and the marginal physical product (MPP) of labor.

Input	Price	MPP
Labor	$1	8
Capital	2	—

Given the information in the table, a producer should hire capital inputs until the marginal physical product of capital declines to equal
(a) 4   (b) 8   (c) 16   (d) 32

33. Which of the following would most likely be an external cost in the production of oil?
(a) royalty payments to landowners
(b) the cost of a pipeline to transport the oil
(c) the cost of drilling an oil well
(d) the cost of the environmental destruction resulting from an oil spill

34. The implicit cost of an input
(a) is determined by its opportunity cost
(b) includes external or third-party costs
(c) is the value of a purchased resource
(d) is not part of the economic cost of producing an item

35. In a model cost diagram, the marginal cost (MC) curve
(a) intersects the average total cost curve (ATC) at the lowest point on the ATC curve
(b) intersects the average variable cost (AVC) curve at the lowest point on the AVC curve
(c) rises beyond some output level because marginal physical product diminishes
(d) exhibits all of these properties

36. If the long-run average cost of production in an industry rises as output and plant size are increased, the industry is said to exhibit
(a) economies of scale
(b) constant economies of scale
(c) diseconomies of scale
(d) none of these conditions because average costs always decline in the long run

37. In order to be classified as a firm, an entity must be
(a) producing a good   (c) privately owned
(b) incorporated   (d) profit oriented in its decision making

38. What is the difference between economic profit and accounting net income?
(a) Many implicit costs that are routinely excluded from accounting costs are included in calculations of economic profit.
(b) Whereas economic profits always equal zero, accounting net income rarely does.
(c) Explicit costs are ignored when economic profits are calculated but not when accounting net income is.
(d) There is no difference. Both terms have the same meaning.

39. A firm should shut down in the short run if the revenue it receives from sales is less than
(a) all private costs of production
(b) the variable costs of production
(c) the fixed costs of production
(d) the sum of the explicit and implicit costs of production

40. If the marginal revenue that a firm receives from the last unit it produces equals $10 and the marginal cost of the unit equals $6, the firm will maximize its profits by
  (**a**) expanding output   (**c**) holding output constant
  (**b**) reducing output   (**d**) shutting down

Part 2: Numerical (20 points)

1. The following schedule shows the quantity demanded and supplied at various prices per unit in the widget market each month:

Quantity demanded	Price	Quantity supplied
1,000	$10	1,450
1,100	9	1,400
1,200	8	1,350
1,300	7	1,300
1,400	6	1,250
1,500	5	1,200
1,600	4	1,150

(**a**) The equilibrium price in the widget market is _____ . The equilibrium quantity in the widget market is _____ .

(**b**) At the equilibrium price and quantity in the widget market, the total revenue received by widget producers equals _____ .

(**c**) The price elasticity of demand for widgets between the prices of $9 and $8, to the nearest hundredth, equals _____ . (Show your calculations.)

2. The following is a partial cost schedule for Acme Gizmos, Limited:

Output/ month	Fixed cost	Variable cost	Total cost	Marginal cost
1	$100	$10	_____	
2	100	16	_____	_____
3	100	26	_____	_____
4	100	40	_____	_____
5	100	58	_____	_____
6	100	80	_____	_____

(**a**) Complete the cost schedule for Acme Gizmos by supplying the missing total and marginal cost figures.

(**b**) If Acme can sell all the gizmos it produces at $18 a gizmo (i.e., if the marginal revenue from each additional unit sold equals $18), Acme's profit-maximizing output level is _____ gizmos a month.

(**c**) At the profit-maximizing output level in part (**b**), Acme's total profit equals _____ . (Show your calculations.)

(**d**) If Acme ceases production, its total profit will equal _____ . The difference between its total profit from shutting down and its total profit in part (**c**) equals _____ . (Show your calculations.)

Part 3: Analytical (20 points)

1. The federal government wants to reduce the surplus wheat in the United States by adopting a payment-in-kind (PIK) program. A PIK program will encourage farmers to produce less wheat by paying them in kind (with wheat) for each acre that they do *not* plant in wheat. The in-kind payments will come from surplus wheat produced in earlier years that the government has purchased and stored. Base your answers to the following three questions on the assumption that the program is effective, that is, that farmers plant fewer acres in wheat and harvest less wheat as a result of the program.

(a) Assume that the market supply and demand curves for wheat are typical. Analyze the effect of the PIK program on the price of wheat and the quantity of wheat exchanged in the U.S. market. Draw an appropriate diagram to support your analysis.

(b) Assume that the market demand for wheat is inelastic at the preprogram output–price level. Analyze the effect of the PIK program on the revenues received by wheat farmers from the sale of wheat. Explain your answer.

(c) Analyze the effect of the PIK program on the market price of wheat seed and the quantity of wheat seed exchanged. Draw an appropriate diagram to support your analysis.

Answers

DIRECTIONS: Score your examination as follows: In Part 1, score 1.5 points for each of the 40 items that you answered correctly. In Part 2, score 2 points for each of the 7 lettered question parts that you answered correctly, plus 2 additional points for each of the 3 calculations that you performed correctly. In Part 3, score 8 points for correct answers to parts (a) and (c) and 4 points for a correct answer to part (b). **Total possible points: 100.**

Part 1

1. (b)	9. (c)	17. (c)	25. (c)	33. (d)
2. (d)	10. (b)	18. (c)	26. (d)	34. (a)
3. (a)	11. (c)	19. (b)	27. (b)	35. (d)
4. (a)	12. (a)	20. (d)	28. (d)	36. (c)
5. (b)	13. (c)	21. (c)	29. (c)	37. (d)
6. (d)	14. (a)	22. (d)	30. (c)	38. (a)
7. (b)	15. (b)	23. (c)	31. (b)	39. (b)
8. (c)	16. (c)	24. (d)	32. (c)	40. (a)

Part 2

1. (a) $7,   1,300

   (b) $9,100

   (c) $E = 0.74$

$$E = \left| \frac{(Q_2 - Q_1)}{(P_2 - P_1)} \times \frac{(P_2 + P_1)}{(Q_2 + Q_1)} \right|$$

$$= \left| \frac{(1,200 - 1,100)}{(\$8 - \$9)} \times \frac{(\$8 + \$9)}{(1,200 + 1,100)} \right|$$

$$= \left| \frac{100}{-\$1} \times \frac{\$17}{2,300} \right|$$

$$= 0.74$$

2. (a) *Total cost* is the sum of fixed cost and variable cost. *Marginal cost* is the change in total cost for a one-unit change in output. Acme's total and marginal costs at each level of output are shown in the following table:

Output/ month	Fixed cost	Variable cost	Total cost	Marginal cost
1	$100	$10	$110	
2	100	16	116	$ 6
3	100	26	126	10
4	100	40	140	14
5	100	58	158	18
6	100	80	180	22

(b) Acme's profit-maximizing output level is five gizmos a month. At that level, its marginal revenue and its marginal cost are equal (MR = MC = $18).

(c) *Total profit* is the difference between total revenue (price times quantity) and total cost (fixed cost plus variable cost):

$$\text{Total profit} = \text{TR} - \text{TC}$$
$$= (P \times Q) - (\text{FC} + \text{VC})$$

At an output level of five gizmos, Acme's total profit equals −$68:

$$\text{Total profit} = (P \times Q) - \text{TC}$$
$$= (\$18 \times 5) - \$158$$
$$= \$90 - \$158$$
$$= -\$68$$

(d) If Acme shuts down, its total revenue and its variable cost will both be zero, so its total profit will equal its negative fixed cost, −$100:

$$\text{Total profit} = \text{TR} - (\text{FC} + \text{VC})$$
$$= 0 - (\$100 - 0)$$
$$= -\$100$$

The difference between −$100 and −$68 is −$32:

$$-\$100 - (-\$68) = -\$100 + \$68 = -\$32$$

Part 3

1. (a) An effective PIK program will reduce the supply of wheat. In other words, as Figure ME-2 shows, it will shift the supply curve for wheat to the left, from *SS* to *S'S'*. As a result, the market price of wheat will increase from *P* to *P'*, and the quantity of wheat exchanged will decline from *Q* to *Q'*.

(b) When demand is inelastic ($E < 1$), increases in price more than offset the decreases in quantity that they produce, so total revenue (price times quantity) increases. Therefore, if the demand for wheat is inelastic before a PIK program is adopted, as it is at point (Q, P) in Figure ME-2, and if the program results in an increase in price and a decrease in quantity exchanged, the total revenue of wheat farmers will increase.

(c) A reduction in the production of wheat will reduce the demand for wheat seed and other factors used to produce wheat. As Figure ME-3 shows, the demand curve for wheat seed will shift left, from *DD* to *D'D'*. As a result, the price of wheat seed will decline from *P* to *P'*, and the quantity of wheat seed exchanged will decline from *Q* to *Q'*.

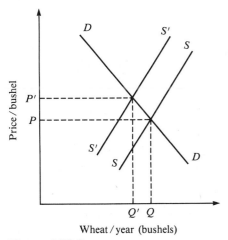

Figure ME-2

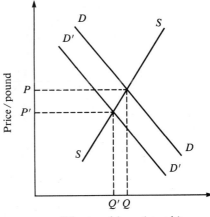

Figure ME-3

12 PERFECT COMPETITION

THIS CHAPTER IS ABOUT

☑ **The Theory of Perfect Competition**
☑ **Short-Run Decisions and the Supply Curve of a Competitive Firm**
☑ **Short-Run Competitive Equilibrium**
☑ **Long-Run Competitive Equilibrium**
☑ **Economic Efficiency and Perfect Competition**
☑ **Long-Run Industry Supply Conditions Under Perfect Competition**

12-1. The Theory of Perfect Competition

Perfect competition is one of the oldest and most widely employed theories in economics. It is used to predict economic phenomena, such as the effect of a crop failure on commodity prices. The theory of perfect competition brings together the material on output and production, economic cost, and profit maximization in the last three chapters.

As you recall from Chapter 2, theories have three components: assumptions, definitions, and the implications or results that follow from the assumptions. In this chapter you will learn about these components as they relate to the theory of perfect competition, and you will come to understand the logic that connects the assumptions of the theory with its implications.

A. The theory of perfect competition includes four major assumptions.

1. There are many buyers and sellers in a perfectly competitive market—enough so that individual decisions about production and consumption do not (and cannot) affect market price. In a perfectly competitive market, a firm does not have price-setting power; it takes the market price as given.
2. All products produced in a perfectly competitive market are homogeneous. Thus no buyer prefers the products of one seller to those of another.
3. All buyers and sellers in a perfectly competitive market have perfect knowledge about the prices of products and the quantities in which they are available.
4. Entry into and exit from a perfectly competitive market are both free from impediment. New firms can enter and existing firms can leave without restriction.

Three other assumptions are implicit in the theory of perfect competition and in the theories of all other market structures. You are already familiar with two of these assumptions.

5. Firms (producers) aim to maximize their profits.
6. Households (consumers) aim to maximize their satisfaction or utility.

7. No external or third-party costs or benefits are associated with any good.

EXAMPLE 12-1: The national markets for grains, such as wheat, are among the few markets that closely fit the four basic assumptions of the theory of perfect competition. First, there are a very large number of buyers and sellers who participate in the national grain markets. Second, market information is extensive and widely reported. Third, products are homogeneous. Wheat, for example, is graded so that # 1 hard red winter wheat is essentially the same no matter who produces it. Fourth, entry into and exit from the market are virtually free from restriction. If they establish accounts with commodity trading firms, farmers, exporters, millers, and speculators can buy or sell wheat simply by phoning their brokers.

B. Each seller in a perfectly competitive market perceives a demand curve that is horizontal at the market price.

Because the market price is given and is not noticeably affected by the actions of any individual buyer or seller, each firm in a perfectly competitive market perceives the demand curve that it faces as horizontal (perfectly elastic) at the market price. This means that each firm perceives that it can sell in any quantity it chooses without affecting the market price of its product.

Of course the demand curve that an individual firm *perceives* is not identical with the market demand curve. As Figure 12-1 shows, whereas the demand curve (*dd*) that a typical firm faces is horizontal at the market price, the market demand curve (*DD*) has a classic downward or negative slope. (Throughout the chapter we will continue to differentiate between the general conditions in a perfectly competitive market and those that face an individual firm participating in the market.)

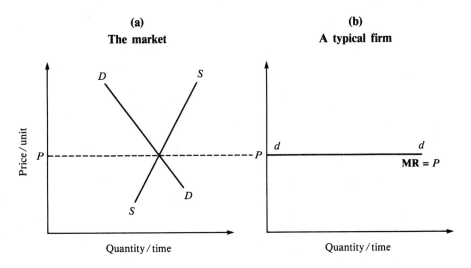

Figure 12-1
In a perfectly competitive market, the market demand curve (*DD*) has a negative slope, but each firm perceives a demand curve (*dd*) that is horizontal at the market price.

C. In a perfectly competitive market, each seller's marginal revenue equals the market price.

In a perfectly competitive market, a firm sells each unit of its product at the market price. Thus, the firm's marginal revenue, which is the change in its total revenue that results from a one-unit change in the quantity it sells, equals the market price at every level of output. If a firm's marginal revenue equals the market price at every level of output, its marginal revenue curve is congruent with the horizontal demand curve that it faces. Both curves, in other words, are horizontal at the market price.

EXAMPLE 12-2: If wheat is selling for $4 a bushel in a perfectly competitive market, the total revenue that a wheat farmer earns is $4 times the number of bushels that he or she sells. The marginal revenue that the wheat farmer earns, no matter how many bushels he or she sells, is $4.

Bushels of wheat	Price per bushel	Total revenue	Marginal revenue
1	$4	$ 4	
			$4
2	4	8	
			4
3	4	12	
			4
4	4	16	

12-2. Short-Run Decisions and the Supply Curve of a Competitive Firm

Since products are homogeneous and price is given, life is relatively simple for a firm in a perfectly competitive market. Assuming that the firm has decided what technology and what mix of inputs it will use, the only other significant decision it has to make is how much it will produce.

A. A firm selects its output level in accordance with the rules for maximizing profits.

A typical firm in a perfectly competitive market selects the level at which it will produce in the short run by following two of the profit-maximizing rules set forth in the last chapter:

Rule 1: If a firm chooses to produce, it should produce that level of output at which its marginal cost (MC) curve intersects its marginal revenue (MR) curve from below. At that level of output its marginal cost equals its marginal revenue, which equals the market price (P) in a perfectly competitive market: MC = MR = P.

Rule 2: In the short run, a firm should produce if the price (P) of its product (the market price) is greater than the average variable cost (AVC) of production: P > AVC.

EXAMPLE 12-3: Figure 12-2 shows the MC and AVC curves of a typical firm in a perfectly competitive market. It also shows the firm's MR curve, which is congruent with the horizontal demand curve (*dd*) that it faces at market price P. The profit-maximizing output level for the firm is q^*, where its MC curve intersects its MR curve from below (MC = MR = P). The firm will produce quantity q^* in the short run because the price of its product is greater than the average variable cost of producing it.

B. A firm's MC curve is its supply curve.

Since a firm's MC curve determines the quantity that the firm will seek to provide at any given price, its MC curve is actually its supply curve. In a perfectly competitive market, a firm's short-run supply curve is represented by the portion of its MC curve that lies above its AVC curve.

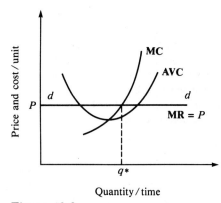

Figure 12-2
A firm applies the MC = MR rule to locate its profit-maximizing output level at q^*. Since P > AVC at q^*, the firm should produce in the short run.

EXAMPLE 12-4: In Figure 12-3, the heavy portion of the MC curve, the portion above the AVC curve, is the short-run supply curve of a typical firm in a perfectly competitive market. It is labeled *ss*. At price P, the firm will maximize its profits by supplying quantity q. At price P', the firm will maximize its profits by supplying quantity q'. At price P''—or at any other price below its average variable cost of production—the firm will maximize its profits by not supplying in any quantity at all. Since price P'' is lower than the average variable cost of production, the firm will lose less in the short run if it shuts down than if it produces.

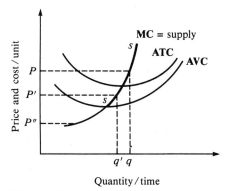

Figure 12-3
In a perfectly competitive market, a firm's short-run supply curve (*ss*) is the portion of its MC curve that lies above its AVC curve.

12-3. Short-Run Competitive Equilibrium

As you may recall from Chapter 5, equilibrium is a state of balance in a market, a state in which there is no internal tendency for the market price, the market quantity, or the output of a typical firm to change. A competitive market equilibrium requires that both the market and the firms serving the market simultaneously achieve a state of equilibrium.

Just as the short run differs from the long run, so short-run competitive equilibrium differs from long-run competitive equilibrium. In the short run, since firms cannot vary their fixed inputs, their options are limited. Therefore, short-run competitive equilibrium is a state of balance for firms *already* serving a market. New firms cannot enter and existing firms cannot exit from the market.

Two conditions are necessary for short-run competitive equilibrium.

A. Markets must be cleared.

For short-run equilibrium, markets must be cleared: that is, quantity supplied must equal quantity demanded. Quantity supplied equals quantity demanded at the point where the market supply curve (*SS*) and the market demand curve (*DD*) intersect, as shown in part (**a**) of Figure 12-4. The intersection of the two curves determines the market price (*P*) and the quantity exchanged in the market (Q^*).

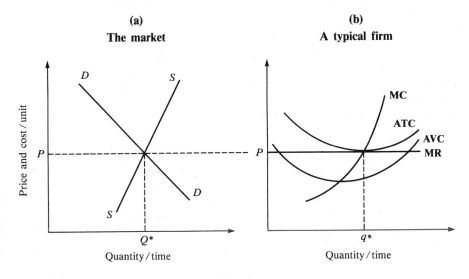

(a)
The market

(b)
A typical firm

Figure 12-4
Two conditions are necessary for short-run competitive equilibrium: (**a**) the market must be cleared and (**b**) a typical firm must be maximizing its profits.

B. Firms must be maximizing profits.

For short-run equilibrium, a firm must be producing at its profit-maximizing output level. Thus, a typical firm in a perfectly competitive market is in short-run equilibrium when (**1**) its marginal cost equals its marginal revenue (the market price) and (**2**) the market price is greater than its average variable cost of production. Output q^* in part (**b**) of Figure 12-4 represents the short-run equilibrium output level for a typical firm in a perfectly competitive market. At that level, it is important to note, the firm's profits may be positive, zero, or negative.

EXAMPLE 12-5: Assume that the trucking industry is perfectly competitive and in long-run equilibrium. Then a government-imposed tax on gasoline and diesel fuel increases the marginal costs (MC) and the average costs (ATC) of a typical firm in the industry, as shown in part (**b**) of Figure 12-5. The firm's supply curve, which is congruent with its marginal cost (MC) curve, shifts upward, and the market supply curve, which is simply a horizontal aggregation of the supply curves of all the individual firms in the industry, shifts left, from SS to $S'S'$, as shown in part (**a**) of Figure 12-5. As a result of the shifts, the market price rises from P to P' and output declines from Q to Q' for the industry and from q to q' for a typical firm. Since the market is cleared at price P' and quantity Q' and since the typical firm is maximizing its profits at output q' (even though its profits are negative), a new short-run equilibrium has been established.

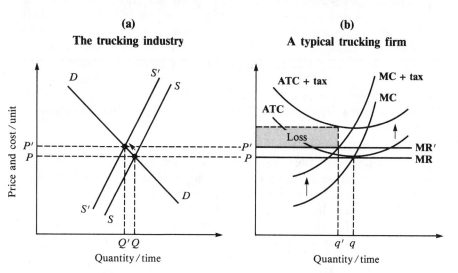

(a)
The trucking industry

(b)
A typical trucking firm

Figure 12-5
In a perfectly competitive market, an increase in costs shifts the cost curves, and thus the supply (MC) curve, of a typical firm upward and the industry supply curve to the left (SS to $S'S'$).

12-4. Long-Run Competitive Equilibrium

In the long run, firms can make more adjustments than they can in the short run. They can alter their plant sizes; they can enter or leave a market. For this reason, the conditions necessary for long-run competitive equilibrium include not only the two for short-run equilibrium but two additional ones, as well.

A. Economic profits must equal zero.

For long-run equilibrium, economic profits of a typical firm must equal zero.

1. If positive economic profits could be earned, new firms, attracted by the above-normal earnings, would enter the market. The entry of new firms would shift the market supply curve to the right, from SS to $S'S'$, as shown in part (**a**) of Figure 12-6. As a result, the market price would be pushed down, from P to P', and market output would be pushed up, from Q to Q'. As part (**b**) of the figure shows, a typical firm would be forced to reduce its output from q to q', and its profits would drop to zero.
2. If economic profits were negative, a typical existing firm, following the third rule for maximizing profits (see Chapter 11), would exit from the market in the long run, and the process that we have just described would reverse itself.

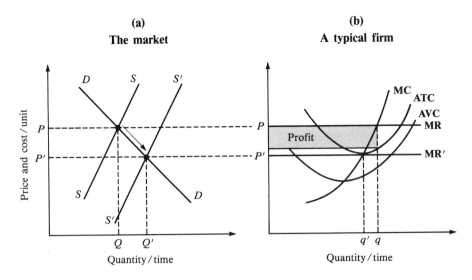

(a)
The market

(b)
A typical firm

Figure 12-6
Positive profits ($P >$ ATC at q) attract new firms to a competitive market. Their entry increases market supply (SS to $S'S'$), reduces market price (P to P'), and pushes the profits of a typical firm down to zero ($P' =$ ATC at q').

EXAMPLE 12-6: Consider the trucking industry in Example 12-5 again. After a tax on gasoline and diesel fuel is imposed by the government, a typical firm in the trucking industry is earning a negative economic profit (operating at a loss). As part **(b)** of Figure 12-5 shows, its average total cost (ATC + tax) is greater than price P' at output q'. Because it is not earning enough to cover its costs, the firm, and others like it, will leave the market in the long run. Their exit will cause the market supply curve to shift even further to the left, as shown in part **(a)** of Figure 12-7, from $S'S'$ to $S''S''$. The market price will increase from P' to P'' and market quantity will decrease from Q' to Q'', at which point the market will be cleared. At price P'', as part **(b)** of Figure 12-7 shows, the profit-maximizing output level for a typical firm that remains in the industry will increase from q' to q'', and its profits will rise to zero. Thus, price P'' and quantity Q'' for the market and quantity q'' for a typical firm represent a new long-run competitive equilibrium.

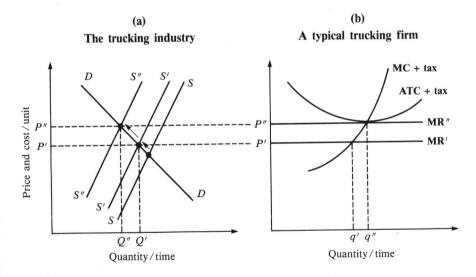

(a)
The trucking industry

(b)
A typical trucking firm

Figure 12-7
Negative profits ($P' <$ ATC at q') induce some firms to exit from a competitive industry. Their exit decreases industry supply ($S'S'$ to $S''S''$), increases price (P' to P''), and pushes the profits of a typical firm up to zero ($P'' =$ ATC at q'').

B. Long-run average costs must be as low as possible.

For long-run equilibrium in a perfectly competitive industry, the average cost of production must be at an absolute minimum: that is, a typical firm must be producing at the lowest point on the LRAC curve for the industry, as shown in part **(b)** of Figure 12-8 on the following page. If it were not—in other words, if the market price were to exceed the minimum long-run average cost of production in the industry—new firms would choose plant sizes that corresponded to the lowest point on the LRAC curve, enter the industry, and earn positive economic profits. The prospect of earning positive economic profits would attract still more new firms to the industry. Their entry would cause the industry supply curve to shift to the right until a typical firm was earning an economic profit of zero and producing at the lowest point on the LRAC curve. Price P and quantity Q in part (a) and price P and quantity q in part (b) of Figure 12-8 fulfill all of the conditions for a long-run competitive equilibrium.

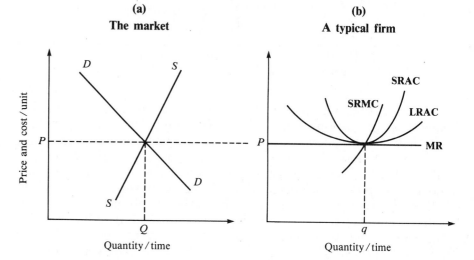

Figure 12-8
In long-run competitive equilibrium, the market is cleared, a typical firm is maximizing its profits ($MC = MR = P$), its profits are zero ($P = AC$), and it is producing at the lowest point (q) on its LRAC curve.

12-5. Economic Efficiency and Perfect Competition

Any allocation of goods and resources that results from a perfectly competitive equilibrium is economically efficient—hence the label *perfect* competition. In fact, the efficiency of resource allocation under perfect competition is the standard by which the efficiency of resource allocation under other market structures, such as monopoly, is evaluated.

A. Productional efficiency is related to allocative efficiency.

Two types of economic efficiency are productional efficiency and allocative efficiency. These two types of efficiency are related.

1. **Productional efficiency** occurs when the average cost of producing a good is at an absolute minimum, as it is under the conditions for long-run equilibrium in a perfectly competitive market. Production is efficient when there are no means of producing a good at a lower cost.

2. **Allocative efficiency** occurs when the price of a good equals the marginal cost of producing it. This equivalence of price and marginal cost, which is a necessary condition for the efficient use of resources by society, results from the profit-maximizing decisions of firms that take prices as given in a perfectly competitive market.

Price = marginal revenue = marginal cost

EXAMPLE 12-7: If the price of wheat is $4 per bushel and its marginal cost is $5 per bushel, society is not allocating its resources efficiently, which means that consumers are not obtaining as much satisfaction as they could with a reallocation. A marginal cost of $5 indicates that society is sacrificing \$5 worth of other goods in order to produce an additional bushel of wheat. The market price of \$4 indicates that society would pay no more than \$4 for an additional bushel; i.e., the value of an additional bushel is \$4 or less. Since society is sacrificing \$5 worth of other goods to gain \$4 worth of wheat, it will enhance its welfare if it reduces production of wheat from Q to Q', as shown in Figure 12-9, and reallocates some of its resources to the production of other goods.

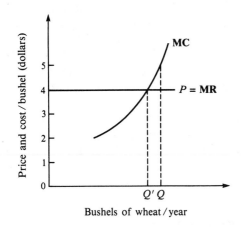

Figure 12-9
Resource use is not efficient when the marginal cost of a good exceeds its price (MC > P at Q). Society will benefit from a reduction in output (Q to Q').

B. An "invisible hand" ensures the economic efficiency of resource allocation under perfect competition.

Adam Smith attributed the economic efficiency of resource allocation under perfect competition to the guidance of an "invisible hand." In *The Wealth of Nations* (1776), he wrote that individuals pursuing their own selfish ends in a competitive market economy would promote the economic welfare of society as a whole "as if guided by an invisible hand." According to Smith, they would not need the direction of government. In fact, he advocated that government adopt a *laissez-faire* policy, a policy of noninterference in economic affairs that allows individuals to do as they choose within the constraints of a competitive market system.

12-6. Long-Run Industry Supply Conditions Under Perfect Competition

So far in our analysis of perfectly competitive markets, we have been assuming that input prices and therefore the production costs of a typical firm in an industry have not been affected by changes in industry output. In reality, however, this is not usually the case. If an increase or decrease in product demand stimulates an expansion or contraction of production in an industry, the prices of inputs are usually affected. When input prices change, they cause the cost curves of the firms in the industry to shift. These shifts, along with the shifts in the industry supply curve, affect the equilibrium price and quantity in the industry.

A. In an increasing-cost industry, input prices and costs increase as output expands.

An **increasing-cost industry** is one in which an expansion of output due to an increase in product demand causes an increase in input prices and production costs in the long run. In an increasing-cost industry, the cost curves of a typical firm shift upward, and both the long-run equilibrium price and the average cost of production increase. Agriculture is an example of an increasing-cost industry. So are most other industries.

EXAMPLE 12-8: Figure 12-10 illustrates the adjustment process that takes place in an increasing-cost industry as a result of an increase in industry demand. In part (**a**) of the figure, as industry demand increases from DD to $D'D'$, the market price rises from P to P' in the short run. At price P', economic profits are positive, attracting new firms and stimulating an expansion of output in the industry. The expansion of output causes the prices of inputs to rise, which in turn causes the average total cost curve of a typical firm to shift upward, from ATC to ATC'', as shown in part (**b**) of the figure. The expansion of output also shifts the industry supply curve to the right, from SS to $S'S'$, as shown in part (**a**), and this shift forces the market price back down from P' to P''. When the adjustment process is complete, a new long-run equilibrium is established at price P'', which is higher than the original long-run equilibrium price, and output Q'' for the industry. At price P'', a typical firm earns an economic profit of zero at output q''.

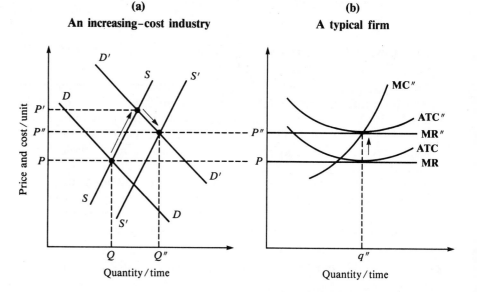

(a)
An increasing–cost industry

(b)
A typical firm

Figure 12-10
In an *increasing-cost* industry, an expansion of industry output (Q to Q'') raises input prices, production costs (ATC to ATC''), and the long-run equilibrium price in the industry (P to P'').

B. In a decreasing-cost industry, input prices and costs decrease as output expands.

A **decreasing-cost industry** is one in which an expansion of output due to an increase in product demand causes a decrease in input prices and production costs in the long run. In their early years, the industries producing such electronic products as calculators and digital watches were good examples of decreasing-cost industries.

EXAMPLE 12-9: Figure 12-11 shows the process of adjustment that occurs in a decreasing-cost industry as a result of an increase in industry demand. It differs from the process of adjustment in an increasing-cost industry in two ways. First, the cost curves of a typical firm naturally shift down rather than up, as shown by the movement from ATC to ATC'' in part (**b**) of the figure. Second, although the market price rises in the short run, from P to P' in part (**a**) of the figure, it declines in the long run to P''. Price P'', the new long-run equilibrium price, is lower than both the short-run price, P', and the original price, P.

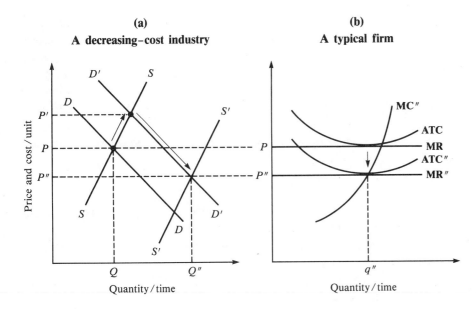

Figure 12-11
In a *decreasing-cost* industry, an expansion of industry output (Q to Q") reduces input prices, production costs (ATC to ATC"), and the long-run equilibrium price in the industry (P to P").

C. In a constant-cost industry, input prices and costs remain constant as output expands.

A **constant-cost industry** is one in which an expansion of output due to an increase in demand has no effect on input prices and production costs in the long run. Costs are most likely to remain constant in industries that account for only a small fraction of the total demand for the inputs or resources they use.

EXAMPLE 12-10: Figure 12-12 illustrates the price adjustment process that results from an increase in industry demand in a constant-cost industry. As you can see in part (a) of the figure, the increase in product demand (DD to D'D') pushes the market price up from P to P' in the short run. However, the entry of new firms and the expansion of industry output gradually force it back down to its original level in the long run. Although the new equilibrium quantity, Q", is greater than the original equilibrium quantity, Q, the new equilibrium price is the same. So, too, is the average total cost of production for a typical firm, as shown in part (b). Since input prices are unaffected by the expansion of output in the industry, the average costs of a typical firm do not change in the long run.

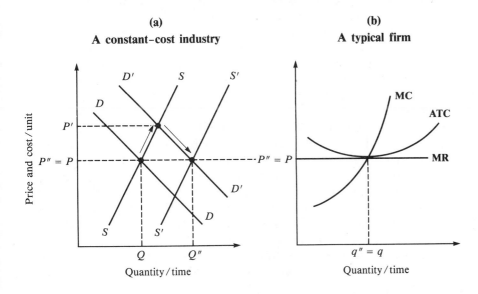

Figure 12-12
In a constant-cost industry, an expansion of industry output (Q to Q") does not affect input prices, production costs, or the long-run equilibrium price in the industry (P" = P).

NOTE: Don't confuse increasing-, decreasing-, and constant-cost industries with diseconomies, economies, and constant economies of scale. The latter refer to the effects of increases in plant size and output on long-run average costs; they determine the *shape* of an LRAC curve. The former refer to the effects of increases in industry output on input prices and long-run average costs in an industry; they determine the *position* of an LRAC curve.

RAISE YOUR GRADES

Can you explain...?

☑ why each firm in a perfectly competitive market perceives the demand curve that it faces as horizontal

☑ why marginal revenue equals the market price in a perfectly competitive market

☑ why a portion of the MC curve of a perfectly competitive firm is its supply curve

☑ why it is necessary for a typical firm to achieve its profit-maximizing output level in order for a competitive equilibrium to exist

☑ why the economic profit of a firm in long-run competitive equilibrium must equal zero

☑ why a firm in long-run competitive equilibrium must be producing at the lowest point on its LRAC curve

☑ why the equivalence of price and marginal cost ($P = \text{MC}$) is a necessary condition for efficient resource use

☑ what happens to input prices when industry demand decreases in an increasing-cost industry

☑ how a decreasing-cost industry differs from an industry that exhibits economies of scale

SUMMARY

1. The theory of perfect competition assumes market conditions in which (1) buyers and sellers are too numerous to affect price individually; (2) goods and resources are homogeneous; (3) knowledge is perfect; and (4) firms may enter and exit freely.

2. Each seller in a perfectly competitive market perceives a horizontal demand curve at the market price. A firm can sell any quantity it desires at the market price, but it does not have price-setting power. It must take the market price as given.

3. In a perfectly competitive market, a firm's marginal revenue is just equal to the market price (MR = P).

4. In the short run, a firm in a perfectly competitive market should produce if the market price exceeds the firm's average variable cost of production ($P > \text{AVC}$). It should produce at the output level at which its marginal revenue equals its marginal cost (MR = MC = P).

5. In a perfectly competitive market, the portion of a firm's MC curve that lies above its AVC curve is the firm's short-run supply curve.

6. Two conditions are necessary for short-run competitive equilibrium: (1) markets must be cleared (quantity supplied must equal quantity demanded) and (2) firms must be maximizing profits. Profits may be positive, zero, or negative in the short run.

7. Four conditions are necessary for long-run competitive equilibrium: (1) markets must be cleared; (2) firms must be maximizing profits; (3) the economic profits of firms must equal zero; and (4) firms must be producing at the lowest points on their LRAC curves.

8. Positive economic profits attract new firms into a competitive market. Their entry shifts the market supply curve to the right and depresses the market price.

9. Negative economic profits induce some existing firms to exit from a competitive market. Their exit shifts the market supply curve to the left and elevates the market price.

10. Perfect competition yields both productional and allocative efficiency.

11. *Productional efficiency* occurs when the average cost of producing a good is at its absolute minimum. *Allocative efficiency* occurs when the price of a good equals the marginal cost of producing it.

12. According to Adam Smith in *The Wealth of Nations* (1776), if individuals are allowed to pursue their own selfish interests in a competitive market economy, they will maximize the economic welfare of society "as if guided by an invisible hand."

13. In an increasing-cost industry, an increase in industry output increases input prices, shifts the cost curves of a typical firm upward, and increases the long-run equilibrium price.

14. In a decreasing-cost industry, an increase in industry output decreases input prices, shifts the cost curves of a typical firm downward, and decreases the long-run equilibrium price.

15. In a constant-cost industry, an increase in industry output has no long-run effect on input prices, the cost curves of a typical firm, or the equilibrium price.

RAPID REVIEW

1. All of the following are principal assumptions of the theory of perfect competition *except* (a) many buyers and sellers, (b) an economic profit of zero, (c) perfect knowledge of prices and quantities, (d) free entry and exit. [See Section 12-1.]

2. The demand curve perceived by a typical firm in a perfectly competitive market is (a) vertical, (b) negatively sloped, (c) horizontal, (d) positively sloped. [See Section 12-1.]

3. The marginal revenue of each firm in a perfectly competitive market is equal to the _____ _____. [See Section 12-1.]

4. Like a firm in any other type of market, a firm in a perfectly competitive market should produce at the output level at which its marginal revenue equals its _____ cost. [See Section 12-2.]

5. A firm in a perfectly competitive market should produce in the short run if its average _____ cost of production is _____ than the market price. [See Section 12-2.]

6. The short-run supply curve of a firm in a perfectly competitive market is the portion of its _____ cost curve that lies above its _____ _____ cost curve. [See Section 12-2.]

7. Which of the following is *not* characteristic of short-run competitive equilibrium? (a) Production costs are at an absolute minimum. (b) There is no internal tendency for the market price or quantity to change. (c) Firms are maximizing their profits. (d) Firms may neither enter nor leave the market. [See Section 12-3.]

8. A market is _____ or in short-run _____ when quantity supplied equals quantity demanded. [See Section 12-3.]

9. Long-run competitive equilibrium differs from short-run competitive equilibrium in that, in the former, (a) firms may enter or leave the industry, (b) economic profits may be positive, (c) firms must be maximizing profits, (d) markets must be cleared. [See Section 12-4.]

10. The exit of firms from a competitive market causes the market demand curve to shift to the right. True or false? [See Section 12-4.]

11. All of the following are characteristics of long-run equilibrium in a perfectly competitive market *except* (a) minimum average costs, (b) an economic profit of zero, (c) extensive government regulation, (d) an equivalence between price and marginal cost. [See Sections 12-4 and 12-5.]

12. The use of resources in a perfectly competitive market is the standard for efficiency. True or false? [See Section 12-5.]

13. Adam Smith, author of *The Wealth of Nations*, advocated a role of _____, or noninterference in the economic affairs of individuals, for _____. [See Section 12-5.]

14. According to Adam Smith, individuals pursuing their own selfish interests in a competitive market economy are guided by an "_____ _____" toward the promotion of the economic well-being of society. [See Section 12-5.]

15. An increase in industry output has no effect on input prices in a(n) _____ industry. [See Section 12-6.]

16. In a decreasing-cost industry, an increase in industry output causes the ATC curve of a typical firm to shift (a) upward, (b) downward, (c) to the right, (d) to the left. [See Section 12-6.]

17. In an increasing-cost industry, a decrease in industry output causes the ATC curve of a typical firm to shift (a) to the left, (b) to the right, (c) downward, (d) upward. [See Section 12-6.]

18. Diseconomies of scale always occur in increasing-cost industries because the two are synonymous. True or false? [See Section 12-6.]

Answers
1. (b)   2. (c)   3. market price   4. marginal   5. variable, less   6. marginal, average variable   7. (a)   8. cleared, equilibrium   9. (a)   10. false   11. (c)
12. true   13. laissez-faire, government   14. invisible hand   15. constant-cost
16. (b)   17. (c)   18. false

SOLVED PROBLEMS

PROBLEM 12-1 Explain why perfect competition is classified as a theory. List the four main assumptions of the theory and three of its implications or results. [*Hint:* You may want to review the material on theories in Chapter 2.]

Answer: Perfect competition is classified as a theory because it is composed of a series of consistent and related statements that provide a logical explanation of observed phenomena and a basis for predicting future events.

The four principal assumptions of the theory of perfect competition are that (1) the number of buyers and sellers in a market is sufficiently large that no one of them can affect the market price, (2) products and resources are homogeneous, (3) all participants have perfect information about prices and quantities available, and (4) entry into and exit from the market are unrestricted.

Three of the implications or results of the theory of perfect competition are that, when a market is in long-run equilibrium, (1) economic profit equals zero, (2) production costs are at their lowest possible level, and (3) price equals the marginal cost of production. [See Section 2-2 in Chapter 2 and Sections 12-1, 12-4, and 12-5 in this chapter.]

PROBLEM 12-2 Explain how an individual firm in a perfectly competitive market can perceive the demand curve that it faces as horizontal when the demand curve for the market has a classic negative slope.

Answer: An individual firm in a perfectly competitive market perceives the demand curve that it faces as horizontal because the firm can sell any quantity of its product that it wants to sell at the market price. An individual firm is too small to have a significant impact on the market price, whether it sells, say, 5 bushels of corn or 50,000. [See Section 12-1.]

PROBLEM 12-3 Chapter 11 lists four decisions that a firm must make. If a firm in a perfectly competitive market has already decided how it will produce (i.e., what technology and what mix of inputs it will use), what is the only other decision that it must make? Why are the other two decisions irrelevant?

Answer: The only other decision that a firm in a perfectly competitive market must make is what quantity it will produce. It does not—in fact, cannot—decide what price it will charge for its product because the price is given by the market. Moreover, since the products in the market are, by assumption, homogeneous, the firm does not have to decide how it will differentiate its product from the products of other firms in the same market. [See Section 12-2.]

PROBLEM 12-4 The following table is the cost schedule for Olie's Widget Works. It shows Olie's average fixed cost (AFC), average variable cost (AVC), average total cost (ATC), and marginal cost (MC) at various levels of output.

Cost Schedule

Output	AFC	AVC	ATC	MC
10	$100	$40	$140	
20	50	35	85	$30
30	33.3	40	73.3	50
40	25	45	70	60
50	20	50	70	70
60	16.7	55	71.7	80

Assuming that the widget market is perfectly competitive, find the quantity that Olie should make available in the short run at each of the following three prices: $70, $50, and $30.

Answer: According to the second rule for maximizing profits, a firm should produce in the short run only if the price of its product exceeds the average variable cost of production. At a price of $30, then, Olie should not produce any widgets. As you can see in the table, his average variable cost is never lower than $35.

According to the first rule for maximizing profits, Olie should produce that level of output at which his marginal revenue equals his marginal cost. In a perfectly competitive market, a firm's marginal revenue equals the market price. At a price of $70 a widget, then, Olie should produce 50 widgets. At a price of $50, he should produce 30. [See Section 12-2.]

PROBLEM 12-5 The answer to the last problem can be presented in the form of a schedule:

Price	Output
$70	50
50	30
30	0

Explain why the schedule is the supply schedule for Olie's Widget Works.

Answer: A supply schedule relates quantity supplied to price. It shows the various quantities of a product that a firm seeks to sell at alternative prices, *ceteris paribus*. The schedule in the problem shows exactly that information for Olie's Widget Works. Therefore it is the supply schedule for the firm. [See Chapter 5 and Section 12-2.]

PROBLEM 12-6 On the basis of the cost information in the table in Problem 12-4, calculate the economic profit that Olie's Widget Works will earn if the market price of widgets is $50. Demonstrate that, at a price of $50, Olie should produce rather than shut down, even though his economic profit will be negative.

Answer: *Total profit* equals total revenue minus total costs. *Total revenue*, as you recall, is the product of price and quantity. Thus, if Olie produces 30 widgets at $50 apiece, his total revenue will be $1,500:

$$\text{TR} = P \times Q$$
$$= \$50 \times 30$$
$$= \$1,500$$

Total cost is the sum of total fixed and total variable costs. Since those costs are not given in the table in Problem 12-4, the easiest way to find Olie's total cost is to multiply his output, in this case 30, by his average total cost, in this case $73.3:

$$\text{TC} = Q \times \text{ATC}$$
$$= 30 \times \$73.3$$
$$= \$2,199$$

For convenience, let's round that off to $2,200. Now we know that if the price of a widget is $50 and Olie produces 30 widgets, his economic profit will be −$700:

$$\text{Total profit} = \text{TR} - \text{TC}$$
$$= \$1,500 - \$2,200$$
$$= -\$700$$

If Olie shuts down, his total profit will be the negative amount of his total fixed costs. To find his total fixed costs, multiply his average fixed costs by his output at *any* level:

$$\text{TFC} = Q \times \text{AFC}$$
$$= 10 \times \$100$$
$$= \$1,000$$

As you can see, if Olie shuts down, he will lose $1,000. If he produces, he will lose only $700. Therefore he will maximize his profits in the short run by producing at a loss. [See Section 12-2.]

PROBLEM 12-7 Explain why short-run competitive equilibrium is a state of balance only for firms *already* serving an industry.

Answer: Since the short run, by definition, is a period insufficiently long for fixed inputs to be varied, it does not allow new firms enough time to acquire the fixed inputs they need to enter a market, nor does it allow existing firms enough time to liquidate their assets and go out of business. Existing firms can shut down in the short run, but only in the long run can they either get rid of such fixed inputs as plants and machinery or modify them for other productive uses. Therefore, short-run equilibrium is a state of balance only for firms already serving a market. [See Section 12-3.]

PROBLEM 12-8 Explain why the combination of price P and quantities Q and q in Figure 12-13 cannot represent a long-run competitive equilibrium.

Answer: The combination of price P and quantities Q and q in Figure 12-13 cannot represent a long-run competitive equilibrium because long-run average costs are not at their lowest possible level. As part (**b**) of the figure shows, price P is higher than the lowest point on the LRAC curve of a typical firm. Therefore the firm can reduce its production

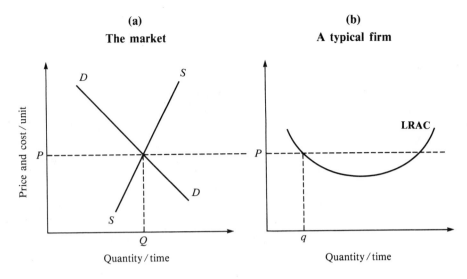

(a)
The market

(b)
A typical firm

Figure 12-13

costs and thereby increase its profits (earn an economic profit greater than zero in the short run) by building a larger plant. Also, new firms can enter the market with plants of the optimal size, and they, too, can earn a positive economic profit. Therefore Figure 12-13 cannot represent a long-run competitive equilibrium. [See Sections 12-3 and 12-4.]

PROBLEM 12-9 Assume that the conditions in a perfectly competitive, constant-cost industry are those shown in Figure 12-13. Describe the adjustment process that will take place in the industry. Explain what will happen in the long run to the equilibrium price, the equilibrium quantity, and the output of a typical firm.

Answer: Since long-run average costs are not at their lowest possible level, the industry offers new and existing firms an opportunity to earn positive economic profits. Existing firms can build larger plants, plants that correspond to the lowest point on the LRAC curve in the industry; new firms can enter the industry with plants of the same optimal size. In either case, the firms with the new plants will produce at output q^*, as shown in part (**b**) of Figure 12-14, and they will earn positive economic profits so long as price remains above P^*.

However, price will not remain above P^* for long. The expansion of output in the industry will eventually shift the industry supply curve to the right, from SS to $S'S'$, as shown in part (**a**) of the figure. That shift will force the market price down from P to P^*. At price P^* and quantities Q^* and q^*, the industry will reach a new long-run equilibrium: the market will be cleared, a typical firm will be earning a maximum economic profit of zero, and long-run average costs will be at their lowest possible level. [See Section 12-4.]

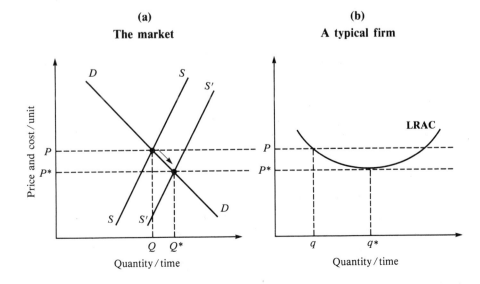

(a)
The market

(b)
A typical firm

Figure 12-14

PROBLEM 12-10 Assume that the pizza market is perfectly competitive. Assume, further, that the market price of pizza is currently $9 and that the marginal cost of producing a pizza is currently $5. Is the pizza market in equilibrium? Are resources being used efficiently? Explain your answers.

Answer: No, the pizza market is not in equilibrium because firms are not maximizing their profits. Firms maximize their profits when their marginal cost equals their marginal revenue. In a perfectly competitive market, that happens when marginal cost equals the market price. In this case, firms can increase their profits by expanding their output because each additional pizza that they produce will add more to their total revenue ($9) than it will add to their total cost ($5).

The discrepancy between the market price of pizza and the marginal or opportunity cost of producing it indicates that resources are not being used efficiently. If people are willing to give up $9 worth of other goods in order to obtain $5 worth of pizza (its marginal cost), some of the resources used to produce other goods should be reallocated to the production of pizza. [See Sections 12-2, 12-3, and 12-5.]

PROBLEM 12-11 Explain what Adam Smith meant by the phrase "invisible hand."

Answer: The "invisible hand" is a metaphor that Adam Smith invented to explain how the competitive market mechanism (supply and demand) could turn selfish behavior into social benefit. Smith argued that if individuals were allowed to pursue their own self-interests in competitive markets, they would promote, and even maximize, the economic well-being of the group as a whole without any direction from a government planning bureau. [See Section 12-5.]

PROBLEM 12-12 Explain the disparate effects that a widespread increase in demand and output would have on the long-run average cost curve in an increasing-cost industry, on the one hand, and a decreasing-cost industry, on the other. Draw appropriate diagrams.

Answer: In an increasing-cost industry a widespread increase in demand and output would cause the prices of inputs to increase (hence the label *increasing-cost* industry). The increase in input prices would cause the LRAC curve in the industry to shift up, as shown in Figure 12-15.

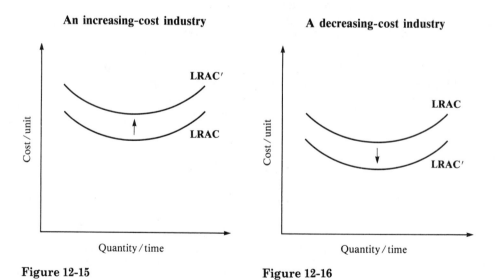

An increasing-cost industry	A decreasing-cost industry
Figure 12-15	**Figure 12-16**

In a decreasing-cost industry, the effect would be just the opposite. A widespread increase in demand and output would cause the prices of inputs to decrease, and the decrease in input prices would cause the LRAC curve in the industry to shift down, as shown in Figure 12-16. [See Section 12-6.]

NOTE: The following three problems are more difficult, but they are typical of the questions that you can expect to find on a test that features either problems or essay questions or both.

PROBLEM 12-13 Assume that the lumber industry is a perfectly competitive, constant-cost industry in long-run equilibrium. Then the demand for housing, and thus for lumber, increases significantly. Analyze the *short-run* impact of the increase in demand on price, industry output, and the output and economic profit of a typical firm in the lumber industry. Draw appropriate diagrams for both the market (i.e., the industry) and the firm.

Answer: An increase in demand will shift the market demand curve to the right, from DD to $D'D'$, as shown in part (**a**) of Figure 12-17. When the demand curve shifts, the market price will increase from P to P', and the market quantity will increase from Q to Q'. The output of a typical firm will also increase, from q to q' in the short run, as shown in part (**b**) of Figure 12-17. At price P' and output q', the firm will earn a positive economic profit in the short run because the price of its product (the market price) will be greater than the average total cost (ATC) of production. [See Section 12-3.]

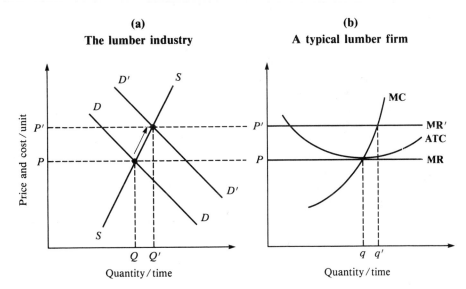

(a)
The lumber industry

(b)
A typical lumber firm

Figure 12-17

PROBLEM 12-14 Assume that the conditions in the lumber industry are the same as those given in Problem 12-13. Now analyze the *long-run* impact of the increase in demand on price, industry output, and the output and economic profit of a typical firm. Draw appropriate diagrams for the market and the firm.

Answer: The short-run impact, as you have already determined, includes economic profit for a typical firm in the lumber industry. The positive economic profit will attract new firms into the industry, and their entry will increase industry output and shift the supply curve to the right, from SS to $S'S'$, as shown in part (**a**) of Figure 12-18 on the following page. New firms will continue to enter the industry until the economic profit of a typical firm returns to zero.

Since we are assuming that the lumber industry is a constant-cost industry, the expansion of industry output will not increase input prices or shift the cost curves of a typical firm upward. Therefore the market price will return to its original level in the long run. As part (**a**) of Figure 12-18 shows, the market price will drop from P' down to P'', its original level, and the market quantity will increase from Q' to Q''. As the market price drops, so will the output of a typical firm. As part (**b**) of the figure shows, a typical firm will reduce its output from q' to q'', its original level, where it will once again earn an economic profit of zero. [See Section 12-4.]

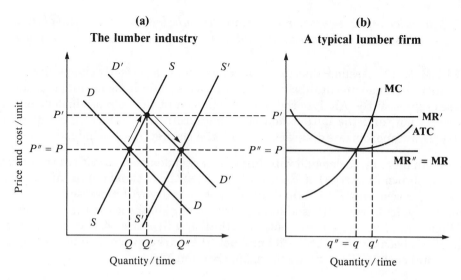

Figure 12-18

PROBLEM 12-15 Revise your long-run analysis in Problem 12-14 on the new assumption that lumber is an increasing-cost industry. Again, draw appropriate diagrams.

Answer: Whether the lumber industry is an increasing- or a constant-cost industry, an increase in industry demand will set off the same chain reaction: the increase in demand will push the market price up, a typical firm will increase its output and earn a positive economic profit in the short run, new firms will be attracted to the industry, the industry supply curve will shift right, the increase in supply will push the market price down, and the economic profit of a typical firm will return to zero.

However, the long-run impact of an increase in demand and an expansion of industry output will be different on an increasing-cost industry than it will be on a constant-cost industry. If lumber is an increasing-cost industry, the expansion of industry output will increase the prices of inputs and shift the average and marginal cost curves of a typical firm upward, as shown in part (**b**) of Figure 12-19. The market price will decline from its short-run level, P' in part (**a**) of the figure, to its new equilibrium level, P'', but the new equilibrium price, reflecting the increase in production costs, will be higher than the initial equilibrium price, P. The quantity of lumber exchanged in the market will increase from Q', its short-run level, to Q'', and the output of a typical firm will decline until the firm is once again earning an economic profit of zero. As Figure 12-19 is drawn, the firm's output returns to its original level ($q'' = q$), but this is not a necessary result of the adjustment process. [See Sections 12-4 and 12-6.]

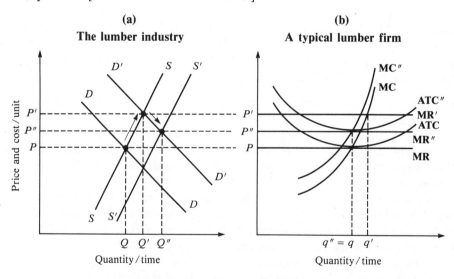

Figure 12-19

13 MONOPOLY

THIS CHAPTER IS ABOUT

- ☑ **The Theory of Monopoly**
- ☑ **Output–Price Decisions Under Monopoly**
- ☑ **Economic Efficiency Under Monopoly**
- ☑ **The Conduct of Monopolists**
- ☑ **Public Policy Toward Monopoly**

13-1. The Theory of Monopoly

The theory of monopoly is perhaps as old as the theory of perfect competition, and, appropriately, its focus is a market structure that, in its pure form, is the diametric opposite of perfect competition. A perfectly competitive market is characterized by a very large number of sellers and free entry; by contrast, a purely monopolistic market is characterized by only one seller and blocked entry. Blocked entry and the lack of competition in a monopoly give a monopolistic firm pricing options that are not available to firms in perfectly competitive markets.

A. The theory of monopoly includes four major assumptions.

As you recall from Chapter 12, three assumptions are common to the theories of all market structures, including both monopoly and perfect competition: (1) that firms aim to maximize their profits, (2) that households aim to maximize their satisfaction, and (3) that no external costs or benefits are associated with any good. In addition to these common assumptions, the theory of monopoly includes four major assumptions:

1. Although there are many buyers in a monopoly, there is only one seller.
2. No close substitutes exist for a product produced in a monopoly.
3. The single seller and the buyers in a monopoly have perfect knowledge of the prices of products and the quantities in which they are available.
4. The entry of other sellers into a monopolized market is blocked. No new firms can enter even in the long run.

EXAMPLE 13-1: Until recently the telephone service provided throughout the United States by the American Telephone and Telegraph Company (AT&T) and its local subsidiaries served as a classic example of a monopoly. Other firms could not compete with AT&T by offering their own brands of telephone service because entry into local markets was blocked by franchise agreements between AT&T and city or county governments. Neither could other firms compete with AT&T by providing close substitutes for telephone service because none exist. In 1984 the company underwent a court-mandated breakup into smaller, regional companies.

These companies, though smaller, still have monopolies on local telephone service in their own areas.

B. Entry barriers prevent new firms from entering a monopoly.

Since new firms are normally attracted to profitable markets, a monopolist earning a positive economic profit can remain the sole seller in a market only if other firms are prevented from entering the market. An obstacle that prevents or deters new firms from entering a market is known as an **entry barrier**. Entry barriers take three common forms.

1. *Government franchises and patents.* A **franchise** is the exclusive right to a market granted by the government to one firm or to a limited number of firms. A **patent** is the exclusive right to make, use, or sell an innovative product or process.
2. *Economies of scale.* Economies of scale, as you recall, are the cost advantages of producing a good or service on a large scale—that is, with a large plant and at a high rate of production. When the economies of scale in an industry are significant relative to industry demand, a market may not be large enough to support more than one plant of a size that corresponds to the lowest point on the long-run average cost curve for the industry. Such industries are natural monopolies.
3. *High sunk costs and risk.* Entering some industries requires an irrevocable commitment to certain resources. When the costs associated with those resources, known as *sunk costs*, are high and the risk of failure is substantial, a firm may decline to enter an industry even though an existing firm may be earning positive economic profits.

C. The demand curve facing a monopolist is the market demand curve.

Since there is only one seller in a monopoly, the demand curve that a monopolist faces is the market demand curve. Like other market demand curves, it has a downward or negative slope, which means that, unlike a firm in a perfectly competitive market, the firm in a monopoly can sell in larger quantities only by reducing the price of its product.

EXAMPLE 13-2: Figure 13-1 shows the demand curve (*DD*) facing the Widget Works, a firm that enjoys a monopoly over the production and sale of widgets in a small geographical area. The Widget Works is currently producing and selling 200 widgets a month at a price of $8 each. Assuming that it must charge the same price for each widget that it sells, if the firm wishes to increase its output and sales to 400 widgets, it can do so only by reducing the price of a widget from $8 to $6. As market demand curve *DD* in Figure 13-1 shows, at a price of $6 the buyers in the market will seek to purchase 400 widgets.

D. For a monopolist, marginal revenue is less than price.

As you recall from Chapter 12, the marginal revenue of a firm in a perfectly competitive market is always equal to the market price because the demand curve that the firm faces is horizontal at the market price. This is not the case in a monopoly. Since the demand curve that a monopolistic firm faces has a negative slope, consumers in the market will buy more only if the firm offers to sell the product at a lower price. Again, assuming that the firm must charge the same price for *all* units, this means that it can produce and sell an additional unit of its product only if it reduces the price of all units. Therefore at any

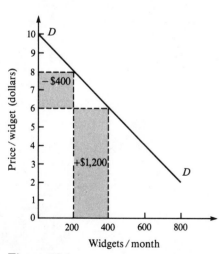

Figure 13-1
A monopolist faces a market demand curve (*DD*) with a negative slope. Therefore a monopolist must reduce price to increase quantity sold.

level of output after the first, the firm's marginal revenue—the revenue that it derives from producing one additional unit of its product—is necessarily less than the price that it charges. In fact, as you may be able to deduce, the difference between the firm's marginal revenue and the price that it charges at any level of output is exactly equal to the sum of the price cuts that it must take on lower levels of output that it otherwise could be selling at a higher price.

EXAMPLE 13-3: By reducing the price of its product from $8 to $6, the Widget Works in Example 13-2 (see Figure 13-1) can gain $1,200 in new revenue by selling 200 additional widgets ($6 × 200 = $1,200). However, if it does so, it will also lose $400 in old revenue because it will have to reduce the price of its first 200 widgets by $2 apiece ($2 × 200 = $400). Thus the net increase in its total revenue (the gain minus the loss) will be only $800 ($1,200 − $400 = $800). A net increase of $800 in total revenue means that the marginal revenue that the Widget Works will derive from each of the 200 additional widgets that it produces will be only $4 ($800 ÷ 200 = $4), which is $2 less than the price that it will charge for each one.

Graphically, the fact that marginal revenue is less than price for a monopolist implies that the monopolist's marginal revenue (MR) curve lies below or to the left of the market demand curve. In fact, a monopolist's MR curve is easy to construct because it bisects the horizontal distance between the *y*-axis and the market demand curve (*DD*), as shown in Figure 13-2.

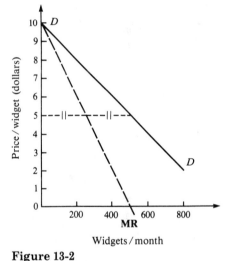

Figure 13-2
A monopolist's marginal revenue (MR) curve bisects the horizontal distance between the *y*-axis and the market demand curve (*DD*).

13-2. Output–Price Decisions Under Monopoly

As you recall from Chapter 12, a firm in a perfectly competitive market has no control over the price of its product because it is only one of a very large number of small firms that sell the same standardized product. For this reason, a firm in a perfectly competitive market is known as a *price taker*. By contrast, a firm in a monopolistic market is the only firm that *can* set the price of its product because it is the sole seller of a unique product for which there are no close substitutes. For this reason, a firm in a monopolistic market is known as a *price setter*. It must decide not only how much to produce, but also what price to charge.

The conditions for equilibrium under monopoly are much less complicated than the conditions for equilibrium under perfect competition. Because there is only one seller, the firm and the market are both in equilibrium when the firm is maximizing its profits.

A. The firm in a monopoly decides how much to produce by following the rules for profit maximization.

Like a firm in a perfectly competitive market (or, for that matter, any other type of market), the firm in a monopoly decides whether or not to produce and, if so, how much by following the three basic rules for profit maximization:

Rule 1: If a firm produces, it should produce at the level at which its marginal revenue equals its marginal cost (MR = MC).

Rule 2: In the short run, a firm should produce if the price of its product is greater than the average variable cost of production ($P > AVC$).

Rule 3: In the long run, a firm should produce if the price of its product is greater than or equal to the long-run average cost of production ($P \geq AC$).

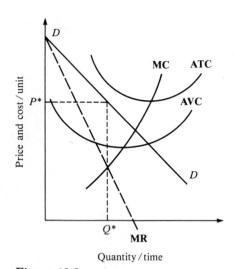

Figure 13-3

The firm in a monopoly finds its optimal output (*Q**) by applying the MR = MC rule and its optimal price (*P**) by measuring the height of the demand curve (*DD*) at that output.

EXAMPLE 13-4: Figure 13-3 shows the market demand (*DD*) and the marginal revenue (MR) curves in a monopolized market, as well as the short-run marginal cost (MC), average variable cost (AVC), and average total cost (ATC) curves of the firm in the market. The firm's MC curve intersects its MR curve from below at quantity *Q**; therefore quantity *Q** is its profit-maximizing output level.

B. The firm in a monopoly decides what price to charge by measuring the height of the market demand curve at its optimal production level.

Once the firm in a monopoly has determined its profit-maximizing output level, it determines the price that it will charge by finding the price that corresponds to that output level on the market demand curve—that is, by measuring the height of the market demand curve at its optimal production level. Graphically, it does so simply by drawing two lines: (1) a vertical line that extends from its profit-maximizing output level on the *x*-axis up to the market demand curve and (2) a horizontal line that extends from that point to the *y*-axis.

EXAMPLE 13-5: Figure 13-3 illustrates the process by which the firm in a monopoly decides what price it will charge for its product. After it has used the MR = MC formula to find its profit-maximizing output level at quantity *Q**, it locates the price that the market will bear at that quantity by drawing a vertical line from *Q** to market demand curve *DD* and a horizontal line from that point to the price axis (the *y*-axis). As you can see in the figure, the firm should charge price *P** for quantity *Q** of its product. If it charges less for quantity *Q**, there will be an excess demand; if it charges more, there will be an excess supply. Price *P**, therefore, is the highest price that will allow the firm to sell its profit-maximizing output. Since price *P** lies above the firm's AVC curve at quantity *Q** (*P** > AVC at *Q**), the firm will produce quantity *Q** in the short run.

Three observations should be made about the method by which the firm in a monopoly determines the price that it will charge for its product.

1. Unlike a firm in a perfectly competitive market, the firm in a monopoly has no supply curve in the conventional sense because no prices are "given" in a monopoly. The firm sets its own price.
2. The price-setting power of the firm in a monopoly is constrained by the market demand curve. Once the firm has located its profit-maximizing output level at the point at which its MC curve intersects its MR curve from below, the market demand curve determines the maximum price that the firm can charge for its product at that output level.
3. The total and marginal revenue of the firm in a monopoly can be derived from the market demand curve or schedule that the firm faces.

EXAMPLE 13-6: The first two columns in the table that follows show the number of gizmos that the consumers in a small market monopolized by the Gizmo Group are willing and able to purchase at various prices each year. In other words, the first two columns in the table are the market demand schedule that the Gizmo Group faces. Since the Gizmo Group is the sole seller in the market, it knows from the demand schedule how many gizmos it can sell if it charges any of various prices for its product. Therefore the Gizmo Group can derive its total and marginal revenue schedules from the demand schedule.

Total revenue, as you recall, is the product of price and quantity sold. Thus, to derive its total revenue schedule, the Gizmo Group need only multiply price and quantity at each level of output. Then, once it has derived its total revenue schedule, it can derive its marginal revenue schedule simply by dividing the change in its total revenue by the change in its output (quantity) from one level to the next. The total revenue (TR) and marginal revenue (MR) schedules for the Gizmo Group are shown in the third and fourth columns of the table.

Demand Schedule

Quantity/time	Price/unit	TR	MR
10	$90	$ 900	
			$70
20	80	1,600	
			50
30	70	2,100	
			30
40	60	2,400	
			10
50	50	2,500	
			− 10
60	40	2,400	
			− 30
70	30	2,100	

If we assume for the sake of simplicity that the Gizmo Group's marginal and average total cost of production are both $30 (MC = ATC = $30), then by applying the MR = MC rule, we can locate its profit-maximizing output level midway between 30 and 40—or at 35—gizmos. For those 35 gizmos, as the second column shows, the firm will be able to charge a price midway between $60 and $70—or $65. Since $65 is greater than $30 (the firm's average total cost of production), it will earn a handsome profit if it produces.

C. Monopolists are not guaranteed positive economic profits.

Monopolists are not guaranteed positive economic profits simply because they have monopolies. As you have already learned, costs and market demand both influence the output and price decisions— and therefore the economic profits—of monopolists. Although monopolists are free, theoretically, to charge any price they like, consumers are also free to restrict their purchases. Therefore, like firms in perfectly competitive markets, monopolists can earn negative, zero, or positive profits in the short run. In the long run, of course, their economic profits must be equal to or greater than zero; otherwise, like competitive firms, they will find it more profitable to shut down.

EXAMPLE 13-7: Local transit companies, such as bus and subway lines, often have monopolies on public transportation in their areas. Yet few of them are able to achieve a positive economic profit. Many, in fact, are not even able to earn an economic profit of zero. Figure 13-4 illustrates just such a situation for a hypothetical metropolitan transit company. As you can see, the firm's profit-maximizing output level is Q^*, where its MC curve intersects its MR curve from below. Market demand allows it to charge price P^* for Q^* rides per month, but even at that optimal output–price combination, its economic profit is negative because it is unable to cover all of its costs (notice the position of the firm's ATC curve at output Q^*). The firm may be able to survive in the short run, but if its losses, represented by the shaded area in the figure, are not offset by government subsidies in the long run, it will shut down.

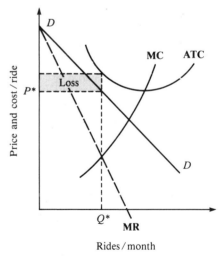

Figure 13-4
The firm in a monopoly is not guaranteed a positive economic profit. Even at its profit-maximizing output level (Q^*) and price (P^*), it may not be able to cover all of its costs ($P^* <$ ATC at Q^*).

13-3. Economic Efficiency Under Monopoly

As you recall from Chapter 12, the economic efficiency achieved under perfect competition is the standard against which the economic efficiency achieved under other market structures is measured. Since cost and demand conditions in perfectly competitive markets often differ dramatically from cost and demand conditions in purely monopolistic markets, comparisons between the two market extremes are difficult. However, analogous comparisons show that, if cost and demand conditions were identical, prices would be higher and output lower in a monopolistic market than in a perfectly competitive one. Such comparisons support the conclusion that monopoly does not allocate resources with the efficiency of perfect competition.

A. Under monopoly, prices are higher and output lower than under perfect competition.

To demonstrate that, if cost and demand conditions were identical, prices would be higher and output lower under monopoly than under perfect competition, let's assume a hypothetical market that is at first perfectly competitive and then becomes monopolized by a cartel with the price-setting power of a purely monopolistic firm.

A **cartel** is a formal organization of sellers to control price and output levels in a market.

Figure 13-5 shows such a hypothetical market with the same cost and demand conditions before and after the formation of a monopolizing cartel. As you can see in the figure, before the cartel is formed, the market is in competitive equilibrium at price P and quantity Q, the point at which the market demand (DD) and market supply (SS) curves intersect. The market supply curve is labeled "MC" (for *marginal cost*), as well as "SS" (for *supply*), because the market supply curve in a perfectly competitive market, as you remember from the last chapter, is an aggregation of the marginal cost curves (which are the supply curves) of the individual firms in the market. Thus at the point of competitive equilibrium in the market, the market price of the good being produced is just equal to the marginal cost of producing it ($P = \text{MC}$). This equivalence between price and marginal cost, as you also remember from the last chapter, is the standard against which the efficiency of resource allocation is measured.

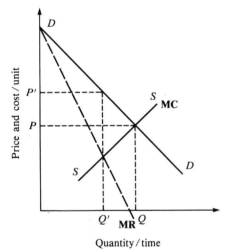

Figure 13-5
If a monopolizing cartel were formed in a perfectly competitive market, price would increase (P to P') and output would decrease (Q to Q'), *ceteris paribus*.

After the monopolizing cartel is formed, the equilibrium price and quantity in the market both change. The cartel selects Q' as its profit-maximizing output level because Q' marks the intersection of its MC and MR curves. Accordingly, it selects P' as its optimal price because demand curve DD indicates that P' is the highest price the market will bear at quantity Q'. As you can see in the figure, price P' is higher than competitive price P, and quantity Q' is lower than competitive quantity Q. As you can also see, price P' is considerably higher than the marginal cost of producing quantity Q' ($P' \neq \text{MC}$). Therefore, prices are higher and output is lower under monopoly (or a close approximation thereof) than under perfect competition, and resource allocation is inefficient.

B. Under monopoly, allocative efficiency is not achieved.

That resource allocation is necessarily inefficient ($P \neq \text{MC}$) in a monopoly follows logically not only from the comparison that we have just made but also from two earlier observations. The first is that monopolists, like other firms, find their profit-maximizing output level at the point at which their marginal cost equals their marginal revenue ($\text{MC} = \text{MR}$). The second is that, for monopolists, marginal revenue is less than price ($\text{MR} < P$). Now, if marginal cost equals marginal revenue (MC = MR) and marginal revenue is less than price (MR < P) for monopolists, then it follows that marginal cost must also be less than price (MC < P) for monopolists:

If MC = MR and MR < P, then MC < P.

Whenever the marginal cost of producing a good is less than the price of the good (MC < P)—that is, whenever the economic cost to society of producing a good is less than the economic value of the good to society—society's resources are being misallocated. Additional resources should be allocated to the production of the good, and the production of the good should be increased to its socially optimal level. Perfect competition provides the incentive (in fact, issues the mandate) for such a reallocation; monopoly does not.

EXAMPLE 13-8: Suppose that a profit-maximizing firm with a monopoly on telephone service in a local market charges a price of 25¢ and incurs a marginal cost of 10¢ for a telephone call made within its area. Is the company utilizing society's scarce resources efficiently? No.

The price of a good is the measure of the marginal economic value of the good to society; it tells how much some individuals in society are willing to pay in order to obtain an additional unit of the good. Thus, a price of 25¢ indicates that the consumers who purchase the telephone service are willing to pay at least that amount for a local telephone call.

The marginal cost of a good is the measure of the opportunity cost of the good to society; it tells how much society must sacrifice in order to obtain an additional unit of the good. Thus, a marginal cost of 10¢ means that society must forgo 10¢ worth of other goods in order to produce an additional local telephone call.

Clearly, if the opportunity cost of a local telephone call is only 10¢ and its economic value is 25¢, society will derive a net benefit of 15¢ (25¢ − 10¢ = 15¢) if the telephone company produces an additional call. Although this potential net benefit to society is relatively substantial, the telephone company has no incentive to produce an additional call because it is maximizing its profits at its current level of output. If it expands its output, it will have to lower its price and sacrifice some of its profits.

As this example demonstrates, even when the firm in a monopoly is maximizing its profits, resource allocation is nevertheless inefficient.

C. Under monopoly, productional efficiency is not likely to be achieved.

As you recall from Chapter 12, productional efficiency is achieved only when production costs are at an absolute minimum—that is, only when production takes place at the lowest point on a long-run average cost curve. Monopolists are not likely to achieve productional efficiency. It is in their best (profit-maximizing) interests, of course, to build plants that minimize their production costs. However, without competition, they are not likely to choose plant sizes and output levels that correspond to the lowest points on their long-run average cost curves. In fact, as Figure 13-6 demonstrates, the plant sizes and output levels that they choose to maximize their profits may not correspond to the minimum points on either their short-run average cost (SRAC) curves or their long-run average cost (LRAC) curves.

13-4. The Conduct of Monopolists

Because they are the only sellers of a product, monopolistic firms have more latitude in their conduct than do perfectly competitive firms. Free from competitive pressures, they may not be diligent in their pursuit of

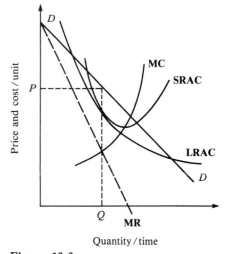

Figure 13-6
Monopoly does not promote either allocative or productional efficiency. Price is always higher than marginal cost (P > MC at Q), and production rarely occurs at the lowest point on a monopolist's LRAC curve.

minimum production costs. Similarly, free from a market-determined price, they may set many different prices for their product.

A. Monopolists may promote X-inefficiency.

Established monopolists may forsake the rigors of profit maximization and instead pursue the quiet life. When monopolists do not devote sufficient effort to minimizing production costs, the result is a phenomenon known as *X-inefficiency*.

X-inefficiency is an increase in production costs above the level shown on a firm's short-run or long-run average cost curves as a result of poor managerial decisions or insufficient administrative effort.

Not all monopolists are guilty of X-inefficiency, but the lack of competition in monopolized markets allows inefficient firms to survive.

B. Monopolists may practice price discrimination.

Price discrimination is the practice of charging different prices for the same or similar products. Because they are the sole sellers of a product, monopolists can engage in several forms of price discrimination. They can charge different prices in different markets; they can charge different prices to different classes of customers; they can charge different prices for different units of a product that they sell to the same customer. Whatever form or forms they engage in, monopolists practice price discrimination for one obvious reason: charging different prices generates more revenue and therefore more profits than charging a uniform price.

EXAMPLE 13-9: Telephone companies, natural gas and electric companies, and other public utilities engage in extensive price discrimination. They discriminate on the basis of class, charging different prices to commercial, industrial, and residential customers. They discriminate on the basis of time of service, charging higher rates during peak hours and lower rates during off-peak hours. They discriminate on the basis of quantity, charging lower rates, for example, after the first 500 kilowatt hours of electricity used each month or after the first 3 minutes of a long-distance telephone call.

C. Two conditions are necessary for effective price discrimination.

1. The elasticity of demand for a product must clearly differ from one class of buyer or from one market to the next.
2. A firm must have a means of segregating the buyers or markets and preventing the resale of its product from one buyer or market to the next.

EXAMPLE 13-10: Telephone, natural gas, and electric companies can practice effective price discrimination for two main reasons. First, the elasticities of demand for their products obviously vary from one class of customer (e.g., industrial, commercial, residential) to another. Second, the use of their services requires the physical presence of a line or pipe from a central source to a customer's location. The lines and pipes limit the potential for resale.

D. Other things being equal, the less elastic the demand, the higher the price a monopolist will charge.

As you recall from Chapter 7, a low elasticity of demand means that consumers are relatively insensitive to changes in the price of a product. It stands to reason, then, that a market with a lower elasticity of demand will bear a higher price than a market with a higher elasticity. Thus, other things being equal, if the firm in a monopoly supplies two distinct markets from a single plant, it will charge a higher price in the market with the lower elasticity of demand (providing, of course, that it can successfully segregate the markets and prevent the resale of its product).

EXAMPLE 13-11: Figure 13-7 shows two monopolized markets with different elasticities of demand for the same product. As the identical marginal and average cost (MC = AC) curves suggest, market A and market B are both being supplied by the same firm from a single plant. Although the firm's marginal and average costs are the same in both markets, the firm will charge a higher price in market A (P_A) because the steeper demand curve (*DD*) in market A indicates a relatively low elasticity of demand for its product. It will charge a lower price in market B (P_B) because the flatter demand curve (*DD*) in market B indicates a relatively high elasticity of demand for its product.

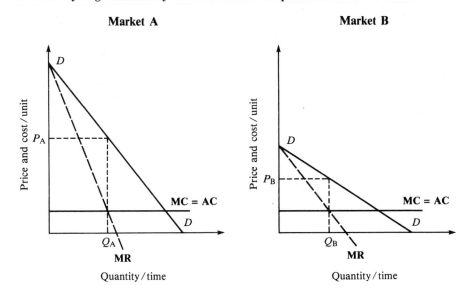

Figure 13-7
A market with a lower elasticity of demand (market A) bears a higher price for the same product than a market with a higher elasticity of demand (market B).

13-5. Public Policy Toward Monopoly

Society frequently intervenes in monopolized markets to seek an efficient use of resources or to change the distribution of incomes resulting from monopolistic profits.

A. Intervention in monopoly takes three main forms.

1. *Prevention.* In the United States, the Sherman Act, the Clayton Act, and other antitrust laws are designed to prevent the formation of monopolies. These laws (**a**) limit mergers between firms that sell products in the same market, (**b**) limit price-fixing and territorial arrangements between firms in the same industry, and (**c**) prohibit monopolization of a market by any firm.

2. *Ownership and operation.* When economies of scale are so substantial that a single plant can satisfy industry demand at a lower cost than can many plants, an industry is efficiently served by a single producer. Under such circumstances, government can "nationalize" or collectively own and operate an industry. The U.S. Postal Service is an example of a collectively owned monopoly.

3. *Regulation.* As an alternative to collective ownership, government can allow privately owned monopolies to exist and empower public

commissions to regulate them. For example, public utility commissions modify the pricing decisions of privately owned natural monopolies in electric power, natural gas, and communications.

B. Regulation limits the return on a monopolist's investment.

Public utility commissions in many states employ "fair-rate-of-return" regulation. They endeavor to limit the price that a utility can charge, say, for electricity or natural gas so that the utility earns no more (but no less, either) than a "fair" rate of return on its investment in its plant and equipment. Effective regulation reduces price and increases output.

EXAMPLE 13-12: From an economist's point of view, an economic profit of zero implies a "normal" rate of return on all inputs, including capital inputs. Thus if "fair" rate of return means "normal" rate of return, a public utility commission employing such regulation will seek to limit the price that a utility can charge for its product to the average cost of producing it. In doing so, it will induce the utility to increase its output.

As Figure 13-8 demonstrates, a monopolizing utility will seek to charge price P for quantity Q. At price P and quantity Q, it will earn a positive economic profit or an "above-normal" return on all inputs because price P is greater than its average cost of producing quantity Q ($P >$ AC at Q). However, a regulatory commission will seek to limit the price that the utility can charge to P' so that the utility will increase its output to Q'. At price P' and quantity Q', the utility will earn an economic profit of zero ($P' =$ AC at Q') or a "normal" ("fair"?) return on all inputs.

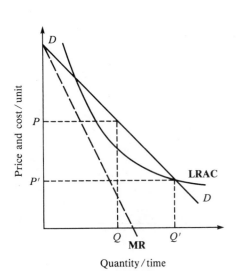

Figure 13-8
Effective rate-of-return regulation forces a profit-maximizing monopolist to reduce price (P to P') and increase output (Q to Q').

RAISE YOUR GRADES
Can you explain...?

☑ why economies of scale in an industry can serve as an entry barrier to new firms

☑ why the demand curve that a monopolist faces has a negative slope

☑ why marginal revenue is less than price for a monopolist

☑ how to locate a monopolist's MR curve given a market demand curve

☑ how the firm in a monopoly determines its profit-maximizing output level and price

☑ how price and output would differ under monopoly and perfect competition if demand and cost conditions were the same

☑ why resource allocation is inefficient under monopoly

☑ why resource allocation is inefficient when the price of a good is greater than its marginal cost ($P >$ MC)

☑ why monopolies tend to foster X-inefficiency

☑ what conditions are necessary for effective price discrimination

☑ why price discrimination increases a monopolist's revenue and profits

☑ why the government allows some privately owned monopolies to exist

☑ how effective rate-of-return regulation affects price and output by a monopoly

SUMMARY

1. The theory of monopoly includes four principal assumptions: (1) there are many buyers but only one seller in a monopoly; (2) there are no close substitutes for the good or service produced in a monopoly; (3) the single seller and the buyers in a monopoly have perfect knowledge of prices and quantities available; and (4) the entry of other firms into a monopolized market is blocked.

2. *Entry barriers* are obstacles that prevent or deter new firms from entering a profitable market.

3. Three common entry barriers are (1) government-granted franchises and patents, (2) significant economies of scale relative to market demand, and (3) high sunk costs combined with a substantial risk of failure.

4. The demand curve facing the firm in a monopoly is the downward-sloping market demand curve. Therefore the firm can sell additional units of its product only by reducing the price of all units.

5. Because a monopolist must reduce price in order to increase output and sales, marginal revenue is less than price for a monopolist.

6. A monopolist's marginal revenue (MR) curve bisects the horizontal distance between the y-axis and the market demand curve.

7. The firm in a monopoly is a *price setter*; by contrast, a firm in a perfectly competitive market is a *price taker*. Thus the firm in a monopoly decides what price to charge as well as how much to produce.

8. The firm in a monopoly decides how much to produce by following the $MR = MC$ rule for profit maximization.

9. The firm in a monopoly decides what price to charge by measuring the height of the market demand curve at its profit-maximizing output level.

10. Because their output and price decisions are constrained both by their costs and by market demand, monopolists are not guaranteed positive economic profits. Their profits may be positive, zero, or negative in the short run.

11. A *cartel* is a formal organization of sellers to control price and output levels in a market. When a perfectly competitive market is cartelized, price increases and output decreases.

12. If cost and demand conditions were identical, price would be higher and output lower under monopoly than under perfect competition.

13. Under monopoly, allocative efficiency is not achieved because marginal economic value (as measured by product price) exceeds marginal economic cost.

14. Under monopoly, productional efficiency is not likely to be achieved: that is, monopolists are not likely to choose plant sizes and output levels that correspond to the lowest points on their long-run average cost curves.

15. Monopoly promotes *X-inefficiency*, an increase in production costs above the level shown on a firm's short-run or long-run average cost curves as a result of poor managerial decisions or insufficient administrative effort.

16. Monopolists may practice price discrimination to increase their revenue and profits. They may charge different prices in different markets, to different classes of customers, or for different units of a product that they sell to the same customer.

17. Two conditions are necessary for effective price discrimination: (1) the elasticity of demand for a product must differ from one buyer or market to the next, and (2) a firm must be able to segregate the buyers

or markets so as to prevent the resale of its product from one to the other.

18. Other things being equal, the firm in a monopoly will set a higher price in a market with a lower elasticity of demand than in a market with a higher elasticity of demand for its product.

19. Society often intervenes in monopolized markets to seek an efficient use of resources or to change the distribution of incomes resulting from monopolistic profits.

20. Intervention in monopoly takes three forms: (1) prevention through antitrust legislation, (2) operation of nationalized or collectively owned monopolies, (3) regulation.

21. Many public utility commissions use "fair-rate-of-return" regulation to limit the price that a privately owned monopoly can charge so that it earns only a "fair" rate of return on its investment.

RAPID REVIEW

1. All of the following are characteristics of monopoly *except* (a) a product for which there are no close substitutes, (b) perfect knowledge of prices, (c) a single seller, (d) free entry into a market. [See Section 13-1.]

2. Obstacles that deter new firms from entering a profitable industry are called _____ _____. [See Section 13-1.]

3. A _____ is the exclusive right to make, use, or sell an innovative product or process. [See Section 13-1.]

4. The demand curve facing a monopolist is (a) positively sloped, (b) horizontal, (c) vertical, (d) negatively sloped. [See Section 13-1.]

5. For a firm in a perfectly competitive market, marginal revenue is equal to price; for the firm in a monopoly, it is greater than price. True or false? [See Section 13-1.]

6. Unlike a firm in a perfectly competitive market, which is a price _____, the firm in a monopoly is a price _____. [See Section 13-2.]

7. The profit-maximizing output level for the firm in a monopoly is the level at which its _____ _____ equals its _____ _____ . [See Section 13-2.]

8. Given its profit-maximizing output, the firm in a monopoly can find its optimal price by consulting the _____ curve that it faces. [See Section 13-2.]

9. In the short run, economic profit in a monopoly may be negative. True or false? [See Section 13-2.]

10. A monopolist's long-run economic profit may be positive. True or false? [See Section 13-2.]

11. If demand and cost conditions were the same, _____ would be higher and _____ lower under perfect competition than under monopoly. [See Section 13-3.]

12. A _____ is a formal organization of sellers to control price and output levels in a market. [See Section 13-3.]

13. The profit-maximizing firm in a pure monopoly never achieves allocative efficiency because the price of its product is always _____ than the _____ _____ of producing it. [See Section 13-3.]

14. _____ is an increase in production costs above the level shown on a firm's short-run or long-run average cost curves as a result of poor managerial decisions or a lack of administrative effort. [See Section 13-4.]

15. _____ _____ is the practice of charging different prices for the same or similar goods. [See Section 13-4.]

16. To engage in effective price discrimination, a monopolist must have a means of preventing the _____ of its product from one buyer or market to another. [See Section 13-4.]

17. Given two segregated markets, a price-discriminating monopolist will charge a lower price in the market with the _____ elasticity of demand. [See Section 13-4.]

18. Government often intervenes in monopoly to seek an efficient use of _____ and to redistribute _____. [See Section 13-5.]

19. In the United States, the _____ Act and the _____ Act are two pieces of _____ legislation designed to prevent or limit the formation of monopolies. [See Section 13-5.]

20. Effective regulation of monopolies results in (**a**) higher prices and increased output, (**b**) higher prices and reduced output, (**c**) lower prices and increased output, (**d**) lower prices and reduced output. [See Section 13-5.]

Answers
1. (d)   **2.** *entry barriers*   **3.** *patent*   **4. (d)**   **5.** false   **6.** taker, setter
7. marginal revenue, marginal cost   **8.** demand   **9.** true   **10.** true
11. output, price   **12.** *cartel*   **13.** greater, marginal cost   **14.** *X-inefficiency*   **15.** *Price discrimination*   **16.** resale   **17.** higher   **18.** resources, income   **19.** Sherman, Clayton, antitrust   **20. (c)**

SOLVED PROBLEMS

PROBLEM 13-1   Explain how economies of scale in an industry can serve as a barrier to entry.

Answer: Economies of scale in some industries are so great relative to total demand that the industry can support no more than one or a few plants of a size corresponding to the lowest point on the long-run average cost (LRAC) curve in the industry, as shown in Figure 13-9. Such economies of scale serve as an entry barrier to new firms for two main reasons. First, unless a firm can enter such an industry with a plant of optimal size, it will be at a disadvantage in a price war and its rivals will easily be able to drive it out of business. Second, even if it can enter such an industry with a plant of optimal size, its entry may very well precipitate a chain reaction that will increase industry output, reduce industry price, and result in losses for *all* firms in the industry. [See Section 13-1].

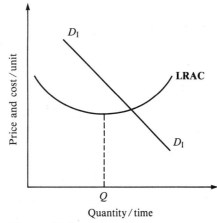

Figure 13-9

PROBLEM 13-2   Explain why marginal revenue is less than price for the firm in a monopoly.

Answer: As the sole seller of a good or service, the firm in a monopoly faces a market demand curve with a downward or negative slope. Assuming that the firm must charge a uniform price for all units of the product that it sells, the downward or negative slope implies that the firm can sell an additional unit only by lowering the price of all units. Thus the revenue that the firm derives from the additional unit—that is, its marginal revenue—is necessarily less than the price that it can charge. Specifically, the firm's marginal revenue is the difference between the revenue that it gains from selling an additional unit (the price of the unit) and the revenue that it loses from lowering the price of previous units. Figure 13-10, for example, shows how much revenue a monopolistic firm will gain and lose if it increases its output by one unit. As you can see, the firm can sell five units instead of four if it reduces the price of the first four units by $1 each and sells all five units at a price of $6

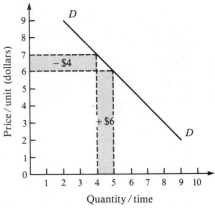

Figure 13-10

apiece. The fifth unit, then, will increase the firm's total revenue by $6, but lowering the price of the first four units from $7 to $6 will reduce its total revenue by $4. Thus the marginal revenue of the fifth unit will be only $2. [See Section 13-1.]

PROBLEM 13-3 Figure 13-11 shows the marginal revenue (MR), marginal cost (MC), and average total cost (ATC) curves for a monopolistic firm, along with the market demand curve (*DD*) that the firm faces. Locate the firm's profit-maximizing output level and price on the figure. Label the output level *Q** and the price *P**. Then shade the area on the figure that represents the firm's positive economic profit at that output level and price.

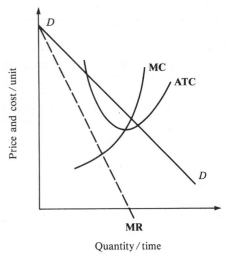

Figure 13-11

Answer: To locate the firm's profit-maximizing output level, follow the MR = MC rule. As Figure 13-12 shows, the firm's marginal cost equals its marginal revenue at the point where its MC curve intersects its MR curve from below. The *x*-coordinate of that point is the firm's profit-maximizing output level, *Q**.

To locate the firm's profit-maximizing price, find the price that corresponds to quantity *Q** on the market demand curve that the firm faces. To do so, just draw a vertical line from *Q** up to demand curve *DD*; then draw a horizontal line from that point to the *y*-axis. As Figure 13-12 shows, price *P** is the firm's profit-maximizing price: at quantity *Q**, its profit-maximizing output level, price *P** is the highest price that the market will bear.

To determine the firm's positive economic profit at output *Q** and price *P**, locate the average total cost on the firm's ATC curve that corresponds to quantity *Q**. That cost,

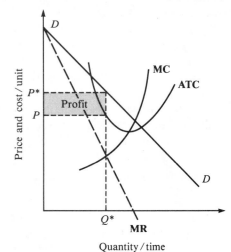

Figure 13-12

labeled *P* in the figure, will enable the firm to cover all of its costs. Any price above that level will enable it to earn a positive economic profit at quantity *Q**. Thus the shaded rectangular area in Figure 13-12 represents the firm's positive economic profit at its profit-maximizing output level and price. [See Section 13-12.]

PROBLEM 13-4 Explain why the firm in a monopoly is a price setter rather than a price taker, like a firm in a perfectly competitive market. How does being a price setter affect the supply curve of a monopolistic firm?

Answer: The firm in a monopoly is a price setter because it is the only seller in the market and therefore the only firm that can determine the "market" price of the product that it sells. Since a monopolistic firm does set the price of its product, it does not have to determine the quantity that it will supply at alternative "given" prices because, unlike a firm in a perfectly competitive market, it is never confronted with a set of alternative "given" prices. Therefore it does not have a supply curve in the conventional sense. [See Section 13-2.]

PROBLEM 13-5 Following is the market demand schedule facing the firm in a monopoly. Prepare a marginal revenue schedule for the firm.

Demand Schedule

Quantity/week	Price/unit
100	$9
150	8
200	7
250	6
300	5
350	4

Answer: To prepare the firm's marginal revenue schedule, first find its total revenue at each level of output by multiplying price times quantity demanded (TR = *P* × *Q*). Then find its marginal revenue by dividing the change in total revenue by the change in quantity demanded from one level of output to the next. The firm's total revenue (TR) and marginal revenue (MR) schedules are shown in the following table [see Section 13-2]:

Demand Schedule

Quantity/week	Price/unit	TR	MR
100	$9	$ 900	
			$6
150	8	1,200	
			4
200	7	1,400	
			2
250	6	1,500	
			0
300	5	1,500	
			− 2
350	4	1,400	

PROBLEM 13-6 Assume that the monopolistic firm in Problem 13-5 has the following cost schedule, which shows its total fixed cost (TFC), its total variable cost (TVC), its total cost (TC), and its marginal cost (MC) at various levels of output. Find the firm's profit-maximizing output and price. Then find its economic profit at that output and price.

Cost Schedule

Quantity/week	TFC	TVC	TC	MC
0	$500	$ 0	$ 500	
				$1
50	500	50	550	
				2
100	500	150	650	
				3
150	500	300	800	
				4
200	500	500	1,000	
				5
250	500	750	1,250	
				6
300	500	1,050	1,550	
				7
350	500	1,400	1,900	

Answer: A monopolistic firm, like any other firm, maximizes its profits by producing that output level at which its marginal cost equals its marginal revenue. If you compare the marginal revenue schedule in the answer to the preceding problem with the marginal cost schedule in this problem, you can see that the firm's marginal cost equals its marginal revenue midway between 150 and 200, or at 175, units a week. According to the demand schedule that the firm faces, it can sell 175 units at a maximum price midway between $8 and $7, or at $7.50. If it sells 175 units a week at $7.50 a unit, its total revenue will be $1,312.50 (175 × $7.50 = $1,312.50), its total costs will be $900, and its total profit will therefore be $412.40 ($1,312.50 − $900 = $412.50) per week. [See Section 13-2.]

PROBLEM 13-7 Suppose that a property tax of $450 per week is imposed on the plant owned and operated by the monopolistic firm in Problems 13-5 and 13-6. Assuming that the firm has to pay the tax regardless of output, find its profit-maximizing output level and price and its profit after the tax is imposed. Will the firm produce in the short run? How about the long run? [*Hint:* The property tax is a fixed cost. Consider the effect that an increase in fixed costs has on variable and marginal costs.]

Answer: An increase in fixed costs has no effect on marginal costs. Hence the $450-a-week property tax will have no effect on the firm's profit-maximizing output level and price. Similarly, an increase in fixed costs has no effect on variable costs. Hence the property tax will have no effect on the firm's decision to produce or not to produce in the short run. (Remember the second rule for profit maximization: A firm should produce in the short run if the price of its product is greater than the average *variable* cost of production.) Thus, even after the property tax is imposed, the firm will continue to produce 175 units a week at a price of $7.50 a unit. However, it will not continue to earn a positive economic profit of $412.50 a week. Since its total costs will be $450 higher each week, it will instead earn a negative economic profit of −$37.50 ($412.50 − $450 = −$37.50). Thus, although it will continue to produce in the short run, the firm will shut down in the long run. [See Section 13-2.]

PROBLEM 13-8 Suppose that your stockbroker called you with a hot tip: "Buy ABCD Robots. They have a monopoly on a new control system, and monopolists always make a profit." How would you respond to the last part of your broker's statement?

Answer: Monopolists are not guaranteed a positive economic profit simply because they have a monopoly on a good or service. Even if they are not regulated by the government, their profits are determined by two variables: (1) their cost curves and (2) the market demand curves that they face. If these variables are unfavorably related, as they are in Figure 13-13, monopolists may not be able to find any output–price combinations for which revenue covers, let alone exceeds, their costs. [See Section 13-2.]

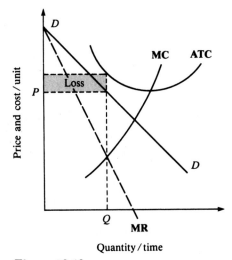

Figure 13-13

PROBLEM 13-9 Point (Q, P) in Figure 13-14 illustrates a hypothetical competitive equilibrium in the dairy industry. Suppose that the government creates a monopolizing cartel in the industry and instructs the cartel to maximize its profits, using supply curve SS as its marginal cost (MC) curve. Construct a marginal revenue (MR) curve to accompany the market demand curve (DD). Then find the profit-maximizing quantity and price for the cartel. What happens to output and price when a competitive industry is cartelized?

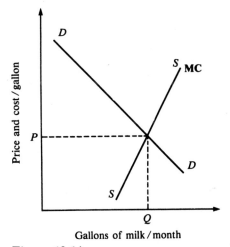

Figure 13-14

Answer: To construct the cartel's marginal revenue (MR) curve, draw a line that bisects the horizontal distance between the y-axis and the market demand curve (DD), as shown in Figure 13-15. The cartel, acting with the power of a monopolist, will set output at Q', where its MC curve intersects its MR curve from below, and price at P', the highest price the market will bear at quantity Q'. As you can see in the figure, the formation of a monopolizing cartel in a formerly competitive industry increases price and reduces output. [See Section 13-3.]

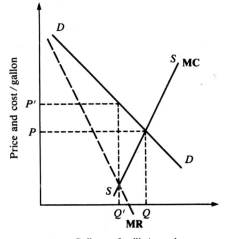

Figure 13-15

PROBLEM 13-10 Explain why the cartelization of the competitive dairy industry in Problem 13-9 results in an inefficient allocation of society's scarce resources.

Answer: At output Q' in Figure 13-15, the price of a gallon of milk, P', exceeds its marginal cost. This discrepancy between price and marginal cost indicates that the value that society places on an additional gallon of milk (the price that consumers are willing and able to pay for it) is greater than the opportunity cost, to society, of producing another gallon. In other words, the marginal economic value of an additional gallon is greater than its marginal economic cost. Therefore the well-being of society, but obviously not the profits of the cartel, will be maximized if the output of milk is increased to its competitive level of Q gallons and the price per gallon is reduced to P. [See Section 13-3.]

PROBLEM 13-11 Turbid Springs, Incorporated, sells bottled mineral water in two distinct and separate markets, Baltimore and Washington, D.C. The water comes from the same spring, goes through the same bottling process, and is shipped an equal distance to both markets. The marginal and average cost of producing a bottle of mineral water is the same in both markets (MC = AC). Given the market demand curves (DD) in Figure 13-16, locate the profit-maximizing quantity and price in each market. Label the quantity and price in the Washington, D.C., market Q' and P', respectively, and label the quantity and price in the Baltimore market Q and P, respectively. Explain why the profit-maximizing output–price combinations are not the same in the two markets.

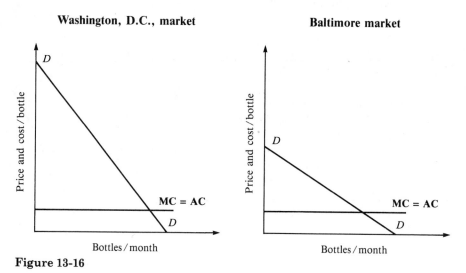

Figure 13-16

Answer: First, construct a marginal revenue (MR) curve for each market by bisecting the horizontal distance between the y-axis and the market demand curve (DD), as shown in Figure 13-17. Second, determine the profit-maximizing output level in each market by locating the point at which the MR curve and the MC curves intersect. Third, find

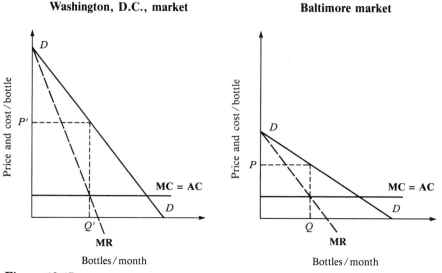

Figure 13-17

the profit-maximizing price in each market by measuring the height of the demand curve at the profit-maximizing output level—that is, by drawing a vertical line up from the profit-maximizing output level to the demand curve and a horizontal line from that point on the demand curve to the *y*-axis.

As Figure 13-17 shows, the profit-maximizing output–price combination in Washington, D.C., is (Q', P'), and in Baltimore it is (Q, P). As the figure also shows, price is considerably higher in the Washington market than it is in the Baltimore market $(P' > P)$. The reason, of course, is that demand is less elastic (the demand curve is more nearly vertical) in the Washington market than it is in the Baltimore market. [See Section 13-4.]

PROBLEM 13-12 Under what conditions could Turbid Springs, Incorporated, charge a different price for its bottled mineral water in two markets in geographical proximity to one another?

Answer: Turbid Springs, Incorporated, could charge a different price for its bottled mineral water in geographically proximate markets on two conditions: (**1**) if the elasticity of demand for bottled water were clearly different in the two markets, and (**2**) if Turbid Springs could effectively segregate the markets so as to prevent the resale of its water from one market to the next. If it could not prevent the water it was selling at a lower price in one market from being resold at a higher price in the second market, Turbid Springs would not be able to maintain a price differential in the two markets. [See Section 13-4.]

PROBLEM 13-13 Consider Figure 13-18, which shows that the profit-maximizing output and price for a hypothetical monopolistic firm are Q^* and P^*, respectively. Now assume that, through rate regulation, the government forces the firm to increase its output to Q' and to decrease its price to P'. Does the regulated price and output combination represent an efficient use of society's scarce resources? Does it allow the firm to earn a fair rate of return on its investment in its plant and equipment?

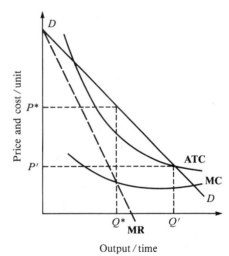

Figure 13-18

Answer: The regulated price and output combination, (Q', P'), still does not meet the standard for allocative efficiency established under perfect competition. As you can see in Figure 13-18, price P' is still higher than the firm's marginal cost (MC) of production at output Q'; therefore the value that society places on an additional unit of the product that the firm is producing (measured by its price) is still higher than the cost of producing the additional unit (its marginal cost).

However, the combination of price P' and quantity Q' does allow the firm to earn a normal (fair?) rate of return on its investment. Since point (Q', P') lies on the firm's average total cost (ATC) curve, it allows the firm to recover the opportunity costs, implicit as well as explicit, of *all* inputs, including plant and equipment. [See Section 13-5.]

14 MONOPOLISTIC COMPETITION

14-1. The Theory of Monopolistic Competition

The theory of monopolistic competition is much newer than the theories of perfect competition and monopoly. It was developed in the 1930s by two economists, Joan Robinson and Edward Chamberlin. As its name suggests, the theory of monopolistic competition has some elements in common with the theory of monopoly and even more elements in common with the theory of perfect competition. In fact, its focus is a market structure that differs from perfect competition in only one fundamental respect: the products in a perfectly competitive market are homogeneous; the products in a monopolistically competitive market are heterogeneous. This heterogeneity of products accounts for the *monopolistic* in *monopolistic competition*. Since each firm in a monopolistically competitive market sells a product that is at least slightly different from the products of all other firms, each firm enjoys a slight degree of monopolistic power.

A. The theory of monopolistic competition includes four major assumptions.

The theory of monopolistic competition includes the three basic assumptions implicit in the theories of all market structures: (1) that firms aim to maximize their profits; (2) that households aim to maximize their satisfaction; and (3) that no external costs or benefits are associated with any good. In addition, it includes four major assumptions, three of which you have already encountered in the theory of perfect competition:

1. There are many buyers and sellers in a monopolistically competitive market, and all of them are too small to have a perceptible effect on other buyers and sellers in the market.
2. The product of each seller in a monopolistically competitive market is slightly different from the product of every other seller. Buyers perceive the differences and may prefer the product of one seller to that of another. Since products are similar but not identical, prices usually vary within product groups.
3. Firms may enter and leave a monopolistically competitive market with ease.
4. All buyers and sellers in a monopolistically competitive market have perfect knowledge of the prices of products, their qualities, and the quantities in which they are available.

EXAMPLE 14-1: Conditions in the wholesale markets for men's and women's clothing, as well as many retail markets, approximate the theoretical conditions for monopolistic competition. There are many firms in the markets, but none of them is large enough to have any significant impact on the sales of its competitors. Moreover, each firm differentiates its products from those of other firms in many ways: style, color, cut, material, sizing, quality of workmanship, brand or trademark, price, and so on. If you wish to purchase any particular article of clothing, such as a suit or a tie, you have a wide selection to choose from at a wide variety of prices.

B. Under monopolistic competition, a firm makes three decisions.

A firm in a perfectly competitive market makes one decision: how much to produce. A firm in a monopolistic market makes two decisions: how much to produce and what price to charge. A firm in a monopolistically competitive market makes three decisions: how much to produce, what price to charge, and how to differentiate its product from the products of other firms in the market.

Product differentiation includes not only the differentiation of one good or service from another but also the differentiation of one seller from another. It takes three principal forms:

1. *Differentiation of the product itself.* This type of differentiation includes any unique physical or substantial characteristic of a product, such as (depending on the product) its design, its durability, its composition, its taste, its effectiveness, and so on.
2. *Differentiation of the image of a product.* This type of differentiation includes the packaging of a product and other superficial characteristics, such as designer labels, as well as the imagery associated with the product through advertising.
3. *Differentiation of the characteristics of the sellers of a product.* This type of differentiation includes location, hours of business, credit policy, returns policy, pricing policy, personnel, quality and variety of merchandise, quality of service, and so on.

EXAMPLE 14-2: In order to acquire and maintain its own share of a monopolistically competitive market, a firm must differentiate the good or service that it is producing from the goods or services that other firms in the same market are producing. It can do so in many ways. In the retail clothing market, for example, product differentiation has resulted in a remarkable variety of stores: from exclusive high-fashion shops to clothing warehouses and factory outlets, from stores for very large men to stores for petite women (and vice versa), from large department stores to tiny boutiques, from stores in shopping malls to stores in neighborhood commercial districts, from stores that carry only sportswear to stores that carry only imported tweeds or furs or maternity clothes or what have you. Each store represents an attempt by a firm to find the type and the optimal degree of differentiation that will secure for it the share of the retail clothing market that it seeks and thus enable it to maximize its profits.

C. Under monopolistic competition, a firm's marginal revenue is less than price.

Since each firm in a monopolistically competitive market produces a unique product, one that is similar to but not identical with the products of other producers in the market, each firm faces a demand curve with a downward or negative slope. As you recall, a downward

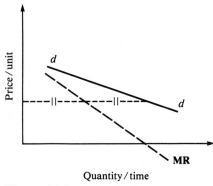

Figure 14-1
Each firm in a monopolistically
competitive market produces a unique
product and thus faces a unique
downward-sloping demand curve (*dd*)
that lies above its marginal revenue
(MR) curve.

or negative slope implies an inverse relationship between price and quantity demanded. This inverse relationship has the same set of implications for a firm in a monopolistically competitive market as it does for a monopolist:

1. The firm can produce and sell an additional unit of its product only if it lowers the price of all units.
2. The marginal revenue that the firm derives from selling an additional unit of its product is less than the price of the product.
3. The firm's marginal revenue (MR) curve, as shown in Figure 14-1, lies below the demand curve that it faces (labeled *dd* in the figure) and bisects the horizontal distance between the *y*-axis and the demand curve.

D. Under monopolistic competition, a firm's demand curve is highly elastic.

As you recall from Chapter 12, one reason that a firm in a perfectly competitive market faces a horizontal (perfectly elastic) demand curve is that the product it produces is standardized and therefore indistinguishable from the products of other firms in the same market. By contrast, one reason that a firm in a monopolistically competitive market and a firm in a monopoly both face downward-sloping demand curves is that the products they produce are unique.

There is a big difference, however, between the product that a monopolistically competitive firm produces and the product that a monopolist produces. For the product that a monopolist produces, there are no close substitutes. For the product that a monopolistically competitive firm produces, there are many close substitutes. When numerous close substitutes for a product are available, consumer brand loyalty is weak, and increases in price bring about significant decreases in quantity demanded, *ceteris paribus*. Buyers simply switch to cheaper brands. Consequently, the demand curve that a monopolistically competitive firm faces, though negatively sloped, is relatively flat, signifying that the demand for its product is highly elastic.

EXAMPLE 14-3: If one clothing store in a shopping mall offers blue jeans at a lower price than competing stores in the same mall, or even in the same general area, it can expect a substantial increase in its sales. Conversely, if it offers blue jeans at a higher price than competing stores, it can expect an equally substantial decrease in its sales.

14-2. Output–Price Decisions Under Monopolistic Competition

Although the profits of a firm in a monopolistically competitive market are affected (though not always in predictable ways) by the decisions that it makes about product differentiation, the firm selects its optimal output level in the same way that any other firm does, and it selects its optimal price in the same way that a monopolist does. The conditions for long-run equilibrium under monopolistic competition are similar to the conditions for long-run equilibrium under perfect competition.

A. A monopolistically competitive firm selects its optimal output level by following the rules for profit maximization.

To determine its profit-maximizing output level, a firm in a monopolistically competitive market applies the MR = MC rule with which you are by now very familiar. It produces at that level in the short run if the price of its product is greater than its average variable cost of production ($P >$ AVC). It produces at that level in the long run if the price of its product is greater than or equal to the average cost of production ($P \geq$ AC)—that is, if it can earn an economic profit greater than or equal to zero.

B. A monopolistically competitive firm selects its optimal price by measuring the height of its demand curve at its optimal output level.

Like a firm in a purely monopolistic market, a firm in a monopolistically competitive market selects its optimal price by finding the price corresponding to its optimal output level on the demand curve that it faces. It does so by drawing a vertical line from its profit-maximizing output level up to its demand curve and a horizontal line from that point to the *y*-axis. Its optimal price is the highest price that the market for its product will bear.

EXAMPLE 14-4: Figure 14-2 shows the marginal revenue (MR), marginal cost (MC), average variable cost (AVC), and average total cost (ATC) curves for a hypothetical firm in a monopolistically competitive market, as well as the demand curve (*dd*) that the firm faces. The firm locates its profit-maximizing output level at Q^*, where its MC curve intersects its MR curve from below (MC = MR). Then it measures the height of its demand curve (*dd*) at Q^* to locate its profit-maximizing price at P^*. Since price P^* is greater than its average variable and its average total cost of production at quantity Q^* ($P^* >$ AVC and $P^* >$ ATC at Q^*), the firm will produce and earn a positive economic profit in the short run.

C. In the long run, a monopolistically competitive firm earns an economic profit of zero.

As you recall from Chapter 12, one of the conditions for long-run equilibrium under perfect competition is that firms be earning an economic profit of zero. The same condition is necessary for long-run equilibrium under monopolistic competition—and for the same reason. Unless entry into a market is blocked, as it is under monopoly but not under perfect or monopolistic competition, positive profits attract new firms into the market in the long run. Their entry reduces the market share of each firm (shifts each firm's demand curve to the left) and pushes each firm's profits down toward zero.

When a monopolistically competitive firm is in long-run equilibrium, its long-run average cost (LRAC) curve must be tangent to the demand curve that it faces, as shown in Figure 14-3. At point *A*, the highest price that the firm can charge for its product is just equal to the average cost of production, and so the firm is earning an economic profit of zero. At any other point, the firm's profits would be either positive, attracting new entrants to the market, or negative, inducing it, or firms like it, to exit from the market.

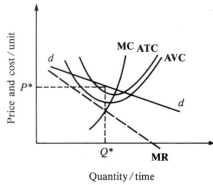

Figure 14-2
A monopolistically competitive firm locates its optimal output (Q^*) by applying the MR = MC rule and its optimal price (P^*) by measuring the height of its demand curve (*dd*) at that output.

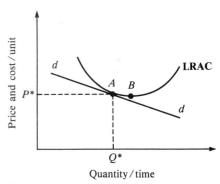

Figure 14-3
When a monopolistically competitive firm is in long-run equilibrium (point *A*), it is earning an economic profit of zero ($P^* =$ AC at Q^*), but it is not producing at the lowest point on its LRAC curve (point *B*).

14-3. Economic Efficiency Under Monopolistic Competition

As you might expect from its name, monopolistic competition doesn't quite measure up to the standards for economic efficiency established under perfect competition.

A. Under monopolistic competition, productional efficiency is not achieved.

As you recall from Chapter 12, productional efficiency is achieved only when production costs are at an absolute minimum, that is, only when production takes place at the lowest point on the long-run average cost (LRAC) curve for an industry. In a monopolistically competitive industry, profit-maximizing firms stop short of that point. They produce at a level that enables them to earn a normal economic profit, but not at a level that enables them to take full advantage of all available economies of scale. Figure 14-3 suggests the reason.

In order for a monopolistically competitive firm to be in long-run equilibrium, the demand curve that it faces must be tangent to its LRAC curve. Because of its downward slope, the demand curve that the firm faces can be tangent to its LRAC curve only at a point where its LRAC curve also has a downward slope—that is, only at a point such as *A* in Figure 14-3, where long-run average costs are *declining*, but not at a minimum. The firm could reduce its average cost of production to an absolute minimum (point B) by increasing its output. However, at an increased level of output, it would not be able to charge a price high enough to cover all of its costs; therefore it would not be able to continue producing in the long run.

Because monopolistically competitive firms produce at levels that are not efficient, monopolistically competitive industries suffer from what economists call *excess capacity*—too many plants producing too little output. Both the industries and society might be better off if fewer plants were producing at higher levels of output, that is, if larger plants were constructed or existing plants were more fully utilized. That way average or unit costs could be reduced to their lowest possible levels, and products could be offered for sale at lower prices. However, the price of productional efficiency would be less variety within product groups.

EXAMPLE 14-5: The next time you wander through the stores in a shopping mall, consider the number and the variety of blue jeans that you, as a consumer, have to choose from. According to the theory of monopolistic competition, those jeans could be produced at a lower cost and sold at a lower price if fewer firms were manufacturing them and fewer stores were selling them in a higher volume. However, if that were the case, you would have fewer "differentiated" blue jeans to choose from—fewer styles, fewer cuts, fewer brand names, fewer sizes, fewer shades of blue, fewer variations in fabric content—and you would also have fewer places to choose to buy them. Many economists argue that the cost of excess capacity in a monopolistically competitive industry is simply the price of product differentiation. As a consumer, you may be willing to pay a little extra just for the privilege of having a wide variety to choose from.

B. Under monopolistic competition, allocative efficiency is not achieved.

Resource allocation under monopolistic competition is inefficient for the same reason that resource allocation under pure monopoly is inefficient. When a monopolistically competitive firm is maximizing its profits, its marginal cost equals its marginal revenue (MC = MR) and its marginal revenue is less than its price (MR < P); therefore, the marginal cost of producing the product is less than the price that the firm charges for the product (MC < P). As you recall from Chapter 12, an equivalence between marginal cost and price (MC = P) is essential for efficient resource allocation.

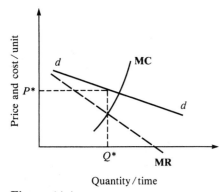

Figure 14-4
For a profit-maximizing firm under monopolistic competition, MR = MC and *P** > MR, so *P** > MC. Therefore resource allocation is inefficient under monopolistic competition.

EXAMPLE 14-6: Figure 14-4 shows the marginal cost (MC), marginal revenue (MR), and demand (*dd*) curves facing a firm in a monopolistically competitive market. The firm's optimal production level is Q^*, where its MC curve intersects its MR curve from below (MC = MR). At output Q^*, the firm maximizes its profits by charging price P^*. Price P^*, as you can see in the figure, is considerably higher than the firm's marginal cost (MC) of production at output Q^*. Whenever the price of a product (its economic value to society) is greater than its marginal cost (its economic cost or the opportunity cost to society of producing it), resources are underallocated to the production of the good.

14-4. Product Differentiation: Advertising

In a monopolistically competitive market, a firm's decisions about product differentiation, particularly advertising, which is the form that we shall focus on here, are as important to the firm's profits as its decisions about output and price are. However, the effects of a firm's decisions about product differentiation are far less predictable than the effects of its output and price decisions. They are also much more controversial.

A. Supporters of advertising list its potential benefits.
1. Advertising informs consumers about products and thus helps them to make rational purchasing decisions.
2. Advertising enables firms to increase their output and thus allows them to realize greater economies of scale.
3. Advertising promotes competition and stimulates product innovation.
4. Advertising provides revenues that support the communications media: newspapers, magazines, radio, television.

B. Critics of advertising dispute its benefits.
1. Most advertising seeks to persuade, rather than to inform, buyers.
2. Advertising increases the cost, and thus the price, of a product.
3. Advertising is a substitute for price competition, and advertisements tend to cancel each other out.
4. Alternative methods of funding for the communications media would result in less biased reporting, more diverse programming, and communications of a generally higher quality.

C. Effective advertising causes a firm's demand curve to shift or rotate to the right.

Advertising allows a firm to choose the market or market segment in which it wishes to compete. An effective advertising campaign produces one or both of two results: (1) it increases the demand for a firm's product, giving the firm a larger share of the market in which it is participating; (2) it reduces the price elasticity of demand for the firm's product, giving the firm more monopolistic power and thus a firmer grasp on its share of the market.

If advertising increases the demand for a firm's product, as Figure 14-5 shows, it shifts the firm's demand curve to the right, from dd to $d'd'$. The rightward shift indicates that, as a result of the campaign, consumers will seek to purchase a larger quantity of the firm's product at each price for which the firm may offer to sell it.

If advertising reduces the price elasticity of demand for a firm's product, as Figure 14-6 shows, it produces a clockwise rotation in the firm's demand curve, from dd to $d'd'$. The steeper slope allows the firm to charge a higher price for its product. It also indicates that consumers are less responsive to changes in the price of the product and will not reduce their consumption quite as dramatically as they would have before the campaign if the firm increases its price.

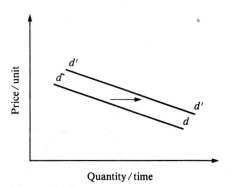

Figure 14-5
A monopolistically competitive firm hopes to increase the demand for its product (dd to $d'd'$) through advertising and other forms of product differentiation.

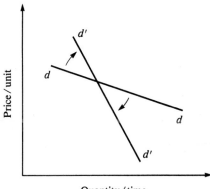

Figure 14-6
An effective advertising campaign may produce a clockwise rotation in a firm's demand curve (dd to $d'd'$) and thus reduce the price elasticity of demand for the firm's product.

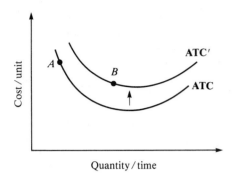

Figure 14-7
Advertising shifts a firm's average total
cost curve upward (ATC to ATC').
However, it may result in lower average
total costs (*B*, as opposed to *A*).

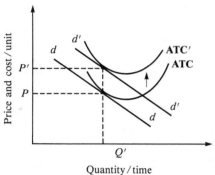

Figure 14-8
Advertising and other forms of product
differentiation may lead to higher costs
with little increase in output when firms
are interdependent. A firm may be
forced to advertise just to preserve its
market share.

D. Advertising causes a firm's cost curves to shift upward.

Advertising is costly, and added costs push a firm's cost curves
upward. If a firm commits itself by contract to a specified level of
advertising, its average fixed cost curve shifts upward. If it varies its
advertising directly with sales, its average variable cost curve shifts
upward. In either case, its average total cost (ATC) curve shifts
upward, as shown in Figure 14-7.

Although advertising causes a firm's ATC curve to shift upward, it
does not necessarily result in a higher average total cost of
production. As the movement from point *A* to point *B* in Figure 14-7
suggests, an effective advertising campaign may enable a firm to
expand its output to a level at which it can realize greater economies
of scale. If that happens, the economies of scale may more than offset
the costs of the advertising, and the firm's average total cost of
production may actually be lower than it was initially.

E. Interdependence may lead to excessive advertising.

When the firms in a market are interdependent, as they are under
oligopoly, which you will learn about in the next chapter, the actions
of one firm noticeably affect other firms. Under such circumstances,
advertising in a market may become excessive. If one firm successfully differentiates its product through advertising, other firms may
be forced to advertise simply to preserve their shares of the market.
The result, then, may simply be an increase in the average costs of all
the firms with no significant increase in the output or sales of any of
them, as shown in Figure 14-8.

RAISE YOUR GRADES
Can you explain . . . ?

☑ why there is a price range rather than a single price for goods
sold in monopolistically competitive markets

☑ why the demand curve facing a firm under monopolistic
competition is highly elastic

☑ how a monopolistically competitive firm selects its profit-
maximizing output and price

☑ why long-run equilibrium under monopolistic competition
requires that economic profits equal zero

☑ why resource allocation is inefficient under monopolistic
competition

☑ why monopolistically competitive industries exhibit excess
capacity

☑ how advertising affects the demand curve that a
monopolistically competitive firm faces

☑ how advertising affects the average cost curves of a firm
under monopolistic competition

☑ when and how advertising may be excessive

SUMMARY

1. The theory of monopolistic competition was developed in the 1930s
by Joan Robinson and Edward Chamberlin.
2. The theory of monopolistic competition assumes market conditions
in which (1) buyers and sellers are both numerous and small,

(2) products are at least slightly differentiated from one another, (3) firms can enter and exit with ease, and (4) buyers and sellers have perfect knowledge of the prices and qualities of products and the quantities in which they are available.

3. A monopolistically competitive firm must make three decisions: (1) how much to produce, (2) what price to charge, and (3) how to differentiate its product from the products of other firms in the same market.

4. Product differentiation takes three principal forms: (1) differentiation of the product itself, (2) differentiation of the image of a product, and (3) differentiation of the sellers of a product.

5. Each firm in a monopolistically competitive market produces a product that is similar to , but not identical with, the products of other firms in the market; therefore, each firm faces its own unique downward-sloping demand curve.

6. Because each firm faces a demand curve with a negative slope, marginal revenue is less than price under monopolistic competition.

7. Under monopolistic competition, a firm's marginal revenue (MR) curve bisects the horizontal distance between the y-axis and the demand curve that the firm faces.

8. The demand curve facing each firm under monopolistic competition is highly elastic (relatively flat) because there are a large number of close substitutes for the firm's product.

9. Under monopolistic competition, a firm selects its optimal output level by applying the MR = MC rule for profit maximization.

10. Under monopolistic competition, a firm selects its optimal price by measuring the height of the demand curve that it faces at its profit-maximizing output level.

11. Since entry into a monopolistically competitive industry is easy, long-run equilibrium requires that a typical firm be earning an economic profit of zero.

12. A typical firm in a monopolistically competitive industry is earning an economic profit of zero when its long-run average cost (LRAC) curve is tangent to the demand curve that it faces.

13. When a firm under monopolistic competition is in long-run equilibrium, its average cost of production is above the lowest possible level. Therefore, productional efficiency is not achieved under monopolistic competition.

14. Monopolistically competitive industries suffer from excess capacity—too many plants producing too little output. Theoretically, production costs could be lower if plants were larger and were utilized more intensively.

15. Allocative efficiency is not achieved under monopolistic competition: price exceeds marginal revenue, which equals marginal cost.

16. The proponents of advertising argue that it informs consumers, allows firms to realize greater economies of scale, promotes competition and innovation, and supports the communications media.

17. The critics of advertising argue that it aims to persuade, not inform; that it increases costs; that it is a substitute for price competition and that ads cancel one another out; and that alternative methods of funding would improve the communications media.

18. A monopolistically competitive firm attempts to select its own demand curve through advertising. An effective advertising campaign increases the demand for a firm's product (shifts the firm's demand curve to the right) or reduces the price elasticity of demand for a firm's product (produces a clockwise rotation in the firm's demand curve).

19. Advertising causes a firm's average total cost curve to shift upward.

20. Advertising may be excessive when the firms in a market are interdependent and are forced to advertise to preserve, rather than to expand, their shares of the market.

RAPID REVIEW

1. Two names associated with the development of the theory of monopolistic competition are _____ and _____ . [See Section 14-1.]

2. Monopolistic competition is characterized by **(a)** a single seller, **(b)** many small sellers, **(c)** a few large sellers, **(d)** a few small sellers and many buyers. [See Section 14-1.]

3. Unlike the products produced under perfect competition, which are _____ , the products produced under monopolistic competition are at least slightly _____ from one another. [See Section 14-1.]

4. Product differentiation includes not only differentiation of the characteristics of the product itself, but also differentiation of the _____ associated with the product and differentiation of the characteristics of the _____ of the product. [See Section 14-1.]

5. Because the demand curve facing a firm in a monopolistically competitive market has a _____ slope, the firm's marginal revenue is _____ than its price. [See Section 14-1.]

6. The demand curve for a firm under monopolistic competition is relatively flat because **(a)** there are many exact substitutes for the firm's product, **(b)** there are only a few close substitutes for the firm's product, **(c)** there are no perfect but there are many close substitutes for the firm's product, **(d)** demand for the firm's product is highly inelastic. [See Section 14-1.]

7. Each firm in a monopolistically competitive market must determine the combination of _____ , _____ , and _____ _____ that will enable it to maximize its profits. [See Section 14-2.]

8. A monopolistically competitive firm will produce and earn a positive economic profit in the short run if the price of its product is greater than its average total cost of production. True or false? [See Section 14-2.]

9. If the firms in a monopolistically competitive market are earning positive economic profits, new firms will enter the market in the long run, and their entry will shift the _____ curves of existing firms to the _____ until the economic profit of a typical firm equals _____ . [See Section 14-2.]

10. Allocative efficiency is achieved under monopolistic competition. True or false? [See Section 14-3.]

11. Many economists argue that the cost of excess _____ in a monopolistically competitive industry is the price of product _____ . [See Section 14-3.]

12. A monopolistically competitive industry cannot be in long-run equilibrium unless **(a)** the demand curve facing a typical firm in the industry is tangent to its LRAC curve, **(b)** each firm is earning a normal economic profit, **(c)** the price of each firm's product is equal to the average cost of producing it, **(d)** all of these conditions prevail. [See Section 14-3.]

13. Whereas the proponents of advertising argue that it _____ consumers and thus helps them to make rational choices, the opponents of advertising argue that it seeks mainly to _____ consumers. [See Section 14-4.]

14. Effective advertising **(a)** shifts a firm's demand curve to the left, **(b)** makes a firm's demand curve less elastic, **(c)** produces a counterclockwise rotation in a firm's demand curve, **(d)** results in either **(a)** or **(c)**. [See Section 14-4.]

15. An advertising campaign shifts a firm's average cost curve downward. True or false? [See Section 14-4.]

Answers
1. (Joan) Robinson, (Edward) Chamberlin   **2. (b)**   3. homogeneous, differentiated
4. imagery, sellers   5. downward or negative, less   **6. (c)**   7. output, price, product
differentiation   **8.** true   **9.** demand, left, zero   **10.** false   **11.** capacity,
differentiation   **12. (d)**   **13.** informs, persuade   **14. (b)**   **15.** false

---

SOLVED PROBLEMS

PROBLEM 14-1   Compare and contrast the assumptions of the theory of monopolistic competition with the assumptions of the theories of perfect competition and monopoly.

Answer: The theory of monopolistic competition is similar to the theory of perfect competition in that both theories assume **(1)** that there are many small buyers and sellers in a market, **(2)** that the buyers and sellers in a market have perfect information about the prices of products and the quantities in which they are available, and **(3)** that new firms can enter and existing firms can leave a market with little or no impediment. The two theories differ in that monopolistic competition assumes heterogeneous or slightly differentiated products whereas perfect competition assumes homogeneous or standardized products.

The theory of monopolistic competition is similar to the theory of monopoly in only one way, the same way in which it is dissimilar to the theory of perfect competition: the products produced and sold under both monopolistic competition and monopoly are assumed to be unique. Of course there are many close substitutes for the products sold under monopolistic competition whereas there are no close substitutes for the products sold under monopoly. However, because there are nevertheless no exact or perfect substitutes for the products sold under either market structure, each monopolist and each monopolistically competitive firm faces its own unique downward-sloping demand curve. [See Section 14-1.]

PROBLEM 14-2   Consider two retail clothing stores in your area. Make a list of the ways in which their products, the retail goods and services that they provide, are differentiated from one another.

Answer: Your list will depend, in part, on the particular stores that you choose. However, it should include such features as size, location, floor plan and organization, credit policy, pricing policy, returns policy, quantity and quality of merchandise, selection of brand names, quality of house brands, number and competence of clerks, speed and quality of service, frequency of sales, quality of sales merchandise, policy on extra services, such as alterations, gift wrapping, mailing, and so on. [See Section 14-1.]

PROBLEM 14-3   Explain why at any one time there is only one price on the Chicago Board of Trade for #1 hard red winter wheat, yet there are many prices in Chicago for blue jeans, even identical pairs of Levi's.

Answer: At any one time there is only one price on the Chicago Board of Trade for #1 hard red winter wheat primarily because #1 hard red winter wheat is a homogeneous good. Since any farmer's #1 hard red winter wheat is indistinguishable from any other farmer's, no farmer can ask for and expect to receive a price higher than the going rate at the Board of Trade. Any farmer who does will sell no wheat.

By contrast, at any one time there are many prices for blue jeans in Chicago not only because blue jeans are a heterogeneous good and vary widely from one manufacturer to another, but also because the retail establishments in Chicago that sell blue jeans are as heterogeneous as the blue jeans that they sell. Because the jeans are different, manufacturers can charge different prices. Because the stores are different, retailers can charge different prices—even for identical pairs of Levi's. [See Section 14-1.]

PROBLEM 14-4 Imagination Unlimited (IU) has developed a new and as yet unnamed product. Sketch a hypothetical demand curve for the product. Then sketch the effect on the demand curve if other firms produce and market close substitutes for IU's product.

Answer: Line *dd* in Figure 14-9 is a hypothetical demand curve for a new product for which no close substitutes exist. As you can see, the curve is fairly steep, which indicates that IU has a considerable amount of monopolistic power. It can charge a higher price for its product than it could if close substitutes were available. It can also vary its price considerably without dramatically affecting quantity demanded and sold.

Line *d'd'* shows the effects that monopolistic competition will probably have on IU's demand curve. New firms producing and marketing close substitutes for IU's product will reduce IU's share of the market for the product group, causing IU's demand curve to shift left. They will also make IU's con-

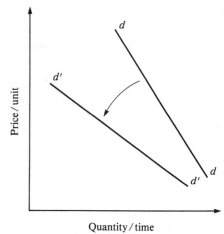

Figure 14-9

sumers more sensitive to changes in price, causing IU's demand curve to rotate in a counterclockwise direction (i.e., to become more elastic). [See Section 14-1.]

PROBLEM 14-5 Figure 14-10 shows the marginal cost (MC), the average variable cost (AVC), and the average total cost (ATC) curves of a firm in a monopolistically competitive market, along with the demand curve (*dd*) that the firm faces. Locate the firm's profit-maximizing output level and price. Label them *Q** and *P**, respectively. Would you proceed any differently if the firm were a monopolist?

Answer: Begin by constructing a marginal revenue (MR) curve for the firm. The procedures for constructing a firm's MR curve are the same whether the firm is a monopolist or a monopolistic competitor.

To construct the firm's MR curve, draw a line that bisects the horizontal distance between the *y*-axis and demand curve *dd*, as shown in Figure 14-11. To locate the firm's profit-maximizing output level, drop a vertical line from the intersection of the firm's MR and MC curves (where MR = MC) to the *x*-axis. That's quantity *Q**. Finally, to locate the firm's profit-maximizing price, draw two lines, a vertical line from *Q** to

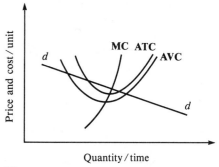

Figure 14-10

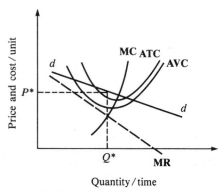

Figure 14-11

demand curve *dd* and a horizontal line from that point to the *y*-axis. As Figure 14-11 shows, that's price *P**, the highest price the market will bear at output *Q**. Since price *P**

exceeds the firm's average total as well as its average variable cost at output Q^* ($P^* > $ AVC and $P^* > $ ATC at Q^*), the firm will produce at that level and earn a positive economic profit in the short run. [See Section 14-2.]

PROBLEM 14-6 Figure 14-12 shows the long-run average cost (LRAC) curve and the demand curve (*dd*) facing a typical firm in a monopolistically competitive industry. Explain why the configuration of the two curves cannot represent a long-run equilibrium in the industry. What will happen to the demand curve facing the firm? Sketch a demand curve in the figure that fulfills the conditions for long-run equilibrium under monopolistic competition. Find the long-run equilibrium price and quantity for the firm; label them Q^* and P^*, respectively.

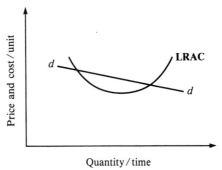

Figure 14-12

Answer: Figure 14-12 cannot represent a long-run equilibrium under monopolistic competition because the LRAC curve of a typical firm *intersects* the demand curve that the firm faces; it is not *tangent* to it. Therefore, the firm can earn a positive economic profit by producing at a point on its LRAC curve that lies below its demand curve. So can other firms in the industry. However, the opportunity for earning positive profits won't last forever. New firms will be attracted to the industry, and their entry will reduce the market shares of existing firms,

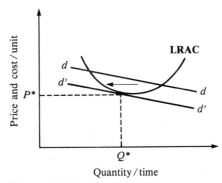

Figure 14-13

shifting the firms' demand curves to the left. The process will continue until the demand curve of a typical firm is tangent to its LRAC curve, as shown in Figure 14-13. At the point of tangency, where its equilibrium quantity will be Q^* and its equilibrium price will be P^*, a typical firm in the industry will just be breaking even (earning an economic profit of zero), and the firm and the industry will both be in a state of long-run equilibrium. [See Section 14-2.]

PROBLEM 14-7 Use the standards established under perfect competition to assess the productional and allocative efficiency achieved under monopolistic competition.

Answer: Neither productional nor allocative efficiency is achieved under monopolistic competition. As you recall from Chapter 12, the standard set for productional efficiency under perfect competition is an average cost of production no higher than absolute minimum. To meet this standard, a firm must produce at a level that corresponds to the lowest point on its long-run average cost (LRAC) curve. A firm under monopolistic competition stops short of that level because the downward-sloping demand curve that it faces does not allow it *both* to produce at the lowest point on its LRAC curve *and* to earn an economic profit of zero in the long run. Therefore, the average cost of production in a monopolistically competitive industry could be reduced if fewer plants of a larger scale were producing a greater output.

Allocative efficiency is not achieved under monopolistic competition for the same reason that it is not achieved under monopoly. Whenever a profit-maximizing firm faces a demand curve with a negative slope, its marginal revenue—and thus its marginal cost—is less than the price that it charges for its product. Whenever marginal cost is not equal to price, resources are misallocated to the production of a good. [See Section 14-3.]

PROBLEM 14-8   Why do monopolistically competitive industries suffer from excess capacity? What gains or losses would be associated with eliminating the excess?

Answer: In the long run, a monopolistically competitive firm must produce at an output level that will enable it to charge a price equal to its average cost of production. That output–price combination corresponds to the point of tangency between the firm's demand curve and its LRAC curve. Since the firm's demand curve slopes downward because of product differentiation, it cannot be tangent to the LRAC curve at the lowest point on the LRAC curve; it can only be tangent to it at a point where the LRAC curve also slopes downward (i.e., where the average cost of production is declining, but is not at an absolute minimum). Therefore, instead of utilizing a plant of optimal size to its fullest capacity, either a firm in a monopolistically competitive industry utilizes a plant of less than optimal size or it utilizes a plant of optimal size at less than optimal capacity. In either case the result is excess capacity in an industry.

As you know from Problem 14-7, the per-unit or average cost of production in a monopolistically competitive industry could be lowered if fewer plants of a larger scale were producing a greater output. However, the cost savings could only be achieved at the expense of variety; the number of producers in the industry and thus the variety of brands made available to consumers would have to be reduced. [See Section 14-3.]

PROBLEM 14-9   Assume that many different brands of widgets are produced, all of them similar to but not identical with the widgets produced by Olie's Widget Works. If Olie undertakes an advertising campaign and the campaign is successful, what will happen to the demand curve that Olie faces? What will happen to Olie's average total cost (ATC) curve? Draw diagrams to illustrate your answer.

Answer: A successful advertising campaign will have one or both of two effects on Olie's demand curve: (**1**) it will shift it to the right, indicating that Olie now has a larger share of the widget market and can sell more widgets at each price; (**2**) it will rotate it in a clockwise direction (make it less elastic), indicating that Olie now has a more secure hold on his share of the widget market and can charge a higher price for his brand of widgets than he could before the campaign. Figure 14-14 illustrates a combination of these two effects. Demand curve $d'd'$, which represents Olie's demand curve after the successful advertising campaign, is both farther right and steeper than demand curve dd.

The advertising campaign, whether it is successful or not, will be costly for Olie and will thus have one simple and predictable effect on his average total cost (ATC) curve: it will shift it upward, as shown in Figure 14-15. [See Section 14-4.]

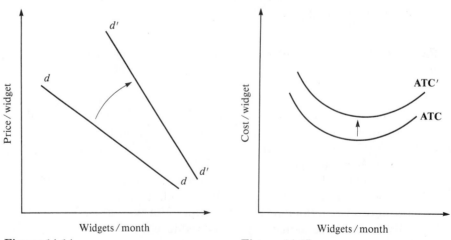

Figure 14-14   Figure 14-15

PROBLEM 14-10   When similar products are differentiated from one another in both real and imaginary ways, consumers need information about the products in order to make rational purchasing decisions. Does advertising provide that information? Under what market conditions might advertising be carried beyond the socially efficient level?

Answer: Some advertising does provide factual, substantive information about products that consumers need to make rational purchasing decisions. However, most advertising provides little or no information. Much of it, in fact, is not even designed to inform consumers; it is designed to persuade, and sometimes even to deceive, them.

Advertising may be carried beyond a socially efficient level in an industry in which firms are interdependent and the actions of one affect the others. In such an industry, advertising begets more advertising because each firm risks losing its share of the market if it stops advertising and its rivals don't. The excessive advertising neither conveys added information nor increases total sales in an industry. It simply increases costs and prices. [See Section 14-4.]

15 OLIGOPOLY

THIS CHAPTER IS ABOUT

☑ **Theories of Oligopoly**
☑ **The Kinked Demand Curve Theory**
☑ **The Cartel Theory**
☑ **Coordinating Behavior by Noncollusive Methods**

15-1. Theories of Oligopoly

Oligopoly is a form of market structure in which there are just a few firms selling a given product, as opposed to the single seller in a monopoly and the many sellers in perfect competition. Oligopoly also differs from monopoly and perfect competition in that any action taken by an oligopolistic firm noticeably affects the firm's rivals. (By contrast, firms in perfect competition are by definition too small to affect their rivals, and a monopolistic firm by definition has no rivals.) Consequently, the rival firms are likely to react to any action by the oligopolistic firm, and the oligopolistic firm must consider those reactions every time it makes a decision.

Oligopolists' decisions are thus complicated by this extra factor of rivals' reactions. And as a result, whereas there are but single theories of monopoly and of perfect competition, there are many theories of oligopoly, each based on different assumptions about the rivals' reactions. This chapter will describe two popular theories of oligopolistic pricing. The *kinked demand curve theory* describes pricing decisions of an individual oligopolistic firm producing a differentiated product. The *cartel theory* describes joint maximization of profits by several oligopolistic firms. Your text may describe still other theories.

A. All theories of oligopoly include four major assumptions.

All theories of oligopoly include the three assumptions common to the theories of all market structures: (**1**) that firms aim to maximize their profits; (**2**) that households aim to maximize their satisfaction; and (**3**) that no external costs or benefits are associated with any good. In addition, all theories of oligopoly include four major assumptions:

1. There are so few sellers of the product produced in an oligopoly that the decisions of each seller noticeably affect the sales of the other sellers.
2. The product produced in an oligopoly may be homogeneous or differentiated.
3. Perfect information is available regarding prices, but not regarding rivals' reactions. Firms do not know in advance how rivals will react to a change in price or in product differentiation.
4. There are barriers that hinder new firms from entering an oligopolistic market.

EXAMPLE 15-1: The steel industry is an example of an oligopoly with a relatively homogeneous product. The automobile industry is an example of an oligopoly with a relatively differentiated product. Each of the four major U.S. automobile manufacturers produces products that are slightly different from those of its rivals. Furthermore, consumers show that they recognize this differentiation by their preferences for the various automobile brands.

B. Oligopolistic firms are interdependent.

Since by definition any action taken by an oligopolistic firm will noticeably affect that firm's rivals, a key characteristic of oligopolistic firms is that they are interdependent and recognize that fact. Each firm's profit-maximizing decisions regarding output, price, and product differentiation depend on corresponding decisions made by rival firms.

EXAMPLE 15-2: The airline industry is in many respects an oligopoly with a differentiated product. Demand for that product can be expressed in terms of the number of passenger miles sold per month, as shown in Figure 15-1 for two airlines: Archaic Airlines and Occidental Airlines. Each airline initially charges price P for the same number of passenger miles (Q), and all other factors, such as advertising and so forth, are the same for the two firms. Archaic's initial demand curve, labeled DD, is shown in part (**a**), and Occidental's initial demand curve, also labeled DD, is shown in part (**b**).

Suppose that Archaic reduces its fare from P to P'. As shown in part (**a**) by the intersection of P' and demand curve DD, Archaic's sales will rise (Q to Q'). However, because of the oligopolistic nature of this market, a part of Archaic's sales increase will come at the expense of its competitors; every time a passenger switches to Archaic, there will be a corresponding decrease in demand for flights on competing airlines. One result will be a lower demand for Occidental flights, as shown in part (**b**) by the shift leftward from the initial demand curve DD to the new demand curve labeled $D'D'$.

However, suppose that Occidental retaliates with a price cut of its own or with a new advertising campaign. The result might be a shift of passengers back to Occidental and a corresponding drop in demand for flights on Archaic, as shown in part (**a**) by the shift leftward to the new demand curve labeled $D'D'$.

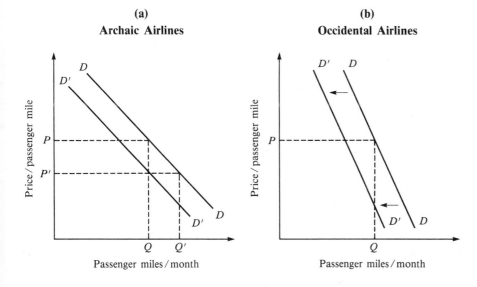

(a)
Archaic Airlines

(b)
Occidental Airlines

Figure 15-1
A price cut or change in advertising strategy by one oligopolistic firm will shift the demand curve for a rival firm.

In sum, each airline's profit-maximizing decisions regarding price depend to a significant extent on the corresponding decisions made by the other airline.

C. The interdependence of oligopolistic firms has three notable consequences.

1. There is no single theory of oligopoly, since decisions and results depend on how rivals react. Instead, there are many different theories of oligopoly based on different assumptions about the reactions of rival firms.

2. Conventional demand curves based only on variations in price and quantity demanded are of limited use to oligopolists. In oligopoly, any firm's price change will cause reactions by rival firms, and those reactions will shift the conventional demand curve used to make the first firm's price change decision.

3. It is difficult to construct a demand curve for an oligopolistic firm that produces a homogeneous good. To do so, you would need to know, for example, how much the firm could sell at a price that was twice that of its rivals or half that of its rivals. For an oligopolistic firm producing a homogeneous good, these are not realistic questions. As a result, most analyses, including the kinked demand curve model presented here, are for oligopolistic firms producing a differentiated good.

D. Oligopolists producing differentiated goods will apply the MR = MC rule to maximize profits.

An oligopolistic firm producing a differentiated good will find its profit-maximizing price and output by applying the MR = MC rule, *ceteris paribus.*

15-2. The Kinked Demand Curve Theory

One popular theory of oligopoly assumes that rival firms will match each other's price reductions but not each other's price increases. If so, the demand curve for an oligopolistic firm will be "kinked" at the existing market price, as shown in Figure 15-2.

If the firm shown in Figure 15-2 increases its price above the existing market price (*P*), the quantity demanded of its product will decline. However, since this market is an oligopoly, the final outcome will also be affected by the reactions of rival firms. In this case, these rivals will be gaining the sales lost by the first firm, so they will have no reason to match the first firm's price increase. If indeed they keep their original price, the first firm will lose an important part of its market share, and the decline in the quantity demanded of its product will be very sharp. Consequently, for all prices above the existing market price, this firm has a relatively *elastic* demand curve (segment *dA*).

On the other hand, if the first firm reduces its price below the existing market price (*P*), the quantity demanded of its product will rise. Once again, however, the final outcome will be affected by the reactions of rival firms. This time these rivals will be losing sales to the first firm, so they will most likely match the first firm's price cut in order to retain their market shares. If indeed these rivals do cut their prices, the first firm will fail to increase its market share, and the rise in the quantity demanded of its product will not be nearly as sharp as was the decline in the quantity demanded when the firm raised its price. Consequently, for all prices below the existing market price, this firm has a relatively *inelastic* demand curve (segment *AD*).

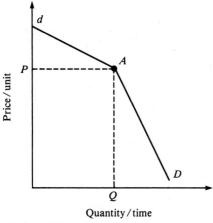

Figure 15-2
If rival firms match price cuts but not price increases, the demand curve for an oligopolistic firm will be "kinked" at the existing market price (*P*).

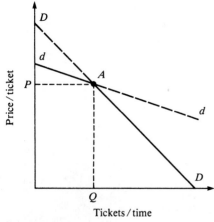

Figure 15-3
An oligopolistic firm's demand curve can differ significantly depending on whether or not rival firms match price cuts and price increases.

EXAMPLE 15-3: Let P be the existing market price of an airline ticket from New York to Frostburg, as shown in Figure 15-3. Suppose that Northern Airlines, one of four carriers on this route, reduces its price below that existing market price. Northern will then be able to sell more tickets, for example, because more people will be induced to fly by the lower fare. However, the final outcome will also be affected by the reactions of the rival carriers. If the rival carriers maintain the original price, Northern will gain a portion of their market shares and the number of tickets that Northern can sell will increase very sharply, as shown in Figure 15-3 by the dashed demand curve segment Ad, which is relatively elastic. However, it is much more likely that the rival carriers will match Northern's price cut and thereby retain their existing market shares. If this is the case, Northern's sales will still rise, but the increase will be much less sharp, as shown by the solid demand curve segment AD, which is relatively inelastic.

Suppose instead that Northern increases its ticket price above the existing market price. The quantity demanded of Northern's tickets will then fall, but again, the final outcome will be affected by the reactions of the rival carriers. If the rivals increase their prices, too, all four carriers will maintain their original market shares, more or less. In this case, the quantity demanded of Northern's tickets will still fall, as shown in Figure 15-3 by the dashed demand curve segment DA, which is relatively inelastic. However, it is much more likely that the rival carriers, who will be gaining the passengers that Northern loses, will not match Northern's price increase. If this is the case, Northern will lose some of its market share to them, and the quantity demanded of Northern's tickets will drop very sharply, as shown by the solid demand curve segment dA, which is relatively elastic.

A. Under a kinked demand curve, a marginal revenue curve typically is not continuous.

A kinked demand curve typically produces a two-piece marginal revenue curve, as shown in Figure 15-4. In that figure, which shows the same basic kinked demand curve as in Figure 15-3, the top portion of the dashed line MR is the marginal revenue curve for the upper portion (segment dA) of the kinked demand curve. The bottom portion of line MR is the marginal revenue curve for the lower portion (segment AD) of the kinked demand curve. The gap or discontinuity between the portions of line MR is typical of a marginal revenue curve under a kinked demand curve.

B. With a kinked demand curve, cost changes may not always result in price changes.

A major implication of the kinked demand curve model is that cost changes do not always result in price changes. Prices will not change as long as shifts in a firm's marginal cost curve are confined to the gap between the two portions of the marginal revenue curve. In this respect, oligopoly may lead to so-called "sticky" prices.

EXAMPLE 15-4: A decrease in the cost of jet fuel will not necessarily lead to a reduction in airline fares. Figure 15-5 shows the kinked demand curve for tickets on Northern Airlines, as described in Example 15-3, along with its two-piece marginal revenue (MR) curve, as described above. Suppose that a decrease in Northern's jet fuel costs causes Northern's marginal cost curve to shift downward from MC to MC'. As long as this shift is confined to the gap in the marginal revenue curve, as shown in the figure—that is, as long as there is no new, lower

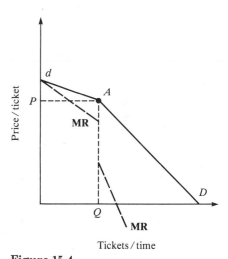

Figure 15-4
Under a kinked demand curve (dAD), a marginal revenue (MR) curve will be discontinuous at the kink.

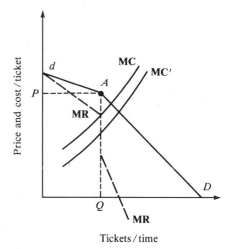

Figure 15-5
Under oligopoly, a shift in a firm's marginal cost curve (MC to MC') that is confined to the gap in the firm's marginal revenue (MR) curve may not lead to a change in product price.

intersection between MC′ and MR—Northern will have no reason to lower its ticket prices. After all, as we have seen, cutting the price will not necessarily increase Northern's market share, and it could set off a price war.

15-3.   The Cartel Theory

Firms in an oligopolistic market may form a cartel. As you recall from Chapter 13, a *cartel* is a formal arrangement among firms in a market to fix prices, output levels, sales territories, production quotas, and the like for the purpose of jointly maximizing profits.

A. An inclusive cartel will behave as a monopolist.

If a cartel is *inclusive*—that is, if it includes all the firms participating in a particular market—it will have the power to organize production, choose an output level, and set prices exactly as a monopolist would. A cartel of this kind in effect becomes a monopolist, as shown in part (**a**) of Figure 15-6. Note that for a monopolizing cartel, the supply curve (*SS*) is identical with the marginal cost (MC) curve for the industry as a whole. Note, too, that in order to keep the price at *P*′, and thus above what would be the strictly competitive level (price *P*), the cartel must restrict industry output from *Q* to *Q*′. The output of a typical member firm in the cartel, as shown in part (**b**) of Figure 15-6, must be restricted from *q* to *q*′. To restrict the output of member firms, cartels use various devices, such as assigning output quotas or sales territories.

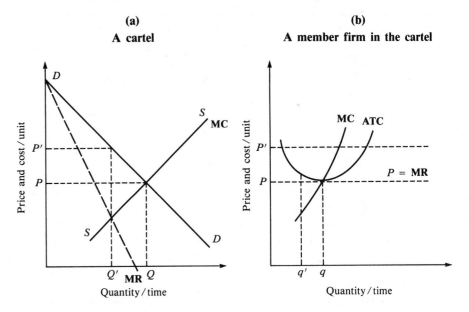

Figure 15-6
Firms in an industry may form a cartel and set prices and output levels in the same way as a monopolist.

B. There are limits on cartel behavior.

There are four important factors limiting the tendency of oligopolists to form cartels and engage in monopolistic behavior.

1. In most industries in the United States, cartels and similar schemes for collusion are illegal; violators can be prosecuted under the Sherman Act, which prohibits combinations and conspiracies in restraint of trade.
2. Members of an illegal cartel have a tendency to cheat on their output quotas. The artificially high price that the cartel enforces tempts individual members to expand output beyond their quotas in order to increase profits. In other words, cartels are inherently unstable.

3. The positive profits earned by the cartel members will attract more sellers into the market unless there are substantial barriers to entry.
4. The larger the number of firms in a cartel, the more difficult it becomes to negotiate and enforce quota or territorial agreements, especially if these agreements are not legal.

EXAMPLE 15-5: In the early 1980s the Organization of Petroleum Exporting Countries (OPEC), the international petroleum producers' cartel, encountered serious difficulties in enforcing petroleum production quotas among its member countries. At that time world petroleum demand was low, so OPEC assigned its members low output quotas in order to keep petroleum prices high. However, for many OPEC members these low quotas meant very low incomes, which caused severe problems for countries that had launched ambitious development schemes. Consequently, certain OPEC members began overproducing their quotas and selling their output at prices lower than those set by OPEC. The result was a decline in the power of the OPEC cartel and lower petroleum prices worldwide.

15-4. Coordinating Behavior by Noncollusive Methods

The structure of the U.S. economy to some extent encourages coordinated behavior among firms in oligopolistic industries. After all, rough-and-tumble competition can lead to lower profits for all firms, bankruptcy for some, and antitrust action against the "winners" if they practice monopolization. However, formal coordination through cartels or collusion is illegal. Given this situation, many firms have developed noncollusive methods to coordinate their behavior.

A. Firms can coordinate their behavior through noncollusive methods.

There are four important noncollusive methods whereby oligopolistic firms coordinate their behavior.

1. *Price leadership.* One firm sets a price and other firms in the industry follow if they perceive that the new price is in their common interest.
2. *Dominant firm pricing.* A dominant firm dictates the price structure for an entire industry.
3. *Administered pricing.* Firms pursue independent pricing policies designed to achieve a mutually satisfactory rate of return on investment.
4. *Nonprice competition.* Firms pursue similar pricing policies and then compete through packaging, service, technology, and other nonprice factors.

B. Coordinated behavior is more likely in static situations.

Firms are more likely to engage in some form of coordinated behavior when the market or production technology is static. By contrast, when new technology and changing tastes create opportunities for enlarging market shares, diversifying, and increasing profits, firms are more likely to be competitive.

C. The legality of noncollusive coordination has been challenged.

The legality of noncollusive coordination among oligopolistic firms has been challenged several times by the U.S. Justice Department and by the Federal Trade Commission (FTC) under the Sherman and Clayton Acts. In one notable case in 1972, the FTC prosecuted the "big four" ready-to-eat cereal makers (Post, Kellogg, General Mills, and Ralston Purina) for "shared monopoly." However, the charges were dismissed.

RAISE YOUR GRADES

Can you explain...?

☑ why oligopolistic firms are interdependent
☑ why there is no single theory of oligopoly
☑ why conventional demand curves have limited relevance to oligopolists
☑ why a demand curve for an oligopolistic firm may be kinked
☑ how a kinked demand curve can lead to a measure of price stability
☑ why cartels are inherently unstable
☑ how the structure of the U.S. economy encourages oligopolistic firms to coordinate their behavior
☑ how oligopolists may coordinate their behavior without forming an illegal cartel

SUMMARY

1. The theory of oligopoly assumes a market structure characterized by (1) a few interdependent sellers, (2) significant barriers to entry, (3) perfect information on prices, and (4) either homogeneous or differentiated products.
2. Oligopolistic firms are interdependent. The profit-maximizing decisions of any one oligopolistic firm depend on the decisions of rival firms.
3. There are many different theories of oligopolistic behavior, each based on different assumptions concerning the reactions of rival firms.
4. Conventional demand curves have limited relevance in analyzing oligopolistic markets.
5. Oligopolists with differentiated products will apply the MR = MC rule in order to maximize profits.
6. An oligopolistic firm's demand curve will be "kinked" at the existing market price if rival firms match price cuts but not price increases.
7. When an oligopolist has a kinked demand curve, the corresponding marginal revenue curve will have a gap or discontinuity at the point corresponding to the kink in the demand curve.
8. An oligopolist's kinked demand curve can lead to "sticky" prices. An oligopolistic firm will not necessarily change its price when its marginal cost changes, as long as the shift in its marginal cost curve is confined to the gap between the two portions of its marginal revenue curve.
9. Firms in an oligopolistic industry may form a cartel to maximize profits jointly by restricting output and raising prices.
10. A *cartel* is a formal arrangement among firms in a market to fix prices, output levels, sales territories, and the like.
11. There are four major factors limiting cartel behavior among oligopolists: (1) cheating by members, (2) entry into the market by

new firms, (3) difficulty in enforcing cartel rules, and (4) (in the United States) antitrust legislation.

12. In the United States, the most important antitrust law is the Sherman Antitrust Act, which prohibits combinations and conspiracies in restraint of trade.
13. The structure of the U.S. economy to some extent encourages coordinated behavior among firms in oligopolistic industries.
14. Oligopolistic firms can coordinate their behavior through non-collusive methods such as price leadership, dominant firm pricing, administered pricing, and nonprice competition. None of these methods necessarily involves formal collusion or cartels.
15. Coordinated behavior among oligopolistic firms is more likely to occur when the market or production technology is static.

RAPID REVIEW

1. Oligopoly is characterized by a _____ firms selling a given product and _____ entry into the market by new firms. [See Section 15-1.]
2. If firm A lowers the price of its product, the demand curve facing oligopolistic rival firm B will shift to the _____ . [See Section 15-1.]
3. The output and price that maximize profits for oligopolistic firm A depend on the output and price decisions of rival firms. True or false? [See Section 15-1.]
4. There is one single theory of oligopoly, as there is for monopoly. True or false? [See Section 15-1.]
5. Conventional demand curves based only on variations in price and quantity demanded are of _____ relevance to the decisions of oligopolists. [See Section 15-1.]
6. The _____ demand curve theory assumes that rival firms match price cuts but not price increases. [See Section 15-2.]
7. Firms A and B are oligopolistic rivals. If firm A lowers its price but firm B does not, firm A's market share will most likely _____ . [See Section 15-2.]
8. When a demand curve is kinked, the corresponding marginal revenue curve typically is not continuous. True or false? [See Section 15-2.]
9. In an oligopolistic market, a kinked demand curve is likely to make prices less stable. True or false? [See Section 15-2.]
10. A _____ is a formal agreement among firms in a market to fix prices or take other cooperative measures for the purpose of jointly maximizing profits. [See Section 15-3.]
11. An inclusive cartel has the power to behave as a _____ . [See Section 15-3.]
12. In most industries, cartels and collusion among firms to fix prices are illegal under U.S. law. True or false? [See Section 15-3.]
13. The structure of the U.S. economy to some extent encourages _____ behavior among firms in an oligopolistic market. [See Section 15-4.]
14. _____ pricing is a market strategy whereby firms pursue independent pricing policies designed to achieve a mutually satisfactory rate of return on investment. [See Section 15-4.]
15. Coordinated behavior among oligopolistic firms is most likely to take place in an industry where technology is rapidly changing. True or false? [See Section 15-4.]

Answers

1. few, restricted   2. left   3. true   4. false   5. limited   6. kinked   7. increase
8. true   9. false   10. *cartel*   11. monopolist   12. true   13. coordinated
14. Administered   15. false

SOLVED PROBLEMS

PROBLEM 15-1   Explain the meaning of *interdependence* as it relates to oligopoly, and explain why the term does not apply to a monopolistic firm or to a perfectly competitive one.

Answer: Interdependence is a key characteristic of firms in an oligopolistic market. By definition, these firms are so few in number in the given market that any action taken by one of them is bound to noticeably affect the others. Moreover, those rival firms are likely to react to any action by the first firm. Consequently, every firm in an oligopolistic market must consider the reactions of its rivals each time it makes a decision. All such firms are thus interdependent and recognize that fact.

By contrast, firms in perfect competition are by definition too small to affect their rivals, and a monopolistic firm by definition has no rivals; thus neither of these kinds of firms can be said to be interdependent. [See Section 15-1.]

PROBLEM 15-2   Protocola is a major firm in the oligopolistic soft drink market. Suppose that as the result of an intensive advertising compaign, sales of Protocola increase dramatically. Draw a diagram to show the effect of the advertising campaign on the demand for Protocola, and draw another diagram to show the effect of Protocola's success on the demand for its chief rival, Cryptocola.

Answer: Demand for Protocola and for Cryptocola can be shown in terms of the number of cases shipped in a given time period, as in Figure 15-7.

Part **(a)** of Figure 15-7 shows the result of Protocola's successful advertising campaign, which is a shift rightward from the initial demand curve *DD* to a new demand curve labeled *D'D'*. This rightward shift means that at each price, a larger quantity of Protocola will be demanded than had been the case previously.

Since, as stated, the soft drink market is oligopolistic, Protocola's success is bound to have an effect on its rivals. Part **(b)** shows that effect on demand for Cryptocola, Protocola's chief rival. The loss of customers to Protocola has caused demand for Cryptocola to fall, as shown by the leftward shift from the initial demand curve *DD* to the new demand curve labeled *D'D'*. [See Section 15-1.]

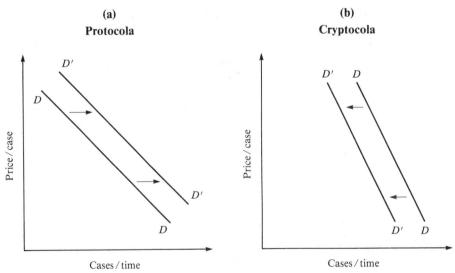

Figure 15-7

PROBLEM 15-3   Given the situation described in Problem 15-2, if you were the sales manager for Cryptocola, what might you do to counteract the effect on your product of Protocola's advertising campaign? Describe two strategies that you might adopt, and for each one, show graphically its desired effect on the demand curve for Cryptocola and also on the demand curve for Protocola.

Answer: The two strategies that Cryptocola's sales manager is most likely to adopt are reducing product price and launching a counteractive advertising campaign.

Reducing the price of Cryptocola will not shift its demand curve, but it will lead to an increase in sales, as shown in part (**b**) of Figure 15-8 by the intersection of the new price, P', and Cryptocola's demand curve, labeled $D'D'$ (the curve that Cryptocola has as the result of Problem 15-2). This strategy will affect Cryptocola's rival, Protocola, by decreasing the demand for the rival product. As shown in part (**a**) of Figure 15-8, this will cause a shift leftward for Protocola's demand curve from $D'D'$ (the curve it has as the result of Problem 15-2) to a new demand curve, labeled $D''D''$.

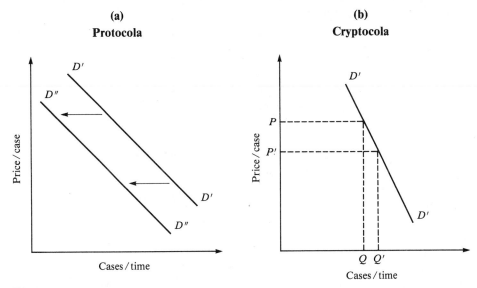

(a)
Protocola

(b)
Cryptocola

Figure 15-8

Launching a counteractive advertising campaign will increase demand for Cryptocola, as shown in part (**b**) of Figure 15-9 by the shift rightward for Cryptocola's demand curve from $D'D'$ (the curve that Cryptocola has as the result of Problem 15-2) to a new demand curve labeled $D''D''$. This strategy will affect Protocola by decreasing the demand for it, as shown in part (**a**) of Figure 15-9 by the shift leftward for Protocola's demand curve from $D'D'$ (the curve that Protocola has as the result of Problem 15-2) to a new demand curve labeled $D''D''$. [See Section 15-1.]

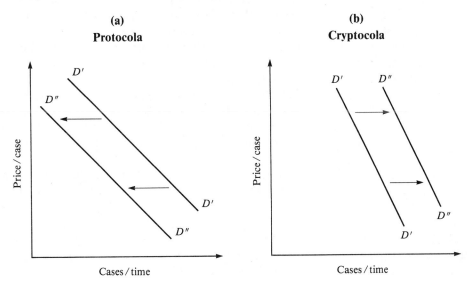

(a)
Protocola

(b)
Cryptocola

Figure 15-9

PROBLEM 15-4   Explain why there is no single theory of oligopoly, but a variety of different theories instead.

Answer: Unlike a monopolist or a firm in perfect competition, an oligopolistic firm must consider the reactions of rival firms whenever it makes a decision. Each time a decision is needed, the oligopolistic firm must make assumptions about how its rivals will react and then make the decision accordingly. Since the rival firms can react in a variety of different ways, many different assumptions are possible, and each assumption supports a different theory of oligopolistic behavior. [See Section 15-1.]

PROBLEM 15-5   Figure 15-10 shows two demand curves (labeled *AA* and *BB*) for the product of Gizmos Limited, a firm in an oligopolistic market. One curve is drawn under the assumption that every price change by Gizmos *will* be matched by rival firms. The other curve is drawn under the assumption that every price change by Gizmos will *not* be matched by rival firms. Identify which curve is which and explain your reasoning.

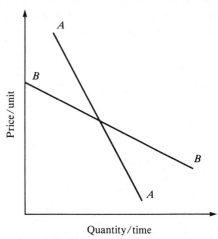

Figure 15-10

Answer: If every price change by Gizmos *will* be matched by rival firms, then none of these price changes will lead to a significant redistribution of market shares among Gizmos and its rivals. Consequently, Gizmos' price changes will not produce sharp increases or decreases in quantity demanded, so in this situation, Gizmos' demand curve will be relatively inelastic. In Figure 15-10, the demand curve that matches this description is curve *AA*.

If every price change by Gizmos will *not* be matched by rival firms, then each change is likely to produce a significant redistribution of market shares among Gizmos and its rivals. Consequently, these changes will result in sharp increases or decreases in quantity demanded, so in this situation, Gizmos' demand curve will be relatively elastic. In Figure 15-10, the demand curve that matches this description is curve *BB*. [See Section 15-2.]

PROBLEM 15-6   The kinked demand curve model is sometimes referred to as a "market share" model of oligopoly. How does this model relate to market shares?

Answer: The kinked demand curve model implicitly assumes that oligopolistic firms wish to preserve or expand their market shares. Consequently, when one firm reduces its price below the existing market price, its rivals are likely to match the reduction in order to preserve their shares of the market. The result is no significant redistribution of market shares and, for the first firm, a relatively inelastic demand curve for all prices below the existing market price.

On the other hand, when one oligopolistic firm increases its price above the existing market price, its rivals are not likely to match the increase since in this situation they have the opportunity to expand their market shares. The result will be a significant redistribution of market shares and, for the first firm, a relatively elastic demand curve for all prices above the existing market price.

The difference between the elastic demand curve above the existing market price and the inelastic demand curve below that price is what creates the "kink" at the existing market price. [See Section 15-2.]

PROBLEM 15-7   In Figure 15-11, let *P* be an oligopolistic firm's initial price and let *Q* be its initial output. If the marginal cost of production falls from MC to MC', what will be the new equilibrium price and quantity?

Answer: Note first in the figure that the firm has a kinked demand curve, and as is typical in this situation, the corresponding marginal revenue (MR) curve has a gap at the point of the kink. Note, too, that the fall in the marginal cost of production from MC to MC′ is confined to that gap. Since MC′ does not intersect MR at some new, lower point, there is no reason for the firm to reduce its price or change its quantity when MC shifts. Instead, the equilibrium levels will remain at P and Q. Indeed, for a firm with a kinked demand curve, this amount of decrease in the marginal cost of production is not enough incentive to reduce price since any price cut is likely to be matched by rival firms, and thus no increase in the firm's market share is to be expected as a result. [See Section 15-2.]

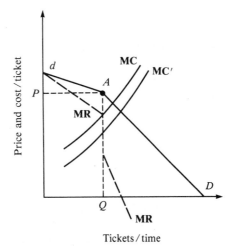

Figure 15-11

PROBLEM 15-8 Why is the kinked demand curve in Figure 15-11 not a conventional or *ceteris paribus* demand curve? [*Hint:* What do we normally assume about demand curves that is not being assumed for segment AD of this curve?]

Answer: Conventional or *ceteris paribus* demand curves are drawn with the assumption that everything other than the price of the good and the quantity demanded—including the prices charged by other firms—is held constant. The kinked demand curve in Figure 15-11 is not a conventional demand curve because its lower portion, segment AD, is drawn with the assumption that any time the firm reduces its price below the existing level, rival firms will react by matching that price cut. [See Section 15-2.]

PROBLEM 15-9 Suppose that the few firms producing widgets (a homogeneous good) have been seriously competing for market shares. What happens if these firms stop competing, form a cartel, and start behaving as a monopolist? What is likely to happen to equilibrium price and quantity in the market?

Answer: A monopolizing cartel, since it includes virtually the entire industry, will perceive the industry demand curve as its own. The cartel will maximize profits at the point where the marginal revenue for the industry as a whole equals the marginal cost for the industry as a whole. In Figure 15-12 this point is where the MR curve intersects the MC curve. Note that for a monopolizing cartel, the MC curve is identical with the supply curve (*SS*) for the industry as a whole. This intersection is at the point where output is Q^* and price is P^*. Note that to keep the price above what would be the strictly competitive level (price P), the cartel must restrict industry output from Q to Q^*. [See Section 15-3.]

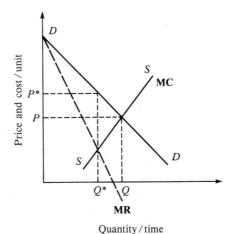

Figure 15-12

PROBLEM 15-10 Consider again the cartel described in Problem 15-9. What arrangement might the leaders of this cartel establish in order to allocate output Q^* among the cartel's various member firms? Why must there be a rule or some kind of agreement assigning output quotas to member firms? Why might a member firm disobey that rule?

Answer: Historically, cartels have allocated output among member firms according to a variety of different arrangements. Sometimes the member firms have been given equal shares of the market. Other times, each firm has been given a share commensurate with that firm's historical importance in the market: that is, the firms that in the past have been the most important in the market have received the largest shares. Still other times, the firms that could produce the desired output most economically have been given responsibility for all production, while profits have been shared by all of the member firms.

A cartel must have a rule or some kind of agreement assigning output quotas to member firms in order to restrict that output and thereby keep prices artificially high. As shown in part **(b)** of Figure 15-13, if the cartel restricts an individual member firm's output to a quota of q^*, an artificially high price of P^* can be maintained. The rule must be enforced, however, because the member firm's profit-maximizing output level is actually q, and thus that firm will be tempted to cheat on its quota in order to increase its income. Indeed, if enforcement is lax, many member firms may disobey the rule and overproduce their quotas, and the cartel will be unable to restrict output to the desired level. If that happens, it will be impossible to maintain the artificially high price, and the power of the cartel will disappear. [See Section 15-3.]

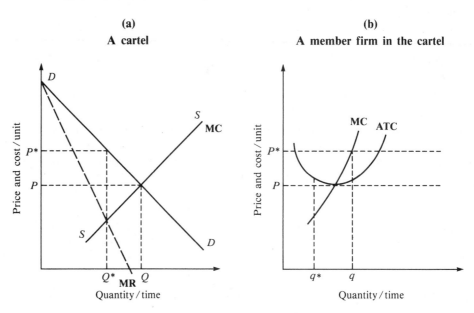

(a)

A cartel

(b)

A member firm in the cartel

Figure 15-13

PROBLEM 15-11 It is sometimes claimed that firms in some oligopolistic industries coordinate their behavior even though they do not resort to illegal collusion or cartel agreements. Coordination of this kind may lead to price and output decisions similar to those of a cartel. One method that these firms use to coordinate their behavior is called *price leadership*. What is this method and how do firms use it to increase their joint profits?

Answer: *Price leadership* is a form of coordinated behavior in which one firm sets a price and other firms in the industry follow if they perceive that the new price is in their common interest. Price leadership will increase industry profits if the demand and cost conditions of the price leader are typical of the industry as a whole. If that is the case, when a price rise benefits the price leader, it will also benefit the other firms in the industry. Alternatively, a price leader might monitor industry demand and cost conditions and seek the profit-maximizing price and output that are best for the industry as a whole. This kind of price leader will resemble a "cartel manager" for the industry. [See Section 15-4.]

16
GENERAL EQUILIBRIUM, MARKET FAILURES, AND PUBLIC POLICY

THIS CHAPTER IS ABOUT

☑ **The Market System and General Equilibrium**
☑ **Economic Efficiency**
☑ **Market Failure: Externalities**
☑ **Market Failure: Public Goods**

16-1. The Market System and General Equilibrium

The U.S. economy is an intricate system of interrelated markets. Consider Figure 16-1, which is a reproduction of the circular flow model of an economy that you first encountered in Chapter 4.

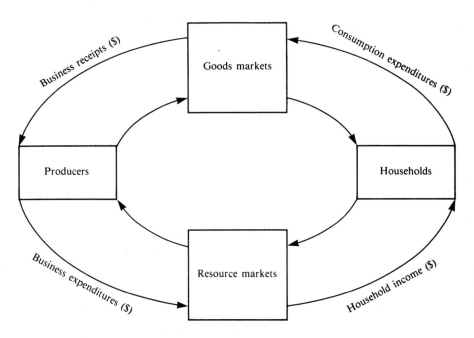

Figure 16-1
The U.S. economy is a flexible but complex system of interrelated markets.

As the model suggests, goods markets are related to resource markets through household income and business receipts. Payments by producers to the factors or resources used in production are the sources of household income. Household income becomes business receipts when it is spent to purchase goods. In addition, demand curves for substitute and complementary goods are interrelated. Supply curves are interrelated through joint production or the production of complementary goods. In short, markets are interrelated in a variety of ways.

A. Interrelation makes the market system flexible but complex.

Interrelation makes the market system flexible and adaptive, but it also makes it very complex. A single change in one market has a ripple effect throughout the system, resulting in a series of adjustments in many related markets. This responsiveness to change allows the system to adapt quickly both to internal shocks, such as unexpected crop failures, and to external shocks, such as huge increases in the price of oil by the Organization of Petroleum Exporting Countries (OPEC). Flexibility is vital in a world in which technology and tastes are constantly changing.

However, interrelatedness also makes a system very complex, and, as a result, very difficult to analyze. When a change occurs in one market, it affects the system as a whole, and its effects on the system as a whole cannot be studied through partial equilibrium analysis. Although you have not been formally introduced to the term yet, you have been exposed to the practice of partial equilibrium analysis in preceding chapters.

Partial equilibrium analysis is the study of movements from one point of equilibrium to another in a particular market or a particular decision-making unit, such as a firm or a household, without regard to the effects of those movements on other markets and decision-making units in the system as a whole.

To examine the effects of change in the system as a whole, economists employ two types of analysis: (1) general equilibrium analysis and (2) input–output analysis.

EXAMPLE 16-1: The OPEC-induced petroleum price increases in 1973 had ramifications far beyond the immediate increases in the price of gasoline and heating oil that they precipitated. Sales of energy-using items, such as air conditioners and automobiles, declined. Sales of substitute or energy-saving goods, such as insulation and mopeds, rose dramatically. Jobs and incomes were lost in the steel and auto industries while earnings rose in the oil industry. The market system generated many price signals that induced firms and households to reduce their use of petroleum products.

B. General equilibrium analysis focuses on the market system as a whole.

When we move from studying a single market to studying the entire market system, we need to expand our concept of equilibrium.

General equilibrium is a condition in which all of the individual markets and decision-making units within a system simultaneously achieve a state of balance, and there is no internal tendency to change.

Although the techniques of general equilibrium analysis are complicated, and thus limited in use, economists employ them to determine the systemwide effects of policies and changes.

C. Input–output analysis provides consistency in planning.

Input–output analysis, another approach to analyzing an entire system, is used by economic planners to achieve consistency. The approach centers around a matrix, called an input–output table, which lists the sectors of an economy that are the producers and users of basic materials. The data in an input–output table is gathered empirically from each sector of the economy. Input–output analysis is used by planners to guarantee that the types and quantities of inputs allotted to each sector are consistent with the production goals of the sector and that the overall allocation is feasible.

EXAMPLE 16-2: The following table is a hypothetical input–output table for a very simple economy:

	Destinations or Uses					
Sources	Steel	Coal	Autos	(Labor)	Export	Total
Steel	10	20	80	100	60	270
Coal	80	10	20	220	110	440
Autos	2	3	1	50	10	66
Labor (households)	20	50	30	20	0	120

Each vertical column in the table lists the units of inputs or resources used by that sector. For example, the coal sector uses 20 units of steel, 10 units of coal (it takes energy to produce coal), 3 units of automobiles, and 50 units of labor. Each horizontal row in the table lists the units of output produced by each sector and distributed to the various sectors. For example, the coal sector produces a total of 440 units (last column), which it distributes as follows: 80 units to the steel sector, 10 units to its own sector, 20 units to the auto sector, 220 units to the household sector, and 110 units to the export sector.

16-2. Economic Efficiency

Economists use the criterion of Pareto efficiency to evaluate the allocation of resources in an economic system. The criterion is named in honor of an Italian sociologist, Vilfredo Pareto. Pareto argued that any change that increases the welfare of one or more persons in a society without decreasing the welfare of any other person in the society represents a clear improvement in the welfare of the society as a whole. Economists using the Pareto criterion contend that a society should continue to alter the allocation of its resources as long as it is possible for someone to gain without someone else losing. Any allocation short of that criterion is not efficient. Thus:

Pareto efficiency is an allocation of resources that cannot be altered to increase the welfare of one or more individuals without reducing the welfare of at least one other person.

A. A perfectly competitive market system achieves Pareto efficiency.

A system of perfectly competitive markets achieves Pareto efficiency when it is in a state of general equilibrium. Pareto efficiency necessarily implies consumptive and productional efficiency as well as allocative efficiency.

1. *Consumptive efficiency* is a distribution of goods that cannot be altered to increase the satisfaction of one or more consumers without decreasing the satisfaction of at least one other consumer.
2. *Productional efficiency*, as you recall from Chapter 12, is the production of goods at the lowest cost possible. When a system achieves productional efficiency, it has exhausted all available means for reducing the per-unit cost of producing every good and every combination of goods.
3. *Allocative efficiency*, as you also recall from Chapter 12, is an allocation of resources that results in an exact equivalence of

price and marginal cost for every good produced. When a system achieves allocative efficiency, the value that society places on each good that it produces (the price of the good) is exactly equal to the economic cost (the opportunity cost to society) of producing the last unit of the good.

B. Efficiency must be distinguished from equity.

There is a difference between efficiency and equity. Equity is fairness or justice. An allocation of resources may satisfy the Pareto criterion for efficiency and yet be judged inequitable by society.

EXAMPLE 16-3: Consider a simple economy consisting of two individuals, individual A and individual B. Individual A owns all of the resources and receives all of the goods produced in the economy. Since any redistribution that will make individual B better off will also make individual A worse off, the allocation of resources in the economy is Pareto efficient. However, most people would consider it inequitable.

The members of a society may collectively decide to promote equity, even at the expense of efficiency, by taking measures to redistribute resources. Such measures include taxation, transfer programs, regulation, licensing, and so on.

EXAMPLE 16-4: A progressive income tax is an example of a program designed to promote equity. In a progressive income tax program, the marginal and average rates of taxation increase as income increases. For example, the tax rate on the first $8,000 of yearly income may be 0 percent. The tax rate on income between $8,000 and $10,000 a year may be 5 percent. The tax rate on income over $200,000 a year may be 50 percent. Although a progressive income tax may distort the income–leisure choices of some households and thus undermine efficiency, society may nevertheless consider it more equitable to tax lower incomes at lower rates.

16-3. Market Failure: Externalities

When a market does not result in an efficient allocation of resources, the market or the system itself is said to "fail." You encountered instances of market "failure" in earlier chapters on monopoly, monopolistic competition, and oligopoly. As you recall, none of these three market structures results in allocative efficiency because marginal value (price) exceeds marginal cost under all of them.

Markets can fail for reasons other than that their structures are noncompetitive or imperfectly competitive. Externalities—external or third-party costs and benefits—and public goods also result in market failures. When markets fail, society often intervenes, as it does in monopoly, to modify resource allocation.

A. External costs lead to overproduction.

As you recall from Chapter 10, *external costs* are costs borne by individuals other than those directly involved in the production or consumption of a good. Even in perfectly competitive markets, external costs result in market failure because underestimation of the true economic cost of a good to society (the private cost *plus* the external cost) leads to overproduction of the good. Since producers and consumers do not have to pay the external costs, those costs do not affect their producing and purchasing decisions and thus are not reflected in the market supply and demand curves for the good. As a result, the market price of the good, which is an index of its marginal economic value (MEV) to society, is never as great as the marginal economic cost (MEC) to society of the production and consumption of the good (MEV < MEC).

EXAMPLE 16-5: Figure 16-2 graphically depicts the reason for market failure when external costs are associated with the production of a good in a perfectly competitive market. As you recall from Chapter 12, the market supply curve in a perfectly competitive market is simply an aggregation of the supply curves—which are the marginal cost curves—of the individual sellers in the market. Since the marginal cost curves of the individual sellers reflect only those costs that the sellers actually pay—namely, their *private* costs—market supply curve SS in Figure 16-2 reflects only the marginal *private* costs of production in this hypothetical market. It does not reflect the full marginal economic costs—the marginal private costs *plus* the marginal external costs—of production. Curve CC does that.

If the mechanism of supply and demand is allowed to operate without interference in this market, quantity Q of the good will be produced, and it will sell at a market price of P per unit. As you can see in the figure, price P will cover the marginal private costs of producing quantity Q, but it will not cover the marginal external costs. Therefore, at quantity Q, the marginal economic value of the good to society, as measured by its price (P), will be less than the marginal economic cost to society of producing the good. This inequality indicates an overallocation of resources to the production of the good.

B. Public policy should restrict output when external costs result in market failure.

Since external costs result in the overproduction of goods, society can promote an efficient allocation of its resources by adopting policies that encourage the producers of such goods to reduce their output. In Figure 16-2, for example, society's aim would be to restrict production to the level represented by point B. At that level, resource allocation would be efficient because the marginal economic value of the good would be just equal to its marginal economic cost.

The inefficiency of resource allocation that results from external costs can be corrected in several ways. Two common ways are taxation and internalization.

1. *Taxation.* Excise taxes can be imposed on goods that generate external costs. As you may recall from Chapter 6, excise taxes that are collected from the producers of a good shift the market *supply* curve for the good up (to the left). If they are collected from the consumers of the good, they shift the market *demand* curve for the good down (to the left). In either case, the result is a reduction in market output. For example, if an excise tax equal to the external cost associated with the good in Figure 16-2 were imposed on the producers of the good, it would shift the market supply curve up, from SS to CC. As a result, as Figure 16-3 shows, output would decline from Q to Q*, its socially correct level (where MEC = MEV).

2. *Internalization.* The producers of goods that generate external costs can be forced to bear *all* of the costs associated with the goods, external as well as private. Forcing the producers of a good to internalize all external costs has the same effect on market

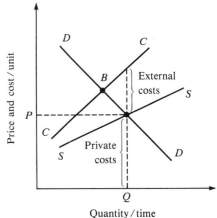

Figure 16-2
External costs lead to overproduction in a competitive market because they are not reflected in the market supply curve (*SS*). At quantity Q, marginal economic (private plus external) cost exceeds marginal economic value (price P).

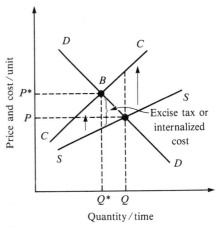

Figure 16-3
Imposing an excise tax equal to external costs on producers or forcing them to internalize all external costs reduces output (Q to Q*) and results in an efficient allocation of resources. At point B, marginal economic value equals marginal economic cost.

output as imposing an excise tax on them. It shifts the market supply (marginal cost) curve upward until it reflects the marginal external as well as the marginal private costs associated with the good (*SS* to *CC* in Figure 16-3). As a result, market output declines to its socially correct level (*Q* to *Q** in Figure 16-3).

Society forces producers to internalize external costs through regulation. For example, it establishes emissions standards and effluent levels that producers must meet. However, regulation is usually an imperfect approach to the problem of external costs. In the first place, regulations must be enacted by a political body, such as the U.S. Congress, and enforced by a government agency, such as the Environmental Protection Agency. As a result, both the enactment and the enforcement of regulations are highly dependent on the political climate. In the second place, the costs of complying with the regulations may have little relationship to the external costs they are designed to eliminate. In other words, the marginal cost of pollution control may far exceed the marginal benefit of pollution control to society. For these reasons, some economists advocate that society create markets for "pollution rights"—that is, for the right to dispose of specified quantities of pollutants into the environment.

EXAMPLE 16-6: Reserve Mining Company in Minnesota for many years dumped waste material or "tailings" from its taconite (low-grade iron ore) production into Lake Superior. The governments of Canada and the state of Wisconsin protested the pollution of the lake. So, too, eventually did the government of the state of Minnesota when unusually high concentrations of asbestos fibers were found in the city water supply in Duluth, Minnesota. The problem was remedied through legal action that forced Reserve Mining to internalize the costs of dumping by establishing an on-land site and hauling its tailings to the site.

C. External benefits lead to underproduction.

As the name suggests, **external benefits** are benefits that accrue to individuals other than those directly engaged in the consumption or production of a good. Like external costs, external benefits result in market failure because underestimation of the true economic value of a good to society (the private value *plus* the external or social value) leads to underproduction of the good. Since consumers and producers do not derive the external benefits generated by a good, those benefits do not affect their consuming and producing decisions and thus are not reflected in the market demand and supply curves for the good. As a result, the marginal economic value of the good to society is always greater than its marginal economic cost (MEV > MEC).

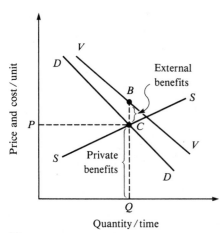

Figure 16-4
External benefits lead to underproduction in a competitive market because they are not reflected in the market demand curve (*DD*). At quantity *Q* and price *P*, marginal economic value (line segment *QB*) exceeds marginal economic cost (line segment *QC*).

EXAMPLE 16-7: Figure 16-4 graphically depicts the reason for market failure when external benefits are associated with the consumption of a good in a perfectly competitive market. Just as supply curve *SS* in Figure 16-2 and 16-3 reflects only the marginal *private* cost of a good that generates external costs in production, so conventional demand curve *DD* in Figure 16-4 reflects only the marginal *private* value of a good that generates external benefits in consumption. The full marginal economic value of the good to society, its marginal private value *plus* its marginal external or social value, is reflected in curve *VV*, which lies above conventional demand curve *DD*.

If society does not interfere with the mechanism of demand and supply, the market will yield an output of Q at a price of P. As you can see in the figure, price P is not an accurate reflection of the full economic value of quantity Q to society. In fact, as you would expect, it reflects only the marginal private value of the good to the people who actually consume it. Thus at quantity Q, the marginal economic value of the good to society (represented by line segment QB) is greater than its marginal economic cost (represented by line segment QC). This inequality indicates an underallocation of resources to the production of the good.

D. Public policy should increase output when external benefits result in market failure.

Just as public policy should restrict output when external costs result in overproduction of a good, so it should expand output when external benefits result in underproduction of a good. A common method for encouraging producers to increase their production of a socially beneficial good is to subsidize production, consumption, or both. If the subsidy is given to producers, it shifts the supply curve for the good down (to the right). If it is given to consumers, it shifts the demand curve for the good up (to the right). In either case, the result is an increase in market output. For example, if a subsidy equal to the value of the external benefits associated with the good in Figure 16-4 were given to the consumers of the good, it would shift the conventional demand curve up from DD to VV, as shown in Figure 16-5. As a result, producers would increase their output from Q to Q^*, its socially correct level (where MEC = MEV).

Subsidies are designed to achieve efficient resource allocation in particular markets. While they may accomplish that purpose, there is no guarantee that they will contribute to the achievement of efficiency in the system as a whole. Subsidies require revenues, revenues are usually raised by taxes, and taxes tend to undermine efficiency. Modifying markets to achieve economic efficiency is a complex process—so complex, in fact, that some economists argue that society should not attempt to alter market allocations even when those allocations are not efficient.

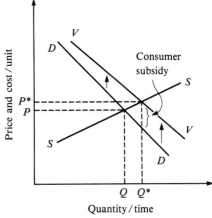

Figure 16-5
Subsidizing the consumption (or production) of a good that generates external benefits increases output (Q to Q^*). At output Q^* and price P^*, resource allocation is efficient (MEV = MEC).

EXAMPLE 16-8: Elementary education is an example of a good that generates external benefits. It provides fundamental knowledge and basic skills, but it also socializes children, inculcating cultural values and adapting the young to the customs, traditions, manners, and mores of society. Since the private benefits, the basic knowledge and skills that each child acquires, are only part of the total benefits that society derives from elementary education, we cannot rely on competitive markets to produce and consume it in socially optimal quantities. Accordingly, we subsidize production through tax-supported public schools and through grants to private schools. We also subsidize consumption by providing tax incentives to parents who send their children to private schools.

E. Externalities are associated with collectively owned resources.

Many external costs arise from the collective ownership of resources. Resources that belong to everybody belong to nobody in particular. Therefore nobody in particular has any selfish interest in protecting or conserving them. On the contrary, it is in every individual's selfish interest to *deplete* collectively owned resources, such as clean air and water, before anyone else has a chance to do so.

16-4. Market Failure: Public Goods

Public goods are goods that are nonexclusive and nondepletive in consumption. They may be simultaneously consumed by more than one individual, and their use by one individual does not reduce the quantity available for consumption by others.

EXAMPLE 16-9: One of the best examples of a public good is a radio or television broadcast. An entire city or country can simultaneously tune in to a broadcast for a special news event; therefore it is nonexclusive. One person's tuning in to the broadcast does not reduce the amount of news available to other consumers; therefore it is nondepletive. Other examples of public goods are national defense, knowledge, the space program, and, to some extent, parks and highways.

A. Competitive markets underproduce public goods.

Markets fail to allocate sufficient resources to the production of public goods because people systematically understate their demand for such goods. When they are required to pay in proportion to their stated demand for a public good, people have no incentive to reveal their true demand for it because the good, by definition, is nonexclusive. Therefore, even if they don't pay anything at all for it, they will still be able to consume the good in the same quantity as the people who do pay for it.

As Figure 16-6 shows, the discrepancy between the revealed demand and the true demand for a public good is depicted graphically by two separate demand curves. Curve *DD* represents the true demand for a public good; curve *RR*, which lies below it, represents the revealed demand. If the mechanism of supply and demand is allowed to operate without interference in the market, quantity *Q* of the public good will be produced. At quantity *Q* the marginal economic value (MEV) of the good to society is greater than its marginal economic cost (MEC). This inequality indicates that the good is being underproduced.

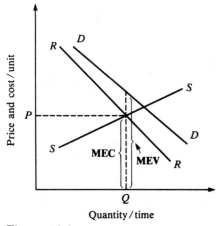

Figure 16-6
Competitive markets underproduce public goods because revealed demand (*RR*) is an understatement of true demand (*DD*). At quantity *Q* and price *P*, marginal economic value (MEV) is greater than marginal economic cost (MEC).

EXAMPLE 16-10: Suppose that we had a system of supporting national defense by voluntary enlistment in military service. Under this system, people would be asked to reveal their demand for national defense by committing from 6 months to 30 years to military duty. Suppose, further, that the pay rate for military duty were kept below the opportunity cost of the services of most volunteers. Under these conditions, how many people do you think would reveal their true demand for national defense by volunteering? Do you think the revealed demand (the number of volunteers and the length of their service) would reflect the true demand for national defense? Not likely. In the absence of a national emergency (and perhaps even in the presence of one), people would systematically understate their demand for national defense by pursuing more lucrative occupations. Hence national defense, a public good, would be underproduced.

B. The production of public goods is often politically determined.

Because of the potential for market failure, the output of such public goods as national defense and national public radio is often determined by the political system rather than the market system. However, there is no reason to expect that the political system will efficiently allocate resources to the production of public goods.

RAISE YOUR GRADES

Can you explain...?

☑ how markets for goods and resources are interrelated in a market economy
☑ why economists employ general equilibrium analysis
☑ how general equilibrium analysis differs from partial equilibrium analysis
☑ what the rationale is behind the concept of Pareto efficiency
☑ why productional efficiency is necessary for Pareto efficiency
☑ why allocative efficiency is necessary for Pareto efficiency
☑ why external costs result in market failure
☑ why external benefits result in market failure
☑ why public goods result in market failure
☑ how a public good differs from a normal good

SUMMARY

1. The U.S. economy is an intricate system of interrelated markets. Interrelation makes the market system flexible but complex.
2. *Partial equilibrium analysis* is the study of movements from one equilibrium position to another in particular markets or decision-making units without regard to the effects of those movements on the system as a whole.
3. Economists employ general equilibrium analysis and input–output analysis to study entire systems.
4. *General equilibrium* is a condition in which all of the individual markets and decision-making units within a system simultaneously achieve a state of balance, and there is no internal tendency to change.
5. Input–output analysis centers around a matrix (an input–output table) that lists the sources and destinations or uses of basic materials in an economy. Economists use input–output analysis to develop feasible output goals for the future and to plan input allocations that are consistent with those goals.
6. *Pareto efficiency* is an allocation of resources that cannot be altered to increase the welfare of one or more individuals without reducing the welfare of at least one other person.
7. A system of perfectly competitive markets achieves Pareto efficiency when it is in a state of general equilibrium. In that state it necessarily exhibits consumptive efficiency, productional efficiency, and allocative efficiency.
8. An allocation of resources may be efficient and yet be judged inequitable by society.
9. Markets are said to "fail" when they do not allocate resources efficiently. Four causes of market failure are **(1)** noncompetitive or imperfectly competitive market structures, **(2)** external costs, **(3)** external benefits, and **(4)** public goods.
10. Competitive markets overproduce goods that generate external costs because producers consider only their private costs when they decide how much to produce. As a result, the marginal economic cost (MEC) of such goods is greater than their marginal economic value (MEV) to society (MEC > MEV).

11. Society may seek to reduce the production and consumption of goods that generate external costs by imposing an excise tax on producers or consumers or by forcing producers to internalize the costs.
12. Competitive markets underproduce goods that generate external benefits because consumers consider only their private benefits when they decide how much to consume. As a result, the marginal economic cost (MEC) of such goods is less than their marginal economic value (MEV) to society (MEC < MEV).
13. Society may seek to increase the production and consumption of goods that generate external benefits by subsidizing production, consumption, or both.
14. External costs often arise from the collective ownership of resources. Collective ownership removes private incentives to conserve or manage resources.
15. *Public goods* are goods that are nonexclusive and nondepletive in consumption.
16. Competitive markets underproduce public goods because the revealed demand for such goods is less than the true demand.
17. Society allocates resources to the production of many public goods through the political system. However, there is no reason to expect political allocations to be Pareto efficient.

RAPID REVIEW

1. The U.S. economy is a complex system of interrelated _____ . [See Section 16-1.]
2. Interrelation makes the market system flexible but _____ . [See Section 16-1.]
3. Economists use _____ equilibrium analysis to study changes in particular markets and decision-making units. [See Section 16-1.]
4. _____ *equilibrium* is a condition in which all of the individual markets and decision-making units within a system simultaneously achieve a state of balance. [See Section 16-1.]
5. If they wanted to analyze the effects of a policy change on an entire economic system, economists would employ _____ _____ analysis. [See Section 16-1.]
6. If they wanted to develop realistic output goals for the future and plan input allocations consistent with those goals, economists would employ (a) partial equilibrium analysis, (b) psychoanalysis, (c) input–output analysis, (d) general equilibrium analysis. [See Section 16-1.]
7. _____ _____ is an allocation of resources that cannot be altered to increase the welfare of one or more individuals without reducing the welfare of at least one other person. [See Section 16-2.]
8. A system of perfectly competitive markets achieves Pareto efficiency when it is in a state of _____ _____ . [See Section 16-2.]
9. Pareto efficiency necessarily implies _____ efficiency, _____ efficiency, and _____ efficiency. [See Section 16-2.]
10. Any allocation of resources that is efficient is also equitable. True or false? [See Section 16-2.]
11. Market _____ occurs when a market does not allocate resources efficiently. [See Section 16-3.]
12. When the production of a good generates external costs, the marginal economic value of the good is greater than its marginal economic cost. True or false? [See Section 16-3.]

13. Forcing a producer to internalize external costs results in (a) a higher price and a lower output, (b) a higher price and a higher output, (c) a lower price and a higher output, (d) a lower price and a lower output. [See Section 16-3.]

14. Competitive markets underproduce goods that generate external benefits. True or false? [See Section 16-3.]

15. Taxing goods that provide external benefits will improve the allocation of resources. True or false? [See Section 16-3.]

16. Subsidizing the producers of a good that generates external benefits will _____ the quantity produced and _____ the market price. [See Section 16-3.]

17. *Public goods* are goods that are _____ and _____ in consumption. [See Section 16-4.]

18. The revealed demand for public goods is _____ than the true demand. [See Section 16-4.]

Answers
1. markets   2. complex   3. partial   4. *General*   5. general equilibrium   6. (c)
7. *Pareto efficiency*   8. general equilibrium   9. consumptive, productional, allocative
10. false   11. failure   12. false   13. (a)   14. true   15. false
16. increase, reduce   17. nonexclusive, nondepletive   18. less

SOLVED PROBLEMS

PROBLEM 16-1 Explain how the income received by the household sector in the circular flow model of an economy is related to the revenue received by the business sector and vice versa.

Answer: Household income becomes business receipts when it is spent to purchase the goods and services produced by the business sector. Business receipts become household income when they are used to pay for the factors of production—the human, natural, and capital resources owned by the households. Thus funds flow back and forth between the two sectors. [See Section 16-1.]

PROBLEM 16-2 Explain the difference between partial and general equilibrium.

Answer: *Partial equilibrium* refers to a state of balance in only one particular market or one particular decision-making unit, such as a firm or a household. Partial equilibrium analysis ignores the effects that changes in one market or unit have on other markets and units in a system as a whole. *General equilibrium* refers to a state of balance in an entire system. In order for a general equilibrium to exist, all of the particular decision-making units and all of the particular markets in a system must simultaneously achieve a state of balance. [See Section 16-1.]

PROBLEM 16-3 Consider the following hypothetical input–output table:

		Destinations			
Sources	Steel	Coal	Autos	Households (labor)	Exports
Steel	10	40	100	20	50
Coal	50	5	10	60	10
Autos	5	10	5	100	30
Labor (households)	40	60	70	0	0

List the types and quantities of inputs allotted to steel production. List the uses to which the output of the coal sector is allotted and the quantities allotted to each use.

Answer: To find the types and quantities of inputs allotted to steel production, read down the steel column: 10 units of steel, 50 units of coal, 5 units of autos, and 40 units of labor. To find the quantities of coal allotted to each use or destination, read across the coal row: 50 units to the steel sector, 5 units to the coal sector, 10 units to the auto sector, 60 units to the household sector, and 10 units to the export sector. [See Section 16-1.]

PROBLEM 16-4 From the hypothetical input–output table in Problem 16-3, calculate the amount of steel required to produce an automobile. How might this information be used to plan for the future?

Answer: To find the amount of steel required to produce an automobile, first find the total number of automobiles produced in the hypothetical economy by adding all of the numbers in the auto row: $5 + 10 + 5 + 100 + 30 = 150$. Then divide that number into 100, the number of units of steel allotted to auto production: $100 \div 150 = 0.67$. Thus, 0.67 units of steel are required to produce one automobile.

A knowledge of input–output ratios is very useful in economic planning. If planners know from past experience the number of units of an input required to produce one unit of a given output (called the *technical coefficient*), they can establish realistic output goals for the future, and they can assign inputs in the amounts required to achieve those goals. [See Section 16-1.]

PROBLEM 16-5 Olie and Lena are the only members of a small society. They are contemplating four plans to reallocate the goods in their society. These plans and the positive or negative changes that they will effect in Olie's and Lena's utility or satisfaction are shown in the following table.

	Change in Utility	
Plan	Olie	Lena
A	+5	+9
B	+20	0
C	+5	−3
D	−2	+40

According to the Pareto criterion, which plan or plans will result in a clear improvement in the well-being of Olie and Lena's society?

Answer: According to the Pareto criterion, only plans A and B will result in a clear improvement in the well-being of Olie and Lena's society. Plan A will increase the utility and thus improve the welfare of both Olie and Lena. Plan B will make Olie better off without making Lena any worse off. The same cannot be said for plans C and D, both of which will decrease the satisfaction of either Lena or Olie. Pareto's criterion does not allow us to evaluate plans C and D because they both necessitate comparison and judgment. [See Section 16-2.]

PROBLEM 16-6 Explain why an economic system cannot achieve Pareto efficiency without also achieving productional efficiency.

Answer: To answer this question, begin with the assumption that a system is not achieving productional efficiency. If it is not achieving productional efficiency, then some goods are being produced at a higher cost—that is, with more inputs or resources— than absolutely necessary. A more efficient organization of production will free up those extra resources for the production of additional goods. The additional goods can then be distributed in such a way that the satisfaction of some or all individuals in the system will be increased. If the satisfaction of some individuals can be increased without the satisfaction of other individuals being decreased, then the initial use of resources is not Pareto efficient. [See Section 16-2.]

PROBLEM 16-7 Explain why the noncompetitive structure of monopoly results in market failure. Draw a diagram to illustrate and support your answer.

Answer: As you recall from Chapter 13, marginal revenue is less than price for the firm in a monopoly because the firm faces a market demand curve with a negative slope. Thus, when the firm equates marginal revenue with marginal cost (MR = MC) to locate its profit-maximizing output level, marginal cost is also less than price. (Symbolically, when MR < P and MC = MR, then MC < P.)

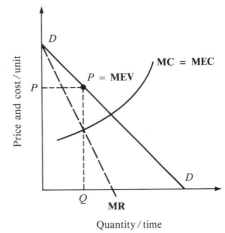

Figure 16-7

Figure 16-7 illustrates the relationship between marginal cost and price in a monopoly. As you can see, the firm locates its profit-maximizing output level at Q, where its MC curve intersects its MR curve from below. At output Q, demand in the market allows the firm to charge price P, which is higher than its marginal cost at that level.

If we assume that no external costs or benefits are associated with the production or the consumption of the monopolist's good, then the monopolist's MC curve reflects the marginal economic cost (MEC) of the good to society (MC = MEC, as shown in the figure). Moreover, the price that the monopolist is receiving for quantity Q of the good reflects the marginal economic value to society of the last unit sold (P = MEV, as also shown in the figure). At output Q, therefore, the marginal economic cost of the monopolist's good is less than its marginal economic value (MEC < MEV), which means that too few resources are being allocated to the production of the good. When a market results in underproduction, as pure monopoly invariably does because of its noncompetitive structure, allocative efficiency is not achieved and the market is said to fail. [See Chapter 13 and Section 16-3.]

PROBLEM 16-8 Explain why, when the production of a good generates external costs, the result is market failure, even in a perfectly competitive market. Should production of the good be increased or decreased?

Answer: Since external costs are not borne by the firm that produces a good, they are not reflected in the firm's marginal cost (MC) curve (unless, of course, the firm is forced to internalize the costs). The firm's MC curve reflects only the marginal *private* costs of producing the good. It does not reflect the full marginal *economic* cost (marginal private cost *plus* marginal external cost) to society. Thus, when the firm selects its profit-maximizing output level by equating marginal private cost with marginal revenue and price in a perfectly competitive market (remember, marginal revenue equals price under perfect competition), the result is overproduction.

The reason is simple. At the firm's profit-maximizing output level, the marginal economic value (MEV) of the good to society, as measured by its price, equals the marginal private cost of the good to the producer. However, it is *less* than the marginal economic cost (MEC) of the good to society (MEV < MEC). This inequality means that society places a lower value on the last unit of the good than it places on the sacrifice that it has to make in order to produce the unit. Therefore the market is failing because it is allocating too many resources to the production of the good. It should allocate fewer resources, and the production of the good should be decreased. [See Section 16-3.]

PROBLEM 16-9 The smoke discharged by the Canon City Electric Company has deleterious effects as far as 10 miles downwind of the plant. It causes health problems in people, sickness in livestock, and deterioration in buildings. In what two ways might society solve the problems caused by the company? What effects would those solutions have on the company's output and the price of its product?

Answer: The Canon City Electric Company is generating pollution, but society is bearing the costs associated with the pollution. To correct the situation, society can impose an excise tax on the company equal to the external costs of the pollution, or it can pass regulations that will force the company to internalize the costs of the pollution. Either policy will induce the company to increase its price and reduce its output. These adjustments should result in the equalization of private cost and economic cost and thus in the equalization of marginal economic cost and marginal economic value. [See Section 16-3.]

PROBLEM 16-10 The City Council of Canon City has decided that its residents can tolerate higher levels of certain pollutants in the air without suffering any ill effects. It has hired you, an economist, to advise it on how to allocate the available "pollutable" air or its equivalent, the right to pollute. As an economist, how will you decide who may pollute and who must internalize the costs of pollution?

Answer: Economists argue that the most efficient method of allocating pollution rights is to sell them to the highest bidders. Therefore you should advise the City Council in Canon City to hold an auction. Since the producers who find it most expensive to internalize the costs of pollution will bid the highest prices for the right to pollute, the auction will ensure that the rights are allocated to their most valuable uses.

Figure 16-8 suggests the reason. As you can see in the figure, the x-axis represents pollution rights, that is, tons of particulates per year. As the number of tons of particulates sent into the air per year increases (the upper x-axis), the quality of the air decreases (the lower x-axis). Demand curve *DD* represents the demand for pollution

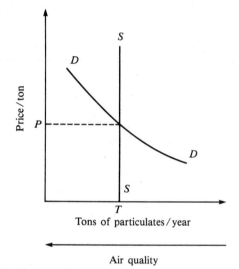

Figure 16-8

rights. It shows the prices that producers are willing to pay to dispose of various quantities of pollution (tons of particulates). Supply curve *SS* represents the available quantity of pollutable air in Canon City—that is, the number of tons of particulates that the City Council has arbitrarily decided to allow into the city's air each year. Notice that supply curve *SS* is vertical. A vertical (perfectly inelastic) supply curve means that Canon City will allow T tons of particulates into the air no matter what price it receives from producers for the rights to send those particulates into the air. Thus, if the City Council wants to ensure an efficient allocation of pollution rights—in other words, if it wants to ensure that the pollution rights go to the producers facing the most expensive pollution control problems—it will sell them under the competitive conditions of an auction at the highest price possible. [See Section 16-3.]

PROBLEM 16-11 Innoculations protect the people who receive them from contracting such diseases as small pox and cholera. However, they also protect other people because they reduce the chances that those other people will be exposed to and infected by the diseases. Do competitive markets allocate resources efficiently to the production of such goods as innoculations? Explain your answer.

Answer: Innoculations generate external or third-party benefits that accrue to individuals who neither produce nor consume them. When external benefits are associated with the consumption of a good such as innoculations, those benefits are not reflected in the demand curve for the good. The demand curve for the good reflects only the private benefits that accrue to the individuals who actually consume it. As a result, competitive markets fail to allocate sufficient resources to the production of the good, the good is underproduced, and the price of the good reflects its marginal economic cost (MEC) but not its full marginal economic value (MEV) to society (MEC < MEV). An inequality between marginal economic cost and marginal economic value is a sign of market failure and the misallocation of resources. [See Section 16-3.]

PROBLEM 16-12 Propose a policy to improve the allocation of a good such as innoculations. Explain the effect that your policy will have on the price of the good and the quantity of the good produced and consumed. Draw a diagram to illustrate your answer.

Answer: Since competitive markets underproduce innoculations and other goods that generate external benefits, you want to propose a policy that will encourage producers to increase their output and consumers to increase their consumption. A subsidy granted to producers, consumers, or both will do just that.

Figure 16-9 illustrates the effect that a subsidy granted to consumers will have on output and price in the market for innoculations. Curve *DD* represents private demand or the marginal private value of innoculations to the persons who actually receive them. Curve *VV* represents social demand or the marginal economic (private plus external) value of innoculations to society. If society does not interfere with the mechanism of supply and demand in the market, quantity *Q* innoculations will be produced and consumed at a price of *P* per dose. If society subsidizes consumers, demand curve *DD* will shift up by the amount of the subsidy and will then coincide with curve *VV*. As a result, the quantity of innoculations produced and consumed will increase from *Q* to *Q'*. The price of an innoculation will also increase, from *P* to *P'*, but the subsidy will actually decrease the out-of-pocket price to the consumer from *P* to *P''*.

A subsidy to the producers of innoculations would also increase output from *Q* to *Q'*. However, since the subsidy would be reflected in a downward shift in the supply curve, it would reduce the market price to *P''*. [See Section 16-3.]

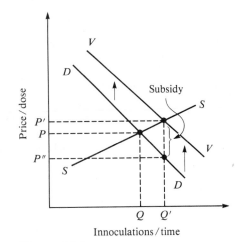

Figure 16-9

PROBLEM 16-13 Explain why competitive markets fail to allocate sufficient resources to the production of public goods.

Answer: Competitive markets fail to allocate sufficient resources to the production of public goods because the revealed demand for public goods is less than the true demand. When people are required to pay for public goods in proportion to their stated demand, they have an incentive to understate their true demand. The reason is simple. Since public goods, by definition, are nonexclusive and nondepletive in consumption, each person hopes to be able to use additional units of the goods paid for by others. As a result, public goods are underproduced. [See Section 16-4.]

PERFECT COMPETITION AND FACTOR MARKETS

17-1. Factor Markets

So far in this outline we have considered three main parts of the circular flow model of a market economy: the household sector, the producer sector, and the goods markets in which the two come together to determine the prices of finished products (producer outputs) and the quantities in which they are exchanged. In this chapter we turn to the fourth part of the circular flow model, the factor markets in which households and producers also come together, but for a different reason: to determine the prices of resources (producer inputs) and the quantities in which they are exchanged. Productive resources, as you may recall from Chapter 1, include natural, capital, and human resources, and their sale by households to producers is the source of household income. The same mechanisms that determine how goods and business receipts are allocated in product markets determine how resources and income are allocated in factor markets. In this chapter, we shall consider the implications of perfectly competitive conditions on factor markets. In the next chapter, we shall consider the implications of imperfectly competitive conditions on factor markets.

A. Labor is the principal factor supplied by households.

National income figures in the United States indicate that employee labor services are the principal factor that households supply to producers. Households also supply land, capital, and entrepreneurial services, but, statistically speaking, the sale of employee labor services accounts for more than two-thirds of household income in the United States. The rest is accounted for by rent, interest, profits, and proprietors' income. Because of this disproportion, the following discussion focuses primarily on labor markets, but most of the principles that you will learn also apply to the markets for other factors as well.

B. Roles and motivations in factor markets differ from those in product markets.

The roles and motivations of the suppliers and demanders of factors differ from the roles and motivations of the suppliers and demanders of goods and services.

1. Roles in factor markets are the reverse of those in goods markets.
   In goods or product markets, firms are suppliers and households

are demanders. In factor or resource markets, households are suppliers and firms are demanders.

2. In goods or product markets, firms produce and sell goods and services to gain economic profits. In factor markets, households sell labor (and other resource) services to earn income so that they can purchase goods and services that satisfy their material needs and wants.

3. The demand for factors is a *derived demand*; the demand for goods and services is not. Households demand goods and services because they obtain intrinsic satisfaction or utility from them. Firms demand factors not because they obtain any intrinsic satisfaction or utility from them, but because they can gain economic profits by using them to produce goods and services that *do* provide intrinsic satisfaction or utility. Thus the demand for factors is derived from the demand for goods and services.

C. Household income depends on factor endowments and factor prices.

The earned income of a particular household depends on two variables: (1) the factor endowments of the household—that is, the number and the quality of the productive factors or resources that it owns and chooses to sell, including its natural and capital, as well as its human, resources; and (2) the prices that those factors or resources command in the marketplace. The household's earned income will be high if it owns and sells a large quantity of factors or if its factors sell for high prices. The household's earned income will be low if it owns and sells few resources or if its resources sell for low prices.

17-2. Individual Demand for a Variable Factor

According to the marginal productivity theory, a firm's demand for a variable factor of production, such as labor, is determined by that factor's contribution to the firm's total revenue. A factor's contribution to a firm's total revenue is known as its *marginal revenue product* (or, in some texts, as its *value of marginal product*).

Marginal revenue product (MRP) is the change in the value of production for a one-unit change in a variable factor.

A factor's marginal revenue product is the mathematical product of two variables: (1) marginal physical product (MPP) and (2) marginal revenue (MR):

$$MRP = MPP \times MR$$

As you recall from Chapter 9, *marginal physical product* is the change in total product (or total output) that results from a one-unit change in a variable input, such as labor. As you recall from Chapter 11, *marginal revenue* is the change in total revenue that results from a one-unit change in quantity sold. Thus a factor's *marginal revenue product* is simply the revenue that a firm derives from selling the marginal physical product or the marginal output attributable to each successive unit of the factor.

A. The marginal physical product of a variable factor diminishes beyond some point in the short run.

When you were introduced to the concept of marginal physical product in Chapter 9, you were also introduced to the law of diminishing returns or the law of diminishing marginal physical product. As you may remember, that law dictates that, if other things remain constant, the marginal physical product of a variable factor

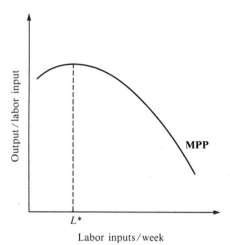

Figure 17-1
The marginal physical product (MPP)
of labor or any other variable input
declines as a result of the law of
diminishing returns.

must decline beyond some point as more and more units of the factor
are added to a production process in which other inputs are fixed.
Because of this law, a firm's MPP curve for labor—or for any other
variable factor of production—has a negative slope beyond the point
at which diminishing returns set in.

EXAMPLE 17-1: Figure 17-1 shows a hypothetical firm's MPP curve for
labor. The point at which diminishing returns set in is L^* units of labor
inputs a week. Beyond that point, the curve has a negative slope, which
means that, after the L^* unit of labor is added to the production process,
each *additional* unit of labor adds less to total output than the unit before
it. As Figure 17-1 suggests, beyond the point of diminishing returns, *increasing* the use of a factor *reduces* its marginal physical product, and
decreasing the use of a factor *increases* its marginal physical product.

The law of diminishing returns has one other important implication
that is relevant to this discussion: Since marginal physical product
(MPP) for a variable input declines beyond some point in the short run,
then its MRP curve for the same input must also decline beyond some
point (have a negative slope) in the short run.

**B. In a competitive product market, marginal revenue equals product
price.**

The second component of marginal revenue product is the marginal
revenue that a firm derives from selling additional units of the
product. If the firm sells its product in a perfectly competitive market,
it can sell any quantity it chooses to sell at the market price. Therefore,
as you already know, the product demand curve that the firm faces is
horizontal at the market price for its product, and the firm's marginal
revenue equals that price (MR $= P$). The formula for determining the
marginal revenue product of a variable factor used by a firm that sells
its product in a perfectly competitive market can be restated as
follows:

$$MRP = MPP \times P$$

EXAMPLE 17-2: Since the Widget Works sells widgets in a perfectly
competitive market for $4 apiece, the marginal revenue that it derives
from selling each additional widget is $4. Thus its MRP schedule for labor
can be found by multiplying its MPP schedule for labor by $4, as shown in
the following table:

Units of labor	Total output	MPP	×	MR	=	MRP
0	0					
		8	×	$4	=	$32
1	8					
		7	×	4	=	28
2	15					
		6	×	4	=	24
3	21					
		5	×	4	=	20
4	26					
		4	×	4	=	16
5	30					

Notice that the MPP column in the table is found by subtracting total
output at one level from total output at the next. For example, the total

output of the first two units of labor is 15 widgets, and the total output of the first three units of labor is 21 widgets; therefore the marginal output or marginal physical product (MPP) of the third unit of labor is six widgets $(21 - 15 = 6)$. By hiring the third unit of labor, the Widget Works increases its total output by six widgets.

The *value* of those six widgets is shown in the fifth column. Since each widget sells for a price of $4, the Widget Works will gain $24 in revenue by selling the six widgets that the third unit of labor produces.

C. In a competitive factor market, marginal factor cost equals factor price.

A firm in a perfectly competitive product market perceives the demand curve that it faces as horizontal at the market price. Similarly, a firm in a perfectly competitive factor market perceives the supply curve that it faces as horizontal at the market price. A horizontal factor supply curve has two important implications. First, it implies that a firm purchasing factor services, such as labor, can purchase any quantity that it chooses to purchase without affecting the market price of those services. Second, it implies that each additional unit of the factor services that the firm purchases adds the same amount, its price, to the firm's total factor costs. That amount is known as *marginal factor cost.* **Marginal factor cost (MFC)** is the change in total factor cost for a one-unit change in the use of a factor.

$$\text{MFC} = \frac{\text{change in total factor cost}}{\text{change in quantity of factor}}$$

Thus in a perfectly competitive factor market, marginal factor cost equals factor price, which, in a labor market, is the wage rate (W) of the factor:

$$\text{MFC} = P \text{ (or } W)$$

EXAMPLE 17-3: The Widget Works hires labor services in a perfectly competitive labor market for $20 a unit. Thus the manager of the Widget Works perceives the labor supply curve that she faces as horizontal at $20. Since the manager can hire any quantity of labor services that she wants to hire without driving that price up, she knows that, if she expands the use of labor inputs at her plant, each additional unit will add the same amount, $20, to her total labor costs. In other words, the marginal factor cost of each unit will be the same as its price or wage rate: MFC = factor price (wage rate) = $20.

D. To maximize its profits, a firm should follow the MRP = MFC rule for optimal factor use.

As you recall from Chapter 11, a firm selects its profit-maximizing output level by applying the MR = MC rule: it continues to produce until the last unit of output adds the same amount to total costs as it adds to total revenue. A firm selects its profit-maximizing input level in much the same way. It continues to add units of a variable factor to its production process until the last unit adds as much to total costs as it adds to total revenue. In other words, a firm continues to add units of a variable factor to its production process until the marginal revenue product (MRP) of the factor declines to equal its marginal factor cost (MFC). Symbolically:

$$MRP = MFC$$

If the marginal revenue product of a factor exceeds its marginal factor cost, a firm can increase its profits by purchasing additional units of the factor because each additional unit will add more to total revenue than it will add to total costs. Conversely, if the marginal factor cost of a factor exceeds its marginal revenue product, a firm can increase its profits by purchasing fewer units of the factor because each unit beyond the MRP = MFC point is adding more to total costs than to total revenue.

Since marginal factor cost equals factor price in a perfectly competitive factor market, the rule for optimal input use can be restated as follows for perfect competition:

$$MRP = P \text{ (or } W)$$

Notice that this rule is simply a particular form of the general MRP = MFC rule. It applies only to perfectly competitive factor markets. As you will learn in the next chapter, the general MRP = MFC rule for optimal factor use applies to *all* factor markets, imperfectly competitive as well as perfectly competitive.

EXAMPLE 17-4: According to Example 17-3, the market wage rate or marginal factor cost of each unit of labor services that the Widget Works hires is $20. If you look again at the MRP schedule for labor given in Example 17-2, you can see that, if the manager of the Widget Works wants to maximize her profits, she should apply the MRP = MFC rule and hire four units of labor: MRP = $20 = W = MFC at four units of labor.

As you can see in the table in Example 17-2, although the first, second, and third units of labor will cost the Widget Works only $20 each, they will produce, respectively, $32, $28, and $24 worth of widgets. Clearly the manager should hire all three of these units. She should also hire the fourth unit because the cost of hiring the fourth unit ($20) will be no greater than the value of the widgets that the fourth unit produces ($20). But after she has hired the fourth unit, the manager should stop hiring because the fifth unit will cost $20 but will produce only $16 worth of additional widgets.

E. A firm's MRP curve (schedule) for a factor is its demand curve (schedule) for the factor.

As Example 17-4 suggests, a firm's MRP schedule or curve for a single variable factor is its demand schedule or curve for the factor. It shows the quantity of the factor that the firm will seek to purchase at each of various alternative prices, *ceteris paribus*.

EXAMPLE 17-5: Look again for a moment at the table in Example 17-2. The first and fifth columns, as you know, are the MRP schedule for labor at the Widget Works. They are also the firm's demand schedule for labor because they show how many units of labor the firm will seek to purchase at various prices (wage rates). If the price of labor (the wage rate) is $32, quantity demanded at the Widget Works will be one unit of labor. If it is

$28, quantity demanded will be two units; $24, three units; $20, four units; $16, five units.

17-3. Market Demand for a Variable Factor

A market demand curve for a variable factor, such as labor, is like a market demand curve for a good or service in that it shows the various quantities of the factor that all of the individual buyers in the market are willing and able to purchase at alternative prices, *ceteris paribus*. It also has the same properties: it has a negative slope, it applies to a particular time only, and it shifts when any of the *ceteris paribus* variables changes.

A. Four variables affect the price elasticity of demand for a factor.

The price elasticity of demand for a variable factor, such as labor, depends on the following:

1. the ease with which another factor, such as capital, can be used as a substitute (the easier it is to use a substitute, the higher the price elasticity of demand for the factor)
2. the price elasticity of demand for the product the factor is being used to produce (the higher the price elasticity of demand for the product, the higher the price elasticity of demand for the factor)
3. the length of time under consideration (the longer the time period, the higher the price elasticity of demand for the factor)
4. the proportion of production costs that the factor represents (the larger the proportion, the higher the price elasticity of demand for the factor)

B. Changes in *ceteris paribus* variables cause the demand curve for a factor to shift.

Just as a change in a *ceteris paribus* variable (a variable other than price or quantity) causes the demand curve for a product to shift, so a change in a *ceteris paribus* variable causes the demand curve for a factor to shift. The demand curve for a factor, such as labor, will shift right (demand for the factor will increase) when any of the following occurs:

1. the demand curve for the product that the factor is being used to produce shifts right (demand for the product increases)
2. the marginal physical product of the factor increases
3. the prices of substitute factors increase

17-4. Factor Supply: Labor

As you have already learned, households supply labor services in order to earn income. They earn income so that they can purchase goods and services that provide them with satisfaction or utility. Goods and services, however, are not the only sources of material satisfaction for households. Households also derive satisfaction from nonwork or leisure. Therefore they must choose between work and leisure—which is to say, between income and leisure—in order to maximize their satisfaction. Less work means more leisure but less income to enjoy it, *ceteris paribus*; more work means more income but less leisure to enjoy it, *ceteris paribus*.

A. The labor supply curves of most households have positive slopes.

Most households are willing to increase the quantity of labor services that they supply as the wage rate rises. As the wage rate rises, the opportunity cost of leisure rises with it, making work—or rather the income to be earned by working—relatively more attractive than leisure. This induces households to substitute work (income) for leisure and thus gives the labor supply curves of most households a positive slope.

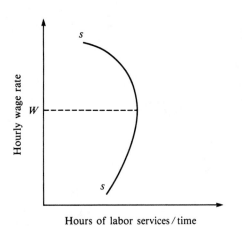

Figure 17-2
The labor supply curve of a household may be backward bending if the household works fewer hours as the wage rate increases beyond a certain level (*W*).

B. The labor supply curves of some households may be backward bending.

Higher wages have two opposing effects, a substitution effect and an income effect. As you have just seen, higher wages increase the opportunity cost of leisure and thus induce households to substitute work for leisure. This is the substitution effect. Higher wages also increase the income derived from a given number of hours worked, and this increase in income induces households to consume more leisure and hence work fewer hours. This is the income effect.

For most households, the substitution effect of a wage increase dominates the income effect and gives the labor supply curve of these households a positive slope throughout its length. For some households, however, the income effect may dominate the substitution effect beyond a certain wage level and give the labor supply curves of these households a negative slope beyond that wage level. The result, in such cases, is a backward-bending labor supply curve, as shown in Figure 17-2. As you can see, the curve has a positive slope until it reaches wage rate *W*; up to that point the substitution effect dominates. Beyond wage rate *W*, the income effect dominates and the household provides fewer hours of labor services as the wage rate increases.

C. A market supply curve for labor has a positive slope.

A market supply curve for labor has the same properties as a market supply curve for a good or service, including a positive slope. A market supply curve for labor has a positive slope even when the supply curves of some individual households in the market are backward bending for three main reasons:

1. A market supply curve for labor is a horizontal aggregation of the supply curves of individual households, most of which have positive slopes.
2. Higher wages attract labor services from other markets and thus increase the number of sellers in the market and the quantity of labor services available at higher rates.
3. Higher wages increase participation in the labor force, which also increases the number of sellers in the market and the quantity of labor services available at higher rates.

EXAMPLE 17-6: Some studies suggest that the labor supply curves of many individual female nurses are backward bending, that is, that many individual female nurses work fewer hours outside the home as the wage rate for their services increases. Nevertheless, the market supply curve for professional nurses has a positive slope. Less than 60 percent of female professional nurses participate in the labor force at any one time; hence higher wages can and do significantly increase labor force participation. The increased participation more than offsets the reductions in hours worked by individual nurses with backward-bending supply curves.

17-5. Wages, Employment, and Earnings

Although economists are not in universal agreement about how wages are determined, many accept the theory that market forces determine wages—the prices of labor services—in the same way that they determine the prices of goods and services. According to this theory, market forces also determine quantity exchanged—that is, employment levels—and thus total wage income or total wage earnings as well.

Wage earnings are the mathematical product of the wage rate and the number of hours worked:

$$\text{Wage earnings} = \text{wage rate} \times \text{hours worked}$$

As Figure 17-3 illustrates, the interaction of supply and demand in a competitive labor market establishes the equilibrium price or wage rate at W^*, where quantity supplied equals quantity demanded. At wage rate W^*, L^* hours of labor services are hired each month, so total wage earnings by workers in the market are $W^* \times L^*$, represented by the shaded area in the figure.

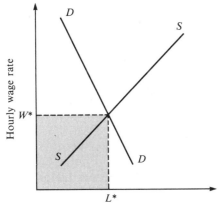

Figure 17-3
The interaction of supply and demand in a competitive labor market determines the wage rate (W^*), the number of hours worked (L^*), and total wage earnings ($W^* \times L^*$, the shaded area).

A. Wage earnings respond to changes in supply and demand.

Changes in demand and supply in labor markets produce the same predictable effects on prices and quantities (wage rates and employment levels) as they do in product markets. Such changes also necessarily affect total wage earnings, but when wage rates increase and employment levels decrease, or vice versa, the effect on total wage earnings depends on the price elasticity of demand for labor. If the demand for labor is elastic, total wage earnings decrease as the wage rate increases; if the demand for labor is inelastic, total wage earnings increase as the wage rate increases. (For a review of the topic of price elasticity of demand, see Chapter 7.)

EXAMPLE 17-7: Figure 17-4 illustrates the effect of an increase in demand on the wage rate, the number of hours worked (the employment level), and the total wage earnings of workers in a hypothetical labor market. As you would expect, when the demand curve in the market shifts right, from DD to $D'D'$, the wage rate increases from W to W', the number of hours worked increases from L to L', and total wage earnings increase by the difference between $W' \times L'$ and $W \times L$ (the shaded area in the figure).

Figure 17-5 on the following page illustrates the effect of an increase in supply on the same market. As you can see, when the supply curve shifts right, from SS to $S'S'$, the wage rate drops, from W to W', and so total wage

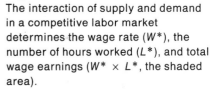
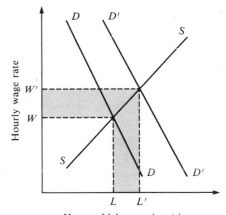

Figure 17-4
An increase in the demand for labor (DD to $D'D'$) will increase both the wage rate (W to W') and the number of hours worked (L to L'). Total wage earnings will increase by the amount shown in the shaded area.

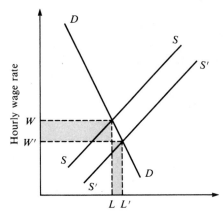

Figure 17-5

An increase in the supply of labor (SS to S'S') will decrease the wage rate (W to W') and increase the hours worked (L to L'), *ceteris paribus*. Total wage earnings will decrease if demand is inelastic, as it is between W and W' in this figure.

earnings *decrease* by the amount represented by the horizontal shaded area. At the same time, the number of hours worked (the employment level) rises from L to L', and so total wage earnings *increase* by the amount represented by the vertical shaded area. In this case the net effect of the decrease in the wage rate and the increase in the level of employment is negative: total wage earnings decrease. The decrease in total wage earnings indicates that the demand for labor is inelastic between wage rates W and W' in Figure 17-5.

B. Wage differentials reflect productivity differentials.

According to the marginal productivity theory, the wage rate paid to a worker in a perfectly competitive labor market is a reflection of the worker's marginal revenue product ($W = \text{MFC} = \text{MRP}$). Since a worker's marginal revenue product in a perfectly competitive product market is determined by the worker's marginal physical product ($\text{MRP} = \text{MPP} \times P$), it follows that a worker's wage rate is a reflection of the worker's productivity. (Worker productivity is commonly measured as output per man-hour or output per worker.) Higher levels of worker productivity are associated with higher wage rates and earnings for labor.

Worker productivity does not depend exclusively on natural aptitudes. It can be enhanced by any of the following means:

1. by increasing the ratio of capital and other inputs to labor inputs
2. by improving technology, *ceteris paribus*
3. by improving the health and the education or training of the labor force (economists refer to such improvements as investments in *human capital*)
4. by improving the organization of production

C. Wage differentials reflect differences in factor scarcity and in product demand.

Market-determined wage rates reflect not only worker productivity but also the relative scarcity of different types of workers. Other things being equal, the higher the relative scarcity, the higher the wage rate; the lower the relative scarcity, the lower the wage rate. For example, as you have already seen in Figure 17-5, an increase in the supply of labor services in a market, which is tantamount to a reduction in the relative scarcity of those services, results in a decrease in the market wage rate.

Market-determined wages also reflect differences in product demand. If you recall that a worker's wage rate is tied to the worker's marginal revenue product and that, in a perfectly competitive product market, a worker's marginal revenue product is tied to product price ($\text{MRP} = \text{MPP} \times P$), you can see why this is so. Other things being equal, the greater the demand for a product, the higher its price; the higher the price of a product, the higher the marginal revenue product of a worker producing the product ($\text{MRP} = \text{MPP} \times P$); the higher the marginal revenue product of a worker, the higher the wage rate paid to the worker.

D. In a competitive labor market, there is a trade-off between wages and hours worked.

The theory of competitive labor markets implies that, in a static market, wages cannot be increased above the equilibrium level unless employment (the number of hours worked) is reduced.

EXAMPLE 17-8: Figure 17-6 illustrates the effect of minimum wage legislation on employment in a perfectly competitive labor market. Before the legislation is passed, the equilibrium wage rate in the market is W, and the equilibrium employment level (the number of hours worked) is L. When the wage rate is increased by law to W', the employment level falls from L to L'. At the higher rate, workers are willing to supply L'' hours of labor services a month, but employers are willing to purchase only L' hours. Thus, although the legislation increases the wage rate, it reduces employment and creates an excess supply of labor in the market.

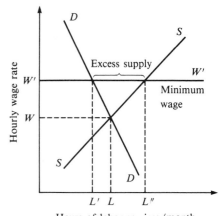

Figure 17-6
In a competitive labor market, raising the wage rate above equilibrium (W to W') will reduce employment (L to L') and result in excess supply.

RAISE YOUR GRADES

Can you explain...?

☑ why the income of a household is only partially determined by resource prices

☑ why the marginal revenue product of a variable factor declines in the short run as additional units of the factor are used in a production process

☑ how the marginal revenue product of a variable factor is calculated

☑ why a firm in a perfectly competitive factor market perceives the supply curve that it faces as horizontal at the market price

☑ why profit-maximizing firms hire a variable factor until its marginal revenue product declines to equal its marginal factor cost (MRP = MFC)

☑ why a firm's MRP curve for a single variable factor is its demand curve for the factor

☑ what variables cause a market demand curve for labor to shift

☑ why a household's supply curve for labor could be backward bending

☑ why a market supply curve for labor has a positive slope

☑ why wage rates might differ among workers in the same industry

---

SUMMARY

1. In the U.S. economy, the same market mechanisms that allocate goods and services in product markets allocate resources or inputs in factor markets.
2. In factor markets, households are suppliers and producers are demanders.
3. Labor is the principal factor supplied by households to producers in the United States; the sale of employee labor services accounts for more than two-thirds of national income.
4. Households sell labor and other factor services to earn income. They earn income so that they can purchase goods and services that provide satisfaction or utility.

5. The demand for factors is derived from the demand for goods and services. Goods and services provide intrinsic satisfaction; factors do not.

6. The income of a household depends on (1) its factor endowments (the quantity and quality of the resources it owns) and (2) factor prices.

7. According to the marginal productivity theory, a firm's demand for a factor is determined by the factor's contribution to the firm's total revenue—that is, by the factor's marginal revenue product.

8. *Marginal revenue product* (*MRP*) is the change in the value of production for a one-unit change in a variable factor.

9. Marginal revenue product is the mathematical product of marginal physical product and marginal revenue: MRP = MPP × MR.

10. Because of the law of diminishing returns, the marginal physical product of a variable factor declines beyond some point in the short run.

11. In a perfectly competitive product market, marginal revenue equals product price (MR = P); therefore marginal revenue product equals marginal physical product times product price: MRP = MPP × P.

12. *Marginal factor cost* (*MFC*) is the change in total factor cost for a one-unit change in the use of a factor.

13. A profit-maximizing firm should hire a variable input until its marginal revenue product declines to equal its marginal factor cost. This is the MRP = MFC rule for optimal input use.

14. In a perfectly competitive factor market, marginal factor cost equals factor price (MFC = factor price); therefore the rule for optimal input use in a perfectly competitive factor market can be restated as follows: MRP = factor price.

15. A firm's MRP curve for a single variable factor is its demand curve for the factor.

16. The price elasticity of demand for a factor increases with all of the following: (1) the ease with which another factor can be used as a substitute; (2) the price elasticity of demand for the product that the factor is being used to produce; (3) the length of time; (4) the proportion of production costs that the factor represents.

17. The demand for a factor increases with all of the following: (1) the demand for the product the factor is being used to produce; (2) the productivity of the factor; (3) the prices of substitute factors.

18. The labor supply curves of most households have positive slopes because increases in the wage rate raise the opportunity cost of leisure and induce most households to substitute work for leisure.

19. The labor supply curves of some households may be backward bending because increases in the wage rate raise income, *ceteris paribus*, and induce some households to consume more leisure and work fewer hours.

20. A market supply curve for labor has a positive slope for three reasons: (1) it is an aggregation of the supply curves of all the individual households in the market, most of which have positive slopes; (2) higher wages increase labor force participation; (3) higher wages attract workers from other markets.

21. The market price of a factor is determined by the interaction of demand and supply in the market for the factor. Wages, employment, and hence total wage earnings respond to market changes.

22. *Wage earnings* are the mathematical product of the wage rate and the number of hours worked: wage earnings = wage rate × hours worked.

23. Differences in wage rates reflect differences in factor productivity, factor scarcity, and product demand.
24. Worker productivity is enhanced by (1) increasing the ratio of capital and other inputs to labor inputs, (2) improving technology, (3) improving the health, education, and training of the labor force (investing in *human capital*), and (4) improving the organization of production.
25. In a perfectly competitive labor market, there is a trade-off between the wage rate and the employment level (number of hours worked).

RAPID REVIEW

1. The sale of employee _____ services accounts for more than two-thirds of national income in the United States. [See Section 17-1.]
2. In factor markets, _____ are suppliers and _____ are demanders. [See Section 17-1.]
3. The demand for factors is a _____ demand because factors provide no intrinsic satisfaction. [See Section 17-1.]
4. The income of a particular household depends on the factor _____ of the household and on factor _____ . [See Section 17-1.]
5. According to the marginal productivity theory, a firm's demand for a variable factor is determined by the factor's contribution to the firm's total (a) revenue, (b) output, (c) costs, (d) product. [See Section 17-2.]
6. _____ _____ _____ is the change in the value of production for a one-unit change in a variable input. [See Section 17-2.]
7. Marginal revenue product is the mathematical product of marginal _____ product and marginal _____ . [See Section 17-2.]
8. Marginal physical product (and therefore marginal revenue product) declines beyond some point in the short run because of the law of _____ _____ . [See Section 17-2.]
9. In a competitive product market, marginal revenue equals product _____ . [See Section 17-2.]
10. _____ _____ _____ is the change in total factor cost for a one-unit change in the use of a factor. [See Section 17-2.]
11. In a competitive factor market, marginal factor cost equals _____ _____ . [See Section 17-2.]
12. The rule for optimal factor use in a perfectly competitive factor market is (a) MRP = product price, (b) MR = MC, (c) MRP = factor price, (d) MPP = MFC. [See Section 17-2.]
13. A firm's demand curve for a single variable factor is its _____ curve. [See Section 17-2.]
14. The price elasticity of demand for a factor is inversely related to the price elasticity of demand for the product that the factor is being used to produce. True or false? [See Section 17-3.]
15. Other things being equal, an increase in the price of a substitute factor will increase the demand for a factor. True or false? [See Section 17-3.]
16. If the productivity of a factor increases, (a) the demand curve for the factor will shift left, (b) the MRP curve for the factor will shift left, (c) the demand or MRP curve for the factor will shift right, (d) demand for the factor will not be affected. [See Section 17-3.]

17. An increase in the wage rate increases the _____ _____ of leisure and induces most households to substitute work for leisure; as a result, the labor supply curves of most households have _____ slopes. [See Section 17-4.]

18. Higher wages in a given market increase labor force participation in that market. True or false? [See Section 17-4.]

19. *Wage earnings* are the mathematical product of the _____ _____ and the number of hours worked. [See Section 17-5.]

20. An increase in the supply of labor will _____ the wage rate and _____ the number of hours worked, *ceteris paribus*. [See Section 17-5.]

21. If the wage rate increases and employment (number of hours worked) decreases, total earnings will (a) always increase, (b) always decrease, (c) increase only if the demand for labor is elastic, (d) increase only if the demand for labor is inelastic. [See Section 17-5.]

22. Spending on education and training in order to enhance worker productivity is referred to as an investment in _____ capital. [See Section 17-5.]

23. Differences in wage rates reflect differences in factor _____ and factor _____ . [See Section 17-5.]

Answers
1. labor   **2.** households, producers (firms)   **3.** derived   **4.** endowments, prices
5. (a)   **6.** *Marginal revenue product*   **7.** physical, revenue   **8.** diminishing returns
9. price   **10.** *Marginal factor cost*   **11.** factor price   **12.** (c)   **13.** MRP (marginal revenue product)   **14.** false   **15.** true   **16.** (c)   **17.** opportunity cost, positive
18. true   **19.** wage rate   **20.** decrease, increase   **21.** (d)   **22.** human
23. productivity, scarcity

SOLVED PROBLEMS

PROBLEM 17-1   Explain how the demand for factors differs from the demand for goods and services.

Answer: The demand for factors (or resources or inputs) differs from the demand for goods and services in two ways. First, whereas *households* demand goods and services, *firms* demand factors. Second, whereas goods and services *directly* satisfy material needs and wants, factors only *indirectly* satisfy material needs and wants by contributing to the production of goods and services that *do*. Hence the demand for factors by firms is a *derived demand*—a demand derived from the demand for goods and services by households. [See Section 17-1.]

PROBLEM 17-2   Explain why the following statement is only partially true: "Incomes are market determined in the United States."

Answer: The statement is only partially true because household income depends on two variables: factor prices and factor endowments. Factor prices are determined in markets in the United States, but factor endowments—that is, the quantity and the quality of the resources or factors of production that each household owns—are not. Households with no factors to sell earn no income (though they may receive income through transfer payments from the government). [See Section 17-1.]

PROBLEM 17-3   Explain what *marginal revenue product* is and how it is calculated.

Answer: Marginal revenue product is the change in the value of production that results from a one-unit change in a variable input. *Value of production* is another way of saying *total revenue.* Thus *marginal revenue product* is simply the change in total revenue that results from a one-unit change in a variable input.

As you might expect from its name, marginal revenue product is the mathematical product of two factors: (**1**) marginal product or marginal physical product (MPP), the change in total product or total output that results from a one-unit change in a variable input, and (**2**) marginal revenue (MR), the change in total revenue that results from a one-unit change in total output or total quantity sold. Thus the formula for determining marginal revenue product (MRP) is this:

$$MRP = MPP \times MR$$

The marginal revenue product of a factor tells you how much a firm will gain by selling the additional output that the factor produces. [See Section 17-2.]

PROBLEM 17-4   Universal Gizmos sells its product in a perfectly competitive market for a price of $5 a unit. The following schedule shows how total output (or total product) at Universal Gizmos increases as successive units of labor are added to the production process:

Labor inputs	Total output
0	0
1	10
2	25
3	45
4	65
5	83
6	99
7	113
8	125
9	135

Prepare a marginal revenue product (MRP) schedule for labor at Universal Gizmos.

Answer: Marginal revenue product is the product of marginal physical product and marginal revenue: MRP = MPP × MR. To prepare an MRP schedule for labor at Universal Gizmos, first find the marginal physical product of each successive unit of labor. To do that, simply subtract the total output associated with the first unit of labor from the total output associated with the second unit of labor, and so on. Then multiply the difference (the change in total output attributable to each additional unit of labor) by marginal revenue. Since Universal Gizmos is selling its product in a perfectly competitive market, where marginal revenue equals product price (MR = *P*), the marginal revenue that the firm derives from each additional gizmo that it sells is the same: $5.

The first and third columns in the following table constitute the marginal physical product (MPP) schedule for labor and the first and fourth columns constitute the marginal revenue product (MRP) schedule for labor at Universal Gizmos. As you can see, the figures in the fourth column are simply the figures in the third column multiplied by $5 [see Section 17-2]:

Labor inputs	Total output	MPP	MRP
0	0		
1	10	10	$ 50
2	25	15	75
3	45	20	100
4	65	20	100
5	83	18	90
6	99	16	80
7	113	14	70
8	125	12	60
9	135	10	50

PROBLEM 17-5 Explain why the marginal revenue product of labor in the last problem begins to decline after the fourth unit of labor is added to the production process at Universal Gizmos.

Answer: The marginal revenue product of labor begins to decline after the fourth unit of labor is added to the production process because the marginal physical product of labor begins to decline at that point. The marginal physical product of labor begins to decline at that point because of the law of diminishing marginal returns. As you recall from Chapter 9, that law states that, if other inputs into a production process are fixed, beyond some point the addition to total output of each successive unit of a variable input (such as labor) begins to decline. The declining marginal physical product of labor in the last problem implies the presence of fixed inputs in the production of gizmos at Universal Gizmos. [See Section 17-2.]

PROBLEM 17-6 Assume that Universal Gizmos in Problem 17-4 is one of a very large number of firms purchasing labor services in a perfectly competitive market. The market price or wage rate for labor services in the market is $90 a unit. Graph the labor supply (*ss*) curve facing Universal Gizmos and the firm's marginal factor cost (MFC) curve for labor.

Answer: Because Universal Gizmos is only one of a very large number of firms purchasing labor services in a perfectly competitive market, it is too small to have any perceptible effect either on the market price for labor (the going wage rate) or on the quantity of labor services exchanged in the market. For this reason, Universal Gizmos perceives the labor supply curve that it faces as horizontal at the market price, $90, as shown in Figure 17-7. A horizontal labor supply curve means that the firm can hire any quantity of labor services it wants to hire without driving the market price for labor services up. For the same reason, Universal Gizmos' MFC curve for labor is horizontal at the market price, too, as also

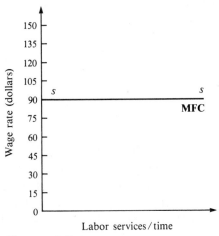

Figure 17-7

shown in Figure 17-7. A horizontal MFC curve means that each additional unit of labor services that Universal Gizmos hires adds the same amount, its market price or wage rate, to the firm's total factor costs. [See Section 17-2.]

PROBLEM 17-7 Given the MRP schedule for labor in Problem 17-4 and the market price (the going wage rate) for labor in Problem 17-6, determine the optimal quantity of labor services that Universal Gizmos should hire. Explain your answer.

Answer: In hiring labor services, Universal Gizmos should follow the rule for optimal input use: that is, it should continue to add units of labor services to its production process until the marginal revenue product of labor declines to equal the marginal factor cost of labor (MRP = MFC). As you know from Problem 17-6, the marginal factor cost of labor for Universal Gizmos is $90, the wage rate set by the perfectly competitive market in which the firm is purchasing labor services. As you can see from the MRP schedule for labor that you prepared for Problem 17-4, the marginal revenue product of labor at Universal Gizmos declines to equal $90 when the fifth unit of labor is added to the production process. Therefore Universal Gizmos should hire five units of labor (MFC = $90 = MRP at five units of labor). [See Section 17-2.]

PROBLEM 17-8 Demonstrate that the MRP schedule for labor in Problem 17-4 is Universal Gizmos' demand schedule for labor.

Answer: An MRP schedule for any factor of production indicates how valuable each additional unit of the factor is to a firm. In other words, it indicates how much the firm will gain by selling the marginal physical product or marginal output of each additional unit of the factor. If the firm follows the rule for optimal input use—that is, if it adds units of a variable factor until the marginal revenue product of the factor declines to equal its marginal factor cost—the firm's MRP curve for the factor will show the quantity of the factor demanded by the firm at each possible price. Therefore a firm's MRP schedule for a factor is the firm's demand schedule for the factor.

For example, according to the MRP schedule for labor in Problem 17-4, Universal Gizmos will gain $90 by selling the marginal output of the fifth unit of labor services. Therefore if the price (wage rate) of labor is $90, the quantity of labor services demanded by Universal Gizmos will be five units. Likewise, Universal Gizmos will gain $60 by selling the marginal output of the eighth unit of labor services. Therefore if the price (wage rate) of labor is $60, the quantity of labor services demanded by Universal Gizmos will be eight units. The same is true for all the other combinations of labor inputs and marginal revenue products in the schedule. Therefore the schedule is Universal Gizmos' demand schedule for labor. [See Section 17-2.]

PROBLEM 17-9 Explain how the price elasticity of demand for a factor of production is affected by the following: (1) the ease with which another factor can be used as a substitute for the factor and (2) the price elasticity of demand for the product that the factor is used to produce.

Answer: The easier it is to substitute one factor of production for a second factor of production, the higher will be the price elasticity of demand for the second factor. For example, if machines can be used as substitutes for labor in the production of widgets, the quantity of labor services demanded by widget producers will decline rapidly as the price of labor services (the wage rate of widget workers) rises relative to the price of machines. Instead of hiring the labor services of widget workers, widget producers will simply purchase widget-making machines.

Similarly, the higher the price elasticity of demand for a product, the higher the price elasticity of demand for any factor used in the production of the product. For example, an increase in the price of a factor used to produce widgets will increase the cost of producing and therefore the price of widgets. If the price elasticity of demand for widgets is high, an increase in the price of widgets will result in a relatively large decrease in the quantity of widgets demanded. A relatively large decrease in the quantity of widgets demanded will in turn result in a relatively large decrease in the quantity demanded of the factors needed to produce widgets. [See Section 17-3.]

PROBLEM 17-10 Explain why a market supply curve for labor has a positive slope even when the supply curves of some individual laborers in the market are backward bending.

Answer: A market supply curve for labor has a positive slope even when the supply curves of some individual laborers in the market are backward bending for two principal reasons. First, a market supply curve for labor is a horizontal aggregation of the supply curves of all the individual laborers in the market, most of which have positive slopes. Most of the supply curves of individual laborers in the market have positive slopes because wage increases raise the opportunity cost of leisure and induce most individual laborers in the market to substitute work for leisure. Second, wage increases attract new participants into a labor market, either individuals who have not been actively participating in the labor force or individuals who have been participating in other labor markets. These new participants in the market increase the quantity of labor services available at higher wage rates. [See Section 17-4.]

PROBLEM 17-11   Analyze the effect that an increase in income tax rates will have on wages and employment in a labor market with a typical supply curve. Draw a diagram to support your analysis. [*Hint:* An increase in income tax rates is equivalent to a reduction in effective wage rates.]

Answer: An increase in income tax rates will reduce all after-tax wage rates. A reduction in all after-tax wage rates will reduce the quantity of labor services supplied at every before-tax wage rate. A reduction in the quantity of labor services supplied at every before-tax wage rate will shift the market supply curve for labor to the left. As Figure 17-8 illustrates, a leftward shift in the market supply curve for labor, from SS to $S'S'$, will result in an increase in the before-tax market wage rate, from W to W', and a decrease in the quantity of labor services hired, from L to L'. [See Section 17-4.]

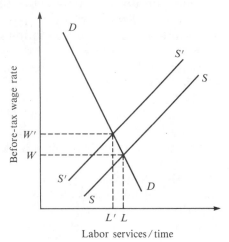

Figure 17-8

PROBLEM 17-12   If factory workers who produce widgets were receiving a higher hourly wage in Massachusetts than in Mississippi, how would an economist explain the wage differential?

Answer: An economist would explain the wage differential in terms of relative scarcity: that is, an economist would say that factory workers who produce widgets in Massachusetts were receiving a higher hourly wage because they were relatively more scarce than factory workers who produce widgets in Mississippi. The higher relative scarcity might be attributable to several factors. The demand for factory workers who produce widgets might be higher in Massachusetts because either the productivity of widget workers or the demand for widgets might be higher there than in Mississippi. Likewise, the supply of factory workers who produce widgets might be lower in Massachusetts because more alternative job opportunities might be available there than in Mississippi. [See Section 17-5.]

PROBLEM 17-13   If you were hired as a consultant by the chief economic planner of a small country to improve worker productivity (output per man-hour or output per worker), what advice could you give the planner?

Answer: You could advise the planner to take any one or more of the following actions, all of which would enhance worker productivity: (**1**) combine larger quantities of natural and capital inputs with labor inputs; (**2**) improve technology; (**3**) improve the health, education, and training of workers; (**4**) improve the organization of production. [See Section 17-5.]

PROBLEM 17-14   The labor market for widget workers in a certain geographical area is perfectly competitive. Then Local 3435 of the Amalgamated Widget Workers successfully organizes widget workers and negotiates a contract with widget producers. The contract calls for a wage rate above the competitive equilibrium level. Analyze the effect of the contract won by the labor union on the employment and total wage earnings of widget workers. Draw a diagram to support your analysis.

Answer: If a labor union raises the wage rate in a perfectly competitive labor market above the competitive equilibrium level, employment in the market will fall. Figure 17-9 suggests the reason. Prior to unionization, the labor market for widget workers is in competitive equilibrium at price (wage rate) W and quantity (employment level) L. Then Local 3435 of the Amalgamated Widget Workers wins a contract with widget pro-

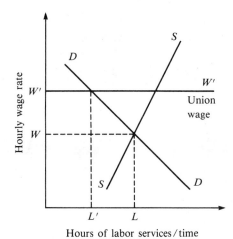

Figure 17-9

ducers that raises the wage rate from W to W'. As demand curve DD shows, at a wage rate of W', widget producers find it profitable to hire only L' hours of labor services because the marginal revenue product of labor equals the marginal factor cost of labor (W') at that level. So the employment of widget workers falls from L to L'.

A decrease in employment due to an increase in the wage rate of widget workers will not necessarily result in a drop in the total wage earnings (wage rate × hours worked) of employed widget workers. Total wage earnings will drop only if the demand for the labor services of widget workers is elastic. If it is inelastic, total wage earnings will increase. [See Section 17-5.]

18 IMPERFECT COMPETITION AND FACTOR MARKETS

THIS CHAPTER IS ABOUT

- ☑ Imperfect Competition and Factor Markets
- ☑ Monopolized Product Markets
- ☑ Unionization: Monopolized Labor Markets
- ☑ Monopsony
- ☑ Bilateral Monopoly and the Minimum Wage

18-1. Imperfect Competition and Factor Markets

The theory of competitive factor markets applies when the conditions in both product markets and factor markets are perfectly competitive. When the conditions in either product markets or factor markets are imperfectly competitive, the theory must be modified. This chapter considers three imperfectly competitive conditions and the modifications that each requires in the competitive theory of factor markets.

18-2. Monopolized Product Markets

Marginal revenue (MR) and marginal physical product (MPP) are the two factors that determine the marginal revenue product (MRP) of—and thus the demand for—labor or any other factor of production. The relationship between marginal revenue and product price is different for a firm under perfect competition than it is for a firm under imperfect competition (e.g., monopoly). Thus the demand for labor is also different. This difference requires a minor modification in the theory of factor markets, which you learned in the last chapter.

A. Marginal revenue is less than price for a monopolist.

A firm in a perfectly competitive product market faces a demand curve that is horizontal at the market price. As a result, (1) the firm's marginal revenue (MR) is always equal to the price (P) of its product (MR = P), (2) its MR curve is always horizontal at that price (the market price), and (3) its demand for labor (its MRP schedule for labor) is found by multiplying the marginal physical product (MPP) of labor at each level of output by the price of its product:

$$MRP = MPP \times P$$

By contrast, a firm in an imperfectly competitive product market, such as a monopoly, faces a demand curve with a negative slope. As a result, (1) the firm's marginal revenue is always less than the price of its product (MR < P), (2) its MR curve always lies below the demand curve that it faces, and (3) its demand for labor (its MRP schedule for labor) is found by multiplying the marginal physical product of labor by the firm's marginal revenue at each level of output:

$$MRP = MPP \times MR$$

In short, calculation of the marginal revenue product of labor in an imperfectly competitive product market requires the use of a firm's marginal revenue schedule rather than the price of its product.

EXAMPLE 18-1: The following table shows the output levels that correspond to various levels of labor inputs at Municipal Monopoly. It also shows how Municipal Monopoly's marginal revenue product (MRP) schedule for labor is calculated from its marginal physical product (MPP) schedule for labor and its marginal revenue (MR) schedule.

Labor inputs	Total output	MPP	×	MR	=	MRP
5	40					
		8	×	$11	=	$88
6	48					
		7	×	10	=	70
7	55					
		6	×	9	=	54
8	61					
		5	×	8	=	40
9	66					
		4	×	7	=	28
10	70					

The third column lists the marginal physical product of labor—that is, the contribution that each additional unit of labor makes to total output at Municipal Monopoly. For example, the sixth unit of labor adds 8 units to total output (48 − 40 = 8); the seventh unit, 7 units (55 − 48 = 7).

The fourth column lists Municipal Monopoly's marginal revenue at the various levels of output—that is, the contribution that each additional unit of output makes to the firm's total revenue. For example, units 40 through 48 contribute an average of $11 each to total revenue; units 48 through 55, an average of $10 each.

The fifth column is simply the product of the third and fourth columns. It shows how much each unit of labor adds to Municipal Monopoly's total revenue. For example, the sixth unit of labor adds 8 units to output that contribute an average of $11 each to total revenue, so the sixth unit of labor contributes $88 (8 × $11 = $88) to total revenue.

B. Under imperfect competition, MR × MPP is less than P × MPP.

When marginal revenue (MR) is less than price (P), as it is under imperfect competition, it follows that marginal revenue times marginal physical product (MPP) is less than price times the same marginal physical product. In symbols:

Given MPP, when $MR < P$, then $(MR \times MPP) < (P \times MPP)$.

This implies that, given two otherwise identical product markets, one perfectly competitive and one imperfectly competitive, the marginal revenue product (MRP) of and thus the demand for a given quantity of labor will be lower in the imperfectly competitive market than in the perfectly competitive one.

EXAMPLE 18-2: Figure 18-1 shows the effect on the MRP or demand curve for labor when a monopolizing cartel is formed in a product market that has previously been perfectly competitive. Curve *DD* is the MRP or demand curve for labor under perfectly competitive conditions. Curve *D'D'* is the MRP or demand curve for labor under imperfectly competitive or monopolistic conditions. Notice that curve *D'D'* lies below curve *DD*. This signifies a lower demand for labor under monopoly than under perfect competition. For example, at wage rate *W*, the quantity of labor services demanded under perfectly competitive conditions is *L*. Under imperfectly competitive conditions, it is only *L'*. This difference is consistent with an observation that we made earlier: namely, that if a cartel is formed in what previously has been a perfectly competitive industry, it will increase its profits by reducing industry output below the competitive level. Lower levels of output naturally require fewer units of a variable input such as labor.

Notice, too, that curve *D'D'* has a steeper slope than curve *DD*, even though the marginal physical product (MPP) curve for labor is the same before and after the formation of the monopolizing cartel. The difference in slopes is attributable to the fact that, in an imperfectly competitive market, marginal revenue (MR) declines more rapidly than price (P) as output (and labor inputs) increase. In a perfectly competitive market, it does not.

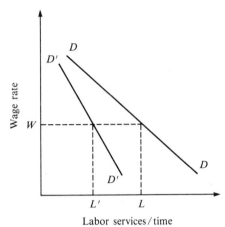

Figure 18-1

If a cartel is formed in a perfectly competitive industry, the cartel's demand curve for labor (*D'D'*) will lie below and have a steeper slope than its competitive counterpart (*DD*).

18-3. Unionization: Monopolized Labor Markets

Just as imperfectly competitive conditions in product markets affect conditions in labor markets, so imperfectly competitive conditions in labor markets themselves affect the pricing and employment of labor. Unionization is one form of imperfect competition in a labor market. It reduces the number of sellers in a labor market and may even monopolize the sale of labor services to a particular employer.

A. Labor unions are subject to government protection and regulation.

A **labor union** is an organization of workers formed to bargain collectively with employers over wages and working conditions. Because labor unions aim to advance the interests of their members by achieving monopolistic power in labor markets, they have been the subject of much legislation in the United States, both regulatory and protective. Three significant pieces of U.S. labor legislation are the Wagner (National Labor Relations) Act, the Taft–Hartley Labor Act, and the Landrum–Griffin Act.

1. The *Wagner Act* (1935) exempts labor unions from prosecution for restraint of trade under antitrust laws.
2. The *Taft–Hartley Labor Act* (1947) prohibits **closed shop** agree-

ments (i.e., agreements requiring union membership before employment); empowers states to pass "right-to-work" laws, which prohibit **union shop** agreements (i.e., agreements requiring union membership as a condition of continued employment); empowers the president of the United States to obtain an 80-day injunction against strikes that imperil the nation's well-being.

3. The *Landrum–Griffin Act* (1959) regulates the internal affairs of unions, such as election procedures, eligibility requirements for holding union offices, and the accountability of union officials to members.

B. Workers may be organized into craft unions or industrial unions.

- A **craft union** is an organization of workers who possess the same skill or practice the same craft or trade. An organization of electricians or plumbers or carpenters is a craft union.
- An **industrial union** is an organization of workers in the same industry without regard to their skills or to the particular jobs they perform. An organization of steelworkers or auto workers or retail workers is an industrial union.

By bargaining collectively—that is, as a single seller—labor unions, whether craft or industrial, can restrict the supply of labor services available to an employer. Ultimately, they can even go out on strike and withhold *all* labor services until they reach an agreement with management that is acceptable to their members.

C. The impact of a labor union depends upon its goals.

The impact that a union has on the wages and employment of its members depends in part on the goals of the union. A union may aim to achieve any of the following reasonable but conflicting goals:

1. It may aim to secure or maintain jobs for most of its members.
2. It may aim to maximize the total wage payment to its members.
3. It may aim to maximize the wage rate of a subset of its members.

EXAMPLE 18-3: Figure 18-2 illustrates the different effects that different goals have on a labor union's wage demands. Curve *DD* represents the demand for labor services in a hypothetical market. Quantity *L* represents the services of all the workers belonging to the union that supplies labor to a particular employer. If the union wishes to ensure the employment of all its members, it will seek a wage rate of *W*. If it wishes to maximize total wage payments to its members, it will seek a wage rate of *W'*. At a wage rate of *W'*, the price elasticity of demand for labor services is 1, which means that *total* wages (though not necessarily the wages of any particular worker) are at a maximum. (If you need to review the concept of price elasticity of demand, return to Chapter 7.) Finally, if the union wishes to maximize the wages of a subset of workers, represented by *L''*, it will seek a wage rate of *W''*. As you can see, each of these different goals has a different effect on wages and employment.

D. Craft unions may restrict supply.

Craft unions can gain higher wages for their members in two ways: (1) by restricting the number of people allowed to learn particular crafts and (2) by restricting membership in their organizations. Over time, these restrictions can cause the supply curve for the services of workers in craft unions to shift to the left. As Figure 18-3 demonstrates, when a labor supply curve shifts to the left, from *SS* to *S'S'*, the wages of employed workers rise from *W* to *W'*, *ceteris paribus*.

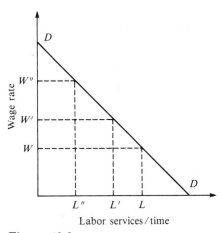

Figure 18-2
The wage demands of a labor union depend on its goals. Wage *W* will maximize employment. Wage *W'* will maximize total wage payments. Wage *W''* will maximize the wage rate of a subset of workers (represented by *L''*).

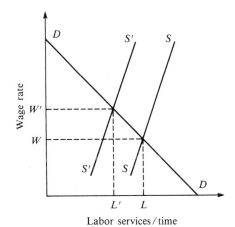

Figure 18-3
A craft union can increase wages for its members by restricting entry into the union. Over time, the supply curve for the union will shift left (*SS* to *S'S'*), and wages will rise (*W* to *W'*).

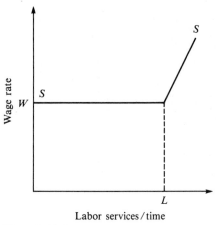

Figure 18-4
An industrial union can reshape the supply curve for workers in its industry by demanding a union-set wage, such as *W*. Workers will refuse to work for less than *W*.

E. Industrial unions may reshape supply.

Industrial unions can gain higher wages for their members by reshaping the supply curves for labor in their industries. Figure 18-4 shows a typical supply curve in a unionized industry. The horizontal portion of the curve represents the wage rate demanded by unionized workers. Unionized workers will refuse to work (i.e., they will strike) for a wage rate less than *W*. At a wage rate of *W*, employers can hire all of the available workers that they choose to hire. However, beyond some point, represented by *L* in the figure, employers must pay higher wages either to induce employees to work overtime or to attract additional workers to the market.

F. Labor unions have probably raised the wages of their members.

The effects of labor unions on wages and earnings in the United States have been studied extensively. Although the results of the studies are not conclusive, they do suggest the following:

1. Labor unions probably have raised the wages of their members by approximately 15 percent over the wages of nonunion workers in the same industries and with similar skills.

2. Labor unions probably have not increased the total wage bill or the total wage income of workers in general. The wage gains that they have made for their members may have come at the expense of wage losses to nonmembers.

18-4. Monopsony

Monopsony is the domination by a single buyer of a market in which there are many sellers. When a labor market is dominated by a single buyer or monopsonistic employer, wages rates and employment levels naturally are different than they would be in a labor market that was perfectly competitive on the demand side.

EXAMPLE 18-4: "Company towns" like Silver Bay, Minnesota, are close approximations of monopsonized labor markets. In Silver Bay, as in other company towns, there is only one major employer, Reserve Mining Company. In fact, Reserve Mining Company built the town of Silver Bay for the express purpose of accommodating the workers at its taconite plant. Company towns—and thus monopsony—are often associated with the mining, lumbering, and textile industries.

A. The supply curve that a monopsonist faces is the market supply curve.

Since a monopsonistic firm is the only buyer of labor services in a market, the supply curve that it faces is the market supply curve. As you recall from the last chapter, a market supply curve for labor, like a market supply curve for any good or service, has a positive slope. The positive slope implies that, if the firm wants to purchase a larger quantity of labor services, it must increase the wage rate that it pays to *all* workers. (This implication is predicated on the assumption that the monopsonist cannot practice wage discrimination.)

B. For a monopsonist, marginal factor cost exceeds factor price.

Because the labor supply curve facing a monopsonistic firm has a positive slope, the firm's marginal factor cost for labor exceeds factor price (the wage rate of labor). The reason for this is the same as the reason that marginal revenue is less than product price for a monopolist. In other words, a monopsonistic employer can hire an additional unit of labor only by increasing the wage rate paid to existing units. Therefore marginal factor cost for a monopsonistic employer is the wage rate paid to the extra worker *plus* the increase in the wage rate paid to workers already on the payroll. Therefore, too, a monopsonistic employer's marginal factor cost (MFC) curve for labor lies above the market supply curve (*SS*) for labor.

EXAMPLE 18-5: Figure 18-5 shows the supply curve (*SS*) in a monopsonized labor market and the monopsonist's MFC curve for labor. As you can see, the MFC curve lies above the supply curve, which indicates that the cost to the firm of hiring an additional worker is greater than the price of (the wage rate paid to) the worker.

Notice that the marginal factor cost (MFC) of the fifteenth worker is $54, but the daily wage rate paid to the fifteenth worker is only $40. The difference, $14, is the sum of the $1-a-day wage increases that the firm must give to the first 14 workers, who are earning only $39 a day, in order to hire the fifteenth worker at $40 a day: $40 + (14 × $1) = $54.

C. A monopsonist equates marginal revenue product with marginal factor cost to determine optimal labor use.

Like any other employer, a profit-maximizing monopsonist hires labor services up to the point at which the marginal revenue product of labor declines to equal the marginal factor cost of labor (MRP = MFC).

EXAMPLE 18-6: Given the MRP and MFC curves for labor in Figure 18-6, a monopsonist will hire L^* hours of labor services each month. Since L^* marks the point of intersection between the monopsonist's MRP and MFC curves for labor, the last worker hired will add as much to total revenue as to total cost. Therefore the monopsonist will maximize profits at that level of employment.

D. A monopsonist sets the wage rate.

Just as the only seller in a product market is a price setter, so the only buyer in a labor market is a wage setter. A monopsonistic firm decides what wage to set by consulting the market supply curve for labor that it faces. It selects the wage on that curve that corresponds to its optimal level of employment.

EXAMPLE 18-7: After applying the MRP = MFC rule to locate its optimal level of employment at L^*, the monopsonistic firm in Figure 18-6 consults supply curve *SS* to determine the wage rate that it should set for labor services. Since wage rate W^* will provide the firm with exactly L^* hours of labor, it sets W^* per hour as its wage rate. A higher rate would lead to a surplus of workers and lower profits for the monopsonist. A lower rate would lead to a shortage of workers.

18-5. Bilateral Monopoly and the Minimum Wage

Two additional departures from perfectly competitive conditions in factor markets remain to be considered: bilateral monopoly and the minimum wage.

A. Economic theory offers no insight into the outcome of bilateral monopoly.

Bilateral monopoly is a combination of monopoly and monopsony in a single market. When a bilateral monopoly occurs in a labor market, a single seller of labor services (a union) is pitted against a single buyer of labor services (a monopsonistic employer). Conventional economic theory offers no insight into the outcome of negotiations between a union and a monopsonistic employer in a

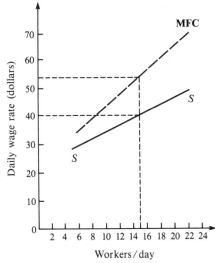

Figure 18-5
A monopsonist's marginal factor cost (MFC) curve for labor lies above the market supply curve (*SS*) for labor. Marginal factor cost exceeds factor price for a monopsonist.

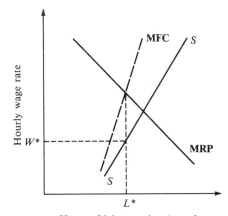

Figure 18-6
A monopsonistic firm will apply the MRP = MFC rule to locate its optimal employment level (L^*). It will consult the market supply curve for labor (*SS*) to select the wage rate corresponding to that level (W^*).

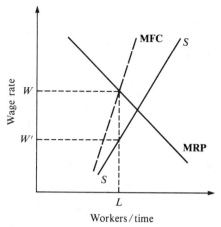

Figure 18-7
In a bilateral monopoly, a labor union may demand wage rate *W* and a monopsonistic employer may offer wage rate *W'*. Economic theory does not predict the outcome of negotiations between the two parties.

bilateral monopoly. For example, as Figure 18-7 shows, in a bilateral monopoly the monopsonistic employer will seek to hire *L* workers at a wage rate of *W'*. If the union wishes to maximize the wage rates of *L* workers, it will seek to win a wage rate of *W*. Which side will prevail? Conventional economic theory does not provide an answer. The outcome will depend on the relative strengths and the bargaining strategies of the two protagonists.

EXAMPLE 18-8: Before 1981, the labor market for air traffic controllers in the United States offered a fairly good example of bilateral monopoly. The Federal Aviation Administration (FAA) was (and still is) essentially the only major civilian employer of air traffic controllers. The Professional Air Traffic Controllers Association (PATCO) had what was at that time very close to a monopoly over the supply of air traffic controllers. When the FAA and PATCO were unable to negotiate an agreement that was satisfactory to both sides, the air traffic controllers went out on strike. Continued negotiations between the FAA and PATCO might have produced any number of compromises. However, President Ronald Reagan placed a firm limit on wage increases, and when PATCO refused to concede to that limit, he fired the striking controllers and ultimately destroyed the union.

B. Minimum wage laws can increase employment and wages in a monopsonized labor market.

A minimum wage law imposed on a monopsonistic employer can increase both wage rates and employment. Figure 18-8 suggests the reason. If a monopsonistic firm is allowed to go about its business without government interference, it will apply the MRP = MFC rule to locate its optimal employment level at *L* hours of labor services a month, and it will be able to obtain *L* hours of labor services a month by paying a wage rate of *W* per hour. Now, if the government imposes a wage minimum at *W'*, the monopsonist's MFC curve for labor will be affected. It will no longer be represented by the dashed line labeled "MFC" in Figure 18-8. Instead, it will be represented by horizontal line *W'W'*, the wage floor, because each hour of labor services will add the same amount, minimum wage *W'*, to the firm's total costs. The firm will then locate its optimal level of employment at *L'*, where its MRP curve intersects the wage floor, *W'W'*. Since *L'* represents more hours of labor services a month than *L*, both employment and wages will rise as a result of the imposition of a minimum wage on the monopsonistic employer. The imposition of a union-set wage would have the same effect.

Figure 18-8
Minimum wage legislation can increase both the wage rate (*W* to *W'*) and the level of employment (*L* to *L'*) in a monopsonized labor market.

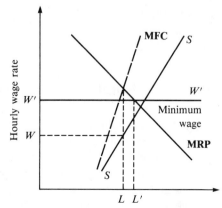

RAISE YOUR GRADES

Can you explain ... ?

☑ why the MRP curve for labor would decline more rapidly if an industry were cartelized than if it were perfectly competitive
☑ how a craft union differs from an industrial union
☑ how a labor union's goals affect its wage demands
☑ how craft unions affect a labor supply curve
☑ how industrial unions affect a labor supply curve
☑ why a monopsonist's MFC curve for labor lies above the supply curve for labor that the monopsonist faces
☑ how wage rates are set in a monopsonized labor market
☑ how wage rates are determined in a bilateral monopoly
☑ how unionization can increase employment and wages under monopsony
☑ how a minimum wage law imposed on a monopsonistic employer can increase both wages and employment

SUMMARY

1. The competitive theory of factor markets must be modified to accommodate imperfectly competitive conditions in both product markets and factor markets.
2. Marginal revenue is less than price for a monopolist (MR $<$ P). Therefore marginal revenue product (MRP) for a monopolist is less than marginal physical product times price (MRP $<$ MPP $\times$ P).
3. If a monopolizing cartel were formed in a perfectly competitive product market, the cartel's demand curve for labor would lie below and have a steeper slope than its competitive counterpart.
4. A *labor union* is an organization of workers formed to bargain collectively with employers over wages and working conditions.
5. Three major pieces of U.S. labor legislation are the Wagner Act (1935), the Taft–Hartley Labor Act (1947), and the Landrum–Griffin Act (1959).
6. A *craft union* is an organization of workers who possess the same skill or practice the same craft or trade. An *industrial union* is an organization of workers in the same industry.
7. The impact of a labor union on wages and employment depends in part on the union's goals. It may seek (1) to maintain jobs, (2) to maximize total wages, or (3) to maximize the wage rate of a subset of its members.
8. Craft unions can gain higher wages for their members (1) by restricting the number of people allowed to learn a craft and (2) by restricting membership in their organizations. Over time, these restrictions shift the supply curve for craft workers to the left.
9. Industrial unions can gain higher wages for their members by reshaping the supply curve for labor in their industries—that is, by making the supply curve horizontal at a union-specified wage rate.
10. Labor unions have probably raised the wages of their members by approximately 15 percent over the wages of nonunion workers in the same industries and with similar skills. However, the wage gains may have come at the expense of wage losses to nonunion workers.

11. *Monopsony* is the domination by a single buyer of a market in which there are many sellers. A *monopsonistic employer* is the sole buyer of labor services in a market.

12. The supply curve for labor that a monopsonistic employer faces is the market supply curve. Since that curve has a positive slope, marginal factor cost (MFC) exceeds factor price for a monopsonist, and a monopsonist's MFC curve lies above the market supply curve for labor.

13. A monopsonistic employer follows the MRP = MFC rule to determine optimal labor use.

14. In a labor market, a monopsonistic firm is a wage setter. It consults the market supply curve for labor to find the wage corresponding to its optimal level of employment.

15. *Bilateral monopoly* is a combination of monopoly and monopsony in a single market. When a bilateral monopoly occurs in a labor market, a single seller of labor services (a union) is pitted against a single buyer of labor services (a monopsonistic employer).

16. Conventional economic theory offers no insight into the outcome of negotiations between a union and a monopsonistic employer in a bilateral monopoly. The outcome depends on the relative strengths and bargaining strategies of the two parties.

17. A minimum wage law imposed on a monopsonistic employer can increase both wage rates and employment. Unionization can have the same effects.

RAPID REVIEW

1. For a monopolist, marginal revenue product equals marginal physical product times product price (MRP = MPP × P). True or false? [See Section 18-2.]

2. If a monopolizing cartel were formed in a perfectly competitive industry and the wage rate remained the same, employment would fall below the competitive level. True or false? [See Section 18-2.]

3. An industry MRP curve for labor would be steeper if the industry were imperfectly competitive than if it were perfectly competitive because _____ _____ declines more rapidly than _____ . [See Section 18-2.]

4. Unions seek to bargain _____ with employers over wages and working conditions. [See Section 18-3.]

5. A(n) _____ *union* is an organization of the workers in an industry. [See Section 18-3.]

6. The _____ Act, also known as the National Labor Relations Act, exempts unions from prosecution under antitrust laws. [See Section 18-3.]

7. The impact of a labor union on wages and employment depends in part on the union's goals. True or false? [See Section 18-3.]

8. If a union seeks a wage rate that corresponds to the point at which the elasticity of demand for labor equals 1, the goal of the union is probably to maximize (**a**) profits, (**b**) the number of jobs available to its members, (**c**) total wage payments to its members, (**d**) the wage rate of a subset of its members. [See Section 18-3.]

9. Restricting membership in a union will shift the supply curve for union labor to the _____ and _____ wages over a period of time, *ceteris paribus*. [See Section 18-3.]

10. If workers refuse employment at any wage below a union-specified rate, the supply curve for their labor will be (**a**) vertical at that wage rate, (**b**) horizontal at that wage rate, (**c**) negatively sloped, (**d**) perfectly inelastic. [See Section 18-3.]

11. If employers do not meet the demands of a union, the members of the union may _____ , that is, refuse to provide labor services. [See Section 18-3.]

12. In the United States, labor unions have raised wages for all workers through their efforts to improve wages for their members. True or false? [See Section 18-3.]

13. A _____ is the sole buyer of an item. [See Section 18-4.]

14. For a monopsonistic employer, factor price is (**a**) less than marginal factor cost, (**b**) equal to marginal factor cost, (**c**) greater than marginal factor cost, (**d**) greater than marginal revenue product. [See Section 18-4.]

15. In order to hire more workers, a monopsonistic employer must reduce the wage rate paid to all workers. True or false? [See Section 18-4.]

16. A _____ _____ combines monopoly with monopsony in a single market. [See Section 18-5.]

17. A union organizing workers in a monopsonized industry can increase wages only by reducing employment. True or false? [See Section 18-5.]

Answers
1. false **2.** true **3.** marginal revenue, price **4.** collectively **5.** *industrial*
6. Wagner **7.** true **8.** (c) **9.** left, increase **10.** (b) **11.** strike
12. false **13.** *monopsonist* **14.** (a) **15.** false **16.** bilateral monopoly **17.** false

SOLVED PROBLEMS

PROBLEM 18-1 The following table shows the quantities of labor inputs that correspond to various levels of output and total revenue at the Gizmo Group. Prepare a marginal revenue product (MRP) schedule for labor for the Gizmo Group.

Labor inputs	Output	Total revenue
18	125	$1,000
19	135	1,046
20	144	1,080
21	152	1,102
22	159	1,113
23	165	1,113

Answer: *Marginal revenue product* is the change in total revenue (the value of production) that results from a one-unit change in a variable input such as labor. To find the marginal revenue product of the nineteenth unit of labor, simply subtract $1,000, the total revenue that the Gizmo Group earns on the first 18 units of labor, from $1,046, the total revenue that it earns on the first 19 units of labor. The difference, $46, is the contribution of the nineteenth unit to the firm's total revenue [see Section 18-2]:

Labor inputs	Output	Total revenue	MRP
18	125	$1,000	
19	135	1,046	$46
20	144	1,080	34
21	152	1,102	22
22	159	1,113	11
23	165	1,113	0

PROBLEM 18-2 If the Gizmo Group in Problem 18-1 purchases labor services in a competitive labor market at $22 a unit, how many units should it hire? What is the price of a gizmo at the firm's profit-maximizing output level?

Answer: The Gizmo Group should follow the MRP = MFC rule to determine its optimal employment level. You know from the last chapter that the marginal factor cost for labor will equal the factor price, $22. Therefore, if you consult the MRP schedule that you prepared for the last problem, you will see that the Gizmo Group should hire 21 units of labor. Since the twenty-first unit will add as much to the Gizmo Group's total revenue as it will add to its total costs, the firm will maximize its profits at that level of employment.

If the Gizmo Group hires 21 units of labor, the table in the last problem indicates that those 21 units of labor will produce an output of 152 gizmos. It also indicates that those 152 gizmos will bring in a total of $1,102 in revenue. Therefore the price or average revenue of a gizmo at the firm's profit-maximizing output level must be $7.25 ($1,102 ÷ 152 = $7.25). [See Section 18-2.]

PROBLEM 18-3   Based on their names, classify each of the following unions as a craft or an industrial union: United Steelworkers of America, Hotel and Restaurant Employees International Union, and Air Line Pilots Association.

Answer: United Steelworkers of America and Hotel and Restaurant Employees International Union are industrial unions; they are organizations of unskilled, semiskilled, and skilled workers in the same industry. Air Line Pilots Association is a craft union; it is an organization of workers who possess the same skill. [See Section 18-3.]

PROBLEM 18-4   Explain the difference between a *closed shop* agreement and a *union shop* agreement. What is the legal status of such agreements in the United States?

Answer: A *closed shop* agreement is an agreement between a labor union and an employer whereby the employer agrees to require membership in the union as a condition of employment. A *union shop* agreement is an agreement between a labor union and an employer whereby the union agrees to allow the employer to hire nonunion workers and the employer, in turn, agrees to require membership in the union within a specified period of time as a condition of continued employment.

Closed shop agreements were declared illegal by the Taft–Hartley Act in 1947. Union shop agreements are illegal in states that have passed "right-to-work" laws. [See Section 18-3.]

PROBLEM 18-5   Members of Local 3435 of the Amalgamated Widget Workers Union have voted not to accept employment for less than $15 an hour. Construct a supply curve for the union.

Answer: The labor supply curve for the union is shown in Figure 18-9. The first part of the curve is horizontal at $15 because the members of Local 3435 will not accept employment for less than that. It then turns up to indicate that, when all of the available widget workers are employed, either widget firms will have to pay the workers time-and-a-half for additional hours of labor services, or they will have to offer a higher wage rate in order to attract new workers into the widget labor market. [See Section 18-3.]

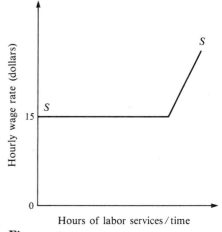

Figure 18-9

PROBLEM 18-6   Analyze the impact of a recession (a period characterized by reduced economic activity) on the employment, wages, and total earnings of the members of the widget union in Problem 18-5. Draw a diagram to illustrate your analysis.

Answer: A recession would probably reduce the demand for widgets, which would reduce both the quantity exchanged and the price of widgets. A reduction in the output and price of widgets would reduce the marginal revenue product of widget workers, which would be reflected in a leftward shift in the demand curve for their labor services. As Figure 18-10 shows, as the demand for the labor services of widget workers shifted from DD to $D'D'$, the number of hours worked would decline from L to L'. The wage rate (the marginal factor cost of labor) would not be affected, but total wage earnings would obviously decline. [See Section 18-3.]

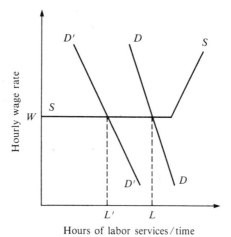

Figure 18-10

PROBLEM 18-7 As you recall from Section 18-3, the wage demands of a labor union depend upon its goals. Assuming that the demand for labor is perfectly competitive, compare the wage demands of a union seeking to maximize total wage payments to its members with the wage demands of a union seeking to maximize the number of jobs available to its members. Draw an appropriate diagram.

Answer: A labor union that seeks to maximize total wage payments to its membership will demand wage rate W' in Figure 18-11, which corresponds to the midpoint of demand curve DD. At a wage rate of W', L' hours of labor services will be hired each month. Since the price elasticity of demand for labor at (L', W') is 1, no higher or lower wage rate will result in an increase in *total* wage payments to union members. (The product of W' and L' is greater than the product of any other wage–employment combination represented along demand curve DD.)

A labor union that seeks to maximize the number of jobs available to its members will demand wage rate W. Actually, since that

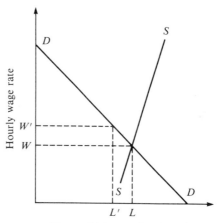

Hours of labor services/month

Figure 18-11

will be the going rate for labor services in a perfectly competitive market (at wage rate W, quantity supplied equals quantity demanded), the union won't have to demand wage rate W. It will only have to accept it. Wage rate W will maximize employment at L hours of labor services a month. [See Section 18-3.]

PROBLEM 18-8 The Widget Works is the only major employer in a small company town. The supply of labor in the town is shown in the following schedule. Find the marginal factor cost of labor for the Widget Works.

Units of labor	Wage rate/hour
50	$ 5
51	6
52	7
53	8
54	9
55	10

Answer: Marginal factor cost is the change in total factor cost that results from a one-unit change in factor use. To find the marginal factor cost of labor for the Widget Works, first find the total factor cost at each level of employment by multiplying the number of units of labor by the hourly wage rate for labor services. Then simply subtract the total factor cost at one level of employment from the total factor cost at the next. The total factor costs (TFC) and the marginal factor costs (MFC) for the Widget Works are shown in the following schedule [see Section 18-4]:

Units of labor	Wage rate/ hour	TFC	MFC
50	$ 5	$250	
51	6	306	$56
52	7	364	58
53	8	424	60
54	9	486	62
55	10	550	64

PROBLEM 18-9 The marginal revenue product (MRP) for labor at the Widget Works is shown in the following schedule. Using the data in the last problem, find the profit-maximizing level of employment and the wage rate corresponding to that level at the Widget Works.

Units of labor	MRP
52	$74
53	68
54	62
55	56
56	50
57	44
58	38
59	32

Answer: Like any other employer, the Widget Works will maximize its profits by applying the MRP = MFC rule. Thus, it will hire 54 units of labor (MRP = $62 = MFC at 54 units). According to the supply schedule in Problem 18-8, the Widget Works can hire 54 units of labor for $9 an hour (which, as you can see, is much lower than the marginal factor cost of the fifty-fourth unit). [See Section 18-4.]

PROBLEM 18-10 Suppose that Local 3435 of the Amalgamated Widget Workers (AWW) organizes the employees of the Widget Works. The AWW demands a wage rate of $38 an hour, plus time and a half for overtime. The Widget Works accepts the union proposal and agrees to pay $38 an hour for labor. Using the information in Problems 18-8 and 18-9, find the number of units of labor that the Widget Works will hire.

Answer: The Widget Works will again apply the MRP = MFC rule to determine its optimal usage of labor, but now its marginal factor cost for labor will be constant at $38. Therefore it will increase its level of employment from 54 to 58 units of labor (MRP = $38 = MFC at 58 units). [See Section 18-5.]

PROBLEM 18-11 Suppose that the Amalgamated Widget Workers does not want to increase employment at the Widget Works from 54 to 58 units. Instead, it wants to maximize the wage rate of the 54 units already employed at the time of unionization. Use the information in the last three problems to determine the wage rate that the AWW should seek in its negotiations with the management of the Widget Works. [*Hint:* What is the maximum wage rate that the Widget Works will pay for 54 units of labor?]

Answer: If the AWW wants to obtain the highest hourly wage possible for the 54 units of labor employed at the Widget Works, it should seek a wage rate of $62 an hour. The

MRP = MFC rule will allow the Widget Works to pay up to $62 an hour for a unit of labor. It will not allow it to pay any more than that. [See Section 18-5.]

PROBLEM 18-12   Suppose that the Amalgamated Widget Workers is seeking a wage rate of $62 an hour and the Widget Works is offering a wage rate of $9 an hour. Given the information in the last four problems, predict the outcome of the negotiations between the AWW and the Widget Works by applying conventional economic theory.

Answer: Conventional economic theory does not predict the outcome of a bilateral monopoly. The Widget Works, remember, is the only major employer in a company town. Therefore the Widget Works is a monopsonist. The AWW, likewise, is a monopolist; it has a monopoly over the supply of labor in the town. The outcome of negotiations between the two parties will depend upon their relative strengths and strategies at the bargaining table. [See Section 18-5.]

19 *PROFITS, INTEREST, AND RENT*

THIS CHAPTER IS ABOUT

- ☑ **Economic Profits**
- ☑ **Interest Rates**
- ☑ **Present Value**
- ☑ **Bond Prices and the Demand for Capital Goods**
- ☑ **Economic Rent**

19-1. Economic Profits

In the last two chapters we have been discussing wages, the primary source of household income in the United States, and how they are determined in factor markets. In this chapter we turn to three other sources of household income—profits, interest, and rent—and the roles they play in a market economy.

As you recall from Chapter 11, *economic profit* is defined as the difference between total revenue and total costs. Since total costs include implicit costs (the opportunity costs of self-owned, self-employed resources) as well as explicit costs (the costs of purchased resources), a positive economic profit is a surplus, an excess of revenue over costs. It implies a higher than normal return on resources devoted to production. The prospect of earning a positive economic profit is a powerful motivating force. It provides the incentive for individuals and firms to perform the entrepreneurial functions in a market economy.

A. Positive profits are a temporary phenomenon in competitive markets.

In competitive markets, positive economic profits occur only during periods of imbalance or disequilibrium. In the long run, competition and the entry of new firms force profits down to zero. In noncompetitive markets, profits may be positive even in the long run because the entry of new firms may be blocked by franchises, patents, or other barriers. However, these barriers do not guarantee positive economic profits.

B. Positive profits provide the incentive to assume the risks of organizing production.

Production, as you may recall from Chapter 13, often entails sunk costs, costs associated with the irrevocable commitment of resources to a particular use. If a firm wishes to undertake production, it must pay the costs and commit the resources in spite of an uncertain future and the possibility of adverse developments. What motivates a firm to assume the risks of organizing production? The prospect of earning a positive economic profit. Were it not for the potential reward, few firms would willingly assume the risk.

C. Potential profits stimulate innovation.

Just as the potential for earning positive profits provides the incentive to assume the risks of organizing production, so it provides the stimulus for research and development and thus for innovation. **Innovation** is the commercial development of a new product or a new production process. By developing a new product, a firm establishes a new market, gains monopolistic power over the market, and earns positive economic profits until other firms develop competing products. By developing a new production process, a firm reduces its costs and thereby creates an imbalance or disequilibrium in the market in which it is participating. Until the market reaches a new equilibrium, the firm can increase its market share and earn positive economic profits. Thus, even in the short run, the potential for earning positive economic profits provides the incentive for innovation.

D. Potential profits encourage competition.

According to Joseph Schumpeter, a major contributor to modern profit theory, the profit incentive is such a spur to competition that even the market positions of monopolists are unsafe in the long run. In Schumpeter's opinion, the prospect of earning positive profits will eventually inspire entrepreneurs to develop substitutes for the products produced in monopolies, and monopolies will be swept aside in a "gale of creative destruction."

19-2. Interest Rates

The **interest rate** is the price of credit or loanable funds. This price is usually expressed as an annual percentage rate. For example, an interest rate of 10 percent means that a borrower will pay a price of 10¢ for the use of $1 for 1 year. The interest rate is market determined; however, the market for credit or loanable funds is not perfectly competitive. The demand for loanable funds is strongly influenced by the borrowings of the federal government. The supply of loanable funds is significantly influenced by the actions of the Federal Reserve Board.

A. *The* interest rate is really a structure of rates.

Although we speak of *the* interest rate, there is really a structure of interest rates systematically related on the basis of risk, term, and liquidity.

1. The *risk* involved in making a loan is the chance that the borrower will default on the loan and will not be able to pay it back. Generally speaking, the higher the risk of default, the higher the interest rate. Lenders request *risk premiums* (higher interest rates) to protect themselves from potential losses.
2. The *term* of a loan is the length of time for which it is granted. Since the future is uncertain, long-term loans are riskier than short-term loans. Thus, generally speaking, the longer the term, the higher the interest rate.
3. *Liquidity* is the ease of converting an asset, such as a bond, into cash. Some types of loans, such as bonds issued by major corporations, are very liquid. They are bought and sold daily on Wall Street. Generally speaking, the lower the liquidity, the higher the interest rate.

B. The interest rate is determined in the market for loanable funds.

The **nominal rate of interest** is the stated rate of interest. The nominal rate of interest is determined in the market for loanable funds. (Again, although we speak of *the* nominal rate of interest, we mean the nominal *rates* of interest for different categories of loans. Those rates are determined not in *the* market for loanable funds, though it is convenient to refer to it as such, but in *many* markets for loanable funds.)

1. *Demand.* There is a demand for credit or loanable funds by households, business firms, and governments. Households borrow to finance current consumption. Business firms borrow to finance investments in new plants and equipment, inventory, and so on. Governments borrow for both reasons.

2. *Supply.* There is a supply of funds to loan from households, business firms, governments, and financial intermediaries. *Financial intermediaries* are banks, insurance companies, pension funds, and all other financial institutions that accept deposits from households and businesses and then lend the funds.

3. *Equilibrium.* The equilibrium rate of interest in the market for loanable funds is the price at which quantity demanded equals quantity supplied.

EXAMPLE 19-1: Figure 19-1 is a diagram of the market supply (SS) and demand (DD) for loanable funds in a hypothetical market. The curves show the quantity of funds that suppliers are willing to lend and demanders are willing and able to borrow at each possible price or rate of interest. As you can see, quantity supplied equals quantity demanded (the market is cleared) at an interest rate of r^*. Thus r^* is the equilibrium rate of interest and M^* is the equilibrium quantity of loanable funds in the market.

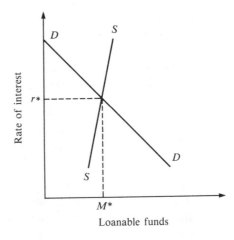

Figure 19-1
The *interest rate* is the price of loanable funds. It is determined by the interaction of supply and demand in the market for loanable funds.

C. **The *real interest rate* is the nominal rate minus the inflation rate.**

There are two different rates of interest: the nominal rate, which, as we have just said, is the stated or market rate, and the real rate. The **real rate of interest** is the nominal rate of interest minus the rate of inflation. Over time, inflation reduces the value or purchasing power of funds. Therefore the funds that a debtor repays are worth less (have less purchasing power) than the funds that the debtor borrows.

EXAMPLE 19-2: Let's say that you took out a loan for $1,000 and you repaid it without interest 1 year later. If the rate of inflation that year was 6 percent, the $1,000 that you borrowed was worth only $940 when you paid it back. In other words, when you borrowed it, the $1,000 was able to purchase goods and services worth $1,000. When you repaid it, since prices had gone up during the year, it was able to purchase goods and services worth only $940 a year earlier.

Lenders or creditors naturally seek to preserve the purchasing power of their loanable funds by adding an inflation premium onto the underlying or real rate of interest that they charge. Thus the nominal rate of interest is simply the real rate of interest plus the inflation premium, and the real rate of interest is simply the nominal rate of interest minus the inflation premium:

nominal interest rate = real interest rate + inflation rate

real interest rate = nominal interest rate − inflation rate

EXAMPLE 19-3: If the nominal interest rate is 12 percent a year and the inflation rate is 9 percent a year, the real interest rate is 3 percent a year. A real interest rate of 3 percent means that a debtor will repay 3 percent more purchasing power than he or she borrowed a year earlier.

19-3. Present Value

The rate of interest is a special price in a market economy. It coordinates decisions on purchasing or holding financial assets (bonds and stocks), capital goods (factory buildings and machines), and money. It also coordinates decisions about consumption and saving by various economic units. To see the tie between the rate of interest, the prices of financial assets, and the demand for capital goods, you must understand the concept of present value.

A. The current worth of future receipts is less than their face value.

To say that the current worth of future receipts is less than their face value is simply to say that a dollar tomorrow is worth less than a dollar today. There are two reasons for this discrepancy in value:

1. Most individuals prefer present consumption to future consumption; therefore they are willing to pay for the use of funds today.
2. Funds not spent today can be lent to earn interest; therefore the amount of funds available tomorrow will exceed the amount of funds lent today.

B. Present value calculations are used to determine the current worth of future revenue.

Present value is the current worth of future revenue—for example, the value today of $100 to be received 2 years from now. Since future revenues are worth less today than their face value, their present value is calculated by discounting their face value. *Discounting* is the opposite of augmenting funds with interest. In other words, instead of multiplying present value by an interest factor to determine future receipts, you divide future receipts by a discount factor to determine present value. The discount factor is simply the inverse or the reciprocal of the interest factor. It represents the opportunity cost of current funds—that is, the amount that the funds could be earning in their next-best use today. Thus:

$$\text{Future receipt (in time } t) = (1 + i)^t \times \text{present value}$$

$$\text{Present value} = \frac{\text{future receipt (in time } t)}{(1 + i)^t}$$

where i is the interest or discount rate and t is the length of time.

EXAMPLE 19-4: If you invest \$82.64 (present value) at 10 percent interest (i) for 2 years (t), you will receive \$100 at the end of the 2-year period:

$$\text{Future receipt (in time } t) = (1 + i)^t \times \text{present value}$$
$$= (1 + 0.10)^2 \times \$82.64$$
$$= 1.21 \times \$82.64$$
$$= \$100$$

Put the other way around, if you are to receive \$100 (future receipt) in 2 years (t), the present value of the \$100 at a discount rate of 10 percent (i) is \$82.64:

$$\text{Present value} = \frac{\text{future receipt (in time } t)}{(1 + i)^t}$$

$$= \frac{\$100}{(1 + 0.10)^2}$$

$$= \frac{\$100}{1.21}$$

$$= \$82.64$$

C. Present values are summed to determine the current worth of multiperiod revenues.

The present value of a stream or sequence of future receipts is the sum of the present values of the receipts in each future time period.

EXAMPLE 19-5: How much should you pay for a machine, a bond, a law degree, or some other asset that will bring you revenue of \$100 a year for the next 4 years? You should pay no more than the present value of the asset, what it is worth today. To determine what it is worth today, first calculate the present value of the asset in each of the next 4 years; then add those values together. Thus, if the current opportunity cost of funds (the interest rate) is 5 percent or 0.05, the present value of the asset is calculated as follows:

$$\text{Present value} = \frac{\$100}{1.05^1} + \frac{\$100}{1.05^2} + \frac{\$100}{1.05^3} + \frac{\$100}{1.05^4}$$

$$= \$95.24 + \$90.70 + \$86.38 + \$82.27$$
$$= \$354.59$$

You should pay no more than \$354.59 for the asset. At a discount rate of 5 percent, that is the present value of the stream of future revenue that it will yield.

19-4. Bond Prices and the Demand for Capital Goods

A **bond** is a certificate of indebtedness that consists of two promises which the issuer makes to the holder: (**1**) a promise to repay the debt or principal on a stated date, known as the *maturity date*, and (**2**) a promise to pay a stated sum of money each year until the bond matures. The yearly payment is often referred to as the interest on the bond, but it should not be confused with the market rate of interest.

Capital goods are similar to bonds in that both yield a stream of future revenues. Just as bonds yield yearly payments, so capital goods, such as buildings and equipment, provide services and revenues over several production periods. Because of this similarity, the price of bonds and the demand for capital goods are both related to the interest rate.

A. The price of a bond is inversely related to the interest rate.

Since bond revenues are received in the future, the worth or the price of a bond is determined by its present value. The rate of return on a bond must equal the rate of interest available in the market for loanable funds. Otherwise, bondholders will simply take advantage of a bond's liquidity by selling it and lending their funds in the market for loanable funds. Therefore the discount rate applied to bonds in calculations of present value is the current market rate of interest. Therefore, too, as the nominal interest rate increases, the present value or the price of a bond decreases.

The inverse relationship between the price of a bond and the nominal interest rate should make sense. A rise in the interest rate increases future receipts from a given current loan; however, it decreases the present value (and hence the price) of a given future receipt. Mathematically this inverse relation holds because the interest rate shows up in the denominator in calculations of present value.

EXAMPLE 19-6: Consider once again the present value of the asset in Example 19-5. Assume for the moment that the asset is a bond, even though there is no principal associated with it. At an interest rate of 5 percent, the present value of the stream of revenue that the bond will yield in the next 4 years is $354.59. What happens if the interest rate rises to 10 percent? The present value of the stream of future revenue declines:

$$\text{Present value} = \frac{\$100}{1.10^1} + \frac{\$100}{1.10^2} + \frac{\$100}{1.10^3} + \frac{\$100}{1.10^4}$$

$$= \$90.91 + \$82.64 + \$75.13 + \$68.30$$

$$= \$316.98$$

As the nominal rate of interest rises from 5 percent to 10 percent, the present value of the stream of future revenue declines from $354.59 to $316.98, and the price of the bond declines with it. The bond will still yield the same amount of money—$100 a year for the next 4 years—but it will yield a higher rate of return, 10 percent rather than 5 percent. The higher rate of return reflects the increased opportunity cost of loanable funds in the current market.

B. Capital goods should be acquired only when their present value equals or exceeds their purchase price.

The rule for purchasing capital goods is simple: A profit-maximizing firm should purchase capital goods only when the present value of the goods equals or exceeds their price ($PV \geq P$). The reasoning behind the rule is also simple. Since capital goods are durable—that is, since they provide services and revenues over several production periods—their worth is determined by their present value, not by their purchase price. If the present value of a capital good does not exceed or at least equal its purchase price, the funds used to purchase the good will generate less future revenue than they would if they were lent at the current market rate of interest. Thus, investing in a capital good whose present value is less than its purchase price will reduce a firm's profits.

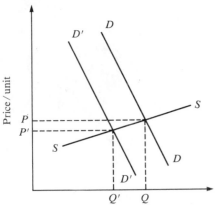

Figure 19-2
The demand curve for a capital good will shift to the left (*DD* to *D'D'*) as the interest rate increases, *ceteris paribus.* As a result, quantity purchased will decline (*Q* to *Q'*).

C. Demand for capital goods varies inversely with the interest rate.

Like the price of bonds, the present value of capital goods declines when the interest rate rises. Other things being equal, then, the demand for capital goods is inversely related to the interest rate. When the interest rate rises, the demand curve for a capital good shifts left, *ceteris paribus.* As Figure 19-2 shows, a leftward shift in the demand curve for a hypothetical capital good, from *DD* to *D'D'*, results in a lower quantity purchased.

D. Increases in the real interest rate have both microeconomic and macroeconomic effects.

1. Increases in the real rate of interest reduce a firm's expenditures on capital goods and thus reduce the capital intensity of its future production. Reductions in the capital intensity of a firm's production tend to reduce the marginal revenue product of—and thus the firm's demand for—labor, *ceteris paribus.*

2. Increases in the real rate of interest reduce aggregate investment expenditures—that is, total expenditures on buildings, equipment, and new housing in the economy as a whole. Reductions in aggregate investment expenditures tend to reduce total output in the economy.

19-5. Economic Rent

Economists have at least three concepts of rent, and the terms that they apply to these concepts vary from one economics textbook to the next. In this book we shall label and define them as follows:

- **Pure economic rent** is a payment for the use of a factor that is completely fixed (perfectly inelastic) in supply to society.
- **Quasi rent** is a payment for the use of a factor that is fixed in supply only in the short run.
- **Economic rent** is any payment for the use of a factor that exceeds the opportunity cost of the factor—that is, the minimum amount needed to retain the factor in its present use.

All three of these concepts have one element in common: rent is a payment for the use of a factor of production in excess of some opportunity cost for the factor.

A. Payment for the use of a factor completely fixed in supply is pure economic rent.

Land is an example of a factor of production that is completely fixed in supply to society. Payment for the services of such a factor exceeds the opportunity cost of the factor to *society* and thus qualifies as pure economic rent. Figure 19-3 suggests the reason. Curve *SS* is the supply curve for land, a factor completely fixed or perfectly inelastic in supply. The curve is vertical because the same quantity of land, designated by *L*, is available to society at any positive price. Since society is not required to sacrifice anything in order to obtain the use of the land—it is there, a gift of nature—its opportunity cost to society is zero. Therefore, from society's perspective, any payment for the services of the land constitutes pure economic rent. (Although pure economic rent is not a cost to society, it is to an individual firm. Individual firms that pay for the use of land perceive the payments they make as costs of production.)

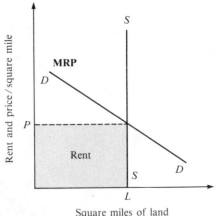

Figure 19-3
Payments for the use of a factor completely fixed in supply, such as land, are pure economic rent.

B. Pure economic rent serves a rationing function in a competitive market.

In a competitive market, pure economic rent serves to allocate resources to their most productive uses. If you look again at Figure 19-3, you will understand why. Curve *DD* represents the demand for land services. Like any other demand curve for a factor of production, curve *DD* reflects the marginal revenue product (MRP) of land, the contribution that each additional unit of land makes to total revenue. Naturally firms that realize a greater increase in total revenue from the use of land are willing to pay a higher price for it. Therefore a competitive market will ensure that land is allocated to those uses with the highest marginal revenue products, that is, to those uses that are most productive. In Figure 19-3, for example, land will be allocated only to those uses that have a marginal revenue product equal to or greater than price *P*; it will not be allocated to any uses with marginal revenue products lower than that. As you can see, although pure economic rent does not affect the quantity of land available (that quantity is fixed), it does affect how the land is used.

C. A single tax on land was proposed in the nineteenth century.

In the late 1800s, Henry George, an American economist, proposed that society adopt a single tax on land in lieu of a variety of taxes on income, sales, inheritances, luxuries, and so on. George argued that, since payments for land services are rent and since rent is a surplus (a payment over and above what is necessary to ensure the availability of land), a single tax on land would not reduce the use of land services. Instead, as Figure 19-4 illustrates, it would simply increase public revenues by reducing private rents and the unearned incomes of landowners. (Since the supply of land is perfectly inelastic, the owners of the land would have to absorb all of the tax. They would not be able to pass it on to renters.)

George's scheme has never been adopted for two principal reasons. First, in some cases it is difficult to separate the value of a plot of land from the value of improvements made on the land. Second, there is no guarantee that a *single* tax will raise sufficient funds to cover the expenses of government, especially today.

D. Urban economists have revived the proposal of taxing land.

Urban economists and city planners have revived the notion of taxing land instead of buildings to prevent the flight of business and manufacturing firms from downtown areas, where property taxes on buildings are high, to suburban areas, where property taxes on buildings are lower. Taxing land instead of buildings would remove much of the incentive for firms to locate in suburban areas rather than in center cities. Of course land taxes in center cities would still be higher, but whereas buildings could be relocated, the land itself could not.

E. Many factors of production receive economic rent.

Payments for land services are not the only payments that qualify as economic rent. Many other factors—notably professional athletes, rock musicians, movie and television stars—also receive economic rent for their services, payments over and above what is necessary to retain them in their current occupations. Since the payments that many of these people receive far surpass the income they could earn in their next-best uses in society, few would change occupations even if their earnings were cut by as much as 30 percent.

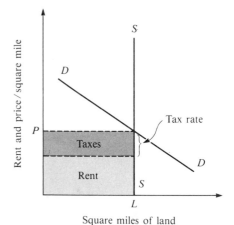

Figure 19-4
A tax on land reduces private rental income without reducing the quantity of land services supplied.

RAISE YOUR GRADES

Can you explain...?

☑ why economic profits are a surplus
☑ what functions pure profits perform in a market economy
☑ why positive profits are a temporary phenomenon in competitive markets
☑ what forces determine the rate of interest in a market economy
☑ how the real interest rate differs from the nominal interest rate
☑ why a future sum of money is worth less than the same sum today
☑ how discounting is related to charging interest on a loan
☑ why bond prices decrease as the interest rate increases
☑ why the demand for capital goods is inversely related to the rate of interest
☑ how pure economic rent serves a rationing function
☑ what the arguments are for the single-tax proposal

SUMMARY

1. A positive economic profit is a surplus, not a cost. It implies a higher than normal return on resources.
2. A positive economic profit is a short-run or temporary phenomenon in a competitive market.
3. The potential for earning a positive economic profit provides the incentive for entrepreneurs to commit resources to production and bear the risks associated with an uncertain future.
4. The potential for earning a positive economic profit, even in the short run, provides the incentive for innovation. *Innovation* is the commercial development of a new product or production process.
5. The *interest rate* is the price of credit or loanable funds. This price is usually expressed as an annual percentage rate.
6. *The* interest rate is really a structure of rates that vary according to (1) level of risk, (2) length of term, and (3) degree of liquidity. Interest rates are higher for high-risk, long-term, low-liquidity loans than they are for low-risk, short-term, high-liquidity loans.
7. The interest rate is determined in the market for loanable funds. Savers are the suppliers of loanable funds; borrowers are the demanders.
8. *Financial intermediaries* are institutions that obtain money from households and business firms and then lend it out. Banks, pension funds, and insurance companies are financial intermediaries.
9. The *nominal interest rate* is the stated or market rate. The *real interest rate* is the nominal interest rate minus the inflation rate.
10. The rate of interest is a special price in a market economy. It coordinates decisions on purchasing and holding financial assets, capital goods, and money.
11. A sum of money to be received in the future is worth less than the same sum today for two reasons: (1) people prefer present to future consumption; (2) money not spent today can be lent to earn interest.

12. *Present value* is the current worth of future revenues. The present value of future revenues is calculated by discounting the face value of those revenues at some rate, called the *discount rate*. Discounting is the inverse of augmenting funds with interest.

13. The formula for determining the present value (PV) of revenue to be received at time t in the future at a discount rate of i is

$$PV = \frac{\text{future revenue}}{(1 + i)^t}$$

14. The present value of a stream or sequence of future receipts is the sum of the present values of the receipts in each future time period.

15. A *bond* is a certificate of indebtedness consisting of two promises that the issuer makes to the holder: (1) to repay the debt or principal on a stated date, the *maturity date*, and (2) to make a fixed annual payment until the bond matures.

16. The price (present value) of a bond is inversely related to the nominal interest rate (the discount rate): as the interest rate increases, the price of a bond decreases.

17. Capital goods provide revenues over several production periods. Hence profit-maximizing firms acquire capital goods only if their present value equals or exceeds their purchase price.

18. The demand for capital goods is inversely related to the rate of interest.

19. *Pure economic rent* is a payment for the use of a factor that is completely fixed in supply to society.

20. *Quasi rent* is payment for the use of a factor that is fixed in supply in the short run.

21. *Economic rent* is any payment for the use of a factor that exceeds the opportunity cost of the factor—that is, the minimum amount needed to retain the factor in its present use.

22. Pure economic rent does not increase the supply of a factor (that supply is fixed), but it rations the resource to its most productive uses.

23. The proposal for a single tax on land is based on the argument that, since payments for land services are pure economic rent (a surplus, not a cost to society), taxing them will provide revenues to improve the public welfare without reducing the quantity of land available.

24. Professional athletes, rock stars, actors, and others in our economy often earn economic rent. The payments they receive are often in excess of what they could earn elsewhere in the economy.

RAPID REVIEW

1. A positive economic profit is a _____ , not a cost. [See Section 19-1.]

2. Positive economic profits are only a short-run phenomenon in competitive markets. True or false? [See Section 19-1.]

3. The potential for earning a positive economic profit is an incentive for entrepreneurs to (a) bear the risks of producing in the face of an uncertain future, (b) develop innovative products and production methods, (c) enter a market, (d) do (a), (b), and (c). [See Section 19-1.]

4. The _____ _____ is the price of loanable funds. [See Section 19-2.]

5. Interest rates are structured according to level of _____ , length of _____ , and degree of _____ . [See Section 19-2.]

6. _____ is the ease of converting an asset into cash. [See Section 19-2.]

7. In the market for loanable funds, the equilibrium rate of interest is the price at which the quantity of loanable funds demanded _____ the quantity of loanable funds supplied. [See Section 19-2.]

8. If the nominal rate of interest is 9 percent and the rate of inflation is 4 percent, the real rate of interest is _____ percent. [See Section 19-2.]

9. The face value of a sum of money to be received in the future is an accurate measure of its current worth. True or false? [See Section 19-3.]

10. _____ _____ calculations are used to determine the current worth of future revenues. [See Section 19-3.]

11. If a loan of $200 made today will yield $266 in 3 years, then the present value of $266 to be received in 3 years is _____ . [See Section 19-3.]

12. A _____ is a certificate of indebtedness issued to a holder with the dual promise that the issuer will repay the debt on the date of _____ and will pay a stated sum of money each year until that date. [See Section 19-4.]

13. An increase in the rate of interest will reduce the present value and thus the _____ of a bond. [See Section 19-4.]

14. A profit-maximizing firm will acquire a capital good only if its purchase price is less than or equal to its present value. True or false? [See Section 19-4.]

15. A decrease in the rate of interest will _____ the demand for capital goods, *ceteris paribus*. [See Section 19-4.]

16. Payments for the use of factors that are completely fixed in supply are called _____ _____ _____ . [See Section 19-5.]

17. _____ _____ is a payment for the use of a factor that is fixed in supply in the short run. [See Section 19-5.]

18. The opportunity cost of land to society is _____. [See Section 19-5.]

19. A single tax on land would reduce the quantity of land available. True or false? [See Section 19-5.]

20. Wanda Yodel gave up her $15,000-a-year job as a taxi driver to become a $315,000-a-year rock star. Of Wanda's income as a rock star, _____ is economic rent. [See Section 19-5.]

Answers

1. surplus   2. true   3. (d)   4. *interest rate*   5. risk, term, liquidity   6. *Liquidity*
7. equals   8. 5   9. false   10. Present value   11. $200   12. *bond*, maturity
13. price   14. true   15. increase   16. *pure economic rent*   17. *Quasi rent*   18. zero
19. false   20. $300,000

SOLVED PROBLEMS

PROBLEM 19-1   Explain why positive economic profits are a temporary or short-run phenomenon in perfectly competitive markets.

Answer: Positive economic profits are a temporary or short-run phenomenon in perfectly competitive markets because they attract new firms to the markets. The entry of new firms increases market supply, depresses market price, and reduces the profits of a typical firm to zero. Positive economic profits are a long-run phenomenon only in markets that are protected from the competition of new firms by barriers to entry. [See Section 19-1.]

PROBLEM 19-2   Evaluate the following statement: "Profits serve no useful function in our economy and should be prohibited."

Answer: First of all, remember the important distinction between economic profits and accounting net income. The accounting net income that a firm reports to its owners is not always an accurate reflection of the firm's economic profits. A firm's accounting net income routinely exceeds its economic profits because calculations of its accounting net income routinely exclude certain implicit costs associated with the firm's self-owned, self-employed resources. These costs are deducted from total revenue when a firm's economic profits are calculated because they represent costs that the firm must cover if it is to continue operation.

Pure or positive economic profits (revenues in excess of all costs) serve at least two important functions in a market economy: (1) they provide the incentive for individuals or firms to assume the entrepreneurial role vital to the economy, and (2) they stimulate innovation. Positive economic profits are the reward that individuals and firms hope to gain by undertaking the risks of production and by investing in research and development. [See Section 19-1.]

PROBLEM 19-3 Assume that the price of stock in company X is directly related to its expected economic profits. In other words, assume that an increase in company X's expected profits will lead to an increase in the price of company X's stock on the New York Stock Exchange. Under what conditions would you expect the profits of and thus the price of stock in company X to increase?

Answer: Company X can increase its profits by developing a new production process that will enable it to reduce its costs below the costs of its competitors. Until its competitors are able either to duplicate the technological innovation or to come up with one of their own, company X will be able to earn a positive economic profit, and the price of its stock will rise.

Company X can also increase its profits by developing a new product, particularly one with patent protection. Developing a new product creates a new market and gives the developer monopolistic power. If entry into the market is blocked by the protection of a patent, company X can expect to earn positive economic profits until the patent runs out or until competing firms develop close substitutes for the product.

Finally, company X will increase its profits and the price of its stock will rise if the demand for a product it is producing increases. This might happen quite naturally and quite unexpectedly as a result of a change in consumer tastes. It might also be accomplished through effective advertising or another form of product differentiation. [See Section 19-1.]

PROBLEM 19-4 Assume that revenues have fallen short of projections and that, for the first time, the federal government must borrow funds. Analyze the effect of the borrowing on the interest rate, on the total quantity of funds loaned, and on the quantity of funds borrowed by the private sector. Draw a diagram to illustrate your analysis.

Answer: If the federal government has not been borrowing funds in the past, its entry into the loanable funds market will shift the market demand curve to the right. As Figure 19-5 shows, this rightward shift in the market demand curve for loanable funds (*DD* to *D'D'*) will increase both the interest rate (*r* to *r'*) and the total quantity of funds lent (*M* to *M'*). However, it will reduce the quantity of funds borrowed by the private sector (*M* to *M''*), *ceteris paribus*.

The reason for this reduction in private borrowing should be clear from Figure 19-5. Curve *DD* represents the demand for loanable funds by private borrowers only. Curve

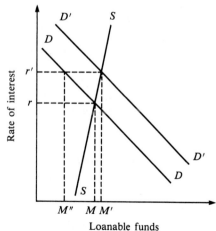

Figure 19-5

$D'D'$ represents the demand for loanable funds by private borrowers *and* the federal government combined. When the federal government enters the market and the demand curve shifts from DD to $D'D'$, the interest rate rises to r'. At a rate of r', private borrowers are willing and able to borrow only M'' funds. The difference between M'' and M', the total funds lent at rate r', is made up by the government. (*Ceteris paribus* may not be the best assumption here. Increased government spending may increase real output and real incomes. These, in turn, may increase the private demand for and the supply of loanable funds.) [See Section 19-2.]

PROBLEM 19-5 Explain why a 90-day bond issued by the federal government and traded daily on a bond exchange will pay a lower rate of interest than a 5-year loan to Joe's Used Computer Emporium.

Answer: Interest rates on loans are determined by three variables: (1) the level of risk, (2) the length of time, and (3) the degree of liquidity. Interest rates on low-risk, short-term, high-liquidity loans like 90-day government bonds are relatively low. Such loans yield only the lowest or "base" rate of return. By contrast, interest rates on high-risk, long-term, low-liquidity loans, such as a 5-year loan to Joe's Used Computer Emporium, are relatively high. When lenders risk more for a longer period of time with fewer opportunities of converting a loan into cash, they demand a higher return on their funds. [See Section 19-2.]

PROBLEM 19-6 What economic entities demand loanable funds and how do they use the funds? What economic entities supply loanable funds?

Answer: All three of the principal economic entities—households, business firms, and governments—demand loanable funds. Households demand funds to finance current consumption. Business firms demand funds to finance the acquisition of capital goods. Governments demand funds to finance current expenditures and capital goods.

The supply of loanable funds comes from the same three economic entities. It also comes from financial intermediaries, such as banks, that accept loans in the form of deposits from households and firms and then reloan the funds to other entities. [See Section 19-2.]

PROBLEM 19-7 Calculate the real rate of interest when the nominal rate of interest is 10 percent and the rate of inflation is 4 percent.

Answer: The real interest rate is the difference between the nominal interest rate and the inflation rate. If the nominal interest rate is 10 percent and the inflation rate is 4 percent, the real interest rate is 6 percent. [See Section 19-2.]

PROBLEM 19-8 If lenders anticipate an increase in the rate of inflation, what will happen to the nominal or market rate of interest? Draw a diagram to support your answer.

Answer: Inflation is a general rise in prices that results in a drop in the purchasing power of money. An anticipated increase in the rate of inflation will have opposite effects on lenders and borrowers. Lenders, expecting to receive in repayment dollars worth less than the dollars they lend out, will reduce the quantity of funds that they are willing to make available to borrowers at each possible rate of interest. As Figure 19-6 shows, this expectation of lenders will be reflected in a leftward shift in the supply curve for loanable funds (SS to $S'S'$).

Borrowers, on the other hand, expecting to repay loans with dollars worth less than the dollars they borrow, will increase the quantity of funds that they are willing and able to borrow at each possible rate of interest. As Figure 19-6 also shows, this expectation of borrowers will be reflected in a rightward shift in the demand curve for loanable funds (DD to $D'D'$).

Whenever demand increases and supply decreases, price—in this case, the rate of interest—rises. As Figure 19-6 is drawn, quantity (loanable funds) exchanged declines, but a drop in quantity is not a necessary consequence of a simultaneous increase in demand and decrease in supply. As you recall from Chapter 5, the effect on quantity in such circumstances depends on the relative magnitude of the two changes. [See Section 19-2.]

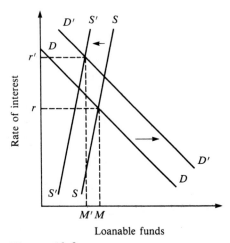

Figure 19-6

PROBLEM 19-9 If you borrow $1,000 for 1 year, how much will you be obliged to pay back at the end of the year if the annual interest rate is 10 percent? How much will you be obliged to pay back if the annual interest rate is 5 percent?

Answer: To determine the amount that you will have to repay on your loan, use the future payment formula:

$$\text{Future payment (in time } t) = (1 + i)^t \times \text{present value}$$

In this problem, time t is 1 year and i is either 10 percent (0.10) or 5 percent (0.05). Thus, if the annual interest rate is 10 percent, you will owe

$$\begin{aligned}
\text{Future payment} &= (1 + 0.10)^1 \times \$1,000 \\
&= 1.10 \times \$1,000 \\
&= \$1,100
\end{aligned}$$

If the annual interest rate is 5 percent, you will owe

$$\begin{aligned}
\text{Future payment} &= (1 + 0.05)^1 \times \$1,000 \\
&= 1.05 \times \$1,000 \\
&= \$1,050
\end{aligned}$$

[See Section 19-3.]

PROBLEM 19-10 Find the present value of $1,100 to be received in 1 year at a discount rate of 10 percent. Find the present value of the same amount to be received in the same time at a discount rate of 5 percent. Which present value is greater?

Answer: If you recall that discounting funds is just the inverse of augmenting them with interest, you can find the answer to the first question in the last problem. In other words, if $1,000 today is worth $1,100 a year from now at an interest rate of 10 percent, then $1,100 to be received a year from now at a discount rate of 10 percent is worth $1,000 today. Alternatively, you can use the present value formula:

$$\text{Present value} = \frac{\text{future revenue (in time } t)}{(1 + i)^t}$$

$$= \frac{\$1,100}{(1 + 0.10)^1}$$

$$= \frac{\$1,100}{1.10}$$

$$= \$1,000$$

To calculate the present value at a discount rate of 5 percent, use the same formula:

$$\text{Present value} = \frac{\$1,100}{(1 + 0.05)^1}$$

$$= \frac{\$1,100}{1.05}$$

$$= \$1,047.62$$

As you can see, $1,100 has a higher present value at a discount rate of 5 percent than it does at a discount rate of 10 percent. The higher the discount rate, the lower the present value. [See Section 19-3.]

PROBLEM 19-11   Explain how to find the present value of an asset that returns revenues for each of the next 5 years.

Answer: The present value of an asset yielding revenues for a series of years is the sum of the present values (PV) for each year [see Section 19-3]:

$$\text{Total present value} = PV_1 + PV_2 + PV_3 + PV_4 + PV_5$$

PROBLEM 19-12   Explain how you would determine the value of a bond without consulting *The Wall Street Journal* or any other financial reporting organ or service.

Answer: Since a bond represents a stream or series of funds to be received in the future, you would determine its value in two simple steps. First, you would calculate the present value of the amount that the bond will pay each year until maturity by discounting that amount at some rate (the market rate of interest). Second, you would calculate the total present value of the bond by summing its present values in all of those years. [See Section 19-4.]

PROBLEM 19-13   Explain the relationship between the rate of interest and the value or price of a bond.

Answer: The present value of a bond is found by discounting the future revenues that it will yield at some rate. That discount rate is necessarily related to the market rate of interest because lending funds at the market rate of interest is an obvious alternative to buying bonds. In other words, the market rate of interest is the opportunity cost of purchasing a bond, the amount that the funds used to purchase the bond could earn in their next-best use. For this reason, the market rate of interest is the appropriate discount rate to use in determining the present value of a bond. For this reason, too, bond prices are inversely related to the market rate of interest: as the market rate of interest rises, bond prices (the present values of existing bonds) decrease. [See Section 19-4.]

PROBLEM 19-14   Explain why a profit-maximizing firm or individual would not acquire a capital good whose purchase price exceeded its estimated present value.

Answer: Because a capital good is durable and thus provides services over several production periods, its worth in today's market is determined not by its purchase price but by the present value of the revenues that it is expected to yield in the future. If the estimated present value of those revenues (i.e., the estimated present value of the capital good) did not exceed, or at least equal, the purchase price of the capital good, a profit-maximizing firm or individual would not buy it because the opportunity cost of the funds needed to purchase it would exceed the rate of return on the capital good. Thus a firm or an individual could generate more future revenue by applying the funds to an alternative use. [See Section 19-4.]

PROBLEM 19-15 Explain why the demand for capital goods varies inversely with the rate of interest.

Answer: Profit-maximizing firms acquire capital goods only if the present value of the revenues the goods are expected to generate exceeds or at least equals the purchase price of the goods. The present value of capital goods, like the present value of bonds, is calculated by discounting anticipated future revenues by the market rate of interest. The market rate of interest is used as the discount rate because it represents the opportunity cost of the funds needed to purchase the goods. An increase in the rate of interest decreases the present value of a capital good and thus reduces the demand for it. [See Section 19-4.]

PROBLEM 19-16 Explain the difference between *pure economic rent* and *economic rent*.

Answer: Pure economic rent is a payment for the use of a factor that is completely fixed in supply to society and therefore has an opportunity cost of zero to society. *Economic rent* is a payment for the use of a factor that exceeds the opportunity cost of the factor—that is, the amount the factor could earn in its next-best use and thus the minimum amount required to retain the factor in its present use. Only factors completely fixed in supply to society can earn pure economic rent. However, any factor earning more than its opportunity cost is earning economic rent. [See Section 19-5.]

PROBLEM 19-17 Explain the rationing function of pure economic rent.

Answer: Figure 19-7 is a graphical explanation of the rationing function of pure economic rent. Vertical line *SS* is the supply curve for land, a factor of production that is always available in the same quantity no matter what the price—a factor of production, in other words, that is completely fixed or perfectly inelastic in supply. Line *DD* is the demand—or marginal revenue product (MRP)—curve for that factor. It relates the quantity of land services demanded for various uses to the marginal revenue product of land in those uses. The intersection of demand curve *DD* and supply curve *SS* sets the market price or rent for land services at price *P* in a competitive market. As Figure 19-7 shows, a rental price of *P*

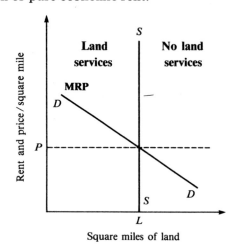

Figure 19-7

ensures that land services will be allocated only to those uses in which the marginal revenue product of land is equal to or greater than the rental price of land. Those uses in which the marginal revenue product of land is lower than rent *P*—those uses that are less productive—will receive no land services. If rent were eliminated (i.e., if the use of land were free), all uses would have an equal claim on land services, land services would be inefficiently allocated, and the value of production would decline. [See Section 19-5.]

20 ALTERNATIVE ECONOMIC SYSTEMS: The Soviet Union

THIS CHAPTER IS ABOUT

- ☑ **Alternative Economic Systems**
- ☑ **Economic Planning**
- ☑ **Economic Planning in the USSR**
- ☑ **The Role of Prices and Incentives in the USSR**
- ☑ **The Soviet Experience**

20-1. Alternative Economic Systems

As you may recall from Chapter 4, economic systems are classified on the basis of two discrete criteria: resource ownership and resource allocation. The two extremes of resource ownership are private ownership, or pure capitalism, and collective ownership, or pure socialism. The two extremes of resource allocation are unplanned allocation through a system of free markets and planned allocation by the command of a central planning bureau. Both sets of extremes are just that—extremes. Between them is a host of intermediate alternatives, a broad spectrum of degrees of private and collective ownership and a broad spectrum of degrees of planned and market allocations.

Thus far in this outline our attention has been focused on the economic system of the United States, which is cross classified as a capitalist market system because most resources are privately owned and are allocated through the interaction of buyers and sellers in an intricate network of markets. In this chapter we shift our attention to alternative economic systems. In particular, we will consider the economic system of the Soviet Union. Although it, too, like ours, is a mixed system, it is cross classified as a socialist planned system. Hence it represents the other end of both spectra and provides an instructive contrast to the system of the United States.

20-2. Economic Planning

Economic planning takes a variety of forms, both in theory and in practice.

- **Indicative planning** is planning by a government bureau that is empowered to coordinate but not directly to influence economic activity. Norway and Sweden are two countries that engage in indicative planning.
- **Participatory planning** is planning by a government bureau that coordinates and directly influences economic activity through its participation in the economy. France and Japan both engage in participatory planning. In France, the government influences the economy through its extensive co-ownership of industrial resources. In Japan, the government influences the economy through a traditionally strong tie with the private sector and through the control of

import and export licenses by the Ministry of International Trade and Industry.

- **Command planning** is planning by a government bureau that directly influences economic activity through ownership of industrial and financial resources or through implementation of an economic plan that has the force of law. The USSR relies heavily on command planning to direct its economic activity.

A. Command planning is not limited to socialist economies.

Although command planning is ideologically associated with socialism, it has appeared at times in capitalist economies. Germany and the United States, for example, both engaged in a form of command planning during World War II. Command planning, however, is not naturally compatible with capitalism because it requires restrictions on some of the customary privileges associated with private property. For example, during wartime many capitalist countries prohibit the private sale of armaments to enemies.

B. Markets are not limited to capitalist economies.

A market system can be used to allocate resources in a socialist economy. In fact, in the 1930s and 1940s, a Polish economist named Oskar Lange advocated just such a combination — an economy in which resources would be owned collectively and would be allocated through a system of markets. Lange envisioned a pseudo market system in which market clearing prices would be generated by a planning board (or by a computer). The purpose of the system would be to duplicate the allocative efficiency of perfect competition. But Lange speculated that a pseudo–market system might actually be superior to a real market system in two ways. First, the system would not be dependent on all of the conditions for perfect competition, such as a very large number of buyers and sellers, homogeneous goods, and so on. Second, planners (or a computer) might be able to arrive at equilibrium prices more rapidly than the mechanism of supply and demand in real markets.

The economy of Yugoslavia combines collective ownership with market allocations. Its socialist market system is often referred to as "worker capitalism."

20-3. Economic Planning in the USSR

The Soviet economy is classified as a socialist economy because all major industries, communication and transportation facilities, the banking system, and most agricultural, as well as other natural, resources are collectively owned by the state.

The Soviet economic system is classified as planned or command because resources are allocated, output quotas are established, prices are set, and the economy in general is directed by the state. In the Soviet Union, two types of economic plans are prepared, Five-Year Plans and One-Year Plans. *Five-Year Plans* chart the general course of the economy for a 5-year period and establish goals and priorities. *One-Year Plans* chart the specific course of the economy for a 1-year period and set forth the particular methods by which the Five-Year Plans are to be carried out. Five-Year Plans naturally are very broad in scope; One-Year Plans are complex and very detailed.

A. The planning process in the Soviet Union is a "top-down" process.

In the Soviet Union, economic planning begins at the top, with Soviet leaders, and filters down through the various levels of the hierarchy to the bottom. For this reason, the process is known as a "top-down" process.

1. Top Soviet leaders set goals and priorities for the economy. Historically, the Soviet leadership has given top priority to the industrial and military sectors of the economy rather than the consumer goods sector.
2. Gosplan, the state planning commission entrusted with the responsibility of formulating and implementing economic plans, collects data from various industrial and regional planners. With these data and the goals and priorities established by the top leadership, Gosplan prepares a preliminary plan or set of directives for subordinate agencies.
3. Subordinate agencies pass down the preliminary plan, or portions of it, to industrial and regional planners, who in turn pass it down to individual plant managers. At each stage in the top-down process, detailed information is supplied and modifications to the plan are suggested. Plant managers, for example, might suggest that their output quotas be lowered and their input levels be raised.
4. Then the process is reversed, and the preliminary plan once again undergoes revision at each level as it makes its way back up through the Soviet hierarchy.
5. When Gosplan receives the detailed information and suggested modifications from the lower echelons, it prepares a final plan. When the plan is approved, it becomes official.

B. Planning in the Soviet Union is done in physical units.

Production goals in the Soviet Union typically are expressed in physical units—metric tons, hours of labor services, and so on. Output quotas or targets are assigned first to each industry and then to each plant within each industry. Basic inputs, such as steel, coal, and oil, are allocated in the same way in accordance with assigned output quotas. The allocation of resources is accomplished by means of material balances.

A **material balance** is a list or ledger of the sources and uses of a particular factor, such as steel.

Material balances are used to ensure the feasibility of production goals—that is, to ensure that the inputs needed to achieve output goals are consistent with quantities available.

EXAMPLE 20-1: The following is a highly simplified, hypothetical material balance for coal:

Material Balance: Coal
(Millions of Metric Tons)

Sources		Uses	
Production	305	Industry	
Stockpiles	40	Electrical power	100
Imports	15	Coke	60
		Other	95
		Stockpiles	—
		Exports	—
		Consumers	105
Total	360	Total	360

Economic planners in the Soviet Union use material balances like this one (though much more complex) to coordinate inputs with outputs and vice versa. In this case, planners need 360 million metric tons of coal to achieve their goals (uses). Therefore they must make sure that 360 million metric tons of coal are either produced or otherwise made available (sources).

An input–output table, which you learned about in Chapter 16, is similar in purpose to a material balance, but because it allows for interdependence between the sectors of an economy, it ensures greater consistency in a highly complex economic plan. For the same reason, it also requires much more data and computing power.

C. Interdependence within a complex economy creates problems for Soviet planners.

The interdependence within a complex industrialized economy like that of the Soviet Union creates enormous coordination problems for economic planners. If one sector of the economy fails to meet its production quotas, all other sectors that depend upon its output are affected. The Soviets address these problems in several ways:

1. As we have just mentioned, they use material balances for basic inputs to coordinate input supplies with input quantities required to meet planned production quotas.
2. They stockpile basic materials to ensure their availability.
3. They include people at all levels of production in their planning process so that problems can be foreseen and realistic adjustments can be made in quotas and allocations before plans are finalized.
4. They establish priorities in their Five-Year Plans to guide economic decision making when unplanned shortages and surpluses arise. These priorities ensure the channeling of available resources to the uses most valued by the Soviet leadership.

20-4. The Role of Prices and Incentives in the USSR

Even though the USSR does not use a price system, prices and economic incentives play significant roles in the Soviet economy.

A. Prices are used to monitor economic activity and to direct consumption in the USSR.

The Soviets use prices in two ways: to monitor economic activity and to influence consumption.

1. Economic planners in the Soviet Union assign prices to inputs and outputs. Gosbank, the state bank, uses the assigned prices to monitor expenditures and receipts at each plant, all of which must pass through the bank. These expenditures and receipts reveal the plant's input use and its progress toward meeting its output quota.
2. Economic planners in the Soviet Union assign prices to consumer goods to influence consumption patterns. They assign prices in part on the basis of the costs of producing the goods and in part on the basis of what is known as a *turnover tax*. A **turnover tax** is a variable excise tax. Soviet economic planners assign low turnover taxes to basic necessities and high turnover taxes to luxury items and goods with low social priority.

B. In the USSR, the signaling and rationing functions of prices are limited.

In a market economy, prices perform signaling and rationing functions. They reflect the relative values of goods, and thus when they change, they send signals to producers to increase or decrease quantity supplied. They also ration goods to those who are willing and able to pay the prices established in the marketplace. In the Soviet Union, the signaling and rationing functions of prices are muted.

1. Yearly output quotas for each plant are established in accordance with the objectives of the current Five-Year-Plan. The quotas are not adjusted to reflect changes in prices or tastes.
2. The prices of necessities, such as food and clothing, are deliberately kept below their equilibrium levels. As a result, consumers must be willing both to stand in a queue or line and to pay the assigned prices in order to purchase these goods.

C. Economic incentives are utilized extensively in the USSR.

Despite Karl Marx's axiom of distribution, "to each according to his needs," the Soviet Union makes extensive use of economic incentives to direct and stimulate economic activity.

1. Plant managers receive substantial bonuses for meeting or exceeding their assigned output quotas.
2. The turnover tax is adjusted to influence consumption patterns.
3. Differential wage rates are offered to induce workers to accept employment in industries or in geographic regions suffering from labor shortages.
4. Workers are frequently paid on a piecework basis so their earnings are directly tied to the quantity they produce.
5. Farmers are allowed to supplement their earnings by selling produce that they raise on small plots of land.

20-5. The Soviet Experience

Economic planning in the USSR has been neither an unqualified success nor a disaster. Since the October Revolution of 1917, the Soviets have made significant economic progress:

1. In spite of two disastrous world wars, the Soviet Union has transformed itself from an agrarian society into a modern industrial nation.
2. Since World War II, the average annual growth rate of the Soviet Union has exceeded that of the United States.
3. The level of general education, housing, and health care has improved dramatically for the average Soviet citizen.

Their success, however, has not been unqualified:

1. Soviet citizens have less economic and personal freedom than their American counterparts.
2. The growth rate of the Soviet Union has been declining in recent years and is now close to the growth rate of the United States.
3. Per capita income in the USSR is significantly lower than it is in the United States. In spite of the progress the Soviets have made, the average Soviet citizen still has a lower standard of living than the average U.S. citizen.

RAISE YOUR GRADES
Can you explain ...?

☑ how a market economy differs from a planned economy
☑ why most nations have mixed economic systems
☑ how indicative planning might be used in the United States
☑ how participatory planning differs from command planning
☑ how prices might be set in Oskar Lange's pseudo market system
☑ why Oskar Lange's market socialism might achieve Pareto efficiency
☑ what role Gosplan plays in the Soviet planning process
☑ why material balances are used in the Soviet economic planning process
☑ why priorities are important in the Soviet planning process
☑ how prices of consumer goods are set in the USSR
☑ how the use of prices differs in the U.S. and Soviet economies

SUMMARY

1. Economic systems are classified on the basis of two criteria: (1) resource ownership (private, collective, or, more commonly, a mixture of the two) and (2) resource allocation (by markets, by planning, or, more commonly, by a mixture of the two).
2. There are three basic types of planning: indicative, participatory, and command.
3. *Indicative planning* is planning by a government bureau that seeks to coordinate but is not empowered to influence economic activity directly.
4. *Participatory planning* is planning by a government bureau that coordinates and directly influences economic activity through its participation in the economy.
5. *Command planning* is planning by a government bureau that directly influences economic activity through ownership of industrial and financial resources or through implementation of an economic plan that has the force of law.
6. Although command planning necessarily implies some curtailment of private property rights, capitalist economies have utilized it to some degree during wartime and other periods of national emergency.
7. A market system can be used to allocate resources in a socialist economy. Oskar Lange argued that a pseudo market system could duplicate the efficiency of a perfectly competitive market system.
8. The Soviet Union prepares Five-Year Plans to chart the course of its economy and to set goals and priorities for economic planners.
9. Soviet Five-Year Plans are implemented through a series of detailed One-Year Plans that assign output quotas and allocate inputs to all industries and plants.
10. Gosplan is the state planning commission in the Soviet Union. It is responsible for formulating and implementing economic plans.
11. Economic planning in the Soviet Union is accomplished through a "top-down" process. Top Soviet leaders set goals and priorities.

Gosplan formulates a preliminary plan. The plan is sent down and then back up again through all levels of the Soviet hierarchy. At each level, it undergoes development, elaboration, and modification.

12. Gosplan's final economic plans are based on the goals and priorities established by the Soviet leadership and on the counterflow of information and suggestions that it receives from lower levels of the hierarchy, including individual plant managers. Its final plans, when approved, are official.

13. Soviet economic planning is done in physical units, such as metric tons. Material balances (lists of sources and uses of particular factors) are prepared for all basic inputs to ensure that quantities needed are consistent with quantities available.

14. The interdependence of a modern industrialized economy creates enormous problems for Soviet planners. They address those problems (1) by preparing material balances, (2) by stockpiling basic materials, (3) by involving all levels of all sectors of the economy in the planning process, and (4) by establishing priorities to guide allocations when material imbalances arise.

15. Economic planners in the Soviet Union assign prices to inputs and outputs. Gosbank, the state banking system, uses those assigned prices to monitor the progress that plants and industries are making toward the achievement of their output quotas.

16. The prices of consumer goods in the Soviet Union depend on (1) production costs and (2) turnover taxes.

17. A *turnover tax* is a variable excise tax used to influence consumption patterns in the Soviet Union.

18. Prices do not perform a signaling function in the Soviet Union. Economic planners assign output quotas, and those quotas are not adjusted when prices change.

19. The prices of basic necessities in the Soviet Union do not perform a rationing function. Since they are deliberately set below equilibrium levels, consumers must be willing to stand in line to purchase the goods.

20. Economic incentives are used extensively in the Soviet Union to direct and stimulate economic activity. For example, plant managers receive substantial bonuses for meeting or exceeding their assigned output quotas.

21. The Soviet Union has made significant economic progress since 1917: it has transformed itself into a modern industrialized nation; it has surpassed the economic growth rate of the United States since World War II; it has dramatically improved the education, housing, and health care of the average citizen.

22. The success of the Soviet system has not been unqualified: Soviet citizens enjoy less political and economic freedom than their American counterparts; the average annual growth rate has been declining in recent years; per capita income is lower in the USSR than it is in the United States.

RAPID REVIEW

1. Economic systems are cross classified on the basis of resource _____ and resource _____ . [See Section 20-1.]

2. In order for an economic system to be classified as socialist, *all* resources must be collectively owned. True or false? [See Section 20-1.]

3. _____ planners encourage the coordination of economic activity, but they do not directly influence that activity. [See Section 20-2.]

4. _____ *planning* is planning by a government bureau that coordinates and directly influences economic activity through its participation in the economy. [See Section 20-2.]

5. The Soviet Union relies primarily on _____ planning to direct its economic activity. [See Section 20-2.]

6. Command planning is limited to socialist economies. True or false? [See Section 20-2.]

7. Oskar Lange, a Polish economist, advocated an economic system that would be cross classified as _____ _____ . [See Section 20-2.]

8. The commission responsible for formulating and implementing national economic plans in the Soviet Union is _____ . [See Section 20-3.]

9. In the Soviet Union, _____ Plans, which establish broad goals and priorities for the economy, are implemented through a series of detailed _____ Plans. [See Section 20-3.]

10. Economic planning in the Soviet Union is accomplished through a (a) bottom-up process, (b) lateral arabesque process, (c) streamlined input–output process, (d) top-down process. [See Section 20-3.]

11. The managers of small industrial plants are not involved in the economic planning process in the USSR. True or false? [See Section 20-3.]

12. When an unexpected shortage arises in one sector of the Soviet economy, adjustments in resource allocations are guided by (a) prices, (b) Gosbank, (c) priorities established in the prevailing Five-Year Plan, (d) consumer preferences. [See Section 20-3.]

13. In the USSR, _____ monitors the progress of plants and industries by maintaining a monetary record of their receipts and expenditures. [See Section 20-4.]

14. A _____ *tax* is a variable excise tax imposed on consumer goods in the Soviet Union. [See Section 20-4.]

15. An increase in the price of a consumer good in the Soviet Union will always result in an increase in the quantity of the good produced. True or false? [See Section 20-4.]

16. The Soviets use the turnover tax to influence consumption patterns. True or false? [See Section 20-4.]

17. In the Soviet Union, the prices of basic necessities are often set below their equilibrium levels; as a result, the prices of those goods do not perform a _____ function. [See Section 20-4.]

18. Which of the following is *not* an incentive used to stimulate economic activity in the USSR? (a) Yearly output quotas are established for all industrial plants. (b) Farmers are allowed to supplement their income by selling produce cultivated on small plots of land. (c) Workers are sometimes paid on a piecework basis. (d) Plant managers receive bonuses for exceeding their output quotas. [See Section 20-4.]

19. The standard of living in the USSR is lower than it is in the United States because the USSR has had a lower economic growth rate than the United States since World War II. True or false? [See Section 20-5.]

20. Per capita income is higher in the United States than it is in the Soviet Union. True or false? [See Section 20-5.]

Answers
1. ownership, allocation   2. false   3. Indicative   4. *Participatory*   5. command
6. false   7. socialist market   8. Gosplan   9. Five-Year, One-Year   10. (d)
11. false   12. (c)   13. Gosbank   14. *turnover*   15. false   16. true   17. rationing
18. (a)   19. false   20. true

SOLVED PROBLEMS

PROBLEM 20-1 Rank the economies of the following countries from least to most on a scale of private resource ownership and on a scale of planned resource allocations: Canada, Hungary, Mexico, Norway.

Answer: On a scale of private resource ownership, the countries rank from least to most as follows: Hungary, Mexico, Norway, Canada. In other words, fewer resources are privately owned in Hungary than in Mexico, in Mexico than in Norway, in Norway than in Canada. On a scale of planned resource allocations, the countries rank from least to most in the opposite order: Canada, Norway, Mexico, Hungary.

These rankings suggest direct correlations between high levels of private resource ownership and low levels of economic planning, on the one hand, and low levels of private resource ownership and high levels of economic planning, on the other. However, such correlations, though common, are not necessary. Yugoslavia, as you recall, combines a *relatively* high level of collective ownership (socialism) with a *relatively* low level of economic planning (a market system). [See Section 20-1.]

PROBLEM 20-2 Explain the difference between indicative and participatory planning.

Answer: The difference between indicative planning and participatory planning is suggested by their names. *Indicative* comes from the verb *indicate*, which means "suggest," and that is precisely what indicative planners do. They make suggestions to private decision makers, and they encourage them to coordinate their economic activities. They do not, however, directly influence those activities.

Participatory comes from the verb *participate*, which means "take part in," and that is precisely what participatory planners do. They take an active part in economic activities, and they participate directly in the decision-making process. [See Section 20-2.]

PROBLEM 20-3 List three methods by which a government planning agency might direct economic activity in an economy characterized by participatory planning and extensive private ownership of resources.

Answer: In an economy characterized by participatory planning and extensive private ownership of resources, a government planning agency might direct economic activity (1) by co-owning industrial plants, (2) by controlling export and import licences, and (3) by maintaining strong ties between the public and private sectors. It might also direct economic activity in other ways, such as by controlling the financial (banking) system. [See Section 20-2.]

PROBLEM 20-4 Comment on the truth value of the following statement: "Command planning is not functionally compatible with private property as we know it."

Answer: The statement is basically true. Although command planning has been used to some extent by capitalist countries, such as the United States, during wartime and other periods of national emergency, it is functionally incompatible with the private ownership of property and other nonhuman resources. Private ownership implies the power to control and the privilege of controlling one's own resources. Command planning would transfer that power and that privilege to the state or to an agency of the state. A temporary combination of the two may be possible, but a permanent one is not likely to be. [See Section 20-2.]

PROBLEM 20-5 Suppose that the economic planning bureau in a socialist country with a pseudo market system wanted to set prices that would result in a duplication of the allocative efficiency of a perfectly competitive market system. What conditions would the prices have to meet? [*Hint:* What conditions are necessary for long-run equilibrium in a perfectly competitive market?]

Answer: If the planning bureau wanted to duplicate the efficiency of a perfectly competitive market system, the prices it set would have to meet the following conditions for long-run competitive equilibrium: (**1**) the price of each good would have to be the price at which quantity supplied equaled quantity demanded; (**2**) the price of each good would have to equal the marginal cost of producing the good; (**3**) the price of each good would have to equal the average cost of producing the good (economic profit on the good would have to equal zero). [See Chapter 12 and Section 20-2.]

PROBLEM 20-6 When would the planning bureau in Problem 20-5 need to adjust (increase or decrease) prices in order to maintain allocative efficiency?

Answer: The planning bureau would have to adjust prices whenever there was an excess supply of or an excess demand for any goods. As Figure 20-1 illustrates, if a good were in excess supply—that is, if quantity supplied exceeded quantity demanded—the bureau would have to lower the price of the good, from P to P^*. If a good were in excess demand—that is, if quantity demanded exceeded quantity supplied—the bureau would have to raise the price of the good, from P' to P^*. These adjustments would move the pseudo market back toward its equilibrium position. [See Chapter 12 and Section 20-2.]

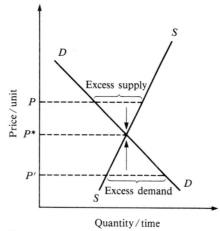

Figure 20-1

PROBLEM 20-7 How could the planning bureau in Problem 20-5 achieve the equality of price and marginal cost necessary for economic efficiency? What incentive would it give to plant managers to promote this equality?

Answer: The planning bureau could achieve the equality of price and marginal cost by tying the compensation of plant managers to profits and by fixing a pseudo market price for all goods. Tying the compensation of plant managers to profits would provide the managers with the incentive to behave as profit maximizers. They would then produce the output at which marginal cost equaled marginal revenue (MC = MR). Fixing a price for all goods would result in an equality of product price and marginal revenue (P = MR, as in perfect competition). Therefore price and marginal cost would be equal for all goods (MC = MR = P). [See Chapters 11 and 12 and Section 20-2.]

PROBLEM 20-8 Explain how the objectives of a Five-Year Plan differ from the objectives of a One-Year Plan in the Soviet Union.

Answer: A Five-Year Plan is a sketch; it provides broad outlines for the Soviet economy and establishes goals and priorities for planners. A One-Year Plan is a blueprint or program of action that specifies, in great detail, how the objectives of the Five-Year Plan are to be carried out. One-Year Plans set output quotas and input allocations for every industry and for every plant within every industry. [See Section 20-3.]

PROBLEM 20-9 Resource ownership in the Soviet economy is classified as collective or socialist. Does this classification mean that *all* resources are owned by the state? What major category of resources is *not* owned by the state?

Answer: The socialist classification means only that most *nonhuman* resources are collectively owned in the Soviet Union. The labor services of each individual are privately owned. Some other resources are also privately owned. [See Section 20-3.]

PROBLEM 20-10 Explain the meaning of *top-down* planning. Explain, too, how the Soviets arrive at internally consistent economic plans through their top-down planning process.

Answer: Top-down planning, as opposed to *bottom-up* planning, is simply planning that begins at the top. In the USSR, it means that the formulation of economic plans begins with the Soviet leadership (the top) rather than with plant managers or local decision makers (the bottom). Plant managers and local decision makers, of course, are very much involved in the planning process, as are all other layers of the Soviet bureaucracy. However, they do not initiate the plans and they do not establish the goals and priorities for the economy. Those are set by the *top* leadership, given to Gosplan, the state planning commission, and passed *down* through the hierarchy for development, elaboration, and modification.

The Soviets use several methods to achieve internal consistency in their economic plans. First, they involve planners and managers at every level of the bureaucracy in the economic planning process so that the quotas they establish are realistic. Second, they coordinate the quantity demanded of each input with the quantity supplied by preparing a material balance. Third, they stockpile basic inputs to ensure their availability. Fourth, they designate priority sectors so that, in the event of an unexpected shortfall in production, inputs can be channeled to those sectors first. [See Section 20-3.]

PROBLEM 20-11 To meet its economic objectives, a hypothetical country plans to produce 900 tons of steel and to import 300 tons. It plans to allocate the steel in the following way: 400 tons to defense, 100 tons to auto production, 200 tons to shipbuilding, 300 tons to construction, 150 tons to consumer goods, and 150 tons to stockpiles. Prepare a material balance to assess the feasibility of the country's plan.

Answer: A *material balance* is simply a list or ledger of the sources and uses of a particular factor. The following material balance shows the planned sources and uses of steel in the hypothetical country:

Material Balance: Steel
(Tons)

Sources		Uses	
Production	900	Defense	400
Imports	300	Automobiles	100
		Shipbuilding	200
		Construction	300
		Consumer goods	150
		Stockpiles	150
Total	1,200	Total	1,300

Since the total steel allocations (uses) exceed the total quantity of steel produced and imported (sources), the country's plan is not feasible. [See Section 20-3.]

PROBLEM 20-12 Explain how the price of a television set is determined in the Soviet Union. Would you expect the price of a television set in the Soviet Union to be approximately equal to or much greater than the cost of producing the set? Explain your answer.

Answer: In the Soviet Union, the price of a consumer good, such as a television set, depends on two variables: **(1)** the cost of producing the good, which depends, in turn, on the somewhat arbitrary prices assigned to inputs, and **(2)** the turnover or variable excise tax assigned to the good. Since a television set is a luxury item, not a necessity, you would expect the turnover tax assigned to it to be relatively high. Therefore you would also expect the price of a television set in the Soviet Union to be much higher than the cost of producing one. [See Section 20-4.]

PROBLEM 20-13 Explain the difference in the role that prices play in a capitalist market economic system, such as that of the United States, and a socialist command economic system, such as that of the Soviet Union.

Answer: Three major differences in the role of prices are the following: **(1)** In a capitalist market economy, the prices of inputs and goods reflect their relative scarcity. In a socialist command economy, the prices of inputs and goods, which are set by economic planners, reflect their social and political value as well as their relative scarcity. **(2)** In a capitalist market economy, price changes serve as signals to producers to adjust their output. A price decrease tells producers to reduce their output; a price increase tells them to expand their output. In a socialist command economy, price changes do not affect output because output quotas are established by a planning bureau. Thus prices do not perform a signaling function. **(3)** In a capitalist market economy, prices perform a rationing function. They apportion goods in limited supply to the individuals that value them the most highly and can also afford to pay for them. In a Soviet-style command economy, the prices of some goods, such as luxury items, perform a rationing function, but the prices of other goods, such as basic necessities, do not. The prices of basic necessities, such as food and clothing, are deliberately set below equilibrium levels. As a result, they do not serve as true rationing devices. Instead, they result in excess demand, and consumers must stand in line to obtain them. The line or *queue*, as it is sometimes called, rations the goods to the consumers who either get there first or who have the time and the patience to wait to purchase them. [See Section 20-4.]

PROBLEM 20-14 List four examples of the use of economic incentives in the Soviet economy.

Answer: **(1)** Plant managers are financially rewarded for meeting or exceeding their production quotas. **(2)** Workers are frequently paid on a piecework basis, which ties their compensation directly to their productivity. **(3)** Earnings differentials are used to encourage Soviet workers to migrate to selected industries and geographical regions. **(4)** The turnover tax is adjusted to encourage or discourage the consumption of certain goods. [See Section 20-4.]

PROBLEM 20-15 How would you respond to the following statement: "The experience of the USSR during the last half century proves that a socialist command economy is inferior to a capitalist market economy like that of the United States"?

Answer: During the last 50 years or so, the USSR has made enormous economic progress. In particular, it has experienced a higher rate of economic growth than the United States has during the same period. It has also brought about dramatic improvements in the level of general education, housing, and health care for the average citizen. Although the standard of living in the Soviet Union is still lower than it is in the United States, and although Soviet citizens enjoy less political and economic freedom than their American counterparts, such a statement would be very difficult to justify. [See Section 20-5.]

FINAL EXAMINATION

Chapters 1–20

DIRECTIONS: This examination is a comprehensive final examination. It concentrates on the topics covered in Chapters 12 through 20, but it also tests your recall and understanding of the material presented in the first 11 chapters of the book. It consists of three types of questions worth a total of **150 points**.

The questions in Part 1 are multiple choice. Select the single best answer to each one. The questions in Part 2 are numerical. Perform the calculations required, and fill in the blanks with the correct answers. The questions in Part 3 are analytical. Write a short-essay answer to each question, applying what you have learned about economic theory and drawing diagrams, as requested, to support your analysis. You should complete the entire examination in **120 minutes**. Answers follow the examination.

Part 1: Multiple Choice   (90 points)

1. A perfectly competitive market is characterized by
   - **(a)** restricted entry and exit
   - **(b)** homogeneous products
   - **(c)** a single seller
   - **(d)** a few sellers

2. Which of the following is the short-run supply curve of a single firm in a perfectly competitive market?
   - **(a)** the portion of the firm's marginal cost curve that lies above its average variable cost curve
   - **(b)** the portion of the firm's average variable cost curve that lies above its marginal cost curve
   - **(c)** the firm's marginal revenue curve
   - **(d)** the portion of the firm's average variable cost curve that lies above its average fixed cost curve

3. When the perfectly competitive market for a good is in long-run equilibrium, the marginal cost of producing the good is just equal to the market price of the good because
   - **(a)** each firm takes the market price as given
   - **(b)** each firm is maximizing its profits
   - **(c)** both **(a)** and **(b)** are true
   - **(d)** perfect information is available

4. After the demand in a hypothetical industry declines, a new long-run equilibrium is established. If the new long-run equilibrium price is higher than the original price, the industry is best classified as
   - **(a)** an increasing-cost industry
   - **(b)** a constant-cost industry
   - **(c)** a decreasing-cost industry
   - **(d)** an industry subject to diseconomies of scale

5. If firms in an industry are earning positive economic profits in the long run,
   - **(a)** the industry must be perfectly competitive
   - **(b)** the industry must be monopolistically competitive
   - **(c)** entry into the industry must be restricted
   - **(d)** marginal cost for the firms must exceed marginal revenue

6. How will an increase in fixed costs affect a monopolistic firm's optimal price and output in the short run?
   (a) The firm's optimal price and output will both increase.
   (b) The firm's optimal price will increase, but its optimal output will decrease.
   (c) The firm's optimal price will increase, but its optimal output will remain constant.
   (d) Neither the firm's optimal price nor its optimal output will be affected.

7. If sellers in a perfectly competitive industry get together and form a cartel,
   (a) industry price will increase and industry output will decrease
   (b) industry price and output will both increase
   (c) industry price and output will both decrease
   (d) industry price will decrease and industry output will increase

8. Under monopoly, a firm's average cost of production
   (a) always corresponds to the lowest point on its long-run average cost (LRAC) curve
   (b) always corresponds to the lowest point on its short-run average cost (SRAC) curve
   (c) exceeds the costs shown on the firm's cost curves if the firm is "X-inefficient"
   (d) declines along its LRAC curve if the firm is in a decreasing-cost industry

9. How will the imposition of effective "fair-rate-of-return" regulation affect the price and output decisions of a monopolist earning above-normal profits?
   (a) The monopolist will increase price and decrease output.
   (b) The monopolist will decrease price and increase output.
   (c) The monopolist will increase both price and output.
   (d) The monopolist will decrease both price and output.

10. Monopolistic competition differs from perfect competition in that
   (a) there are many buyers and sellers in perfect competition
   (b) products are homogeneous in perfect competition
   (c) perfect information about prices and quantities exchanged is available in monopolistic competition
   (d) substantial barriers prevent new firms from entering monopolistically competitive markets

11. How does effective advertising affect a firm's demand or cost conditions?
   (a) It causes the demand curve that the firm faces to shift to the left.
   (b) It causes the firm's average cost curve to shift upward.
   (c) It always increases the firm's average cost of production.
   (d) It causes the demand curve that the firm faces to shift to the right and the firm's average cost curve to shift downward.

12. A long-run equilibrium in a monopolistically competitive market will result in
   (a) economic profits equal to zero
   (b) productional efficiency
   (c) allocative efficiency
   (d) all of these

13. In a monopolistically competitive industry,
   (a) all products are homogeneous
   (b) all goods sell for the same price
   (c) the elasticity of demand for any one seller's product is very high
   (d) all of these are true

14. What does it mean to say that firms in an oligopoly are interdependent?
    (a) The firms must charge identical prices for their products.
    (b) The firm's economic profits must equal zero in the long run.
    (c) Barriers block the entry of new firms into the industry.
    (d) The output–price decisions of one firm affect the output–price decisions of other firms in the industry.

15. What is the reason for the "kink" in the kinked demand curve model of oligopoly?
    (a) The products sold by oligopolistic firms are substantially different from one another.
    (b) Rival firms in an oligopoly match price cuts but not price increases.
    (c) Marginal cost conditions differ significantly for rival firms in an oligopoly.
    (d) The product sold in an oligopoly is not regarded as a necessity by consumers.

16. The demand curve for Take-a-Flier Airlines, which operates a fleet of passenger jets, is kinked at the current market price for air transportation. How will a decline in the price of jet fuel affect the fares that Take-a-Flier charges and the number of passengers it carries?
    (a) Take-a-Flier may reduce its fares.
    (b) The number of passengers that Take-a-Flier carries may increase.
    (c) Take-a-Flier's fares and the number of passengers it carries may remain constant.
    (d) Any of these results may occur.

17. Which of the following would tend to promote stable cartel agreements?
    (a) laws prohibiting cartel agreements
    (b) unrestricted entry into cartelized markets
    (c) a large number of diversified producers
    (d) none of these

18. What term do economists use to refer to the simultaneous achievement of a consistent state of balance by all the markets in a system?
    (a) *partial equilibrium*
    (b) *general equilibrium*
    (c) *dynamic equilibrium*
    (d) *marginal equilibrium*

Questions 19 and 20 are based on the following simplified input–output table:

	Destinations		
Sources	Steel	Wheat	Consumers
Steel	10	15	30
Wheat	1	20	79

19. According to the table, how much steel is allocated to wheat production?
    (a) 10 units   (b) 15 units   (c) 1 unit   (d) 20 units

20. According to the table, how much wheat is scheduled for production?
    (a) 55 units   (b) 35 units   (c) 100 units   (d) 79 units

21. An allocation of resources that cannot be altered to increase the satisfaction of any one individual without reducing the satisfaction of at least one other individual satisfies the requirements for
    (a) allocative efficiency   (c) equity
    (b) Pareto efficiency   (d) productional efficiency

22. If the production of a good generates external costs, a competitive market will produce
  (a) too little of the good at too high a price
  (b) too much of the good at too high a price
  (c) too little of the good at too low a price
  (d) too much of the good at too low a price

23. If the producers of a good are forced to internalize pollution costs that society has been bearing,
  (a) the quantity of pollution will not be affected
  (b) the producers will increase their production of the good
  (c) the supply curve for the good will shift to the left
  (d) the price of the good will remain constant

24. An appropriate way to deal with market failure caused by the generation of external benefits in the consumption of a good is to
  (a) impose a tax on the producers of the good
  (b) adopt regulations that will force the consumers of the good to internalize the external benefits
  (c) subsidize consumption of the good
  (d) prohibit production of the good

25. To be classified as a public good, a good must be
  (a) produced by some unit of government
  (b) nonexclusive and nondepletive in production
  (c) allocated through the political, rather than the economic, system
  (d) nonexclusive and nondepletive in consumption

26. The largest component of national income is
  (a) employee compensation   **(c)** rents
  (b) profits and dividends   **(d)** interest

27. Acme Widgets can sell all the widgets it produces for $1.65 a widget. If Acme installs a new machine that increases the productivity of widget workers,
  (a) employment at Acme's factory will increase
  (b) employment at Acme's factory will decrease
  (c) Acme will reduce the wage rate that it pays to its widget workers
  (d) the supply of widget workers will increase

28. According to the marginal productivity theory, the most important determinant of relative wages is the
  (a) race and sex of a worker
  (b) productivity and relative scarcity of a factor
  (c) contribution of a factor to social welfare
  (d) political connections of a resource owner

29. A market supply curve for labor has a positive slope because
  (a) all the workers in the market seek to work more hours as the wage rate increases
  (b) labor force participation in the market increases as the wage rate increases
  (c) the number of workers in the market declines as the wage rate increases
  (d) the demand for labor increases as the wage rate increases

30. Which of the following will *not* increase the demand for labor?
  (a) an improvement in the technology of production
  (b) an improvement in the training of the labor force
  (c) a reduction in wage rates
  (d) an improvement in the organization of production

31. A craft union may try to raise wages for its members by
    (a) threatening to strike
    (b) reducing the supply of workers trained to practice the craft
    (c) increasing the demand for the products its members produce
    (d) taking any of these actions

32. What effect have labor unions had on wage rates and earnings (wage rate times hours worked) in the United States?
    (a) They have decreased wages but increased earnings for union workers.
    (b) They have increased wages and earnings for both union and nonunion workers.
    (c) They have increased wages but reduced earnings for union workers.
    (d) They have increased wages for union workers, but they have not significantly increased the total wage payment to workers in general.

33. A monopsonist's marginal factor cost curve for labor
    (a) lies below the monopsonist's demand curve for labor
    (b) lies above the monopsonist's demand curve for labor at all points
    (c) lies above the market supply curve for labor at all points
    (d) is horizontal at the market price for labor

34. If Canoe Mills is the only employer in a small town, how will wages and employment at Canoe Mills compare with wages and employment in a competitive labor market?
    (a) Wages will be higher, but employment will be lower.
    (b) Wages will be lower, but employment will be higher.
    (c) Both wages and employment will be lower.
    (d) Both wages and employment will be higher.

35. A positive economic profit may be viewed as all of the following *except*
    (a) a surplus or rent
    (b) a reward for bearing the risks of organizing production
    (c) a return on funds invested in the development of a technological innovation or a new product
    (d) a necessary cost of production

36. Which of the following will result in an increase in the rate of interest charged on a loan?
    (a) a shortening of the term for which the loan is granted
    (b) a decrease in the likelihood that the borrower will default on the loan
    (c) a reduction in the liquidity of the loan
    (d) none of these

37. If the nominal or stated rate of interest is 10 percent and the rate of inflation or the inflation premium charged by a lender is 6 percent, the real rate of interest is
    (a) 4 percent
    (b) 10 percent
    (c) 16 percent
    (d) impossible to determine without further information

38. How does an increase in the market rate of interest affect the present value of a commercial bond issued 5 years ago by IBM?
    (a) It increases the present value of the bond.
    (b) It decreases the present value of the bond.
    (c) It does not affect the present value of the bond.
    (d) The question cannot be answered on the basis of the information given.

39. Which of the following is the best definition of *pure economic rent*?
   (a) a return to a factor of production fixed in supply
   (b) a cost of production
   (c) a payment for the use of a building
   (d) a return earned by members of society that own and control natural resources (land)

40. To an economist, *socialism* means that
   (a) an economy is centrally planned
   (b) the nonhuman resources of production in an economy are collectively owned
   (c) the Communist Party is the dominant political party in a country
   (d) all of these are true

41. The economy of a nation that allocates resources by means of a plan that has the force of law is best classified as a
   (a) socialist economy
   (b) traditional economy
   (c) command economy
   (d) capitalist economy

42. Economic planners in the Soviet Union use material balances to
   (a) monitor the use of raw materials by industries and plants
   (b) check the feasibility of production quotas
   (c) maintain parity with the United States in the production of basic materials
   (d) set economic priorities

43. What measures does Gosplan, the state economic planning commission in the Soviet Union, take to minimize the disruptions that result from unfilled production quotas?
   (a) It designates priority sectors.
   (b) It maintains stockpiles of basic materials.
   (c) It allows plant managers to participate in setting quotas.
   (d) It takes all of these measures.

44. What role do prices play in the Soviet economy?
   (a) They perform the same signaling and rationing functions that they perform in a market economy.
   (b) They perform a limited rationing function, distributing some, but not all, consumer goods to the buyers who are willing and able to pay for them.
   (c) They give the impression that the Soviet economic system is a market system.
   (d) They play none of these roles.

45. Which of the following will cause a society's production possibilities boundary (PPB) to shift outward (to the right)?
   (a) a change in the society's preferences for guns and butter
   (b) an improvement in the society's knowledge of production
   (c) a reduction in unemployment in the society
   (d) an increase in the quantity of goods and services actually produced in the society

46. *Microeconomics* is best defined as the study of
   (a) economic policy (what ought to be)
   (b) the economic activity of individual decision-making units and the functioning of individual markets
   (c) economic aggregates
   (d) the economic activity of small business firms

47. Economists accept a theory
   (a) only if its assumptions accurately and fully describe the real world
   (b) if it includes assumptions, definitions, and implications
   (c) if it predicts economic phenomena more accurately than competing theories
   (d) if the logic of the theory is correct

48. Specialization and the division of labor are directly responsible for all of the following conditions in an economy *except*
    (a) pollution of the environment
    (b) economic interdependence
    (c) the necessity of coordinating economic activity
    (d) the need for exchange

49. In modern industrial economies, governments commonly do all of the following *except*
    (a) regulate economic activity
    (b) own labor resources
    (c) directly produce some goods and services
    (d) ensure minimum levels of nutrition and education

50. An increase in the supply of corn would most likely be caused by
    (a) an increase in the price of corn
    (b) an increase in the cost of growing corn
    (c) an improvement in the technology of growing corn
    (d) an increase in the demand for corn

51. What will happen if the demand for automobiles decreases and the supply of automobiles simultaneously increases?
    (a) The price of automobiles will decrease, but the effect on the quantity of automobiles sold cannot be predicted.
    (b) Both the price of automobiles and the quantity sold will increase.
    (c) Both the price of automobiles and the quantity sold will decline.
    (d) The price of automobiles will increase, but the effect on the quantity of automobiles sold cannot be predicted.

52. If other things remain constant, how will an increase in the price of paint most likely affect the demand for and the price of paintbrushes?
    (a) Both demand and price will increase.
    (b) Demand will increase, but price will decrease.
    (c) Both demand and price will decrease.
    (d) Demand will decrease, but price will increase.

53. If an excise tax is collected from the sellers of a good, who will bear the burden of the tax in the short run?
    (a) Sellers will bear the burden if the demand curve for the good is vertical.
    (b) Sellers will bear the burden because the tax will be collected from them.
    (c) Buyers will bear the burden if the good is a luxury item.
    (d) Buyers and sellers will share the burden.

54. The price elasticity of demand for bus service on Metropolitan Bus Lines (MBL) is 1.1. If MBL raises its fare from 50¢ to 75¢ a ride,
    (a) ridership will increase
    (b) MBL's total revenue will increase
    (c) MBL's total revenue will decrease
    (d) MBL's total revenue will not be affected

55. An increase in the price of bananas can be expected to result in
    (a) a decrease in the marginal utility that consumers derive from bananas
    (b) an increase in the quantity of bananas that consumers purchase
    (c) an increase in the total utility that consumers derive from bananas
    (d) an increase in the consumption of substitute goods

56. The law of diminishing returns implies that, as more units of a variable input are added to a production process, beyond some point
(a) total output must decline
(b) the marginal physical product of the variable input must decline
(c) the average physical product of both variable and fixed inputs must decline
(d) a doubling of all inputs will less than double output

57. The *long run* is a production period during which
(a) all inputs can be varied
(b) most inputs can be varied
(c) at least one input is fixed in quantity
(d) all inputs other than plant size can be varied

58. The costs associated with self-owned, self-employed resources are known as
(a) *external costs*
(b) *third-party costs*
(c) *explicit costs*
(d) *implicit costs*

59. If the economies of scale in an industry are significant relative to industry demand, the industry is most likely to be served by
(a) one firm (monopsony)
(b) a few firms (oligopoly)
(c) many firms (monopolistic competition)
(d) a very large number of firms (perfect competition)

60. If typical firms in an industry are earning an economic profit of zero,
(a) some firms in the industry will cease production in the long run
(b) the firms are earning a normal return on all the resources they are devoting to production
(c) the accounting net incomes of the firms must also be zero
(d) many other firms will seek to enter the industry

Part 2: Numerical   (20 points)

1. The following schedule shows the relationship between various quantities of labor inputs and total output at Gizmos International (GI):

Labor inputs	Total output	Marginal physical product	Marginal revenue product
1	10		
2	21	_____	_____
3	32	_____	_____
4	42	_____	_____
5	51	_____	_____
6	59	_____	_____
7	66	_____	_____
8	72	_____	_____

(a) Complete the schedule by filling in the marginal physical product and the marginal revenue product of each successive unit of labor added to the production process at GI. Assume that GI can sell all the gizmos it produces at $5 apiece.

(b) Assume that labor inputs at GI initially command a price of $40 a unit. At that price, GI's optimal employment level is _____ units of labor. Then a minimum wage for labor is established at $50 a unit. At the new minimum wage, GI's optimal employment level is _____ units of labor.

(c) The difference between GI's optimal employment level at the initial wage of $40 and at the minimum wage of $50 is _____ units of labor. The difference between GI's total wage payment to workers at the initial wage of $40 and at the minimum wage of $50 is _____ .

2. The World Widget Works, known as 3W, for short, is the only producer of widgets in the United States. The demand for widgets in the U.S. market is shown in the following schedule:

Quantity/ day	Price/ widget	Total revenue	Marginal revenue
1	$100	_____	
2	90	_____	_____
3	80	_____	_____
4	70	_____	_____
5	60	_____	_____
6	50	_____	_____
7	40	_____	_____

(a) Complete the schedule by supplying 3W's total and marginal revenue at each level of output.

(b) If the marginal cost of producing a widget at 3W is $40, 3W's profit-maximizing output level is _____ widgets a day. At that output level, its optimal price is _____ per widget.

Part 3: Analytical   (40 points)

1. Assume that the lumber industry in the United States and Canada is perfectly competitive and that the United States imports much of its lumber from Canada. Then the U.S. government imposes a tariff on lumber imported from Canada.

(a) Analyze the short-run effect of the tariff on the price and quantity of lumber purchased in the U.S. market and on the output and profits of a typical U.S. lumber firm. Draw two diagrams to support your analysis, one for the market and one for a typical firm.

(b) Analyze the long-run effect of the tariff on the price and quantity of lumber exchanged in the U.S. market and on the output and profits of a typical U.S. lumber firm. Assume that the lumber industry in the United States is a constant-cost industry. Draw two diagrams to support your analysis, one for the market and one for a typical firm.

2. The nation of Erudition is considering a legislative proposal to make college education compulsory for its young people. The proposal provides generous loans for every student, and it allows students to repay the loans over a long period of time. Senator Sophist favors mandatory college education, but he objects to the proposed method of funding that education. Sophist recommends that the funding be provided in the form of tax-supported scholarships, rather than loans, for all students. He contends that tax-supported scholarships, though equal in amount to the proposed loans, will be less costly to society because they will not require the payment of interest.

(a) Explain how economists measure the economic cost to society of such proposals as the one to make college education compulsory in Erudition. [*Hint:* Construct a hypothetical production possibility boundary (PPB) for Erudition, and use it to depict the cost of the program. Label the axes.]

(b) Analyze Senator Sophist's argument that a compulsory college education program will be less costly to society in Erudition if it is funded through tax-supported scholarships rather than long-term student loans.

(c) Compare the cost of funding compulsory college education in Erudition through loans and through tax-supported scholarships to an individual college student and to a taxpayer with no children.

Answers

DIRECTIONS: Score your examination as follows: In Part 1, score 1.5 points for each of the 60 items that you answered correctly. In Part 2, score 4 points for each of the 5 lettered question parts that you answered correctly. In Part 3, score 8 points for each of the 5 lettered question parts that you answered correctly. **Total possible points: 150.**

Part 1

1. (b)	11. (b)	21. (b)	31. (d)	41. (c)	51. (a)
2. (a)	12. (a)	22. (d)	32. (d)	42. (b)	52. (c)
3. (c)	13. (c)	23. (c)	33. (c)	43. (d)	53. (d)
4. (c)	14. (d)	24. (c)	34. (c)	44. (b)	54. (c)
5. (c)	15. (b)	25. (d)	35. (d)	45. (b)	55. (d)
6. (d)	16. (d)	26. (a)	36. (c)	46. (b)	56. (b)
7. (a)	17. (d)	27. (a)	37. (a)	47. (c)	57. (a)
8. (c)	18. (b)	28. (b)	38. (b)	48. (a)	58. (d)
9. (b)	19. (b)	29. (b)	39. (a)	49. (b)	59. (b)
10. (b)	20. (c)	30. (c)	40. (b)	50. (c)	60. (b)

Part 2

1. (a) *Marginal physical product (MPP)* is the change in total product that results from a one-unit change in a variable input such as labor. Since labor inputs are added in increments of one at Gizmos International, you can fill in the MPP schedule for labor at GI simply by subtracting the total output associated with one input of labor from the total output associated with the next.

   Marginal revenue product (MRP) is the change in total revenue that results from a one-unit change in a variable input such as labor. GI's total revenue schedule is not given in the question, but since GI can sell any number of gizmos it wants to sell at a price of $5 each, you know that its marginal revenue is $5 at every level of output. Therefore, to fill in the MRP schedule for labor at GI, all you need do is multiply the marginal physical product of each successive unit of labor by $5 (MRP = MPP × MR). GI's MPP and MRP schedules for labor are shown here:

Labor inputs	Total output	Marginal physical product (MPP)	Marginal revenue product (MRP)
1	10		
2	21	11	$55
3	32	11	55
4	42	10	50
5	51	9	45
6	59	8	40
7	66	7	35
8	72	6	30

   (b) GI's optimal employment level is the level at which the marginal revenue product (MRP) of labor equals the marginal factor cost (MFC) of labor. Since labor inputs initially command a price of $40 a unit at GI, the marginal factor cost of each unit of labor that GI employs is the same: $40. Thus GI's optimal level of employment initially is six units of labor (MRP = MFC = $40 at six units of labor).

   When the minimum wage is established, the marginal factor cost of each unit of labor rises from $40 to $50. As a result, GI's optimal level of employment falls from six units of labor to four units (MRP = MFC = $50 at four units of labor).

(c) The difference in GI's optimal level of employment at the initial wage of $40 and at the minimum wage of $50 is two units of labor (6 − 4 = 2). The difference in GI's total wage payment to workers is $40:

$$(6 \times \$40) - (4 \times \$50) = \$240 - \$200 = \$40$$

In other words, the imposition of a minimum wage on GI results in a drop both in employment and in total earnings.

2. (a) *Total revenue* is the product of price and quantity sold (TR = P × Q). *Marginal revenue* is the change in total revenue that results from a one-unit change in quantity sold. Since 3W is a monopolist, its total and marginal revenue schedules can be derived from the market demand schedule that it faces. Those schedules are shown here:

Quantity/ day	Price/ widget	Total revenue	Marginal revenue
1	$100	$100	
2	90	180	$80
3	80	240	60
4	70	280	40
5	60	300	20
6	50	300	0
7	40	280	− 20

(b) Like any other firm, 3W applies the MR = MC rule to locate its profit-maximizing output level. Thus, if the marginal cost of producing a widget is $40, 3W's profit-maximizing output level is four widgets a day (MR = MC = $40 at four widgets a day). Its optimal price is the price that buyers are willing and able to pay for four widgets. According to the demand schedule, that's $70.

Part 3

1. (a) As part (a) of Figure FE-1 illustrates, a tariff on Canadian lumber will shift the supply curve for lumber in the U.S. market to the left. As the supply curve shifts left, from SS to S'S', the market price of lumber will rise, from P to P', and the quantity of lumber purchased will decline, from Q to Q', in the short run.

As part (b) of Figure FE-1 illustrates, as the price of lumber rises from P to P', the output of a typical firm in the U.S. lumber market will increase, from q to q', and the firm's economic profits will be positive in the short run (P' > AC at q').

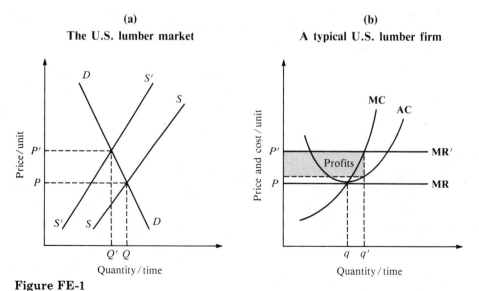

(a)
The U.S. lumber market

(b)
A typical U.S. lumber firm

Figure FE-1

(b) After the imposition of the tariff, typical firms in the U.S. lumber market will be earning positive economic profits in the short run. Those profits will attract new firms into the market in the long run. As part **(a)** of Figure FE-2 illustrates, the entry of new firms will shift the market supply curve for lumber to the right, from $S'S'$ to $S''S''$. Since we are assuming that the lumber industry is a constant-cost industry, one in which input prices and therefore production costs are not affected by expansions and contractions of industry output, the rightward shift of the supply curve will push the market price of lumber back down to P, its original level, and quantity purchased will rise again to Q in the long run.

As part **(b)** of Figure FE-2 illustrates, as the market price of lumber returns to its original level, so will the output of a typical U.S. lumber firm (q' to q). At price P and output q, the firm will once again be earning an economic profit of zero ($P = AC$ at q).

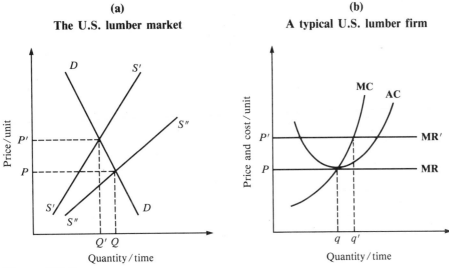

(a)
The U.S. lumber market

(b)
A typical U.S. lumber firm

Figure FE-2

2. **(a)** Economists measure the economic cost of anything by its opportunity cost to society, that is, by the value of the goods that society must sacrifice in order to obtain it. The hypothetical production possibility boundary (PPB) for Erudition in Figure FE-3 illustrates this point. As you can see, the x-axis represents education or total years of schooling; the y-axis represents all other goods and services that Erudition produces. If Erudition adopts the legislative proposal and makes college education compulsory, it will have to increase its production of education, say from E to E'. In order to do that, it will have to reduce its production of other goods, say from

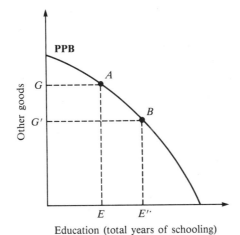

Education (total years of schooling)
Figure FE-3

G to G'. The value of the other goods that it will have to sacrifice (G minus G') is the economic cost of the proposal to society in Erudition.

(b) The tax-supported scholarships proposed by Senator Sophist will not change the economic cost of the program to society. Whether the proposal is funded through tax-supported scholarships or through long-term loans, Erudition will still have to sacrifice the same quantity of other goods (G minus G') in order to move from point A to point B in Figure FE-3.

(c) Although the economic cost of compulsory college education to society in Erudition will be the same whether the program is funded through long-term student loans or through tax-supported scholarships, the cost to individual members of that society will be different. If the program is funded through long-term student loans, the students themselves (or their parents) will bear the cost. If it is funded through tax-supported scholarships, taxpayers—including those with no children—will bear the cost. Thus the original proposal will be more costly for individual students than Senator Sophist's proposal, and Senator Sophist's proposal will be more costly for taxpayers with no children than the original proposal.

GLOSSARY

allocative efficiency An allocation of resources that results in an exact equivalence between price and marginal cost for every good produced.

average cost (AC) or **average total cost (ATC)** Total cost divided by total output; unit or per-unit cost.

average physical product (APP) Output per unit of a variable input (also known as *average product*).

barter The practice of exchanging resources and products directly, without using money.

bilateral monopoly A combination of monopoly and monopsony in a single market.

bond A certificate of indebtedness consisting of two promises that the issuer makes to the holder: (1) a promise to repay the debt or principal on a stated date, known as the *maturity date*, and (2) a promise to pay a stated sum of money each year until the bond matures.

budget line A set of points representing various combinations of two goods, at given prices, that a consumer can purchase with a given expenditure.

capital Any man-made item used in production, such as a machine or a factory.

capitalism An economic system in which the nonhuman resources of production are privately owned.

cartel A formal organization of sellers to control price and output levels in a market.

ceteris paribus "Other things being equal"; a condition that allows economists to describe the isolated effect of one economic variable on another.

circular flow model A simplified picture of how economic activity is organized in a specialized society faced with the problems of interdependence, coordination, and exchange.

closed shop agreement An agreement between a labor union and an employer whereby the employer agrees to require membership in the union as a condition of employment.

command planning Planning by a government bureau that directly influences economic activity through ownership of industrial and financial resources or through implementation of an economic plan that has the force of law.

complementary good A good that is used in conjunction with another good.

constant economies of scale Neither increases nor decreases in the long-run average cost of production as plant size and rate of output increase (represented graphically by a horizontal LRAC curve).

constant-cost industry An industry in which an expansion of industry output has no effect on input prices and production costs in the long run.

consumptive efficiency A distribution of goods that cannot be altered to increase the satisfaction of one or more consumers without decreasing the satisfaction of at least one other consumer.

coordinate axes A pair of crossed number lines (known as the *x-axis* and the *y-axis*) that provide the framework for a graph.

coordinates Paired numbers, such as (3, 7), that locate points on a graph; the first is known as the *x-coordinate* and the second, the *y-coordinate*.

corporation A firm that is legally distinct from the individuals who own and may control it and who reap the profits but do not bear the liability for the debts of the organization.

craft union An organization of workers who possess the same skill or practice the same craft or trade.

decreasing-cost industry An industry in which an expansion of industry output causes a decrease in input prices and production costs in the long run.

demand A curve or schedule that relates the various quantities of an item that buyers are willing and able to purchase at any given time to alternative prices, *ceteris paribus. Change in demand* refers to a shift in a demand curve, that is, to a change in the quantity that buyers are willing and able to purchase at each possible price.

derived demand A secondary demand, such as the demand for inputs, that springs from the primary demand for goods and services.

differentiated product A product that is made to be or to seem different, if only slightly, from other products in the same class.

diseconomies of scale Increases in the long-run average cost of production as plant size and rate of output increase (represented graphically by an LRAC curve with a positive or upward slope).

division of labor The distribution of the activities of production among the members of a society.

earnings See *wage earnings.*

economic cost The value of the alternatives that society must forgo in order to produce a good; the opportunity cost of a good to society.

economic profit The difference between total revenue and total private costs.

economic rent Any payment for the use of a factor that exceeds the opportunity cost of the factor, that is, the minimum amount needed to retain the factor in its present use.

economic system A set of institutions for making basic economic choices and for coordinating economic activity in a society.

economics The study of how individuals and societies choose to use their scarce resources in order to best satisfy their material wants.

economies of scale Decreases in the long-run average cost of production as plant size and rate of output increase (represented graphically by an LRAC curve with a negative or downward slope).

elastic demand A relationship between price and quantity demanded such that a 1 percent increase in price results in more than a 1 percent decrease in quantity demanded.

elasticity See *price elasticity of demand, price elasticity of supply,* and *income elasticity of demand.*

entrepreneur An individual who organizes production, bears the associated risks, and reaps any resultant profits.

entry barrier An obstacle that prevents or deters new firms from entering a market in which existing firms are earning positive economic profits.

equilibrium A state in which all forces or variables are balanced and there is no internal tendency to change.

equilibrium price The market price at which quantity demanded equals quantity supplied.

equilibrium quantity The quantity exchanged at the equilibrium price in a market.

excise tax A tax levied on a particular good.

explicit cost The market value of a resource purchased for use in production.

external benefit A benefit that accrues to an individual who is not directly engaged in the consumption or production of a particular good.

external cost The value of a sacrifice borne by an individual not directly involved in the production or consumption of a particular good; also known as *third-party cost.*

factor A productive resource or input.

fallacy of composition The mistake of drawing unwarranted inferences from the part to the whole.

financial intermediary An institution, such as a bank, that obtains money from households and business firms and then lends it out.

firm A profit-oriented decision-making unit with an internal organization for producing or trading a good.

fixed cost (FC) A production cost that does not vary with output and is incurred even if output falls to zero in the short run; a cost associated with a fixed input.

fixed input A factor of production that does not vary in quantity as output changes.

franchise An exclusive right to serve a particular market or territory.

general equilibrium A condition in which all of the individual markets and decision-making units within an economic system simultaneously achieve a state of balance, and there is no internal tendency to change.

good Any item or service that satisfies a material want.

heterogeneous product A product that varies, from the consumer's perspective, depending on who produces it.

homogeneous product A standardized product, one that is essentially the same no matter who produces it.

human capital An increase in the productive capability of an individual as a result of education, training, or an improvement in health.

human resource Any human skill used in production, including labor and entrepreneurial ability.

implicit cost The value (opportunity cost) of any self-owned, self-employed resource used in production.

income See *money income* and *real income*.

income effect The change in the quantity of a good demanded that is directly attributable to the effect of a change in the price of the good on the real income of consumers (as distinct from the *substitution effect*).

income elasticity of demand The percentage change in quantity demanded that results from a 1 percent change in income.

income-independent good A good whose consumption does not vary with changes in income.

income-inferior good A good whose consumption decreases as income increases.

income-superior good A good whose consumption increases as income increases.

increasing-cost industry An industry in which an expansion of industry output causes an increase in input prices and production costs in the long run.

independent good A good that is unrelated to another good in usual consumption patterns.

indicative planning Planning by a government bureau that is empowered to coordinate but not directly to influence economic activity.

indifference curve A set of points representing various combinations of two goods that yield the same level of satisfaction to a consumer.

industrial union An organization of workers in the same industry.

industry A group of firms engaged in the production of the same or similar goods or services.

inelastic demand A relationship between price and quantity demanded such that a 1 percent increase in price produces less than a 1 percent decrease in quantity demanded.

innovation The commercial development of a new product or a new production process.

input A factor or resource used in production.

input–output analysis A procedure for economic planning that systematically coordinates the quantities of basic materials produced by (output) and needed by (input) the various sectors of an economy.

interest rate The price of credit or loanable funds, usually expressed as an annual percentage rate.

kinked demand curve For a firm in an oligopoly, a demand curve that has a bend or "kink" at the existing market price because rival firms match price cuts but not price increases.

labor union An organization of workers formed to bargain collectively with employers over wages and working conditions.

laissez-faire A policy of noninterference, especially by government, in the economic affairs of individual decision-making units.

land Any naturally occurring resource (any natural resource) used in production.

law A hypothesis that has been widely confirmed by empirical observations.

law of demand Law which states that price and quantity demanded are inversely related: as price increases, quantity demanded decreases; as price decreases, quantity demanded increases.

law of diminishing marginal utility Law which states that the satisfaction a consumer derives from each additional unit of a good declines with consumption.

law of diminishing returns Law which states that, when other inputs are fixed, beyond some point the addition to output from each successive unit of a variable input declines.

law of increasing opportunity costs Law which states that, because resources are not equally productive in all uses, beyond some point the production of one good can be increased only if larger and larger quantities of other goods are sacrificed.

long run A time period in production long enough for all inputs to be varied.

long-run average cost (LRAC) The unit cost of production when all inputs are adjusted to cost-minimizing levels.

macroeconomics The study of how money and aggregate expenditure or investment behavior determine the levels of output, employment, and prices in an entire economy.

marginal cost (MC) The change in total cost that results from a one-unit change in total output.

marginal factor cost (MFC) The change in total factor cost that results from a one-unit change in factor use.

marginal physical product (MPP) The change in total output (or total product) that results from a one-unit change in a variable input (also known as *marginal product*).

marginal rate of substitution (MRS) The number of units of one good that a consumer maintaining a constant level of satisfaction will give up in order to obtain an additional unit of a second good.

marginal revenue (MR) The change in total revenue that results from a one-unit change in quantity sold.

marginal revenue product (MRP) The change in the value of production (total revenue) that results from a one-unit change in a variable factor.

marginal utility The satisfaction that a consumer derives from the consumption of each additional unit of a good; more technically, the change in total utility that results from a one-unit change in quantity consumed.

market An area or setting in which buyers and sellers (the forces of demand and supply) interact to determine prices and quantities exchanged.

market economy An economy in which goods and resources are allocated according to the decisions of individual buyers and sellers.

market failure Lack of success by a market or a market economy in achieving an efficient allocation of resources.

material balance A list or ledger of the sources and uses of a particular factor of production.

microeconomics The study of how the choices of individual decision-making units, such as households and producers, and the functioning of individual markets determine the allocation of society's scarce resources and the distribution of income.

mixed economy An economy that combines, in varying degrees, private ownership with collective ownership or market allocations with planned allocations or both.

money Anything generally accepted as a medium of exchange, a store of value, and a unit of account.

money flows In the circular flow model, the movement of money from producers to households in exchange for resources (called *household income*) and from households to producers in exchange for goods and services (called *business receipts*).

money income Money gained, usually during a given time period, from the sale of labor and other resource services.

monopolistic competition A market structure characterized by (**1**) many buyers and sellers, (**2**) products at least slightly differentiated from one another, (**3**) easy entry, and (**4**) perfect knowledge of product prices, qualities, and quantities.

monopoly A market structure characterized by (**1**) a single seller and many buyers, (**2**) a product for which no close substitutes exist, (**3**) blocked entry, and (**4**) perfect knowledge about product prices and quantities.

monopsony A market structure characterized by many sellers but only one buyer.

natural monopoly A market structure characterized by economies of scale so extensive that a single producer–seller can serve the market at minimum cost.

nominal interest rate The stated or market rate of interest.

normative economics The study of economic policy (what should be).

oligopoly A market structure characterized by (1) a few interdependent sellers, (2) either homogeneous or differentiated products, (3) significant barriers to entry, and (4) perfect information about product prices.

opportunity cost The amount of a good or goods that must be sacrificed or forgone to obtain a unit of another good.

Pareto efficiency An allocation of resources that cannot be altered to increase the satisfaction of one or more individuals without reducing the satisfaction of at least one other person.

partial equilibrium analysis The study of movements from one equilibrium position to another in particular markets or decision-making units without regard to the effects of those movements on the economic system as a whole.

participatory planning Planning by a government bureau that coordinates and directly influences economic activity through the ownership or control of resources or through other forms of participation in an economy.

partnership A firm that is owned and controlled by two or more individuals who share the profits and the debt liability of the organization.

patent An exclusive right to make, use, or sell an innovative product or process.

per-unit cost Average cost.

perfect competition A market structure characterized by (1) a very large number of buyers and sellers, (2) homogeneous products, (3) free entry and exit, and (4) perfect knowledge of product prices and quantities.

planned economy An economy in which goods and resources are allocated according to the central directions of a government agency.

plant A physical facility, including land, buildings, and equipment, owned or operated by a firm or producer (usually the fixed input in a production process).

positive economics The study of economic theory (what is).

***post hoc, ergo propter hoc* fallacy** "After this, therefore because of this"; the mistake of inferring that a preceding event caused a subsequent event.

present value The current worth of future revenue.

price ceiling An upper limit imposed on a market price.

price discrimination The practice of charging different prices for the same or similar products.

price elasticity of demand (*E*) The percentage change in quantity demanded that results from a 1 percent change in price (usually expressed as a positive number even though price and quantity demanded are inversely related).

price elasticity of supply The percentage change in quantity supplied that results from a 1 percent change in price.

price floor A lower limit imposed on a market price.

price system A market system; so-called because prices send signals and ration products and resources to households and producers.

private cost The value of a sacrifice borne by an individual directly involved in the production or consumption of a particular good, whether an implicit cost or an explicit cost.

production function An expression relating the maximum amount of a good that can be produced in a time period to the available technology and to various combinations of natural, capital, and human resources.

production possibilities boundary (PPB) A schedule or curve illustrating the various combinations of goods that a society is capable of producing at any given time if its technology and resources are fixed and all its resources are fully and efficiently employed.

productional efficiency The production of a good at the lowest possible average cost, that is, at the lowest point on a long-run average cost (LRAC) curve.

productivity A measure of output per unit of labor input.

public good A good that is nonexclusive and nondepletive in consumption.

pure economic rent A payment for the use of a factor that is completely fixed (perfectly inelastic) in supply to society.

quantity demanded The amount of an item that buyers are willing and able to purchase at a particular price. *Change in quantity demanded* refers to movement along a given demand curve.

quantity supplied The amount of an item that vendors are seeking to sell at a particular price. *Change in quantity supplied* refers to movement along a given supply curve.

quasi rent A payment for the use of a factor that is fixed in supply in the short run.

real flows In the circular flow model, the movement of resources from households to producers and the movement of products (goods and services) from producers to households.

real income The purchasing power of money income, that is, the quantity of goods and services that can be purchased with a given amount of money income.

real interest rate The nominal rate of interest minus the rate of inflation.

resource Any natural, human, or manmade item used to produce a good; also known as a *factor* or *input*.

scarcity The gap between society's limited means of producing material goods and its unlimited desire for their free availability.

short run A time period in production during which the quantity of at least one input is fixed.

socialism An economic system in which the nonhuman resources of production are collectively owned.

sole proprietorship A firm that is owned and controlled by one individual who reaps the profits and bears the liability for the debts of the organization.

specialization The concentration of effort in a particular activity of production.

substitute good A good that can be used in place of another good.

substitution effect The change in the quantity of a good demanded that is directly attributable to the effect of a change in the price of the good *relative* to the prices of other goods (as distinct from the *income effect*).

supply A curve or schedule that relates the various quantities of an item that vendors are seeking to sell at any given time to alternative prices, *ceteris paribus*. *Change in supply* refers to a shift in a supply curve, that is, to a change in the quantity that vendors are seeking to sell at each possible price.

technology Society's knowledge of alternative methods of production.

theory A set of consistent and related statements that provides a logical explanation of observed phenomena and a basis for predicting future events.

third-party cost See *external cost*.

total cost (TC) The sum of the fixed and variable costs of production (TC = FC + VC).

total product Total output.

total revenue (TR) The product of price and quantity exchanged (TR = $P \times Q$).

total utility The cumulative satisfaction that a consumer derives from the consumption of successive units of a good.

traditional economy An economy in which goods and resources are allocated according to historical patterns.

transfer payment An expenditure (such as for unemployment compensation) for which no currently supplied goods and services, no interest, and no other financial returns are received.

turnover tax A variable excise tax imposed on consumer goods in the Soviet Union.

union shop agreement An agreement between a labor union and an employer whereby the union agrees to allow the employer to hire nonunion workers and the employer, in turn, agrees to require membership in the union within a specified period of time as a condition of continued employment.

unit cost Average cost.

variable cost (VC) A production cost that varies directly with output; a cost associated with a variable input.

variable input A factor of production that varies directly in quantity as output changes.

wage earnings The mathematical product of the wage rate and the amount of time (such as the number of hours) worked.

wage rate The price of a unit (such as an hour) of labor services.

X-inefficiency An increase in production costs above the level shown on a firm's short-run or long-run average cost curves as a result of poor managerial decisions or insufficient administrative effort.

INDEX